The Mammoth Book of
Jack the Ripper

Also available

The Mammoth Book of
Jack the Ripper

Edited by
Maxim Jakubowski
& Nathan Braund

Robinson
LONDON

Acknowledgments

To Murder One, without whom … (MJ)

Special thanks to Kirsten, Adam Gamble, Marcus Moore and Mathew Risdon for their help and support. (NB)

ROBINSON

First published in the UK by Robinson,
an imprint of Constable & Robinson, 1999

This edition published in the UK by Robinson, 2008

Copyright © Maxim Jakubowski and Nathan Braund, 1999, 2008

9 10 8

The moral right of the authors has been asserted.

A CIP catalogue record for this book
is available from the British Library.

ISBN 978-1-84529-712-1

Printed and bound by CPI Group (UK) Ltd, Croydon CR0 4YY

Papers used by Robinson are from well-managed forests and
other responsible sources

MIX
Paper from
responsible sources
FSC® C104740

Robinson
An imprint of
Little, Brown Book Group
Carmelite House
50 Victoria Embankment
London EC4Y 0DZ

An Hachette UK Company
www.hachette.co.uk

www.littlebrown.co.uk

Contents

Introduction

When I was approached back in 1998 to put this book on Jack the Ripper together for the Mammoth list, I was initially somewhat taken aback. After all, I considered myself more of a crime and mystery fiction writer than a true crime specialist and the little I then knew of the notorious case was dizzying in its multiple choice solutions and endless speculation. No theory about the identity of the culprit stood out as the logical one, and despite the plethora of specialists, historians and "ripperologists" around, no one could provide an ideal answer to the eternal question of, who was Jack the Ripper?

It soon became apparent that it would work best, in my opinion, if the book did not actually pretend to provide any specific answers, but instead gave an idea of the sheer complexity and contradictions the case offered. My colleague Nathan Braund, who was then in charge of the true crime section at London's Murder One bookshop, was recruited and did an incredible job sorting out the theories, the facts and the claims and we hit on the idea, for the central part of the book, of asking some of the more prominent experts on the case each to summarize their opinions and views.

Of course, they all strongly disagreed but, I think the final result was both enlightening and fascinating for the lay reader who then had to make a personal choice amongst all the suspects and possibilities presented to him or her.

It seems this approach was welcomed by the public and the book remained in print for many years. While updating the bibliography of books on Jack the Ripper for this newly revised edition, I was truly amazed to see that the interest in this subject has not abated in the least, with handfuls of new books still appearing in the UK and the US every single year since, including the notorious intervention of leading US crime writer Patricia Cornwell, which made headlines worldwide. There have been yet further theories and fingers pointed and it was felt the time had come to update the book. We've excluded some of the original essays and have welcomed five brand new writers to the fold, some of whom have actually published some of the more interesting books on the Ripper case since our initial edition appeared. Barry Forshaw, of *Crime Time Magazine*, examines the whole Patricia Cornwell affray with wit and insight, and there is also a curiosity; a short essay by the late Derek Raymond written for a small French magazine and which has never appeared in English previously, with a novelist's distinct take on the affair.

I have no doubt as we march into the twenty-first century in earnest that more books and theories will keep on surfacing on a regular basis as this unsolved mystery keeps on fascinating new generations. For now, these are some of the facts and possibilities. You pay your money and choose your solution!

Maxim Jakubowski, 2008

Introduction to the First Edition

Who was Jack the Ripper? This question has plagued policemen, doctors, journalists, historians and enthusiasts for over a hundred years.

Jack the Ripper has been portrayed as a slaughterer, fishporter, lodging-house keeper, policeman, barrister, doctor and clergyman. In fact, it would be easier to list the things he has not been described as.

A whole host of individuals have been labelled "Saucy Jack": Montague John Druitt, Aaron Kosminski, Michael Ostrog, William Henry Bury, Dr Francis Tumblety, Joseph Barnett, James Kelly and James Maybrick. There are famous suspects like Prince Albert Victor (the Duke of Clarence), Dr William Withey Gull (Queen Victoria's physician) and Lord Randolph Churchill (Sir Winston Churchill's father). Even children's friends like Doctor Barnardo and Lewis Carroll have been eyed with suspicion.

In 1988, one hundred years after the autumn of terror, the FBI produced a psychological profile of Jack the Ripper for a TV docudrama. They suggested that he was an employed, white, single working-class male in his late 20s who had been abused as a child. He had no police record and no anatomical knowledge. Obviously, the FBI offered the profile as a form of speculation but, if we accept the assessment, it simply adds to the mystery because it does not name a particular individual.

Not all Ripperologists agree that the murders were the work of one man. The late Stephen Knight argued that the Whitechapel Murders were part of a conspiracy that involved the Freemasons, the government and members of the Royal Family. Peter Turnbull argues in this anthology that the murders were a series of "copycat" killings by different men. And we should not necessarily assume that Jack was a man. He could have been Jill the Ripper. William Stewart suggested that the killer was a female abortionist and Edwin T Woodhall insisted that the murderer was Olga Tchkersoff, a Russian immigrant.

Because of the tireless, ongoing debate about the Ripper and his presence both in fact and fiction, he feels strangely familiar. Although he is faceless, he lurks within the shadows of our own subconscious. The identity of Jack the Ripper could greatly depend on who we are and who we wish to perceive as a brutal killer. At the time of the murders, foreign immigrants, particularly Jews, were often accused of being the Whitechapel fiend. With the passing of time and the shifting of social trends, the Ripper's identity will continue to change. Therefore, we should attempt to analyze the writers themselves (if possible) in order to assess their theories. A frequent and valuable criticism of certain "experts" is that they choose a suspect and then find facts to authenticate their belief. Another criticism is that the Ripper debate often turns into a battle of egos where individuals make personal and almost libelous jibes at their contemporaries. Putting 16 Ripperologists in the same room could be regarded as being as sensible as leaving Jack the Ripper in a brothel. However, most Ripperologists would no doubt agree that their desire is to find the truth and, in the words of someone far wittier, the truth is rarely pure and never simple. Lively debate is, therefore, a necessary part of tracking down the elusive East End killer.

Beyond the troubling but fascinating lull of sexual violence that hangs around the murders like a Sherlockian fog, the killings remain so intriguing because the suspect was not found and, consequently, a motive was not discovered (if indeed the murderer had a motive). It is a whodunnit and a whydunnit that attracts earnest historians and obsessive crackpots alike. Thankfully, the following seventeen essays are written by notable and serious Ripperologists, offering compelling and often conflicting arguments on the identity of Jack the Ripper.

We, the editors, do not know who Jack the Ripper was. Therefore, we have no interest in offering essays of our own to strengthen personal, half-baked theories. Instead, we have gathered seventeen persuasive and carefully researched theories with the hope of introducing the Ripper debate to new readers and offering updated arguments for experienced Ripperologists.

Who was Jack the Ripper? Please decide for yourself. Even if you do not find the answer within, you will certainly become addicted to the Ripper mystery. Please tread carefully and keep away from the shadows; you are about to enter the abyss.

Maxim Jakubowski and Nathan Braund, 1999

Undisputed Facts

A Complete Chronology
of the Whitechapel Murders

1887
Summer: the hottest on record. Rats treat the streets as their own. Riots in Mayfair. London stinks. The unemployed pitch camp in West End parks and gardens. Trafalgar Square is closed off by order of Chief Commissioner, Charles Warren.

June: Israel Lipski poisons Miriam Angel at 16, Batty Street.

13 November: Bloody Sunday, a political rally of the unemployed. One demonstrator dies, 150 are injured.

1888
17 January: The *Star*, a new radical newspaper, is printed for the first time.

25 February: Annie Millwood, 38, widow, of Spitalfields, is repeatedly stabbed in the legs and lower torso by an unknown man with a clasp-knife.

28 March: Ada Wilson, 39, machinist of Mile End, victim of attempted robbery, is stabbed twice in the throat by an unknown man with a clasp-knife at the door of her home. She recovers.

31 March: Annie Millwood dies, apparently of natural causes at South Grove Workhouse.

3 April: Emma Elizabeth Smith, 45, widow, of Spitalfields, is assaulted and raped with a blunt instrument.

4 April: Emma Smith dies of peritonitis.

4 April: Oswald Puckridge, trained as a surgeon but confined since threatening to "rip people up", is released from an asylum. John Pizer is charged with indecent assault. He is subsequently discharged.

6 August: Bank Holiday.

7 August: 4.45 am, Martha Tabram, 39, hawker and prostitute, of Spitalfields, is found murdered in George Yard off Whitechapel High Street. She has been stabbed an incredible 39 times.

9 August: Inquest on Martha Tabram. "One of the most horrible crimes that has been committed for certainly some time past," declares the coroner. Verdict: "Wilful murder against some person or persons unknown."

18 August: The *East London Advertiser* complains of police reticence on the subject of Tabram's murder (resumed and amplified, 8 September).

28 August: Annie Chapman fights with Eliza Cooper over a bar of soap.

31 August: 2.30 am, Mary Ann Nichols is seen by Ellen Holland at the corner of Whitechapel Road and Odborn Street.
   3.40 am, Nichols's mutilated body is found by Charles Cross in Buck's Row (now Durward Street), Whitechapel.
   L. & P. Walter & Son of Spitalfields, clothing manufacturers, write to the Home Secretary requesting that a reward be offered in light of the recent murders. The request is refused. James Monro, Assistant Commissioner of CID, resigns after a disagreement with Sir Charles Warren, Chief Commissioner, over the appointment of Monro's nominee, Sir Melville Leslie Macnaghten. He is succeeded by Dr Robert Anderson.

1 September: The *Star* posits a connection between the deaths of Smith, Tabram and Nichols. The Nichols inquest opens.

4 September: The Home Office (Home Secretary, Rt. Hon. Henry Matthews) replies to L. & P. Walter & Son, rejecting their request for a reward.

5 September: "Leather Apron" first identified as the prime suspect by the *Star*.

6 September: Mary Ann Nichols is buried.

7 September: Dr Robert Anderson leaves London for Switzerland, suffering from fatigue. Inspector Helson concedes that "not an atom of evidence" connects any person with Nichols' murder and concludes that there is no evidence whatever against a man called John Pizer, believed to be Leather Apron.

8 September: 5.30 am, Elizabeth Long (Mrs Darrell) sees Annie Chapman talking with a man on the pavement by 29, Hanbury Street, Spitalfields.

5.15–5.32 am, Albert Cadosch hears a voice apparently emanating from the back yard of No. 29, then a sound as if of something falling against the intervening palings.

6.00 am, John Davis, carman, finds Chapman's body mutilated in the back yard.

9 September: William Henry Piggott, 53, suspect, is arrested.

10 September: Chapman inquest opens. Description of a man seen with Annie Chapman entering a passage at 29 Hanbury Street (see Elizabeth Long's statement) is circulated by the police. Samuel Montagu, a local Jewish MP, offers £100 reward for the discovery and conviction of the murderer. His proposal is forwarded to the Home Office. The Whitechapel Vigilance Committee, under George Lusk, is formed in the Crown public house, Mile End Road, in order to assist the police. By

noon, according to the *Star*, seven men are being held for questioning at various police stations. One of these is John Pizer, reputed to be Leather Apron.

11 September: Emmanuel Delbast Violenia identifies Pizer as one of two men supposedly seen arguing with a woman in Hanbury Street on the morning of the 8th, and threatening to knife her. Violenia, however, is discredited and Pizer released.

12 September: Elizabeth Long (Mrs Darrell) makes a statement to the police and identifies Chapman's body. Pizer is summoned to the Chapman inquest. Joseph Isenschmid, butcher, is arrested.

13 September: The Home Office rejects Montagu's offer of a reward. The *Star* suggests that Chapman's eyes be photographed in the hope that the killer's image might be seared on the retina.

14 September: Annie Chapman is buried at Manor Park. Ted Stanley, "The Pensioner" and Dr Phillips give evidence at the inquest. Phillips withholds the gory detail. *The Times* reports Piggott to have been cleared. Edward McKenna, itinerant pedlar, is arrested.

16 September: The Whitechapel Vigilance Committee first seeks Home Office assistance. It is rebuffed, as it will be many times.

17 September: The foreman of the jurors at the Nichols inquest protests that Chapman and Nichols could have been saved had the government offered a reward after Tabram's murder and gives it as his opinion that the authorities would have behaved very differently had the victims been rich. A young man in Hoxton, persuaded that he is wanted for the murders, cuts his throat.

18 September: Lord Sidney Osborne first advances a "Jill the Ripper" theory, suggesting in *The Times* that a jealous woman might be responsible for the killings. Sir Charles Warren, Chief Commissioner of the Metropolitan Police, complains to the Home Office of press

intrusion into police activities. Charles Ludwig, hairdresser, is arrested after pulling a knife on prostitute Elizabeth Burns at Three Kings Court, Minories, and threatening Alexander Freinberg at a coffee stall in Whitechapel High Street. Ludwig is charged with being drunk and disorderly and threatening to stab. He is held on remand until the "double event" proves that he is not the killer. Abberline considers Isenschmid the principal suspect.

19 September: Henry Matthews, the Home Secretary, is attacked for incompetence in the *Daily Telegraph*. Inspector Abberline concurs with his colleague Helson that there is no evidence against Leather Apron. Elizabeth Long gives evidence at the Chapman inquest, giving rise to rumours of a Jewish killer. Dr Phillips reluctantly gives detailed evidence of Chapman's mutilations to a Court cleared of women and boys. These details were not for the most part reported by the press. Wynne Baxter, the coroner, introduces his extraordinary tale of an American prepared to pay £20 each for human uteri for inclusion in an unnamed publication. He therefore concludes that the killer has surgical expertize. Sir Charles Warren sends a progress report to the Home Office, listing three suspects: a lunatic, Issensmith (sic.), Puckeridge and an unnamed man suspected by a brothel-keeper.

22 September: The Nichols inquest is concluded.

26 September: The Chapman inquest is concluded. John Fitzgerald confesses to having murdered Chapman. He is released three days later. Dr Barnardo sees Elizabeth Stride at her lodging house, 32 Flower and Dean Street.

27 September: The first "Jack the Ripper" letter – "Dear Boss" – arrives at the Central News Agency, dated 25 September.

29 September: 11.00 pm, Elizabeth Stride is seen by two witnesses, J Best and John Gardner, leaving the Bricklayer's Arms in the company of a man.

   11.45 pm, William Marshall sees a man talking for about ten minutes to Elizabeth Stride opposite 58 Berner Street. The pair walk past him towards Ellen Street.

Some time after 11.00 pm Matthew Packer supposedly sells some grapes to a man and woman walking up Berner Street from Ellen Road. They stand opposite his shop for more than half an hour.

30 September: 12.30 am, PC 425H William Smith sees Stride talking to a man in Berner Street.

12.45 am, James Brown sees a man and a woman standing talking at the junction of Fairclough Street and Berner Street.

12.45 am, Israel Schwartz sees a man walk up to and argue with Stride in Berner Street, then turn her round and throw her down.

1.00 am, Louis Diemschutz, street jewellery hawker, steward of the International Workingmen's Educational Club, discovers Stride's body.

1.30 am, a man is seen wiping his hands in Church Lane, between Berner Street and Mitre Square, according to a seldom reported story in the *Star* of 1 October.

1.35 am, Joseph Lawende, Joseph Levy and Harry Harris see Catharine Eddowes talking with a man at the corner of Church Passage.

1.45 am, the mutilated body of Eddowes is discovered in Mitre Square by PC 881 Edward Watkins of the City Police.

2.55 am, PC 254A Alfred Long discovers a piece of Eddowes's apron with stains of wet blood and faecal matter in the entry to a staircase at 108–19, Wentworth Model Dwellings, Goulston Street. The words "The Juwes are The Men That Will not be blamed for nothing" are written in white chalk on the edge of the doorway.

5.30 am, the words are wiped off on Sir Charles Warren's express orders.

PC 101H Robert Spicer (subsequently discharged for being drunk on duty) encounters Rosy, a prostitute, sitting on a dustbin off Heneage Street with a Brixton doctor who had blood on his cuffs. Spicer claims to have arrested him, but to have been reprimanded for his pains.

1 October: The "Saucy Jack" postcard (see "Ripper" letters) is received at the Central News Agency. The Lord Mayor authorizes a £500 reward for information leading to the conviction of Eddowes's killer. The Stride

inquest opens. Jenny, an otherwise unnamed prostitute, claims to be certain of the murderer's identity. Michael Kidney, Stride's lover, appears drunk at Leman Street Police Station, declaring that, had he been the constable responsible for patrolling the beat embracing Berner Street, he would have committed suicide.

2 October: Dr Lyttleton Stewart Forbes Winslow, self-appointed expert in medico-legal investigations of lunacy, offers his services to the police. A parcel containing a dismembered female torso is found in the corner of a cellar of the new Metropolitan Police headquarters.

3 October: The police publish facsimiles and the transcribed text of the "Dear Boss" letter and the "Saucy Jack" postcard and post handbills. Warren and Matthews initiate hostilities concerning rewards.

4 October: Newspapers copy and publicize the "Jack the Ripper" letters. The Eddowes inquest opens.

5 October: The Home Secretary, the Rt. Hon. Henry Matthews, MP, PC, defends himself in a letter to his secretary for his refusal to offer rewards. Dr Anderson returns from Switzerland (probable date).

6 October: Elizabeth Stride is buried in grave No. 15509, East London Cemetery, at the expense of the parish.

8 October: Catharine Eddowes is buried in an unmarked grave in Ilford. Crowds line the streets for the procession.

10 October: Warren declares that he believes the "Jack the Ripper" letters to be hoaxes.

11 October: Lawende appears as a witness at the Eddowes inquest.

13 October: The *East London Observer* recounts that Eddowes stated, two days before her death, that she knew the identity of the Whitechapel Murderer and intended to claim the reward.

15 October: Emily Marsh of Mile End Road is asked by a mysterious man who sounds Irish for the address of George Lusk.

16 October: George Lusk receives a parcel containing a letter subscribed, "Catch me if you can Mishter Lusk" and half of a human kidney. Robert D'Onston Stephenson writes to the City of London police explaining the spelling of "Juwes".

17 October: The *East Anglian Daily Times* states that the police have been in possession since 30 September of a bloodstained shirt, which they believe to have been left in a house in Batty Street by the murderer.

19 October: Eighty people have been detained in connection with Stride's murder, declares Chief Inspector Donald Sutherland Swanson, and the movements of more than 300 have been investigated.

21 October: Maria Coroner of Bradford is charged with a breach of the peace for writing letters signed "Jack the Ripper".

23 October: The Stride inquest closes.

26 October: The *Police Gazette* publishes a description of Michael Ostrog, calling "special attention…to this dangerous man".

8 November: During the evening, Joseph Barnett, fish porter, visits his girlfriend Mary Jane Kelly at Miller's Court for the last time, leaving at around 8 pm. At 11.45 pm, Mary Jane Kelly is seen by Mary Ann Cox, "a widow and an unfortunate," of 5 Miller's Court, coming home with a livid-faced man with a "carrotty" moustache. Sir Charles Warren submits his resignation.

9 November: The Lord Mayor's Show.
  1.00 am, Mary Ann Cox hears Mary Jane Kelly singing in her room.
  2.00 am, George Hutchinson, on his way to Flower and Dean Street, sees Kelly and strikes up a conversation. She walks off towards Thrawl Street and is joined by a man whom Hutchinson observes very closely.

Kelly and the man disappear into Miller's Court.

2.30 am, Sarah Lewis, laundress, temporarily residing at Miller's Court, sees Kelly with a man (presumably Hutchinson).

4.00 am, Sarah Lewis hears a single loud scream of "Murder!"

4.00 am, Elizabeth Prater, living immediately above Kelly, hears a cry or cries of "Murder!"

8.30 am, Caroline Maxwell sees and speaks to Kelly (according to her testimony) at the corner of Miller's Court. Kelly "has the horrors of drink on her". Maxwell sees her again, she is to maintain, at 9 am.

10.00 am, Maurice Lewis, tailor, of Dorset Street, "sees" Kelly drinking in the Britannia public house at the north corner of Commercial Street and Dorset Street.

10.45 am, Thomas "Indian Harry" Bowyer, Indian Army pensioner of 37 Dorset Street, collecting rent for landlord John McCarthy, discovers Kelly's terribly mutilated body.

10 November: The Cabinet agrees to authorize a pardon to any accomplice of Kelly's murderer. Queen Victoria telegraphs to the Prime Minister, the Marquess of Salisbury, urging "some very decided action". Sir Charles Warren's resignation is accepted. The police, who have already received 1,400 letters since the "double event", are now deluged with information and speculation.

12 November: The Kelly inquest opens. Hutchinson gives his first deposition at Commercial Street police station. John Avery confesses to the murders, and is sentenced to 14 days' hard labour as drunk and disorderly.

14 November: Michael Ostrog is convicted of theft in Paris.

17 November: Nikaner Benelius, a Swedish traveller who had previously been questioned in relation to Elizabeth Stride's murder, is under suspicion.

19 November: Mary Jane Kelly is buried at Walthamstow Catholic Cemetery. Benelius is apparently exonerated. *The New York Times* claims

that Francis Tumblety has lately been arrested in connection with the murders.

23 November: The Home Secretary expresses the view, confirmed by the pardon, that the murderer had assistance at the scene of Kelly's murder.

24 November: Francis Tumblety, having jumped bail and fled to France, now sails for the United States.

3 December: Scotland Yard files record that "certain members of a quasi-religious organization...have been closely watched for some time past".

19 December: Rose Mylett, drunkard, is found dead but unmutilated in Clarke's Yard. Although initially thought to have been strangled, the police suspect death by natural causes, a verdict supported by Dr Thomas Bond. Wynne Baxter, the opinionated coroner, protested at police interference and rejected Bond's evidence. A verdict of murder was brought in.

28 December: Joseph Denny, in an astrakhan coat, is observed accosting a woman. He is cleared.

31 December: Montague John Druitt's body is found floating in the Thames with a railway ticket dated 1 December on his person. Inspector Walter Andrews has arrived in New York and is rumoured to be searching for the murderer there.

1889

January: Alfred Gray, vagrant, is arrested in Tunis on the unfounded suspicion of being the murderer.

2 January: Druitt adjudged to have been a suicide.

26 January: Assistant Police Commissioner James Monro starts to phase out special patrols.

February: Toynbee Hall students withdraw their assistance from the St Jude's Vigilance Committee.

12 February: *The New York Times* suggests wife-killer William Bury as the Whitechapel Murderer.

June(?): Melville Macnaghten joins the Metropolitan Police.

17 July: Alice McKenzie, washerwoman and part-time prostitute, is found murdered in Castle Alley, her throat punctured by two stabs (not slashes), her abdomen and genitals tentatively mutilated. Monro reintroduces special patrols.

18 July: Dr Thomas Bond states that he believes McKenzie to be a victim of the Whitechapel murderer. Dr Phillips dissents.

25 July: A letter received by Scotland Yard appears to refer to the involvement of spiritualist medium, Robert James Lees.

August: The Cleveland Street Scandal, involving rent boys and apparently implicating the Duke of Clarence, first breaks.

1890
10 January: The *Western Morning News* reports that police are watching the Plymouth docks against the murderer's return.

11 February: Thomas Sadler, ship's fireman and probable murderer of Frances Coles, is discharged from his ship.

April: Special patrols finally cease.

1891
13 February: Frances Coles is found dying, her throat cut, in Swallow

Gardens between Chambers Street and Rosemary Lane (now Royal Mint Street).

16 February: Sadler is charged with Coles's murder.

27 February: Sadler is acquitted.

23 April: Carrie Brown, a prostitute known as "Old Shakespeare", is strangled and mutilated in New York.

13 February 1894: The *Sun* names Thomas Cutbush as the murderer.

23 February 1894: The Macnaghten Memoranda are written, refuting the *Sun's* claims.

February 1895: William Grainger, ship's fireman, is arrested for stabbing a woman in Spitalfields. On 7 May, The *Pall Mall Gazette* records that a witness in the Whitechapel Murders investigation has identified Grainger as the murderer.

July 1902: George Sims, journalist, declares that the murderer was a lunatic found drowned in the Thames.

March 1903: Inspector Abberline, interviewed by the *Pall Mall Gazette*, states that the cases have yet to be solved, but names Chapman as the likeliest suspect.

7 April 1903: George Chapman, alias Severin Klosowski, is hanged for murder.

23 September 1913: John Littlechild, former head of Special Branch, writes to George Sims about Dr Tumblety.

24 March 1919: Aaron Kosminski, suspect, dies in Leavesden Hospital, an asylum.

26 September 1919: *The People's Journal* publishes Sergeant Stephen White's account of his encounter with an unnamed suspect hard by the scene of one of the murders.

1937: Hugh Pollard, editor of *Sporting Life*, gives his assistant Dorothy Stroud a knife said to be the murderer's, now in the possession of Ripperologist Donald Rumbelow.

1938: Inspector Walter Dew's memoirs, including his account of the Kelly murder scene, are published.

1959: Daniel Farson gains access to a copy of the Macnaghten Memoranda.

1966: "Best", a journalist, is identified in *Crime and Detection* as the self-confessed author of the "Ripper" letters.

1976: Surviving Metropolitan Police files on the Whitechapel Murders are opened.

1986: Surviving Home Office files are opened to researchers.

1987: The "Dear Boss" letter, together with other original material missing since the murders, is anonymously posted to Scotland Yard.

1993: Stewart Evans obtains the "Littlechild Letter". Michael Barrett produces a diary purporting to have been written by James Maybrick, a Liverpool cotton merchant, in which he confesses to the murders. A further allegation is made that the murderer was William Evans Thomas, a Welsh doctor who committed suicide in 1889.

Just the Facts

Maxim Jakubowski and Nathan Braund

In 1888, five prostitutes were brutally murdered within a tiny area of the East End of London. The killings rapidly occurred over an 11-week period but they have both haunted and fascinated people for over a hundred years.

Nineteenth-century Whitechapel, the home of numerous prostitutes, thieves and impoverished immigrants, was described by Jack London as "the Abyss". Senior detectives on the Ripper case reported to the Home Secretary that there were roughly 233 common lodging houses with 8,530 occupants, 62 permanent brothels and 1,200 prostitutes in the East End of London. Prostitutes were frequently bullied by gangs who demanded "protection" money and many people were killed in Whitechapel, but the murders of five prostitutes were so sinister that it shook the nation.

Ripperologists quarrel over the exact number of deaths. Some believe that Jack the Ripper killed seven women and others argue that it was closer to 13. At the time of the murders, various policemen associated with the case disputed over the number of killings. Inspector Reid believed that Jack the Ripper committed nine murders, Inspector Abberline believed he killed six victims, Sir Melville Macnaghten believed that there were five murders and Superintendent Arnold felt that only four killings could be attributed to the Whitechapel Murderer. Most of the policemen at the time and most Ripperologists, however, agree that the following five murders were unquestionably the brutal work of "Saucy Jack". In order to remain impartial and avoid developing a lengthy and highly speculative theory, we will concentrate on the five canonical murders. A great deal of the information comes from eyewitness accounts and is sometimes contradictory. The eyewitness accounts should be viewed cautiously because they depend on human memory, which tends to be inconsistent.

Mary Ann Nichols (1845–88): The First Victim

Mary Ann Nichols, commonly known as Polly, was born in Dean Street, off Fetter Lane, on 26 August 1845. She was the daughter of Edward Walker, a locksmith of Dean Street, and his wife Caroline. Mary Ann married William Nichols, a printer's machinist, in 1864. They had five children but their relationship did not last, because of William's brief affair with the midwife who had helped at the birth of Mary Ann's fourth child in 1877 and Mary Ann's love of alcohol. In 1880, Mary Ann and William separated. William kept the children (except for Edward John, who moved to his grandfather's house) and paid Mary Ann a weekly allowance of 5 shillings. The allowance stopped in 1882 when William discovered that Mary Ann was a prostitute. Between 1883 and 1887, she lived with her father but they did not get on because she drank heavily. She moved from workhouse to workhouse until 12 May 1888, when she became a domestic servant with Samuel and Sarah Cowdry in Wandsworth. Within two months, she had absconded, stealing clothes worth £3 10 shillings. She took lodgings at 18 Thrawl Street, sharing a room with Emily Holland and four other women.

Appearance

At the time of her death, Mary Ann Nichols was 43 years old and 5 feet, 2 inches tall. She had dark hair, high cheekbones and grey eyes. There was a scar on her forehead from a childhood accident and her front teeth were missing from a fight.

The Murder

30 August 1888, 11.00 pm, Mary Ann Nichols was seen walking in Whitechapel Road.

31 August 12.30 am, she was seen leaving the Frying Pan public house.

1.20 am, she sat in the kitchen of the common lodging house at 18 Thrawl Street. The deputy-lodging house keeper demanded four pence for her bed. She did not have the money and was thrown out. She merrily claimed that she would soon get her doss money and said, "See what a jolly bonnet I've got now."

2.30 am, she was seen by Emily Holland at the corner of Osborn Street and Brick Lane. Holland had gone to watch a fire at Shadwell dry dock, which was a common pastime because there were so many fires in London in 1888. She was Mary Ann's friend and shared a room with her and four other women at 18 Thrawl Street. Nichols was extremely drunk and leaning against a wall. Holland stopped to speak to Nichols and tried to encourage her to come back to 18 Thrawl Street but Nichols said, "I've had my lodging money three times today and I've spent it. It won't be long before I'm back." The two women parted.

3.15 am, PC John Thain passed the entrance to Buck's Row on his beat. At a similar time, PC John Neil walked down Buck's Row. Sergeant Kerby also walked down Buck's Row. None of them saw anything suspicious.

Roughly 3.40 am, Charles A. Cross, a carman, was walking along Buck's Row when he saw something lying against the gates leading to the stables that were next to New Cottage. He thought it was a tarpaulin sheet and crossed the road to see if he could salvage it. He soon realized that it was the body of a woman, lying on her back, lengthways along the footway, with her hands by her sides. Her legs were extended and slightly apart, and her eyes were wide open. By her side was a black straw bonnet trimmed with black velvet.

Robert Paul, another carman, arrived on the scene and was called over to the body by Cross. The two men looked at the body. It was Mary Ann Nichols. Her skirts were raised almost to her stomach. After feeling her cold hands, Cross decided that she was dead. However, Paul felt her face which was warm and believed that he could detect her heart beating. The two men decided to find a policeman and left Buck's Row.

Roughly 3.44 am, within minutes of the two men departing, PC John Neil entered the street. He found the body and studied it with a lantern. Nichols was unquestionably dead. Her throat was cut from ear to ear.

Blood was still oozing from the wound. Neil believed that she had died recently because her arm was warm from the elbow upwards when he touched it.

Meanwhile, Cross and Paul met PC Mizen at the corner of Hanbury Street and Baker's Row and told him of their terrible find. PC Mizen hurried towards Buck's Row while Cross and Paul went to work, parting company at the corner of Hanbury street.

Roughly 3.47 am, PC Thain passed the entrance of Buck's Row and was beckoned by PC Neil, who signalled with his lantern. After showing him the body, PC Neil told Thain to go and fetch Dr Rees Ralph Llewellyn. PC Thain rushed to Dr Llewellyn's surgery at 152 Whitechapel Road and woke the doctor.

PC Mizen reached Buck's Row and was told by PC Neil to fetch an ambulance (a wheeled stretcher) and further assistance from Bethnal Green police station.

Dr Llewellyn and PC Thain arrived at the murder site. PC Neil had been joined by two slaughtermen, Henry Tomkins and James Mumford, from Barber's Knacker's yard in Winthrop Street which ran parallel to Buck's Row. Dr Llewellyn made a preliminary examination of the body, noting the severe cuts to the throat and discovering that the legs were warm even though the hands and wrists were cold. He observed that there was very little blood in the gutter beside Nichols but believed that she had been killed on the spot. He guessed that she could not have been dead for more than 30 minutes. Dr Llewellyn ordered the body to be removed to the mortuary shed at Old Montague Street Workhouse Infirmary.

Sergeant Kerby arrived with another officer from H Division while Dr Llewellyn was making his examination. He accompanied the body to the mortuary while PC Thain waited in Buck's Row for Inspector John Spratling and watched Mrs Green's son, one of the residents, wash the blood away.

Sightseers were starting to gather.

4.30 am, Inspector John Spratling arrived at Buck's Row and was led by PC Thain to the place where the body was found. There was only a slight stain of blood on the pavement. The small amount of blood caused speculation at the time, leading some to believe that Nichols had been killed at a different location and that her body had been carried and then dumped at Buck's Row. Many policemen, including Inspector Abberline and Inspector Helson, asserted that the murder took place where the body was found in Buck's Row.

5.00 am, Spratling told PC Cartwright to search the murder scene and surrounding area. Spratling and PC Neil went to the mortuary and took down a description of the body. Spratling discovered that the abdomen had been slashed and damaged and the intestines were exposed. He sent for Dr Llewellyn to make a further examination and returned to the murder site where he made a thorough search of the nearby East London and District railway lines and embankments with Sergeant Godley. They did not find any clues.

6.30 am, James Hatfield and Robert Mann, two inmates from the Whitechapel workhouse, stripped and washed Nichols's body even though Detective Sergeant Enright specified that the body should not be touched. The inmates dumped her clothes in the yard.

6.45 am, Inspector Helsen heard of the murder and went to the mortuary where the body was being stripped. After seeing the body, he went to the murder scene.

The Post-Mortem

1 September, 10.00 am, Dr Llewellyn made a full post-mortem examination of Mary Ann Nichols at the mortuary. A bruise on the right side of the face looked as if it was created by the pressure of a thumb and a circular bruise on the left side of the neck. All of the bruises were recent, which led Dr Llewellyn to surmise that the killer had steadied Mary Ann's head before slitting the throat. There were two cuts in the throat. Both of them started on the left side of the neck below the ear and ran below the jaw, one 4 inches and the other 8 inches in length. Both cuts reached through to the vertebrae. The large vessels of the neck on both sides were severed. There were no other injuries to the upper part of the body.

A knife had been thrust into the lower part of the abdomen, creating a very deep wound 2–3 inches from the left side, running in a jagged manner. The tissues were cut through. There were several cuts across the abdomen and three or four similar cuts running downwards on the right side.

All of the cuts were caused by the same instrument, probably a moderately sharp long-bladed knife. Dr Llewellyn guessed that the killer was left-handed and that he would have attacked Nichols from the front and not from behind. He surmised that the mutilations had taken about four or five minutes and were the work of a person with some rough anatomical knowledge.

The Inquest

The inquest was held at the Whitechapel Working Lads' Institute on 1 September 1888 and was conducted by Wynne Edwin Baxter who was the coroner for the South-Eastern Division of Middlesex. The inquest drew a large crowd of journalists and curious spectators. Three witnesses were heard on the first day and after the second day, when eight other witnesses made depositions, the inquest was adjourned for a fortnight so that the police had time to make further investigations. The inquest was not closed until 24 September and, in summing up, Baxter criticized the police for not noticing the abdominal mutilations before the body was taken to the mortuary.

Nichols's body was identified by her friend, Emily Holland, and Mary Ann Monk from Lambeth Workhouse. On 1 September, William Nichols, Mary Ann's husband, was taken to the mortuary with one of her sons. When he saw the mutilated corpse, he said, "Seeing you as you are now, I forgive you for what you have done to me."

Nichols was buried at Ilford Cemetery on 6 September 1888.

The police set about solving the murder. It had happened on J Division's territory but it had been reported by PC Mizen, an H Division constable, so H Division maintained an interest. Inspector Abberline, the former head of the Whitechapel CID, was moved back from Scotland Yard to organize the investigation of the detectives on the ground.

On the same day as the inquest, Robert Anderson became Assistant Commissioner of the CID but had to take a month's leave in Switzerland because of bad health. He left a week later and put

Detective Chief Inspector Donald Sutherland Swanson in charge of the investigation.

The police started to speculate about likely suspects. They firstly believed that Nichols had been murdered by one of the gangs who were known to demand money from local prostitutes. They briefly suspected the slaughterers who had been working at the yard of Harrison, Barber and Co. Ltd in Winthrop Street, but they had sufficient alibis. The police made enquiries at common lodging houses and among prostitutes but they had no suspects and no clues. There was a killer on the loose.

Eight days after the murder, before the final outcome of the inquest, the Ripper struck again.

Annie Chapman (1841–88): The Second Victim

Annie Chapman, commonly known as "Dark Annie", was born in Paddington in 1841, daughter of George Smith, a Lifeguardsman, and Ruth. She married John Chapman, a coachman, in 1869 and had three children. They moved to Windsor in 1881. One of her daughters, Emily Ruth, died of meningitis when she was 12 in 1882. Her son, John, was disabled and ended up in a "cripple's home." The other daughter, Annie Georgina, was sent to an institution in France. Annie left her family at about the time of her daughter's death. She returned to London and received a weekly allowance of 10 shillings from John Chapman until his death in 1886. During 1886, she lived at 30 Dorset Street with Jack Sivey, a sievemaker. Annie liked to drink and they soon separated. At the time of the murder, she lived at Crossingham's lodging house at 35 Dorset Street, Spitalfields.

Appearance

At the time of her death, Annie Chapman was 47 years old and 5 feet in height. She had dark brown wavy hair, blue eyes and a thick nose, and was plump and had a fair complexion. Two teeth were missing from her lower jaw and she had a black eye and bruises on her chest from a recent fight with a woman called Eliza Cooper. She was malnourished and had a disease of the lungs and membranes of her brain which would have eventually killed her if she had managed to escape the Ripper's knife.

The Murder

7 September 1888, roughly 5.00 pm, Chapman was seen by her friend, Amelia Palmer, in Dorset Street. Chapman said that she felt too ill to do anything but that she would have to pull herself together and get some money for her lodgings. They parted company.

8 September, 12.12 am, She was seen by William Stevens in the kitchen of Crossingham's lodging house. She was drunk and took a box of pills from her pocket. She told him that she had been to hospital. The box broke so she put the contents (two pills) in a torn piece of envelope, taken from the kitchen floor.

1.35 am, she was seen by John Evans, the nightwatchman at Crossingham's lodging house. He demanded the four pence fee. She said that she did not have enough money but would soon get it. She went up to the office of Timothy Donovan, the deputy, and told him to save a bed for her because she would go out and earn her money. Evans saw her off the premises. In his opinion she was drunk. She headed up Little Paternoster Row in the direction of Brushfield Street. That was the last time that she was definitely seen alive.

3.30 am, Mr Thompson, a carman who lived at 29 Hanbury Street, left for work. He did not go into the yard and did not hear anything suspicious.

29 Hanbury Street was just a few yards away from Crossingham's lodging house. It was a crowded building with eight rooms and 17 occupants. The yard was 13–14 square feet. The only entrance and exit to and from the yard was through a passage that led onto the street.

4.40–4.45 am, John Richardson, son of one of the residents of 29 Hanbury Street, stopped at the yard on his way to work at Spitalfields Market. He regularly did this because someone had broken the padlock on the cellar door a few months before. He walked through the yard and opened the yard door. One of his boots was hurting a toe so he sat on a step and cut a piece of leather from the boot with a table knife. He could see that the padlock on the cellar door was secure, and left. He had sat for about two minutes and did not see anything unusual.

5.20–5.30 am, Albert Cadosch, a carpenter who lived at 27 Hanbury Street, stepped outside and heard people talking in the yard of 29 Hanbury Street. A fence that was 5 feet, 6 inches in height divided his house from the yard. He heard a woman say "no." A few minutes later he heard a scuffle and someone or something fell against the fence. He heard nothing more and was not suspicious. As he walked along Hanbury Street past Spitalfields church on his way to work, he noticed that it was 5.32 am. He did not see anyone suspicious in Hanbury Street.

5.30 am, Elizabeth Long (also known as Darrell) walked down Hanbury Street on her way to Spitalfields Market. She was on the same side of the street as No 29 and saw a man and a woman standing on the pavement. She could not see the man's face because it was turned away, but she could see the woman whom she later identified as Annie Chapman. Long described the man as being about 40 years old and little taller than Chapman (who was 5 feet tall). She said that he had a dark complexion and a "shabby genteel appearance" with a brown deerstalker hat and a dark coat. She asserted that he looked and sounded like a foreigner. The man asked Annie, "Will you?" and Chapman replied, "Yes." Mrs Long continued on her journey towards Spitalfields. She was convinced that she saw the couple at 5.30 am because she heard the clock of the Black Eagle Brewery in Brick Lane strike the half hour as she reached Hanbury Street.

5.45–6.00 am, after a restless night, carman John Davis, who was one of the residents of 29 Hanbury Street, went downstairs and into the yard. He saw a body lying down between the steps and the fence. It was Annie Chapman. She was lying parallel to the fence. Her head was about 6 inches in front of the level of the bottom step, her feet were pointing towards the shed at the bottom of the yard, and her left arm was placed across her left breast. Her face was covered in blood and her throat had been severely cut. Her clothing was up to her knees.

Davis rushed out into the street and shouted to Henry John Holland, who was on his way to work, and to James Green and James Kent, who were employees of John and Thomas Bayley, a packing case manufacturer, and were standing outside 23a Hanbury Street, waiting to start work. All of the men hurried over to the body. They then rushed off in different directions in search of policemen, except for James Green, who returned to his place of work. James Kent was unsuccessful and went for a brandy to steady his nerves before fetching a piece of canvas with which to cover the body. Henry John Holland found a policeman at Spitalfields Market but he was on "fixed-point" duty and could not leave his position under any circumstances. Davis reached the Commercial Street police station shortly after 6.00 am and told Inspector Joseph Chandler of his discovery. With his men, Inspector Chandler hurried to 29 Hanbury Street, where a crowd had already gathered. He saw the body and then sent for Dr George Bagster Phillips, the divisional police surgeon, an ambulance, further assistance and for news to be sent to Scotland Yard. He covered the body with some sacking.

6.30 am, Dr Phillips arrived at the scene and viewed the body. The left arm was placed across the left breast and the legs were drawn up with the knees turned outwards. The face was swollen and turned on the right side, and the tongue, which was swollen, protruded between the front teeth, but not beyond the lips. The limbs had started to stiffen. The throat was deeply cut and the jagged incisions reached right round the neck. There were smears of blood on the fence about 14 inches from the ground corresponding to the place Chapman's head lay. The smears on the fence were directly above the blood on the ground that had flowed from the slit neck. Phillips guessed that Annie had been dead for at least two hours. He was convinced that the murder occurred in the yard because there were no other blood stains in the passage nor in the vicinity of the house.

Phillips and Chandler made a careful search of the yard. They discovered the contents of Chapman's pocket, which had been cut open, lying in a neat pile. The contents were a piece of coarse muslin, a small-tooth comb and a pocket comb in a paper case. They also found a screwed-up piece of envelope containing two pills. The portion of envelope had the letter "M" in a man's handwriting and a post office stamp on one side. On the other side was a seal of the Sussex Regiment. This was the piece of envelope that Chapman had picked up at the lodging house. Phillips later told the inquest that he believed that the contents had been placed significantly by the victim because the muslin and combs were placed at Annie's feet and the piece of envelope and pills were placed by Annie's head. Two or three brass rings, which Chapman had been wearing at the lodging house, were missing from her finger. A folded and saturated leather apron was also found but this was later identified as belonging to a local resident.

Dr Phillips ordered that the body should be taken to the Whitechapel Workhouse Infirmary Mortuary in Eagle Street, off Old Montague Street. Sergeant Edmund Berry accompanied the body.

Detective Sergeant Thick, Sergeant Leach and others arrived in the yard at Hanbury Street. A telegram had been sent to Inspector Abberline at Scotland Yard and he soon arrived at the scene. Sergeant Thicke went to the mortuary and took a description of the body. Hanbury Street was within the jurisdiction of the Metropolitan Police's H Division. Inspector Abberline, Inspector Helson, J Division, and Acting Superintendent West, who was in charge of H Division, consulted with each other and agreed that Annie Chapman was murdered by the same man who killed Mary Ann Nichols.

The Post-Mortem

Dr Phillips performed his post-mortem on 8 September. He was annoyed that two nurses from the infirmary had stripped and washed the body and was irritated by the insanitary conditions of the shed.

As with his earlier examination, he observed that the face and tongue were swollen and that the throat had been sliced from left to right through to the spine. There was a fresh bruise over the right temple and a bruise on the upper eyelid. There were two distinct bruises, each the size of a man's thumb, on the forepart of the top of the chest, and another on the right hand. He surmised from the facial bruising that the killer had held Chapman by the lower jaw when he cut her throat. The abdomen was laid open and the intestines had been severed from their attachments, lifted out and placed on the ground above the right shoulder. Part of the stomach and a large quantity of blood lay above the left shoulder. The body was cold except for the remaining heat under the intestines in the body. The uterus and its appendages with the upper portion of the vagina, the posterior and two-thirds of the bladder had been completely removed from the body and the murder site. The incisions avoided the rectum and divided the vagina low enough to avoid damage to the *cervix uteri*. This made Phillips assert that the killer had some anatomical knowledge, stating that he could not have performed all of the injuries himself in less than fifteen minutes. If the mutilations had been done in a deliberate manner within the duties of a surgeon they would have taken roughly an hour. He believed that the injuries to the throat and abdomen were probably inflicted with the same knife which would have been a sharp weapon with a thin narrow blade at least 6–8 inches long. The knife would not have been a bayonet or a knife used in the leather trade. It would have been more like a ground-down slaughterman's knife or a small amputating knife.

Phillips surmised that the murderer strangled or suffocated Chapman to death before making a long cut into the neck and mutilating her, because the face, lips and hands were livid as they would be from asphyxia.

The Inquest

The inquest was held on 10 September before Wynne E Baxter at the Working Lads' Institute. Dr Phillips reported his examination on 13 September but did not give a full report because he did not want to upset the jury and the public. In his considered opinion, Chapman had been dead for at least two hours, which would mean that the murder occurred at about 4.20 am. If the estimate was correct then many eyewitness accounts were inaccurate. It was accepted at the inquest that the noise Cadosch heard from the yard of No 29 came from Chapman and the Ripper. However, Baxter questioned the time when it occurred, because Mrs Long claimed to have seen Chapman at 5.30 am. Rightly or wrongly, Baxter decided that Cadosch's estimate of the time was inaccurate. The police, however, doubted Mrs Long's observation because it did not comply with Dr Phillips's estimated time of death. Chandler suspected that the body was in the yard when Richardson came to check the cellar lock at 4.40 a.m. but, because he did not go down the steps into the yard, he did not see it. The time of the murder remains uncertain and depends on whether we question the accuracy of the eyewitness accounts or Dr Phillips's estimation of the time of death.

Wynne E. Baxter concluded the inquest on 26 September. In summing up, he said that the killer had anatomical knowledge and believed that an animal slaughterer would not have been able to remove the organs so accurately. Baxter developed a theory which was accepted by many members of the public at the time. He had heard a story from a London medical school that an American had approached their pathology museum with the intention of buying sample organs. Baxter suggested that perhaps the killer was simply obtaining human organs in order to sell them. However Baxter did not develop this idea at the later Ripper inquests.

The murderer had made an incredible escape on a busy morning with blood on his hands, carrying a knife and organs.

The police questioned residents of 29 Hanbury Street and nearby neighbours. They inquired at all of the common lodging houses and questioned anyone who behaved suspiciously in the streets. Over the weekend, large crowds gathered at 29 Hanbury Street with mounting curiosity and concern. Costermongers took advantage of the situation and sold refreshments from their stands while residents in the buildings either side of No 29 charged people to view the murder scene.

The Home Office was against offering a reward for information about the killer because it felt that a reward would tempt people to give false information in order to make money. A common feeling amongst the public at the time of the murders was that the sinister, bloodthirsty killings could not be the work of an Englishman. "Foreigners" were suspected, particularly Jews. On the day of the murder, crowds gathered in parts of East London and screamed abuse at Jewish immigrants. The police prevented any riots.

Leather Apron

There were a number of suspects, such as William Henry Piggott, Joseph Isenschmid and Charles Ludwig, but the one who attracted a great deal of media coverage was "Leather Apron". Jack Pizer, nicknamed Leather Apron because he was frequently seen wearing a leather apron, bullied prostitutes. The newspapers published lengthy stories about Leather Apron, reporting that he was the only name linked with the Whitechapel murder. He was described as a Jewish slipper-maker with a sinister expression, an unusually thick neck, black hair and a small black moustache. He was said to carry a leather-knife and move without making a noise. In other words, he was turned into a melodramatic villain.

Sergeant Thicke and a few other officers arrested Pizer on 10 September. Pizer, a boot finisher, was 5 feet, 4 inches tall with a dark face, dark moustache and side whiskers. He was taken to Leman Street police station. Five long-bladed knives were found at his home. A temporary resident in Hanbury Street, Emanuel Delbast Violenia, identified Pizer as a man who had threatened a woman with a knife in the early hours of 8 September.

Things did not look good for Pizer. However, Violenia could not identify Chapman's body at the morgue as the body of the woman who had been threatened by John Pizer and, after three hours of cross-questioning, proved to be contradictory and unreliable as a witness. Pizer was able to provide a suitable alibi for his whereabouts on the nights of the two murders. After about 36 hours, Pizer was released but he had received a torrent of abuse from the press who called him a "crazy Jew" and "half man, half beast".

On 11 September, the police issued a description of a man wanted for questioning in connection with the murder. He was described as 37 years old, 5 feet, 7 inches tall, with a dark beard and moustache. He was wearing a dark jacket, dark vest and trousers, black scarf and black felt hat. He spoke with a foreign accent. It is unclear where the police found the description.

As the month progressed and the killer was not found, the police, the Home Secretary Henry Matthews, the coroner Wynne Baxter, and Dr Phillips were criticized and accused of incompetence by the press and the public. East Enders were so shocked and terrified by the horrific nature of the killings that they set up their own Whitechapel Vigilance Committee which offered police help in finding the killer.

Chapman's body was identified by Amelia Palmer, Timothy Donovan and Fountain Smith (Chapman's brother). Annie Chapman was secretly buried at Manor Park cemetery on 14 September.

As if Annie Chapman's murder was not gruesome in itself, the following two killings, known as the double murders, were shocking because they occurred on the same evening within mere hours of each other.

Elizabeth Stride (1843–88): The Third Victim

Elizabeth Stride, commonly known as "Long Liz", was born near Gothenburg in Sweden on 27 November 1843. Her father was Gustaf Ericsson, a farmer, and her mother was Beata. In 1865, the police of Gothenburg registered Stride as a prostitute (No 97). On 21 April 1865, she gave birth to a still-born girl and she was twice treated for venereal diseases.

In 1866, she moved to London, and married John Thomas Stride on 7 March 1869. John Stride died in Bromley in 1884. However, Stride said that her husband and two children died aboard the *Princess Alice*, which collided in the Thames with *Bywell Castle*, a large screw steamer, and sank in 1878. Between 600 and 700 people died. She said that she was also on the steamer and that her front teeth were accidentally kicked out by someone as she was climbing a rope to safety. There was no evidence to back up her exciting story.

Stride lived with Michael Kidney, a waterside labourer, for roughly three years from 1885. He said that she was drawn to alcohol. During 1887–88, Stride had a record of eight drunk and disorderly charges at Thames Magistrates Court. On 27 September 1888, Stride took lodgings at 32 Flower and Dean Street after breaking up with Kidney on 25 September.

Appearance

Elizabeth Stride was 44 years old and 5 feet, 2 inches tall. She had dark brown curly hair and light grey eyes. She had a pale complexion and an oval face. Her upper front teeth were missing.

The Murder

29 September 1888, 6.30 pm, she was seen in the Queen's Head public house, Commercial Street, by Elizabeth Tanner, deputy of the common-lodging house at 32 Flower and Dean Street. Tanner had paid Stride sixpence earlier in the day for cleaning two rooms at 32 Flower and Dean Street. They drank together and then walked back to the lodging house.

7.00–8.00 pm, she was seen by Charles Preston, a barber, and Catharine Lane, a charwoman, at 32 Flower and Dean Street, where she was preparing to go out. She borrowed a clothes brush from Charles Preston. Stride left a piece of velvet with Lane to look after until she came back. She did not say where she was going, but showed Lane the sixpence she had earned earlier in the day.

About 11.00 pm, two labourers, J Best and John Gardner, saw a woman whom they believed to be Stride with a man outside the Bricklayer's Arms in Settles Street. Stride and the man had just left the public house as the two men were entering. Best noticed that they were hugging and kissing in the rain, which surprised him because the man was respectably dressed. Best said that the man was 5 feet, 5 inches tall and smartly dressed in a black morning suit and coat with a black billycock hat. He had a thick black moustache. Best and Gardner teased the couple, saying that the man was Leather Apron. The couple soon left.

11.00–12.00 pm, at some point in the hour, Mathew Packer sold fruit to a man and a woman from his front room at 44 Berner Street (two doors down from Dutfield's Yard). The man was 30–35 years old, of a medium height, with a dark complexion. Packer later identified the woman as Stride. However, Packer, an elderly man, made a number of contradictory statements to the press and police and was consequently seen as an unreliable witness.

11.45 pm, William Marshall, a labourer, was standing outside his lodgings at 64 Berner Street. He saw a man and a woman standing outside No 63. Neither of them appeared to be drunk. The couple kissed and the man remarked, "You would say anything but your prayers." The couple then walked down the street in the direction of Dutfield's

Yard. Marshall said that the man was about five feet, six inches tall, middle-aged, stout and clean-shaven. He was decently dressed like a clerk, wearing a small black cutaway coat, dark trousers and a round cap with a peak (like a sailor's hat). The police did not place great importance on William Marshall's evidence because he did not see the man's face. However, Marshall was one of the witnesses at the inquest.

30 September, 12.30 am, while walking on his beat, PC William Smith observed a man and woman in Berner Street, on the opposite side of the street to where the body was later discovered. The man was about 5 feet, 7 inches tall, 28 years old and had a small dark moustache and a dark complexion. He was wearing a black diagonal cutaway coat, a hard felt hat, a white collar and a tie and was carrying a parcel wrapped up in newspaper about 18 inches long and 6–8 inches wide. The woman, whom Smith later identified as Stride, was wearing a red flower pinned to her jacket. He did not hear any of their conversation.

12.30 am, Charles Letchford, resident of 39 Berner Street, saw nothing suspicious as he walked up the street.

12.35–12.40 am, Morris Eagle returned to the International Working Men's Educational Club in 40 Berner Street. The club was founded in 1884 by a group of Jewish Socialists. Eagle had walked his girlfriend home. He went through the gates of Dutfield's yard because the front door of the club was locked. He strolled down the passage to the rear door and did not see anything strange, nor anyone by the gates of the yard. However, the yard was very dark and Eagle could not be certain, when later questioned, that there was no one there.

12.45 am, Israel Schwartz walked past the gateway of the club in Berner Street. He saw a man stop and speak to a woman who was standing in the gateway. She had a flower pinned to her jacket. He later identified Stride's body as the woman he had seen. The man was 5 feet, 5 inches tall, 30 years old with a fair complexion, dark hair, a small brown moustache, a full face and broad shoulders. He was wearing a dark jacket, dark trousers and a black cap with a peak. The man tried to pull the woman into the street but he turned her around and threw her down on to the footway. The woman screamed three times but not loudly.

On crossing to the opposite side of the street, Schwartz noticed a second man standing on the opposite side of the street, lighting a clay pipe. The second man was 5 feet, 11 inches tall and 35 years old, with a fresh complexion, light brown hair and a brown moustache. He wore a dark overcoat and an old black hard felt hat with a wide brim. The man who threw the woman to the ground called out "Lipski" to the man on the opposite side of the road. This was a term of abuse and was a reference to Israel Lipski, a Polish Jew, who murdered Miriam Angel in 1887. Schwartz thought at the time that the first man was addressing his accomplice and that the second man was following him. Schwartz ran away as far as the railway arch but the second man did not follow him. The second man might not have been following Schwartz and could have been walking away from the man with the woman. The police took Schwartz's evidence seriously and printed his description of the first man on the front page of the *Police Gazette* on 19 October 1888.

Between 12.30 and 1.00 am, Fanny Mortimer stood outside of her house at 36 Berner Street, two doors from the scene of the murder, for ten minutes. She saw no one enter or leave the gates of Dutfield's Yard in Berner Street.

12.45 am, James Brown, a dock labourer, was returning home with his supper at the corner of Fairclough Street and Berner Street when he saw a man and a woman standing outside the Board School in Fairclough Street. The woman had her back to the wall and was facing the man, who was bending over her, resting his arm against the wall above her head. The man looked as though he were impeding her. The man was 5 feet, 7 inches tall, stout and wearing a long dark overcoat. As Brown walked past the couple, he heard the woman say, "No. Not tonight. Some other night." He looked at the woman. When Brown saw Stride at the mortuary, he was almost certain that she was the woman he had seen.

Roughly 15 minutes after Brown reached his home at 35 Fairclough Street, he heard cries of "Police!" and "Murder!" Brown and Schwartz's sightings supposedly occurred at exactly the same time. One or both of the witnesses could have made a mistake about the time of their sighting and one or both of them might not have seen Stride. Such confusion is perfect food for Ripper speculation. For example, greater importance could be placed on the second man observed by Schwartz if one wanted to argue that the murders were part of a conspiracy.

1.00 am, Louis Diemschutz, a Russian Jew who sold cheap jewellery and was the Steward of the Berner Street club, returned in his pony and cart. He intended to drop off some goods before taking his pony on to its stables in George Yard. He lived on the premises with his wife. His pony was reluctant to enter the yard and shied to the left.

Diemschutz looked down and noticed a small heap on the ground. He prodded it with the handle of his whip and then descended and struck a match. It was the body of a woman. Her face was turned towards the wall. Diemschutz rushed into the club. Diemschutz later suggested that the Ripper might have been a few feet away from him in the darkness when he first discovered the body and that the killer ran away when he entered the club. Diemschutz ran to an upstairs room and asked for his wife. When he found her with others, he told them all that there was a woman outside but that he could not tell if she was drunk or dead. Diemschutz found a candle and went back into the yard with Isaacs Kozebrodski, a young tailor's machinist, and others. They could see blood by the body. Her right arm was over her belly, her hands and wrists were covered in blood, and her throat was cut.

Many of them hurried off in search of constables, including Morris Eagle. Diemschutz and another member of the club were unsuccessful in finding a policeman. They passed Edward Spooner, horse-keeper, at the corner of Fairclough Street and Christian Street. He asked them what was going on and then returned with them to Berner Street. There were about 15 people in the yard. Spooner looked at the body and lifted up Stride's chin. It was reasonably warm and he noticed that blood was flowing from her throat and running up the yard towards the side door of the club. He found that there was a piece of paper doubled up in Stride's left hand (this was a packet of cachous, pills used by smokers to sweeten the breath). He also noticed a red and white flower pinned to her jacket.

1.04–1.07 am, Morris Eagle and a companion arrived with PC Henry Lamb and PC Edward Collins. Lamb looked at the body and put his hand against Stride's face. The face was slightly warm. He felt her wrist, but could not find a pulse. Her clothes did not appear to have been disturbed and there was no sign of a struggle. Lamb sent Collins off to fetch Dr Frederick William Blackwell from 100 Commercial Road. He sent Eagle off to get further assistance from Leman Street police station. The number of people in the yard had increased.

PC Collins woke Dr Blackwell at 100 Commercial Road. As Dr Blackwell was getting dressed, he sent Edward Johnston, his assistant, with Collins to Berner Street. Johnston felt the body and found that it was warm except for the hands which were cold. The wound in Stride's throat had stopped bleeding. While Johnston was examining the body, PC Lamb shut the gates of the yard to make sure no one left and made a cursory investigation of the club premises and checked people's hands and clothes for any signs of blood. He found nothing suspicious and so searched the neighbouring houses.

1.16 am, Dr Blackwell arrived at Berner Street and estimated that Stride had been dead for only 20–30 minutes, which meant that she could have died between 12.46–12.56 am.

Roughly 2.00 am, when Dr Phillips arrived at the murder scene, Chief Inspector West and Inspector Charles Pinhorn were in possession of the body and Superintendent Arnold and several other policemen were at the scene of the crime. Dr Blackwell and Dr Phillips examined the body. Stride was lying on her left side and her face was pointing towards the right wall. Her legs were drawn up and her feet were close against the wall of the right side of the passage. The neck, chest and legs were quite warm, and the face was slightly warm. Her right hand was open, smeared with blood and resting on her chest, and her left hand was lying on the ground, partially closed and containing a small packet of cachous wrapped in paper. Her mouth was slightly open and she was wearing a check silk scarf around her neck. Elizabeth Stride had a 6-inch gash across her throat. The cut started on the left side roughly 2.5 inches below the angle of the jaw. The cut severed the windpipe in two and ended on the right side about 2.5 inches below the angle of the right jaw. The incision was clean and deviated a little downwards. The left carotid artery had been severed. There was roughly 1 pound of clotted blood near the body and a stream led all the way from the body to the back door of the club. Unlike those of Nichols and Chapman, the gash was not a deep cut to the spine.

The newspapers called her "Lucky Liz", because Jack the Ripper did not disembowel her. There are numerous theories why she was not mutilated, such as the idea that the killer was interrupted by Diemschutz, or that the killer was not Jack the Ripper. Senior policemen such as Abberline, Anderson, Macnaghten, Smith and Swanson believed that Stride was a Ripper victim because the killing seemed to be part of a sequence where the victims were all middle-aged prostitutes who had their throats cut from left to right. There is no evidence to explain why Stride was not disembowelled.

Neither Dr Phillips nor Dr Blackwell could find any spots of blood on Stride's clothes or on the wall of the club.

4.30 am, Stride was taken to St George's Mortuary.

The Post-Mortem

The post-mortem started at 3.00 pm on 1 October at St George's Mortuary. Dr Phillips and Dr Blackwell conducted the autopsy; Blackwell performed the dissection, while Phillips took notes. Unlike the bodies of the first two victims the body was stripped by the doctors themselves. Dr Phillips described their findings at the inquest on 3 October. He said that they found a long gash in Stride's throat, a clean incision from left to right about 6 inches in length. There were no other cuts or marks to suggest strangulation. There were pressure marks over both shoulders, under the collar bones and in front of the chest, apparently caused by the pressure of two hands upon the shoulders.

Both doctors agreed that the cause of death had been haemorrhage resulting from the partial severance of the left carotid artery and the division of the windpipe. Blackwell believed that the throat was cut while Stride was falling to the ground or when she was lying on the ground because blood would have spurted about if she had been standing up. He surmised that the murderer had grabbed the victim by the shoulders and pushed her down to the ground. The murderer had been on her right side and had cut her throat from left to right. The injury could have been inflicted in two seconds.

Contrary to a few histrionic newspaper reports at the time of the murders, Stride was not clutching grapes in her hand when she was killed, and no grape skins or pips could be found in her stomach at the post-mortem.

The Inquest

The inquest started on 1 October at the vestry hall of St George-in-the-East in Cable Street. The coroner was Wynne Baxter. The inquest was adjourned four times and ended on 23 October.

Identifying Stride proved to be a drawn-out process because Mrs Mary Malcolm, who lived at 50 Eagle Street, mistakenly identified the body as that of her sister, Mrs Elizabeth Watts, on 1 October. Malcolm said at the inquest that the victim was undoubtedly Elizabeth Watts. The police and the coroner were not happy with Malcolm's identification and soon discovered that Malcolm was wrong when the real Elizabeth Watts, now Mrs Elizabeth Stokes, turned up. Malcolm had wasted a great deal of police time. Stride was finally identified by John Arundell and Charles Preston.

Elizabeth Stride was buried in a pauper's grave (No 15509) in an East London cemetery on 6 October 1888.

During the early hours of 30 September 1888, while the police were busy with their investigations and Dr Blackwell was examining Stride's body in Dutfield's Yard, Jack the Ripper struck for the second time. The fourth victim was not called "Lucky" by the newspapers.

Catharine Eddowes (1842–88): The Fourth Victim

Catharine Eddowes was born i[...] father was George Eddowes, a [...] Catharine. Eddowes's mother [...] and 1863, she lived with Thoma[...] from the 18th Royal Irish Regime[...]

They lived in Birmingham a[...] but were not registered as marr[...] separated and Catharine had c[...] past seven years, she had lived [...] at 55 Flower and Dean Street.

Appearance

At the time of her death, Catharine Eddowes was 46 years old and 5 feet tall. She had dark auburn hair and hazel eyes. "TC" (Thomas Conway's initials) was tattooed in blue ink on her left forearm. Among other things, she was wearing a black straw bonnet trimmed with green and black velvet and black beads, a black cloth jacket with imitation fur edging around the collar and sleeves, a dark green chintz skirt, a brown linsey dress bodice and a piece of old white apron.

The Murder

On 27 September 1888, Eddowes and Kelly returned, after several months, from hop-picking in Kent. They spent the night in a casual ward at Shoe Lane. On the following day, Kelly managed to earn six pence in London. Eddowes took two pence and told Kelly to use the remaining four pence to get a bed at the lodging house at 55 Flower and Dean Street. Eddowes said that she would get a bed in the casual ward at Mile End.

29 September 10.00–11.00 am, Eddowes was turned out of the casual ward at about 8.00 am and went to Flower and Dean Street to see Kelly. They pawned a pair of boots and were seen eating breakfast in the lodging-house kitchen by Frederick William Wilkinson, the lodging-house deputy.

2.00 pm, Eddowes and Kelly parted company in Houndsditch because Eddowes was going to see if she could get some money from her daughter in Bermondsey. She promised Kelly that she would be back no later than 4.00 pm.

8.30 pm, PC Louis Robinson and PC George Simmons took ...wes to Bishopsgate police station because she had been drunkenly ... a disturbance by imitating a fire engine outside 29 Aldgate ... At the police station, she was asked her name and replied ... e was placed in a cell by James Byfield, the station

...inson looked in on her. She was asleep and stank of

9.45 pm, PC George Hutt came on duty and regularly inspected the cells.

30 September, 12.15 am, Eddowes was awake and singing quietly to herself. At 12.30 am she asked PC Hutt when she would be released and was told, "When you are capable of taking care of yourself."

12.55. am, a sober Eddowes was brought from the cells. When she discovered the time she told PC Hutt that she would get "a damn fine hiding" when she got home. PC Hutt said, "And serve you right. You have no right to get drunk." When she was asked her name for the second time, she answered "Mary Ann Kelly" and said that her address was "6 Fashion Street, Spitalfields."

1.00 am (the time when Elizabeth Stride was discovered in Berner Street), PC Hutt guided Eddowes through the passage and asked her to close the outer door as she left. Eddowes replied, " All right. Goodnight, old cock." Those were her last recorded words. She turned towards Houndsditch. Hutt later estimated that it would have taken Eddowes eight minutes to reach Mitre Square.

1.30 am, PC Edward Watkins passed through Mitre Square on his beat. He did not see anything suspicious. Mitre Square was about 24 yards square and could be approached in three ways: a carriageway, which led into the square from Mitre Street; Church Passage which joined to Duke Street; and a passage which ran from St James's Place to the northern point of Mitre Square.

1.34 am, Joseph Lawende (or Lavende), a commercial traveller, Joseph Hyam Levy, a butcher, and Harry Harris, a furniture dealer, left the Imperial Club at 16–17 Duke's Place. At the corner of Duke's Place, the entrance to Church Passage (which lead to Mitre Square), the three Jewish men saw a man and a woman talking. Lawende and Levy later identified Eddowes' clothes as the same as those worn by the woman. However, they did not see the woman's face. Lawende observed the man's appearance. The man was roughly 5 feet, 8 inches tall and about 30 years old. He was wearing a pepper-and-salt-coloured loose jacket, a grey cloth cap with a peak and a red neckerchief and had a fair complexion and a moustache. The woman had her hand on the man's chest. Levy said to the other two men that he did not like going home on his own when he saw those "sorts of characters about".

1.40–1.42 am, PC James Harvey walked down Church Passage on his beat. He reached the entrance of Mitre Square but did not enter. He saw no one and did not hear anything suspicious.

1.45 am (three-quarters of an hour after Stride had been discovered in Dutfield's yard), PC Edward Watkins entered Mitre Square on his beat (from the opposite side) and discovered the body of Catharine Eddowes in the southwest corner of the square, lying on her back in a pool of blood. The corner was a popular place for prostitutes and their clients. Watkins flashed his light on to Eddowes. Her throat was cut. Her clothes were above her waist, her stomach was ripped up and her bowels were protruding.

PC Watkins ran to Kearley and Tonge's warehouse on the opposite side of the square to get help from George James Morris, the nightwatchman and a former Metropolitan policeman. Watkins told Morris of his discovery and they both rushed to Eddowes's body. Morris then ran out of the square into Mitre Street and then into Aldgate in search of a constable. Watkins stayed with the body. Morris attracted the attention of PC James Harvey and told him about the body. PC Harvey called over to PC James Thomas Holland, who was across the street. They all went to Mitre Square. PC Holland then went to fetch Dr George William Sequeira at 34 Jewry Street, Aldgate. When Dr Sequeira reached the scene of the crime, he believed that the woman had not been dead for more than 15 minutes, but he did not touch the body until Dr Gordon Brown arrived.

1.55 am, Inspector Edward Collard heard news of the murder at Bishopsgate Street police station, telegraphed the information to headquarters, sent a constable to get Dr Frederick Gordon Brown, the City police surgeon, and rushed to Mitre Square.

The police investigation into the murder was led by Major Henry Smith, who was the acting Commissioner of the City of London Police, and Inspector James McWilliam, head of the City Detective Department. Unlike the other three murders, this murder had been committed on City Police territory. Major Smith, Inspector McWilliam, Inspector Collard, Detective Superintendent Albert Foster and others soon arrived at the scene. Sergeant Jones found three small black metal buttons, a thimble and a mustard tin containing two pawn tickets beside the body. One ticket was for John Kelly's boots and the other ticket was for a flannel shirt given to Eddowes by her friend, Emily Birrell (or Burrell).

2.03–2.18 am, Dr Brown arrived at Mitre Square and examined the body. The body was on its back with the head turned to the left shoulder and the arms were by the side of the body. The left leg was extended in a line with the body and the right leg was bent at the thigh and knee. A thimble was lying off the finger on the right side. The throat had been cut and below the cut was a neckerchief. The abdomen was exposed and the intestines were drawn out and placed over the right shoulder. Part of the intestines (about 2 feet in length) were separated from the body and placed between the body and the left arm. The eyes, nose, lips and cheeks had been horribly mutilated. The lobe and auricle of the right ear was cut through. There was a quantity of clotted blood on the pavement on the left side of the neck, around the shoulder and upper part of the arm. There was fluid blood-coloured serum which had flowed under the neck to the right shoulder. There were no superficial bruises and no blood on the skin of the abdomen or any kind of secretion on the thighs. There was no blood on the front of the clothes and there was no spurting of blood on the bricks or pavement surrounding Eddowes.

When Dr Brown touched the body it was quite warm and he guessed that Eddowes died within the previous 30 minutes.

The body was taken to the City Mortuary in Golden Lane.

Goulston Street Graffito

2.20 am, PC Alfred Long passed through Goulston Street on his beat, but saw nothing peculiar.

2.55 am, PC Long passed through Goulston Street for the second time on his beat. This time he saw a piece of bloody apron on the floor of a stairway leading to 108–119 Wentworth Model Dwellings, Goulston Street. The stairway was used by the tenants of the building. The piece of ripped material matched the apron worn by Catharine Eddowes. It was (and is) commonly accepted that Jack the Ripper went through Goulston Street during his escape, and that he stopped by the stairs and wiped his hands or cleaned his knife on the piece of material and deposited it on the stairway. Above the piece of apron on the wall was a message written in white chalk. PC Long reported that the message read, "The Juwes are the men That Will not be Blamed for nothing". The Metropolitan Police and the Home Office agreed with Long's wording but the City Police believed that the message read, "The Juwes are not the men That will be Blamed for nothing".

There has been a great deal of dispute over the meaning of the message, because it is not clear if the Jews should be blamed or excluded from the murders or whether the word "Juwes" actually means "Jews". Superintendent Arnold asserted that the writing had nothing to do with the murder, but Detective Constable Halse believed that the words were written recently because he had passed the doorway at 2.20 am and not noticed the message. The message was seen by many as the Ripper's "calling card", but it could have been on the wall before he entered the building. The message was connected with the murders because it seemed to be a comment on the rise in anti-Semitism during the Whitechapel Murders.

There is no photographic evidence of the message because Sir Charles Warren ordered the writing to be erased, which was against the wishes of Inspector McWilliam and the City Police. The Metropolitan Police erased the graffito at about 5.30 am, with the hope of preventing further anti-Semitism. The piece of apron was given to Dr Phillips at Golden Lane Mortuary. It was the only physical clue ever left by Jack the Ripper.

3.00 am, Two murder investigations were going on at the same time. The investigation of the Berner Street murder was the responsibility of the Metropolitan Police and the Mitre Square murder was the responsiblity of the City force.

The Post-Mortem

Dr Brown made a post-mortem examination of Eddowes at 2.30 pm on 30 September at the mortuary. He was observed by Dr Sequeira who was the first medical man on the scene of the crime, Dr Saunders, the City's public analyst, and Dr Phillips.

For the first time in the series of Whitechapel Murders, the killer mutilated his victim's face. There was a cut about a quarter of an inch through the lower left eyelid, dividing the structures completely through, and there was a scratch through the skin on the left upper eyelid near to the angle of the nose. The right eyelid was cut through to about half an inch. There was a deep cut over the bridge of the nose, starting from the left border of the nasal bone, down near to the angle of the jaw on the right side of the cheek. The cut went into the bone, dividing all the structures of the cheek except the mucous membrane of the mouth. The tip of the nose was sliced off.

There was a downwards cut from where the wings of the nose joined on to the face, dividing the upper lip and cutting through the substance of the gum. There was an incision on each side of the cheek which peeled up the skin and created a triangular flap. The throat was slit across and the gash was about 6–7 inches in length. The cut started about 2.5 inches below and behind the left ear and extended across the throat to about 3 inches below the lobe of the right ear. The big muscle across the throat was divided through on the left side, and the larynx was severed below the vocal chord.

The cause of death was haemorrhage from the left common carotid artery. Brown believed that the death was immediate and that the mutilations were inflicted after death.

The front walls of the abdomen were laid open from the breast bone to the pubes. The incision went upwards. The liver was stabbed as if by the point of a sharp instrument. There was another incision into the liver of about 2.5 inches and below this the left lobe of the liver was slit through by a vertical cut. The abdominal walls were divided in the middle line to within a quarter of an inch of the navel. The cut then took a horizontal course for 2.5 inches towards the right side. It then divided around the navel on the left side and made a parallel incision to the former horizontal incision. The cut then went down the right side of the vagina and the rectum. There was a stab on the left of the groin and an incision of about 3 inches below this. There was a cut from an inch below the crease of the left thigh down the inner side of the thigh, separating the left labium, forming a flap of skin up to the groin. There was also a flap of skin formed from the right thigh, caused by an incision. The pancreas was cut, but not removed. The left kidney was carefully taken out and removed by the killer. Dr Brown believed that someone who knew the position of the kidney must have done it. The womb was cut through horizontally and taken away with some of the ligaments, leaving a stump of three-quarters of an inch. The press left out the gory details of Dr Brown's inquest deposition with the hope of protecting the public.

Dr Brown surmised that the victim must have been lying on the ground when the wounds were inflicted and all of the injuries were performed by a sharp pointed knife that was roughly 6 inches in length. He believed that the mutilations were the work of one man and had happened at the spot where the body was found. There was a theory at the time that Eddowes had been murdered somewhere else and then dumped in Mitre Square. Brown felt that this was inaccurate because the blood on the left side of the body had clotted, which meant that it must have fallen at the time that the throat was cut.

The Inquest

The inquest started on 4 October 1888, before Samuel Frederick Langham, the City coroner. It was adjourned until 11 October and the jury gave their verdict on the second day – wilful murder by some person unknown. At the inquest, which started two days after Baxter's inquest on Stride, there were arguments over whether the brutal cuts were the work of someone with anatomical knowledge. Both Dr Sequeira and Dr Saunders believed that the mutilations did not show that the killer had great anatomical skill and did not believe that the stolen organs were intentionally sought.

Dr Brown, however, felt that the murderer possessed a reasonable amount of knowledge, because he carefully removed a kidney. He felt that the person was not necessarily a doctor or a surgeon, but could have been an animal slaughterer. Dr Phillips made no report to the inquest and his opinion is unclear.

The police questioned the residents of Mitre Square, but they had not heard anything suspicious. The killer had managed to strike for the second time in one evening with horrifying efficiency. He had managed to travel over half a mile from the last murder site without being stopped by policemen. After killing and mutilating Eddowes, the Ripper escaped from Mitre Square, carrying a knife, a piece of torn apron, a kidney and a womb. He seemed to be viciously efficient and virtually invisible. The police had two new murders in one night and no suspects. The public were understandably fearful. Police secrecy meant that the public and the press could only speculate on the competence of the police.

At 3.00 pm on 30 September 1888, there were public meetings in London. The meeting in Victoria Park attracted nearly 1,000 people. The gathering unanimously agreed that it was time for both Sir Charles Warren and Home Secretary Henry Matthews to resign.

The City Police offered a reward of £500 for information leading to the arrest of Jack the Ripper on 1 October. The Lord Mayor offered a further £500 in the name of the Corporation of London. The Home Office refused to offer a government reward despite requests from the public.

"Dear Boss"

On 27 September 1888, the Central News Agency received a letter from someone who called himself "Jack the Ripper". This was the first time that the nickname was used and it soon replaced the "Leather Apron". Dated 25 September, the letter was treated as a hoax by the Agency and it was not given to Chief Constable Williamson at Scotland Yard for two days. It did not become public knowledge until 30 September.

The letter, which started "Dear Boss", was written in red ink as the writer could not use blood because it went "thick like glue". The writer firstly mocked the police investigation, particularly their suspicion of the Leather Apron, and then stated that he was "down on whores" and would not stop "ripping" them until he was "buckled". He proudly asserted that he gave the last victim no time to "squeal" and said that he intended to clip the next victim's ears off and send them to the police "just for jolly". He requested that the letter should be kept back until he had done "a bit more work". The letter ended with "Yours truly/Jack the Ripper".

On 1 October, the day after the double murders, a postcard, which was apparently bloodstained, was sent to the Central News Agency from "Jack the Ripper". It told the Agency that they would hear about a "double event" caused by "Saucy Jack" on the following day. He wrote that the first victim (Elizabeth Stride) "squealed a bit" and that he could not kill her immediately. He did not have time to get the victim's ears for the police. He then thanked the Agency for holding back the letter until he had killed more people (obviously unaware that the letter had been held back because it was regarded as a hoax).

The postcard would suggest that the writer had knowledge of the double murders and sent this information before it had become public knowledge. The lobe of Kate Eddowes's right ear had been severed as if an attempt had been made to cut it off. However, news of the double murders had reached the late newspapers on 30 September. The writer could have read about the murders and sent the postcard early on Monday morning. This could have then reached the Central News Agency the same day. Many believed that the correspondences were written by the killer and the Metropolitan Police took them seriously enough to print the letter and postcard on posters, requesting the public to contact them if they recognized the handwriting. They also sent facsimiles of the correspondences to the press.

Sadly, the publicity of the correspondences created a mass of fake Jack the Ripper letters, wasting a great deal of police time. Sir Robert Anderson was convinced that the correspondences were a hoax written by an enterprising London journalist because the writer knew that if the letter was sent to the Central News Agency it would receive maximum publicity. The letter was printed in the morning edition of the *Daily News* and the postcard was published in the evening edition of the *Star* on 1 October 1888. Most modern researchers believe that the correspondences were a hoax but they have not been proven without question to be fraudulent.

"From Hell"

At 5.00 pm on 16 October 1888, George Lusk, chairman of the Whitechapel Vigilance committee, received a letter and a small cardboard box wrapped in brown paper. The letter was addressed "From Hell" and read, "Mr Lusk. Sor (sic), I send you half the Kidne (sic) I took from one woman prasarved (sic) it for you tother (sic) piece I fried and ate it was very nise (sic) I may send you the bloody knif (sic) that took it out if you only wate (sic) a whil (sic) longer. Signed Catch me when you can Mishter (sic) Lusk". The small box contained a kidney.

At first, Lusk and the committee thought that it was a hoax but decided to take the kidney to the surgery of Dr Frederick Wiles of 56 Mile End Road on 18 October 1888. Dr Wiles was not in, so they handed the kidney to his assistant, F S Reed. Reed believed that the organ was human and that it had been preserved in spirits of wine. He wanted to be certain of his examination, so the kidney was taken to Dr Thomas Horrocks Openshaw, Curator of the Pathological Museum at the London Hospital. Dr Openshaw believed that it was half of a left human kidney but could not say how long it had been removed from the body and whether it originally came from a woman.

The Vigilance Committee took the kidney to Leman Street police station and gave it to Inspector Abberline. The kidney was sent by the Metropolitan Police to the City Police where it was examined by Dr Gordon Brown, the City Police Surgeon. Unlike organs used for dissection purposes in hospitals, the human kidney was not charged with fluid. The kidney, therefore, had been directly taken from a body, but none of the doctors could say with unquestionable certainty that it was Eddowes's missing kidney.

The police were not idle in their investigations even if they were unsuccessful. By 19 October, 80 people had been detained by the Metropolitan Police and the movements of more than 300 others had been investigated. Abberline said that the Metropolitan Police made about 1,600 sets of papers about their investigations.

Eddowes was identified by John Kelly on 2 October and his identification was confirmed by Mrs Gold (Catharine's sister) on the following day.

Catharine Eddowes was buried in an unmarked grave in Little Ilford on 8 October (two days after Elizabeth Stride had been buried). Crowds lined the streets.

The double murders terrified people because they occurred in quick succession. However, the worst was yet to come. Jack the Ripper's fifth and final victim (or, at least, his final canonical victim) was horrifically mutilated in her own room and on her own bed.

Mary Jane Kelly (1863–88): The Fifth Victim

All events in the early life of Mary Jane Kelly, known to a few of her friends as Marie Jeanette Kelly, perhaps remain uncertain. She was born in Castletown, Limerick in 1863, daughter of John and Mary Kelly. As a young child she moved with her father, who worked as a foreman at an ironworks, to Wales. She married John Davies, a collier, in 1879. He died a few years later in a pit explosion. She moved to Cardiff, where her cousin lived, and became a prostitute. In 1884, she arrived in London and started work in a brothel. One of the customers took her to France, but she soon returned to England. The brief excursion is probably the reason why her name was sometimes changed to Marie Jeanette Kelly.

On 8 April 1887, she met Joseph Barnett, a porter at Billingsgate Market. They decided to live together on the following day and lodged in various places within the "wicked quarter mile" like George Street, Little Paternoster Row, Dorset Street and Brick Lane. At the beginning of 1888, they finally lived in a single room at 13 Miller's Court, which was the back room of 26 Dorset Street. It was a cramped room, 12 feet by 15 feet square. Kelly had taken the room in her own name. The weekly rent was 4 shillings and sixpence and Kelly owed nearly 30 shillings rent. Joseph Barnett had lost his job which caused Kelly to return to prostitution. Her profession, and the fact that she let prostitutes stay in their room, caused Barnett to leave. Kelly had told friends that she was frightened by the Whitechapel Murders and was thinking about leaving London. When Barnett lived with her, she would get him to read aloud from the newspaper about the Whitechapel Murders.

Appearance

The youngest of the victims, at the time of her death Mary Jane Kelly was about 25 years old and 5 feet, 7 inches tall. She had long blonde hair, blue eyes and a fair complexion.

The Murder

8 November, 7.30–7.45 pm, Joseph Barnett called on Kelly at 26 Dorset Street. Although they had split up, he visited her most days. Lizzie Albrook left the couple in the room at 8.00 pm. Barnett left a short time after 8.00 pm.

11.45 pm, Mary Ann Cox, who lived at 5 Miller's Court and had known Kelly for about eight or nine months, saw Kelly as she entered Dorset Street from Commercial Street. Kelly was just ahead of Cox and was walking with a man. She was wearing a linsey frock and a red knitted crossover shawl pulled around her shoulders.

Cox described the man as about 35 or 36 years old and 5 feet, 5 inches tall. He was stout, blotchy-faced and had a full carroty moustache and wore a long shabby overcoat and a billycock hat. He was carrying a quart pail of beer. Cox followed them into Miller's Court and they stopped outside No 13.

As she passed them, Cox said, "Goodnight". Kelly said goodnight back. Cox believed that Kelly was drunk. Cox went to her own room and soon heard Kelly singing, "A violet I plucked from Mother's grave when a boy".

12.00 pm, Cox returned to the streets and could hear Kelly singing the same song.

9 November, 12.30 am, Catharine Picket, a flower seller and neighbour, was annoyed by Kelly's singing and wanted to complain. Her husband stopped her.

1.00 am, Cox returned to her room to warm up for a few minutes because it was raining. She could hear Kelly singing and had noticed that the light in her room was still on. She went out again.

Roughly 1.00 am, Elizabeth Prater, another prostitute, stood at the entrance to Miller's Court for roughly 30 minutes waiting for her partner. He did not turn up so she went to Mr McCarthy's shop and talked to the owner for about ten minutes. In all that time, Prater did not see anyone enter or leave Miller's Court. She did not hear Kelly singing and went to her room (No 20), which was directly above Kelly's and went to sleep.

2.00 am, George Hutchinson, a casual labourer who was a resident at Victoria Home in Commercial Street, had returned from Romford. He saw Mary Kelly by Flower and Dean Street. They stopped and talked because they knew each other well. She asked him if he would lend her sixpence but Hutchinson replied that he had spent all of his money at Romford. Kelly informed him that she must go and look for some money and headed in the direction of Thrawl Street. Hutchinson felt that Kelly was not drunk but that she was a little bit "spreeish". Hutchinson watched her walk towards the corner of Thrawl Street where a man put a hand on Kelly's shoulder and said something that made the pair of them laugh. Kelly said, "All right" and the man said, "You will be all right for what I have told you." He then placed his right arm around Kelly's shoulders and they walked back towards Dorset Street in the direction of Hutchinson. As they passed him outside the Queen's Head public house at the corner of Fashion Street, Hutchinson observed the man. The man was 5 feet, 6 inches tall and about 35 or 36 years old. He had a heavy moustache which curled up at the ends, dark eyes, bushy eyebrows and a dark complexion. Hutchinson said that he had a "Jewish appearance". The man had a soft felt hat drawn over his eyes and was wearing a long dark coat trimmed with astrakhan, a dark jacket underneath, black trousers, a white collar, a black necktie with a horseshoe pin, a massive gold chain and a watch chain which had a large seal with a red stone hanging from it. He wore a dark pair of "spats" with light buttons over button boots and carried a pair of brown kid gloves in his right hand and a small package, about 8 inches in length with a strap around it, in his left. Kelly and the man crossed Commercial Street and turned down into Dorset Street. Hutchinson followed them. The couple stood talking outside the passage leading to Miller's Court for about three minutes. The man said something to Kelly and she replied, "All right, my dear. Come along. You will be comfortable". The man put his arm around Kelly who kissed him and said, "I've lost my handkerchief!" The man pulled a red handkerchief out of his pocket and gave it to her. The couple went to Miller's Court. Hutchinson stood and waited until 3.00 am. As the clock struck the hour, he walked away. Neither Kelly nor the man had appeared during this time. For some unknown reason, Hutchinson did not give his information to the police until 6.00 pm on 12 November.

2.30 am, Sarah Lewis, who possibly reported a similar story to the press under the name of Mrs Kennedy, was staying with a couple (called Keyler), who lived opposite Kelly in Miller's Court, because she had had an argument with her husband. When she arrived in Dorset Street, she saw a man leaning against the wall of the lodging house opposite the passage that lead into Miller's Court (this could have possibly been Hutchinson). Just before 4.00 am she heard a single loud scream of "Murder!" It sounded like the cry of a young woman not far away. However, she was not seen as a reliable eyewitness by the police because she kept contradicting herself on matters of times and details.

3.00 am, Cox returned to her room. She could not hear Kelly singing, nor could she see a light coming from her room. Cox went to bed.

Roughly 4.00 am, Elizabeth Prater was woken by her pet cat who was walking across her neck. She guessed that the time was about 4.00 am but she did not check. She heard a cry of "Oh murder", which sounded as if it were nearby. Her room was directly above Kelly's room. She took no notice because this was a common cry in the East End, and she did not hear anything else.

5.00–5.30 am, Prater left her room and went to the Ten Bells public house, at the corner of Commercial Street and Church Street, for a glass of rum. She saw no one in the court and, after her drink, returned to her lodgings and slept until 11.00 am.

5.45 am, Cox heard what she thought to be a man's footsteps leaving Miller's Court but she did not look out of her room.

8.00 am, Catharine Picket left her room to go to the market. She went to Kelly's room to borrow a shawl because it was raining. She knocked on the door but there was no reply. Picket assumed that Kelly was asleep and went to the market.

8.00 am, at roughly the same time as Picket went to Kelly's room, Maurice Lewis, a tailor who lived in Dorset Street, saw Kelly leave her room and return a few moments later.

8.00–8.30 am, Caroline Maxwell, wife of the deputy of the lodging house at 14 Dorset Street opposite Miller's Court, was on her way to the milk shop in Bishopsgate Street and saw Mary Kelly at the entrance to Miller's Court. Kelly was wearing a dark skirt, black velvet bodice and a maroon shawl. She enquired why Kelly was up so early and Kelly replied that she felt sick because she had "the horrors of drink" upon her. Maxwell suggested that she should go to the Britannia public house and have a drink. Kelly said that she had already drunk half a pint of ale, which had caused her to vomit. Maxwell expressed sympathy and then walked away towards the milk shop.

Roughly 9.00 am, on her way home, Maxwell saw Kelly for the second time outside the Britannia public house. Kelly was talking to a stout man who looked like a market porter and was wearing dark clothes and a plaid coat.

10.00 am, Maurice Lewis said that he saw Kelly in the Britannia public house drinking with some people.

10.45 am, John McCarthy, Kelly's landlord and the owner of a Chandler's shop at 27 Dorset Street, told Thomas "Indian Harry" Bowyer, his assistant, to visit Kelly's room and try to get some of her long overdue rent. Bowyer went to room 13 and knocked on Kelly's door. There was no answer. He knocked again but there was no reply. He looked through the keyhole but could not see anything. One of the window panes in Kelly's room was broken so Bowyer reached through the broken pane and pulled back the curtain. He saw two lumps of flesh on the bedside table. He looked at the bed and saw Kelly's badly mutilated corpse

Bowyer rushed back to Mc Carthy and told him about what he had just seen. McCarthy hurried back to room 13 with Bowyer and looked through the window. He later told *The Times* on 10 November 1888, that the murder looked more like the "work of a devil than of a man".

McCarthy and Bowyer rushed to the Commercial Street police station, where they told Inspector Walter Beck and other constables the dreadful news. They all hurried to the scene of the crime.

Beck saw the body through the window and sent for Dr George Bagster Phillips, the divisional surgeon, further police asssistance and for the news to be telegraphed to Scotland Yard, requesting bloodhounds. Luckily, extra constables arrived quite quickly to control the panicking crowd of people that had developed in Commercial

Street. The constables were in the area because the murder occurred on the same day as the Lord Mayor's Show and there had been concern that there would be socialist disturbances. Beck cordoned off each end of Dorset Street and closed Miller's Court. No one was allowed to enter or leave the street.

11.15 am, Dr George Bagster Phillips arrived at Miller's Court and viewed the body through the window.

11.30 am, Inspector Frederick George Abberline arrived and held a brief conversation with Inspector Beck and Dr Phillips. Phillips suggested not entering room 13 until the bloodhounds were brought in. The police questioned residents. A photographer was brought to the scene and took photographs through the window, after a great deal of delay.

1.30 pm, Superintendent Thomas Arnold, head of H Division, arrived and said that the bloodhounds were not available and ordered the door to be forced open. The door to room 13 was smashed open with a pick-axe by McCarthy. The first person through the door was Dr Phillips. Mary Kelly was lying on her back in the middle of the bed and was dressed only in a linen undergarment. Her head was turned on the left cheek and the left arm was close to the body with the forearm lying across the abdomen. The right arm rested on the mattress with the elbow bent and the fingers clenched. Phillips believed that the body had been moved from the right-hand side of the bed after receiving the death wound because the pillow and sheet at the top right-hand corner of the bed were saturated in blood. The blood was produced by the severing of the carotid artery, which was the immediate cause of death.

Abberline inspected the room. The remains of a fire lay in the grate, which contained burned clothes, including a woman's bonnet. The spout and handle of a kettle in the grate had been melted. Abberline believed that the killer had made a fire in order to illuminate the room. Kelly's clothes were found on a chair at the foot of the bed.

2.00 pm, Dr Bond arrived at Miller's Court. Both Dr Phillips and Dr Bond examined the body in greater detail. The throat had been cut from ear to ear down to the spinal column and the face had been hacked beyond recognition. The breasts were cut off. The arms had several jagged wounds and the legs were wide apart. The surface of the abdomen and thighs had been removed. The abdominal cavity had been emptied of its viscera. The uterus and kidney had been placed with one of the breasts under the head, while the other breast was found by the right foot. The liver had been placed between the feet, the intestines by the right side of the body and the spleen by the left side of the body. The flaps that had been removed from the abdomen and thighs were resting on a table. Rigor mortis had set in, which meant that Bond could not say with unquestionable certainty when Kelly had been killed. He guessed that she had been killed at about 1.00–2.00 am. Beneath the right corner of the bed was a pool of blood on the floor. The wall by the right side of the bed had a number of bloodstains in line with the neck. Bond believed that Jack the Ripper had no anatomical knowledge and did not even possess the technical knowledge of a butcher or horse slaughterer.

About 4.00 pm, the body of Mary Kelly was taken to the Shoreditch Mortuary. The windows of room 13 were boarded up and the door was padlocked. The police searched common-lodging houses and questioned lodgers.

The Post-Mortem

A post-mortem examination of Mary Jane Kelly was performed by Dr Phillips, Dr Bond, Dr Brown and Dr Phillips's assistant on 10 November. The number of doctors present suggested that the investigation of the Whitechapel Murders was being treated with greater care.

The face had been cut in all directions and the nose, cheeks, eyebrows and ears were partly removed. The lips were blanched and cut by several incisions running down to the chin. The neck was cut through the skin and other tissues down to the fifth and sixth vertebrae of the spinal column and the air passage was cut at the lower part of the larynx, through the cricoid cartilage. Both breasts were removed by rough circular incisions and the skin and tissues of the abdomen from the costal arch to the pubes were removed in three large flaps. The right thigh was cut to the bone, the left thigh was stripped of skin, fascia and muscles as far as the knee, and the left calf had a long gash through the skin and tissues to the deep muscles, which reached from the knee to 5 inches above the ankle. The lower part of the right lung was broken and torn away. The heart was missing. Partly digested food, consisting of fish and potatoes, was found in the abdominal cavity along with the remains of the stomach.

The Inquest

Kelly's inquest started at 11.00 am on 12 November 1888, at Shoreditch Town Hall. Dr Roderick Macdonald, coroner for North-East Middlesex, was in charge of the inquest. Macdonald was criticized by one of the jury at the inquest, who said that the body had been found in Whitechapel and was therefore the responsibility of Wynne E Baxter, who had been in charge of the first three inquests. Macdonald correctly argued that the body was taken to a mortuary in his district, which made him responsible for the inquest. He asserted that Annie Chapman had been killed in his area but taken to a mortuary in Mr Baxter's area which had meant that Baxter performed Chapman's inquest.

Macdonald briskly heard various testimonies from nine local residents. Dr Bond surmised that Kelly had been killed at about 1.00 or 2.00 am. If his supposition was correct then neither Maurice Lewis nor Caroline Maxwell could have seen Kelly from 8.00 am onwards. Their evidence was undervalued because it did not relate to Bond's estimation of death. It was assumed that they had the date or the time of day confused. Lewis and Maxwell had no particular reason to confuse the day of the Lord Mayor's Show with any other day, and the time of murder remains a grey area, which is often used to support the idea that someone other than Kelly was murdered or that Jack the Ripper escaped in Kelly's clothes. Phillips, Beck and Abberline said little at the inquest in case it hindered their investigation. Macdonald was happy with their evidence and then encouraged the jury to decide on the cause of death. Their verdict was wilful murder by some person unknown. Unlike the other four inquests, the inquest only lasted one day. Macdonald was criticized for his methods in the inquest, because he did not give a full description of the injuries, establish the identity of the deceased nor speculate on the time of death. The press criticized him for the speed of the inquest, which was brief considering the fact that Kelly was the first victim to be murdered indoors and was the most horribly mutilated.

On 9 November, Sir Charles Warren, the Metropolitan Police Commissioner, resigned. The public had accused him of being incompetent and of slowing down the capture of Jack the Ripper. He was replaced by James Munro, the ex-head of CID, on 27 November.

On 10 November, the government decided that the Home Secretary Henry Matthews should continue to refuse an offer of a reward but should offer a free pardon to any accomplice of the murderer of Mary Kelly who would betray the killer into the hands of the police.

Kelly was buried at Leytonstone Roman Catholic Cemetery on 19 November 1888. Her family did not attend.

Conclusion

It is not clear why Jack the Ripper stopped killing after Mary Kelly (if indeed he did stop killing). There are many arguments – that the extreme mutilation of Kelly fulfilled his bloodlust or that he was placed in a mental asylum, or that he committed suicide, or that he was killed.

The only conclusion that we can safely make about the Whitechapel Murders is that they are frustratingly inconclusive. Discovering the identity of the killer is complicated. The eyewitness accounts are frequently contradictory, the victims (by nature of their profession) would have been seen with numerous men, and the murderer does not appear to have a motive for killing the five women.

The police files on Jack the Ripper were closed in 1892, four years after the murders. In 1894, Sir Melville Macnaghten, Chief Constable of the CID, wrote a confidential report with the intention of disproving claims by the *Sun* newspaper that Thomas Cutbush was Jack the Ripper. The report, simply known as the "Macnaghten Report", or the "Macnaghten Memoranda" names three people whom he believed were more likely to be Jack the Ripper than Thomas Cutbush.

The first suspect was Montague John Druitt, a middle-aged schoolmaster and barrister, who disappeared at the time of the Miller's Court murder and whose body was found floating in the Thames on 31

December 1888, seven weeks after the Miller's Court murder, though it had been in the Thames for at least a month. Druitt's own family suspected him of being Jack the Ripper and it was alleged that he was sexually insane.

The second suspect in the Macnaghten Report was Kosminski, a Polish Jew and resident in Whitechapel. Macnaghten said that Kosminski became insane because of too many years of "solitary vices" and had a great hatred of women, particularly prostitutes. He had strong homicidal tendencies and was placed in a lunatic asylum in 1889.

The third and final suspect was Michael Ostrog, a Russian doctor and a convict, who was detained in a lunatic asylum as a homicidal maniac. Ostrog was known to be habitually cruel to women and often carried surgical knives and other instruments. Macnaghten said that Ostrog had a bad criminal record and his whereabouts at the time of the murders could not be ascertained. Macnaghten's principal suspect was Druitt.

Since Macnaghten's report there have been an inexhaustible number of suspects pushed forward. Many grey areas surround the case, as well as gaps caused by lack of evidence, which helps people to create a whole host of theories on the identity of Jack the Ripper. Interestingly, no one has managed to unmask the Whitechapel Murderer. The arguments over his identity are as heated today as they were among the police, press and public in 1888.

Key Texts

Witness Statements

Elizabeth Long (aka Mrs Darrell)

Elizabeth Long is a contentious witness, in that her evidence casts into doubt Dr George Bagster Phillips's statement that Chapman had been dead for two hours when he examined her body at around 6.30 am. Those who believe Mrs Long – and the coroner, Wynne Baxter, was among them – point to the apparently corroborative evidence of Albert Cadosch, who testified that, at 5.30 am, he heard a voice in the yard of 29 Hanbury Street saying "No!" as well as something falling against the wooden fence dividing the yards. Those who side with Phillips, allowing for half an hour either way, point out that Long's evidence is vague and inconsistent. Why did she particularly observe the time when she passed No. 29? And if this couple which she observed were of such interest, why did she not turn to see the man's face? She *thought* he wore a dark coat, but was not quite certain of that... She couldn't say what his age was...but he *looked* over forty... He *appeared* to be a little taller than Chapman...appeared to be a foreigner... Few have pointed out that Cadosch's evidence fits the notion of someone, drunk or otherwise, coming upon the body and lurching into the fence with an ejaculation quite as well as the notion that this was Chapman's last moment, for there must have been other sounds attendant upon the killing – notably the splashing of the blood on such a dry night.

Baxter: Did you see the man's face?
Mrs Long: I did not and could not recognize him again. He was,

however, dark complexioned, and was wearing a brown
deerstalker hat. I think he was wearing a dark coat but
cannot be sure.

Baxter: Was he a man or a boy?

Mrs Long: Oh, he was a man over forty, as far as I could tell. He
             seemed to be a little taller than the deceased. He looked
             to me like a foreigner, as well as I could make out.

Baxter: Was he a labourer or what?

Mrs Long: He looked what I should call shabby genteel.

William Marshall

Marshall, a labourer of 64 Berner Street, denied seeing the flower which
others reported on Stride's bodice, but that does not mean that he was
an unreliable witness. His description of the man's coat and cap tallies
with that of PC Smith, while his overall description of the man closely
resembles that given by J Best and John Gardner, who, shortly before
11.00 pm, saw Stride leaving the Bricklayer's Arms, Settles Street, with
a man about 5 feet 5 inches tall, with a black moustache and weak,
sandy eyelashes, and wearing a morning suit and a billycock hat.
Gardner corroborated Best's evidence in every regard. Marshall
testified that the man he saw had been kissing Stride and that he heard
him say, in a mild, educated voice, "You would say anything but your
prayers," at which Stride laughed. This is a very natural response to
Stride saying (roughly): "Then I'd better say my prayers" (suggestive of
a threat).

Baxter: Did you notice how he was dressed?

Marshall: In a black cutaway coat and dark trousers.

Baxter: Was he young or old?

Marshall: Middle-aged he seemed to be.

Baxter: Was he wearing a hat?

Marshall: No, a cap.

Baxter: What sort of a cap?

Marshall: A round cap, with a small peak. It was something like
             what a sailor would wear.

Baxter:	What height was he?
Marshall:	About 5 feet 6 inches.
Baxter:	Was he thin or stout?
Marshall:	Rather stout.
Baxter:	Did he look well dressed?
Marshall:	Decently dressed.
Baxter:	What class of man did he appear to be?
Marshall:	I should say he was in business, and did nothing like hard [meaning manual) work.
Baxter:	Not like a dock labourer?
Marshall:	No.
Baxter:	Nor a sailor?
Marshall:	No.
Baxter:	Nor a butcher?
Marshall:	No.
Baxter:	A clerk?
Marshall:	He had more the appearance of a clerk.
Baxter:	Is that the best suggestion you can make?
Marshall:	It is.
Baxter:	You did not see his face. Had he any whiskers?
Marshall:	I cannot say. I do not think he had.
Baxter:	Was he wearing gloves?
Marshall:	No.
Baxter:	Was he carrying a stick or umbrella in his hands?
Marshall:	He had nothing in his hands that I am aware of.

Israel Schwartz

He was an immigrant of Hungarian origin, and one of our best witnesses. He testified that he had seen a strange encounter shortly before the murder of Elizabeth Stride. He subsequently gave an interview to the *Star* in which he elaborated his original description. The first man, he said, had been walking "as though partially intoxicated", while the second man, leaving the pub, carried a knife rather than a pipe, with which he threatened Schwartz. It seems plain that Schwartz's evidence was believed by the police, which makes the absence of any account of his giving evidence at the inquest remarkable.

12.45 am, Israel Schwartz of 22 Helen Street, Backchurch Lane, stated that at this hour, on turning into Berner Street from Commercial Street and having got as far as the gateway where the murder was committed, he saw a man stop and speak to a woman, who was standing in the gateway.

The man tried to pull the woman into the street, but he turned her round and threw her down on the footway and the woman screamed three times, but not very loudly. On crossing to the opposite side of the street, he saw a second man standing lighting his pipe. The man who threw the woman down called out, apparently to the man on the opposite side of the road, "Lipski" and then Schwartz walked away, but finding that he was followed by the second man, he ran so far as the railway arch, but the man did not follow so far.

Schwartz cannot say whether the two men were together or known to each other. Upon being taken to the Mortuary Schwartz identified the body as that of the woman he had seen. He thus describes the first man, who threw the woman down: age, about 30; height, 5 feet 5 inches; complexion, fair; hair, dark; small brown moustache, full face, broad shouldered; dress, dark jacket and trousers, black cap with peak, and nothing in his hands. Second man: age, 35; height, 5 feet 11 inches; complexion, fresh; hair, light brown; dress, dark overcoat, old black hard felt hat, wide brim; had a clay pipe in his hand.

Joseph Lawende

A commercial traveller in cigarettes of 45 Norfolk Road, Dalston, he left the Imperial Club at 16–17 Duke Street at 1.35 am in company with Harry Harris, a furniture dealer, and Joseph Hyam Levy, a butcher. At the corner of Duke Street and Church Passage, they saw a man and a woman in conversation. Levy and Harris took little notice of the pair, but Lawende was more observant.

The description of the man furnished by Lawende but withheld in the following exchange is that of a man of medium build and the look of a sailor. He wore a loose salt-and-pepper jacket, a grey cloth cap and a red or reddish "kingsman" or neckerchief. His age was about 30. He was 5 feet 7 inches or 5 feet 8 inches tall and had a fair complexion and moustache. The following conversation was between Joseph Lawende, Mr Langham (the Coroner) and Mr Crawford (solicitor for the police).

Lawende: I was at the Imperial Club with Mr Joseph Levy and Mr Harry Harris. We could not get home because it was raining. At half past one we left to go out, and left the house about five minutes later. I walked a little further from the others. We saw a man and a woman at the corner of Church Passage, in Duke Street, which leads into Mitre Square.

Coroner: Were they talking at the time?

Lawende: She was standing with her face towards the man. I only saw her back. She had her hand on his chest.

Coroner: What sort of woman was she?

Lawende: I could not see her face, but the man was taller than she was.

Coroner: Did you notice how she was dressed?

Lawende: I noticed she had a black jacket and black bonnet. I have seen the articles at the police station, and I recognize them as the sort of dress worn by that woman.

Coroner: What sort of woman was she?

Lawende: About 5 feet in height.

Coroner: Can you tell us what sort of man this was?

Lawende: He had a cloth cap on, with a peak of the same material.

Mr Crawford: Unless the jury particularly wish it, I have special reason for not giving details as to the appearance of this man.

Jury: No.

Coroner: You have given a special description of this man to the police?

Lawende: Yes.

Coroner: Do you think you would know him again?

Lawende: I doubt it, sir.

Mr Crawford: The Club is 16 and 17 Duke Street, about 15 or 16 feet from where they were standing at Church Passage. By what did you fix the time?

Lawende:	By seeing the club clock and my own watch. It was five minutes after the half hour when we came out, and to the best of my belief it was 25 to when we saw these persons.
Coroner:	Did you hear anything said?
Lawende:	No, not a word.
Coroner:	Did either of them appear in an angry mood?
Lawende:	No.
Coroner:	Was there anything about them or their movements that attracted your attention?
Lawende:	No, except that Mr Levy said the court ought to be watched, and I took particular notice of a man and woman talking there.
Coroner:	Was her arm on his breast as if she was pushing him away?
Lawende:	No, they were standing very quietly.
Coroner:	You were not curious enough to look back to see where they went?
Lawende:	No.

George Hutchinson

George Hutchinson was unemployed, and a resident of Victoria Home, Commercial Street. His testimony appears trustworthy, not least because he seems to have known Kelly well. It has been surmised, indeed, that he may have been among Kelly's occasional clients when he could afford her, or may have been, in the slang of the time, "mashed on" her, which would explain his close interest and her request for the loan of sixpence (Hutchinson told journalists that he occasionally gave her a shilling) and, possibly, his subsequent elaboration of his description of the man sighted.

Hutchinson told the press that the man was of respectable Jewish appearance, that he wore a long dark coat with an astrakhan collar and cuffs, a dark jacket and trousers, light waistcoat, dark felt hat turned down in the middle, button boots, gaiters with white buttons, a linen collar, black tie with a horseshoe pin, and a thick gold chain. His age was 34 or 35, his height 5 feet 6 inches. His complexion was fair, his hair and eyelashes dark, his moustache slight and curled up at the ends. He carried a small parcel wrapped in American cloth (a glazed calico or oilcloth). Hutchinson believed he saw this suspect in Petticoat Lane on 11 November. The theatricality of this description – this appears to be a swell or "masher" – grows with each retelling. The "red handkerchief" is a curious motif. Most of the Whitechapel Murderer's victims wore a "kingsman" or neckerchief. Eddowes's, at least, was of red silk. Why did Kelly tell this man that she had lost her handkerchief? Does this imply that he had already given her a significant handkerchief, and why was he so ready to hand her a red handkerchief? Mayhew – admittedly 30 years earlier – writes of a fence who bought stolen silk handkerchieves, paying ninepence apiece for them although they might be worth as much as four or five shillings, so this was no insubstantial gift.

The following statement was made at Commercial Street police station by Hutchinson following the conclusion of the Kelly inquest on 12 November.

About 2.00 am I was coming by Thrawl Street, Commercial Street, and just before I got to Flower and Dean Street, I met the murdered woman Kelly, and she said to me Hutchinson will you lend me sixpence. I said I can't I have spent all my money going down to Romford, she said good morning I must go and find some money. She went away toward Thrawl Street. A man coming in the opposite direction to Kelly, tapped her on the shoulder and said something to her they both burst out laughing. I heard her say alright to him, and the man said you will be alright, for what I have told you: he then placed his right hand around her shoulders. He also had a kind of small parcel in his left hand, with a kind of a strap round it. I stood against the lamp of the Queen's Head Public House, and watched him. They both then came past me and the man hung down his head, with, his hat over his eyes. I stooped down and looked him in the face. He looked at me stern. They both went into Dorset Street. I followed them. They both stood at the corner of the court for about 3 minutes. He said something to her. She said alright my dear come along you will be comfortable. He then placed his arm on her shoulder and (she) gave him a kiss. She said she had lost her handkerchief. He then pulled his handkerchief a red one and gave it to her. They both then went up the Court together. I then went to the court to see if I could see them but I could not. I stood there for about three quarters of an hour to see if they came out. They did not so I went away.

Autopsy Reports

Mary Ann Nichols

Mary Ann Nichols was the first of the universally accepted "canonical" victims of the Whitechapel Murderer. She was a drab, but had nonetheless retained some vanity. According to her own statement, made on admission to Mitcham workhouse on 13 February, she was born in Dean Street off Fetter Lane in August 1845. Her father, however, locksmith Edward Walker, declared that she was 42. In 1864, she had married William Nichols and had five children. It appears that William had an affair in or around 1877, and, whether this was cause or effect, it was around this time that Mary Ann's lethal relationship with the gin bottle took over her life.

In 1880, the couple separated, and Mary Ann rapidly became a lodging-house dosser and shilling-shag market dame. On 12 May 1888, she made a last bid for respectability, taking a job as a domestic servant in Rosehill Road, Wandsworth. "They are teetotallers, and very religious," she wrote optimistically of her employers, "so I ought to get on."

For all her efforts to convince herself, the lure of the streets, the rowdy companionship, the intoxicating uncertainty of the vagabond life and, above all, the gin, was stronger by far than that of respectability won by solitary service in suburbia. In July, she absconded with clothing to the value of three pounds and ten shillings. We are uncertain where she spent the last five or six nights of her life, though Ellen Holland, her friend and bedfellow, was given the impression that

Nichols had been lodging at the White House, a common lodging house in Flower and Dean Street. This, however, is unconfirmed, and Nichols's last days remain a mystery.

On the last night of her life, she reeled into her favoured lodging house at 18 Thrawl Street, where, until the previous week, she had shared a bed with Holland. The deputy turned her out because she did not have the requisite 4 shillings for her bed. She was good-natured and confident that she would soon have the fee. She drew attention to her new bonnet, saying, "See what a jolly bonnet I've got now." At 2.30 am, Holland saw her again, now staggering, at the corner of Brick Lane and Whitechapel High Street. Holland tried to persuade her to return to Thrawl Street, but Nichols informed her that she had earned her "doss money" three times over that day, but had spent it. At 3.40 am or thereabouts, Charles Cross and Robert Paul, carmen, discovered her body at the entrance to the stableyard in Buck's Row. She was dying or newly killed.

The post-mortem report on Mary Ann Nichols by Dr Rees Ralph Llewellyn demonstrates the killer's savagery and familiarity with the process of killing with the knife. He slashed Nichols' throat with the cutting edge of the blade, whereas anyone who had never killed an animal by this means, or wanting confidence in his knife, would have gouged with the point and ripped in order to be sure at once of achieving his ends and of the victim's silence. It is possible that the killer was interrupted in his work, and might otherwise have extended his exploration of his victim's viscera, but the cuts in the abdomen, though deep, are curiously many and random and want deliberation. The emotive language used by the *Star*, which helped to establish the legend, bears little relation to Llewellyn's account: "No murder was ever more ferociously or brutally done. The knife, which must have been a long and sharp one, was jabbed into the deceased at the lower part of the abdomen and then drawn upwards not once but twice. The first cut veered to the right, slitting up the groin and passing over the left hip, but the second cut went straight upward along the centre of the body, and reaching to the breastbone."

Dr Llewellyn's autopsy report:

Five of the teeth were missing, and there was a slight laceration of the tongue. There was a bruise running along the lower part of the jaw on the right side of the face. That might have been caused by a blow from a fist or pressure from a thumb. There was a circular bruise on the left side of the face, which also might have been inflicted by the pressure of the fingers. On the left side of the neck, about 1 in. below the jaw, there was an incision about 4 in. in length, and ran from a point immediately below the ear. On the same side, but an inch below, and commencing about 1in. in front of it, was a circular incision, which terminated at a point about 3 inches below the right jaw. That incision completely severed all the tissues down to the vertebrae. The large vessels of the neck on both sides were severed. The incision was about 8 inches in length. The cuts must have been caused by a long-bladed knife, moderately sharp, and used with great violence. No blood was found on the breast, either of the body or clothes. There were no injuries about the body until just about the lower part of the abdomen. Two or three inches from the left side was a wound running in a jagged manner. The wound was a very deep one, and the tissues were cut through. There were several incisions running across the abdomen. There were also three or four similar cuts running downwards, on the right side, all of which had been caused by a knife which had been used violently and downwards. The injuries were from left to right, and might have been done by a left-handed person. All the injuries had been caused by the same instrument.

Annie Chapman

This autopsy disposes of two myths which should never have come into being. The first is that of the ritualistic ordering of Chapman's rings and a variable number of shiny farthings, at her feet. There were no farthings, and the three brass rings which Chapman habitually wore were not found at the scene of the murder. They may have been removed by the murderer. The second is the notion of the left-handed Ripper, introduced but subsequently rescinded by Dr Llewellyn at the

Nichols inquest. Had there been any doubt with Nichols, there was none here.

Chapman was killed as she lay on the ground. As to how she was persuaded or forced to lie on the ground in silence, it is worth referring to Mark Daniel's theory relating to the "two distinct bruises, each the size of a man's thumb, on the forepart of the top of the chest". For difficulties relating to the timing of the murder, and discrepancies between Dr Phillips' estimate of the time of death and that fixed upon by the coroner, see our comments on the statement of Elizabeth Long.

Chapman's inquest also gave rise to the most pervasive and enduring of all the Ripper myths, that of the Ripper as a surgeon. Only Wynne Baxter, again flying in the face of expert testimony, believed that the Ripper had expert anatomical knowledge, basing his supposition on the discredited notion that the killer had been hunting for uteri to sell to an unknown American (Tumblety?).

The Central Officers' Special Report, headed, "Subject: Hanbury Street murder of Annie Chapman" is still more specific than is the autopsy with regard to the killer's want of discrimination in his collecting of organs: "the following parts were missing: part of belly wall including naval (*sic*), the womb, the upper part of vagina and greater part of bladder."

Ever since Stephen Knight's fanciful and ingenious *Final Solution*, there has been an attempt to afford significance to the placing of the intestines at one or other shoulder. In fact, the murderer, who plainly wanted to remove the guts in order to obtain unhindered access to the viscera, placed "a flap of the wall of the belly, the whole of the small intestines and attachments" above Chapman's right shoulder, while "two other portions of wall of belly and 'pubes' were placed above left shoulder in a large quantity of blood."

Dr Phillips's autopsy report, as given before the coroner:

He noticed the same protrusion of the tongue. There was a bruise over the right temple. On the upper eyelid there was a bruise, and there were two distinct bruises, each the size of a man's thumb, on the forepart of the top of the chest. The stiffness of the limbs was now well marked. There was a bruise over the middle part of the bone of the right hand. There was an old scar on the left of the frontal bone. The stiffness was more noticeable on the left side, especially in the fingers, which were partly closed. There was an abrasion over the ring finger, with distinct markings of a ring or rings. The throat had been severed as before described. The incisions into the skin indicated that they had been made from the left side of the neck. There were two distinct clean cuts on the left side of the spine. They were parallel with each other and separated by about half an inch. The muscular structures appeared as though an attempt had been made to separate the bones of the neck. There were various other mutilations of the body, but he was of the opinion that they occurred subsequent to the death of the woman, and to the large escape of blood from the division of the neck. At this point Dr Phillips said that, as from these injuries he was satisfied as to the cause of death, he thought that he had better not go into further details of the mutilations, which could only be painful to the feelings of the jury and the public. The Coroner decided to allow that course to be adopted. Witness, continuing, said, – The cause of death was apparent from the injuries he had described. From these appearances he was of the opinion that the breathing was interfered with previous to death, and that death arose from syncope, or failure of the heart's action in consequence of loss of blood caused by severance of the throat…

This evidence could only be reproduced in *The Lancet*:

The abdomen had been entirely laid open and the intestines severed from their mesenteric attachments which had been lifted out and placed on the shoulder of the corpse; whilst from the pelvis, the uterus and its appendages with the upper portion of the vagina and the posterior two thirds of the bladder had been entirely removed. Obviously the work was that of an expert – or one, at least, who had such knowledge of anatomical or pathological examinations as to be enabled to secure the pelvic organs with one sweep of the knife.

Elizabeth Stride

There are several oddities about Stride's killing. Several authorities, indeed, are prepared to assert that this was a domestic murder and does not properly belong in the canon. Preferring, however, to rely on contemporary primary sources and experts, we have little doubt, as had the police and the doctors at the time, that Stride was the victim of "the Knife", as the Whitechapel Murderer was known until the publication of the "Jack the Ripper" letters. The most striking common factor, which must have influenced the police at the time, is the killer's technique of compelling the victim to lie down on her back, then slashing, not stabbing, the throat.

It may be, as is generally assumed, that Louis Diemschutz, returning home, interrupted the murderer and prevented him from performing his usual mutilations. It may be, however, that he was interrupted rather by Schwartz and the man leaving the pub in Schwartz's testimony, and that Schwartz, then scared off by the other man, witnessed the last seconds of Stride's life. With his victim able to identify him, and with two witnesses to his assault on her, the murderer had to rapidly kill the woman and vanish before the witnesses return.

The witnesses to Stride's activities before the murder are several, although we know nothing of her movements for five days prior to this. We know that she was in the Queen's Head public house at 6.30 pm. At 7.00 p., she was back at her lodging house, where she entrusted "a piece of velvet" to Catherine Lane's safekeeping. At 11.00 pm, J Best and John Gardner saw her leaving the Bricklayer's Arms in Settles Street with a "clerkly" young man. At 11.45 pm, William Marshall saw her with a man in Berner Street. At some time between 11.00 pm and midnight, the unreliable Matthew Packer claims to have sold some grapes to her companion and to have watched them for a full half hour outside Dutfield's Yard. PC William Smith saw her again with a man outside Dutfield's Yard at 12.30 am, then we have Schwartz's account and that of James Brown, one of which places Stride outside Dutfield's Yard, the other on Fairclough Street at 12.45 pm. Diemschutz found her at about 1.00 am, killed mere minutes earlier. Although the weather cleared later, there was heavy rain until 1.30 am. One cannot but wonder just why

Stride was, apparently, loitering on the streets for so long in these conditions.

Dr Phillips's autopsy report:

The body was lying on the near side, with the face turned towards the wall, the head up the yard and the feet towards the street. The left arm was extended and there was a packet of cachous in the left hand… The right arm was over the belly. The back of the hand and wrist had on it clotted blood. The legs were drawn up with the feet close to the wall. The body and face were warm and the hand cold. The legs were quite warm. Deceased had a silk handkerchief round her neck, and it appeared to be slightly torn. I have since ascertained it was cut. This corresponded with the right angle of the jaw. The throat was deeply gashed, and there was an abrasion of the skin about one and a half inches in diameter, apparently stained with blood, under her right brow. At 3.00 pm on Monday at St George's Mortuary…Dr Blackwell and I made a postmortem examination… Rigor mortis was still thoroughly marked. There was mud on the left side of the face and it was matted in the head… The body was fairly nourished. Over both shoulders, especially the right, and under the collar-bone and in front of the chest there was a blueish discoloration, which I have watched and have seen on two occasions since. There was a clean-cut incision on the neck. It was 6 inches in length and commenced 2 and a half inches in a straight line below the angle of the jaw, a quarter of an inch over an undivided muscle, and then becoming deeper, dividing the sheath. The cut was very clean and deviated a little downwards. The artery and other vessels contained in the sheath were all cut through. The cut through the tissues on the right side was more superficial, and tailed off to about 2 inches below the right angle of the jaw. The deep vessels on that side were uninjured. From this it was evident that the haemorrhage was caused through the partial severance of the left carotid artery. Decomposition had commenced in the skin. Dark brown spots were on the anterior surface of the left chin. There was a deformity in the bones of the right leg, which was not straight, but bowed forwards. There was no recent external injury save to the neck. The body being washed more thoroughly I could see some healing sores. The lobe of the left ear was torn as if from the removal or wearing through of an earring, but it was thoroughly healed. On removing the scalp there was no sign of bruising or extravasation of blood... The heart was small, the left ventricle firmly contracted, and the right slightly so. There was no clot in the pulmonary artery, but the right ventricle was full of dark clot. The left was firmly contracted so as to be absolutely empty. The stomach was large, and the mucous membrane only congested. It contained partly digested food, apparently consisting of cheese, potato and farinaceous powder. All the teeth on the left lower jaw were absent... Examining her jacket, I found that while there was a small amount on the right side, the left was well plastered with mud...

Catharine Eddowes

Eddowes was the fourth of the Whitechapel Murderer's victims, the most savagely mutilated to that date and the subject of the most thorough and detailed autopsy yet surviving. Dr Brown's precision leaves little room for parsing or construing. He concludes, however, that the murderer possessed anatomical knowledge and surgical skill, basing this assumption upon the notion that the killer set out to extract a kidney, as Wynne Baxter had assumed much the same on the assumption that the killer sought a uterus. It is rather safer to assume, as, it appears, did Sequeira and Sanders (Phillips also attended the post mortem) that, having removed the obtruding intestines and being given liberty to plunder what he could in the crimson cavern of the abdomen, the killer excised stray treasures at will and without prior design. Even Brown concedes, "Such a knowledge might be possessed by someone in the habit of cutting up animals," while Sequeira, asked if the deed had been perpetrated by an expert, was unequivocal, "No", he said, "not by an expert, but by a man who was not altogether ignorant of the use of the knife." With this more temperate verdict we can with assurance concur. The part of the lobe of Eddowes's ear which was cut off may well have been an accidental casualty of the cutting of her throat, especially in that the remainder of the facial mutilations were symmetrical.

Dr Brown's autopsy report:

The body was on its back, the head turned to left shoulder. The arms by the side of the body as if they had fallen there. Both palms upwards, the fingers slightly bent... Left leg extended in a line with the body. The abdomen was exposed. Right leg bent at the thigh and knee...

The throat cut across...

The intestines were drawn out to a large extent and placed over the right shoulder – they were smeared over with some feculent matter. A piece of about two feet was quite detached from the body and placed between the body and the left arm, apparently by design. The lobe and auricle of the right ear was cut obliquely through.

There was a quantity of clotted blood on the pavement on the left side of the neck round the shoulder and upper part of the arm, and fluid blood-coloured serum which had flowed under the neck to the right shoulder, the pavement sloping in that direction.

Body was quite warm. No death stiffening had taken place. She must have been dead most likely within the half hour. We looked for superficial bruises and saw none. No blood on the skin of the abdomen or secretion of any kind on the thighs. No spurting of blood on the bricks or pavement around. No marks of blood below the middle of the body. Several buttons were found in the clotted blood after the body was removed. There was no blood on the front of the clothes. There were no traces of recent connection.

When the body arrived at Golden Lane (mortuary) some of the blood was dispersed through the removal of the body to the mortuary. The clothes were taken off carefully from the body. A piece of deceased's ear dropped from the clothing.

I made a post-mortem examination at half past two on Sunday afternoon. Rigor mortis was well marked; body not quite cold. Green discoloration over the abdomen.

After washing the left hand carefully, a bruise the size of a sixpence, recent and red, was discovered on the back of the left hand between the thumb and first finger. A few small bruises on right shin of older date. The hands and arms were bronzed. No bruises on the scalp, the back of the body or the elbows.

The face was very much mutilated. There was a cut about a quarter of an inch through the lower left eyelid, dividing the structures completely through. The upper eyelid on that side, there was a scratch through the skin on the left upper eyelid, near to the angle of the nose. The right eyelid was cut through to about half an inch.

There was a deep cut over the bridge of the nose, extending from the left border of the nasal bone down near to the angle of the jaw on the right side of the cheek. This cut went into the bone and divided all the structures of the cheek except the mucous membrane of the mouth.

The tip of the nose was quite detached from the nose by an oblique cut from the bottom of the nasal bone to where the wings of the nose join on to the face. A cut from this divided the upper lip and extended through the substance of the gum over the right upper lateral incisor tooth. About half an inch from the top of the nose was another oblique cut. There was a cut on the right angle of the mouth as if the cut of a point of a knife. The cut extended an inch and a half, parallel with the lower lip.

There was on each side of cheek a cut which peeled up the skin, forming a triangular flap about an inch and a half.

On the left cheek there were two abrasions of the epithelium…under the left ear.

The throat was cut across to the extent of about six or seven inches. A superficial cut commenced about an inch and a half below the lobe below (and about two and a half inches below and behind) the left ear, and extended across the throat to about three inches below the lobe of right ear. The big muscle across the throat was divided through on the left side. The large vessels on the left side of the neck were severed. The larynx was severed below the vocal chord. All the deep structures were severed to the bone, the knife marking intervertebral cartilages. The sheath of the vessels on the right side was just opened. The carotid artery had a fine hole opening. The internal jugular vein was opened an inch and a half – not divided. The blood vessels contained clot. All these injuries were performed by a sharp instrument like a knife, and pointed.

The cause of death was haemorrhage from the left common carotid artery. The death was immediate and the mutilations were inflicted after death.

We examined the abdomen. The front walls were laid open from the breast bone to the pubes. The cut commenced opposite the enciform cartilage. The incision went upwards, not penetrating the skin that was over the sternum. It then divided the enciform cartilage. The knife must have cut obliquely at the expense of the front surface of that cartilage.

Behind this, the liver was stabbed as if by the point of a sharp instrument. Below this was another incision into the liver of about two and a half inches, and below this the left lobe of the liver was slit through by a vertical cut. Two cuts were shewn by a jagging of the skin on the left side.

The abdominal walls were divided in the middle line to within a quarter of an inch of the navel. The cut then took a horizontal course for two inches and a half towards right side. It then divided round the navel on the left side, and made a parallel incision to the former horizontal incision, leaving the navel on a tongue of skin. Attached to the navel was two and a half inches of the lower part of the rectus muscle on the left side of the abdomen. The incision then took an oblique direction to the right and was shelving. The incision went down the right side of the vagina and rectum for half an inch behind the rectum.

There was a stab of about an inch on the left groin. This was done by a pointed instrument. Below this was a cut of three inches going through all tissues making a wound of the peritoneum (*sc.* perineum) about the same extent.

An inch below the crease of the thigh was a cut extending from the anterior spine of the ilium obliquely down the inner side of the left thigh and separating the left labium, forming a flap of skin up to the groin. The left rectus muscle was not detached.

There was a flap of skin formed from the right thigh, attaching the right labium, and extending up to the spine of the ilium. The muscles on the right side inserted into the frontal ligaments were cut through.

The skin was retracted through the whole of the cut in the abdomen, but the vessels were not clotted. Nor had there been any appreciable bleeding from the vessels. I draw the conclusion that the cut was made after death, and there would not be much blood on the murderer. The cut was made by someone on the right side of body, kneeling below the middle of the body.

I removed the content of the stomach and placed it in a jar for further examination. There seemed very little in it in the way of food or fluid, but from the cut end partly digested farinaceous food escaped.

The intestines had been detached to a large extent from the mesentery. About two feet of the colon was cut away. The sigmoid flexure was invaginated into the rectum very tightly.

Right kidney pale, bloodless, with slight congestion of the base of the pyramids.

There was a cut from the upper part of the slit on the under surface of the liver to the left side, and another cut at right angles to this, which were about an inch and a half deep and two and a half inches long. Liver itself was healthy.

The gall bladder contained bile. The pancreas was cut, but not through, on the left side of the spinal column. Three and a half inches of the lower border of the spleen by half an inch was attached only to the peritoneum.

The peritoneal lining was cut through on the left side and the left kidney carefully taken out and removed. The left renal artery was cut through. I should say that someone who knew the position of the kidney must have done it.

The lining membrane over the uterus was cut through. The womb was cut through horizontally, leaving a stump of three quarters of an inch. The rest of the womb had been taken away with some of the ligaments. The vagina and cervix of the womb was uninjured.

The bladder was healthy and uninjured, and contained three or four ounces of water. There was a tongue-like cut through the anterior wall of the abdominal aorta. The other organs were healthy.

There were no indications of connexion.

I believe the wound in the throat was first inflicted. I believe she must have been lying on the ground.

The wounds on the face and abdomen prove that they were inflicted by a sharp pointed knife, and that in the abdomen by one six inches long.

I believe the perpetrator of the act must have had considerable knowledge of the positions of the organs in the abdominal cavity and the way of removing them. The parts removed would be of no use for any professional purpose. It required a great deal of medical knowledge to have removed the kidney and to know where it was placed. Such a knowledge might be possessed by some one in the habit of cutting up animals.

I think the perpetrator of this act had sufficient time, or he would not have nicked the lower eyelids. It would take at least five minutes.

I cannot assign any reason for the parts being taken away. I feel sure there was no struggle. I believe it was the act of one person.

The throat had been so instantly severed that no noise could have been emitted. I should not expect much blood to have been found on the person who had inflicted these wounds. The wounds could not have been self-inflicted.

My attention was called to the apron. It was the corner of the apron, with a string attached. The blood spots were of recent origin. I have seen the portion of an apron produced by Dr Phillips and stated to have been found in Goulston Street. It is impossible to say it is human blood. I fitted the piece of apron which had a new piece of material on it which had evidently been sewn on to the piece I have, the seams of the borders of the two actually corresponding. Some blood and, apparently, faecal matter was found on the portion found in Goulston Street. I believe the wounds on the face to have been done to disfigure the corpse.

Mary Jane Kelly

We would have thought that the facts about Mary Jane Kelly's death and mutilation were gruesome enough without further ornamentation. Alas, Ripperology attracts ghouls and romancers and only occasionally serious historians. Entrails, we have been assured, were festooned about the room like Christmas decorations and hung upon the pictures on the walls, Kelly was three months pregnant – and so on *ad infinitum* and *ad nauseam*.

The scene in Miller's Court was grotesque, but the gore was restricted to the bed, the wall beside it and the floor beneath it. For the rest, the room was no messier than a butcher's shop, for the murderer had, as ever, most definitively killed before he started his work, slashing Kelly's throat right down to the spinal column, which was notched by the blade. It appears, however, that he was not as humane as was his wont, and that, for a mere second at least, Kelly may have been aware of her impending doom, and raised her arms and the sheet over her head in self-defence. The injuries to the forearms, the chemise which Kelly was wearing (Bond believed that she was naked, but Phillips testified that she was wearing a linen chemise, which is borne out by the photographs), the cut and bloodied sheet and the locked door of the room all suggest that she may have been asleep until seconds before her death. She had no time to struggle, however, but may have had time to shriek, "Murder!" as heard by Prater and Lewis.

There were further mysteries in Kelly's room. A fierce blaze in the fireplace had melted the solder on the kettle's spout. Subsequent theorists have surmised that this may have happened on another occasion, but it seems highly improbable. The police and doctors at the time were convinced that the fire had been burning at the time of the murder, and it is improbable that the kettle would have been left on the hob without spout or handle. Inspector Abberline believed that the fire had been lit in order to provide light for the murderer's work. It may be so, but there was still a length of unburned candle in the room which must surely have sufficed for a man who had thus far killed in shadow. Initially, the doctors believed that all the body parts were accounted for, but, on Saturday afternoon, Phillips and Dr Roderick Macdonald returned to sift the ashes from the grate. We now know that the heart at least was missing, but we have no idea whether it was burned or taken away by the murderer.

The only identifiable articles in the grate were remnants of women's clothing, said by *The Times* to be a piece of burned velvet and the rim and wirework of a woman's felt hat. Significantly, Walter Dew, who had often seen Kelly "parading" around the area, tells us that Kelly never wore a hat. This gives rise to the improbable supposition that the Ripper, anticipating *Psycho*, lulled his victims by dressing as a woman, and having, on this occasion lingered way into daylight, had to destroy his disguise.

But, whatever his motives, clothing of natural fibres smoulders slowly, so what fuel did he use to generate such heat? After all, the kettle was designed to withstand heat, yet the solder had melted. There were two or three chairs in the room, two tables, one by the bedside, a washstand and a print over the fireplace. The murderer had used none of these, nor did anyone record the increased heat, the light or the sound of a persistent blaze. Prater, who lived directly above, must have heard the fire in the chimney and felt the warmth which it generated. It seems more likely that this was a sudden intense blaze, generated by an inflammable material such as paraffin or alcohol.

The sentimentality attached by now to the Ripper's victims – and, perhaps, the discretion of the police who wished to persuade witnesses to testify – has obscured the nature of "McCarthy's Rents", as this set of Miller's Court rooms were known. John McCarthy must have been aware that Prater and Kelly were "unfortunates", and the fact that he was prepared to allow Kelly to fall nearly 30 shillings behind with the rent suggests that, informally at least, he might have been a "prosser" as well as a landlord, and able to recoup his money with ease.

Dr Bond's autopsy report:

Position of body

The body was lying naked in the middle of the bed, the shoulders flat, but the axis of the body inclined to the left side of the bed. The head was turned on the left cheek. The left arm was close to the body with the forearm flexed at a right angle and lying across the abdomen. The right arm was slightly abducted from the body and rested on the mattress, the elbow bent and the forearm supine with the fingers clenched. The legs were wide apart, the left thigh at right angles to the trunk & the right forming an obtuse angle with the pubes.

The whole of the surface of the abdomen and thighs was removed and the abdominal Cavity emptied of its viscera. The breasts were cut off, the arms mutilated by several jagged wounds and the face hacked beyond recognition of the features. The tissues of the neck were severed all round down to the bone.

The viscera were found in various parts viz: the uterus and Kidneys with one breast under the head, the other breast by the right foot, the Liver between the feet, the intestines by the right side and the spleen by the left side of the body. The flaps removed from the abdomen and things were on a table.

The bed clothing at the right corner was saturated with blood, and on the floor beneath was a pool of blood covering about 2 feet square. The wall by the right side of the bed and in a line with the neck was marked by blood which had struck it in a number of separate splashes.

Post-mortem examination

The face was gashed in all directions; the nose, cheeks, eyebrows and ears partly removed. The lips were blanched and cut by several incisions running obliquely down to the chin. There were also numerous cuts extending irregularly across all the features.

The neck was cut through the skin and other tissues right down to the vertebrae the fifth and sixth being deeply notched. The skin cuts in the front of the neck showed distinct ecchymosis.

The air passage was cut at the lower part of the larynx through the cricoid cartilage.

Both breasts were removed by more or less circular incisions, the muscles down to the ribs being attached to the breasts. The intercostals between the fourth, fifth and sixth ribs were cut through and the contents of the thorax visible through the openings.

The skin and tissues of the abdomen from the costal arch to the pubes were removed in three large flaps. The right thigh was denuded in front to the bone, the flap of skin, including the external organs of generation and part of the right buttock. The left thigh was stripped of skin, fascia and muscles as far as the knee.

The left calf showed a long gash through skin and tissues to the deep muscles and reaching from the knee to 5 inches above the ankle.

Both arms and forearms had extensive and jagged wounds.

The right thumb showed a small superficial incision about 1 inch long, with extravasation of blood in the skin and there were several abrasions on the back of the hand moreover showing the same condition.

On opening the thorax it was found that the right lung was minimally adherent by old firm adhesions. The lower part of the lung was broken and torn away.

The left lung was intact: it was adherent at the apex and there were a few adhesions over the side. In the substances of the lung were several nodules of consolidation.

The Pericardium was open below and the Heart absent.

In the abdominal cavity was some partly digested food of fish and potatoes and similar food was found in the remains of the stomach attached to the intestines.

Subsequently, Bond wrote a report for Abberline on all five murders:

I beg to report that I have read the notes of the four Whitechapel Murders, viz:

1 Buck's Row

2 Hanbury Street

3 Berner's (*sic*) Street

4 Mitre Square.

I have also made a Post-Mortem Examination of the mutilated remains of a woman found yesterday in a small room in Dorset Street –

1 All five murders were no doubt committed by the same hand. In the first four the throats appear to have been cut from left to right. In the last case owing to the extensive mutilation it is impossible to say in what direction the fatal cut was made, but arterial blood was found on the wall in splashes close to where the woman's head must have been lying.

2 All the circumstances surrounding the murders lead me to form the opinion that the women must have been lying down when murdered and in every case the throat was first cut.

3 In the four murders of which I have seen the notes only, I cannot form a very definite opinion as to the time that had elapsed between the murder and the discovering of the body. In one case, that of Berner's (*sic*) Street, the discovery appears to have been made immediately after the deed. In Buck's Row, Hanbury Street, and Mitre Square three or four hours only could have elapsed. In the Dorset Street Case the body was lying on the bed at the time of my visit, two o'clock, quite naked and mutilated as in the annexed report –

Rigor Mortis had set in, but increased during the progress of the examination. From this it is difficult to say with any degree of certainty the exact time that had elapsed since death as the period varies from 6 to 12 hours before rigidity sets in. The body was comparatively cold at 2 o'clock and the remains of a recently taken meal were found in the stomach and scattered about over the intestines. It is, therefore, pretty certain that the woman must have been dead about twelve hours and the partly digested food would indicate that death took place about 3 or 4 hours after the food was taken, so 1 or 2 o'clock in the morning would be the probable time of the murder.

4 In all the cases there appears to be no evidence of struggling and the attacks were probably so sudden and made in such a position that the women could neither resist nor cry out. In the Dorset Street case the corner of the sheet to the right of the woman's head was much cut and saturated with blood, indicating that the face may have been covered with the sheet at the time of the attack.

5 In the four first cases the murderer must have attacked from the right side of the victim. In the Dorset Street case, he must have attacked in front or from the left, as there would be no room for him between the wall and the part of the bed on which the woman was lying. Again, the blood had flowed down on the right side of the woman and spurted on to the wall.

6 The murderer would not necessarily be splashed or deluged with blood, but his hands and arms must have been covered and parts of his clothing must certainly have been smeared with blood.

7 The mutilations in each case excepting the Berner's (*sic*) Street one were all of the same character and showed clearly that in all the murders the object was mutilation.

8 In each case the mutilation was inflicted by a person who had no scientific nor anatomical knowledge. In my opinion he does not even possess the technical knowledge of a butcher or horse slaughterer or any person accustomed to cut up dead animals.

9 The instrument must have been a strong knife at least six inches long, very sharp, pointed at the top and about an inch in width. It may have been a clasp knife, a butcher's knife or a surgeon's knife. I think it was no doubt a straight knife.

10 The murderer must have been a man of physical strength and of great coolness and daring. There is no evidence that he had an accomplice. He must in my opinion be a man subject to

periodical attacks of Homicidal and erotic mania. The character of the mutilations indicate that the man may be in a condition sexually, that may be called satyriasis. It is of course possible that the Homicidal impulse may have developed from a revengeful or brooding condition of the mind, or that Religious Mania may have been the original disease, but I do not think either hypothesis is likely. The murderer in external appearance is quite likely to be a quiet inoffensive looking man probably middle-aged and neatly and respectably dressed. I think he must be in the habit of wearing a cloak or overcoat or he could hardly have escaped notice in the streets if the blood on his hands or clothes were visible.

11 Assuming the murderer to be such a person as I have just described he would probably be solitary and eccentric in his habits, also he is most likely to be a man without regular occupation, but with some small income or pension. He is possibly living among respectable persons who have some knowledge of his character and habits and who may have grounds for suspicion that he is not quite right in his mind at times. Such persons would probably be unwilling to communicate suspicions to the Police for fear of trouble or notoriety, whereas if there were a prospect of reward it might overcome their scruples.

The "Ripper Letters"

The police and the authorities in the East End received thousands of letters during the course of the Whitechapel murders: letters helpful, letters suggestive, letters malicious and letters plain loopy. Everyone, it seems, had a theory as to who the murderer might be (one insistently posited a giant eagle), how he gulled or soothed his victims, what trade he might pursue. From this huge number of documents, two, though almost certainly by a hand unrelated to the killer's, were instrumental in the creation of the legend of Jack the Ripper. One – the "From Hell" letter to George Lusk, accompanying part of a kidney – may well come from the Whitechapel Murderer. The latest discovery, dated 17 September 1888, has just about everything wrong with it and is almost certainly spurious.

The "Dear Boss" letter below was received on 27 September 1888 at the Central News Agency. Originally dismissed as one of many hoaxes, the double murder three days later caused the police to examine the letter a little more closely, particularly when they learned that part of Eddowes's earlobe had been cut from the body (probably, in fact, accidentally in the process of slitting her throat).

Dear Boss,

I keep on hearing the police have caught me but they wont fix me just yet. I have laughed when they look so clever and talk about being on the *right* track. That joke about Leather Apron gave me real fits. I am down on whores and I shant quit ripping them till I do get buckled. Grand work the last job was. I gave the lady no time to squeal. How can they catch me now. I love my work and want to start again. You will soon hear of me with my funny little games. I saved some of the proper *red* stuff in a ginger beer bottle over the last job to write with but it went thick like glue and I cant use it. Red ink is fit enough I hope *ha.ha.*. The next job I do I shall clip the ladys ears off and send to the police officers just for jolly wouldn't you. Keep this letter back till I do a bit more work, then give it out straight. My knife's so nice and sharp I want to get to work right away if I get a chance. Good Luck.

Yours truly

Jack the Ripper

Dont mind me giving the trade name

(PS) Wasnt good enough to post this before I got all the red ink off my hands curse it No luck yet. They say I'm a doctor now. *ha ha*

The "Saucy Jacky" postcard was received on 1 October 1888, again at the Central News Agency. It may be by the same hand as the "Dear Boss" letter, which was published on the same day. Certainly it makes reference both to the earlier letter and to the double event of the previous night. For all that we have improved information technology, however, the post was considerably faster in Victorian London, and a hoaxer could have seen both the details of the letter and the murders in an early edition of the papers.

I wasnt codding dear old Boss when I gave you the tip. You'll hear about Saucy Jackys work tomorrow double event this time number one squealed a bit couldnt finish straight off. Had not time to get ears for police thanks for keeping last letter back till I got to work again.

Jack the Ripper

The "From Hell" letter arrived on 16 October in a three inch square cardboard box delivered to George Lusk, president of the Whitechapel Vigilance Committee. Also inside the box was half a human kidney.

This letter, with its apparently natural errors (and its indications of Irishness in "Sor" and "presarved"?) has none of the polished, slangy jauntiness of its predecessors, and is plainly in a different hand.

Emily Marsh, whose father traded in hides at 218 Jubilee Street, was minding the shop on 15 October when a man came in and requested Lusk's address, which she read to him from a newspaper. The man was around 45, 6 feet tall, and slim. He had a dark beard and moustache and he spoke with "what was taken to be an Irish accent". Could this have been the sender of the kidney? It may also be worth noting that, in October, Lusk lived in fear of a sinister bearded man watching his house, and even asked for police protection.

From hell.
Mr Lusk,
Sor
I send you half the Kidne I took from one women, prasarved it for you tother piece I fried and ate it was very nise I may send you the bloody knif that took it out if you only wate a whil longer
signed
Catch me when you can Mishter Lusk

Police Views

Abberline's Opinions

Inspector Frederick Abberline, though not the most senior member of the Metropolitan Police involved in the Whitechapel Murders investigation, was in charge of detectives on the ground and so intimately concerned in day-to-day operations. His knowledge of the area was unparalleled.

Until 1903, Abberline was plainly sceptical with regard to the various so-called solutions put forward. "Theories!" he is reported to have cried. "We were almost lost in theories; there were so many of them."

In the course of 1903, however, following newspaper suggestions that the murderer was George Chapman (recently convicted of murder) he gave two important interviews to the *Pall Mall Gazette*. His wide-ranging observations do not inspire total confidence. It is not clear, for example, to what he refers when he writes of a similar series of murders in America. He still believes the Whitechapel Murders to be the work of an expert surgeon. He still attaches importance to Wynne Baxter's demonstrably untrue thesis that the procuring of uteri for sale was among the murderer's motives. In asserting that witnesses only saw the murderer's back, he discounts or, more probably, has forgotten the evidence of Schwartz or Lawende, for example.

When a representative of the *Pall Mall Gazette* called on Mr Abberline yesterday and asked for his views on the startling theory set up by one of the morning papers, the retired detective said: "What an extraordinary thing it is that you should just have called upon me now. I had just commenced, not knowing anything about the report in the newspaper, to write to the Assistant Commissioner of Police, Mr Macnaghten, to say how strongly I was impressed with the opinion that Chapman was also the author of the Whitechapel murders. Your appearance saves me the trouble. I intended to write on Friday, but a fall in the garden, injuring my hand and shoulder, prevented my doing so until today."

Mr Abberline had already covered a page and a half of foolscap, and was surrounded with a sheaf of documents and newspaper cuttings dealing with the ghastly outrages of 1888.

"I have been so struck with the remarkable coincidences in the two series of murders," he continued, "that I have not been able to think of anything else for several days past – not, in fact, since the Attorney-General made his opening statement at the recent trial and traced the antecedents of Chapman before he came to this country in 1888. Since then the idea has taken full possession of me, and everything fits in and dovetails so well that I cannot help feeling that this is the man we struggled so hard to capture fifteen years ago…

"As I say," went on the criminal expert, "there are a score of things which make one believe that Chapman is the man; and you must understand that we have never believed all those stories about Jack the Ripper being dead, or that he was a lunatic, or anything of that kind. For instance, the date of the arrival in England coincides with the beginning of the series of murders in Whitechapel; there is a coincidence also in the fact that the murders ceased in London when Chapman went to America, while similar murders began to be perpetrated in America after he landed there. The fact that he studied medicine and surgery in Russia before he came over here is well established, and it is curious to note that the first series of murders was the work of an expert surgeon, while the recent poisoning cases were proved to be done by a man with more than an elementary knowledge of medicine. The story told by Chapman's wife of the attempt to murder her with a long knife while in America is not to be ignored, but something else with regard to America is still more remarkable."

He continues with a rehearsal of Wynne Baxter's tale of an American attempting to buy uteri, speculating that the murderer was seeking to supply this demand, first in London, then in America.

"There are many other things extremely remarkable. The fact that Klosowski when he came to reside in this country occupied a lodging in George Yard, Whitechapel Road, where the first murder was committed, is very curious, and the height of the man and the peaked cap he is said to have worn quite tallies with the descriptions I got of him. All agree, too, that he was a foreign-looking man, but that, of course, helped us little in a district so full of foreigners as Whitechapel. One discrepancy only have I noted, and this is that the people who alleged that they saw Jack the Ripper at one time or another, state that he was a man about thirty-five or forty years of age. They, however, state that they only saw his back, and it is easy to misjudge age from a back view."

Altogether Mr Abberline considers that the matter is quite beyond abstract speculation and coincidence, and believes the present situation affords an opportunity of unravelling a web of crime such as no man living can appreciate in its extent and hideousness.

Chapman has other supporters including, most notably, Philip Sugden. According to H L Adam, Abberline never wavered in his conviction that Chapman was the Whitechapel murderer. He is even said to have questioned Lucy Baderski, whom Chapman had married in October 1889, about his habits at the time of the East End killings, (although Baderski almost certainly had not met him until months afterward). The dramatic difference between the two murderers' modi operandi – Chapman used poison – is still a major stumbling-block. Abberline attempted to address this problem in his second interview. In the extracts from that interview here included, he confirms that the police had no idea as to the killer's identity, dismissing suspicions of an unnamed candidate, possibly Kosminski:

"You can state most emphatically," said Mr Abberline, "that Scotland Yard is really no wiser on the subject than it was fifteen years ago. It is simple nonsense to talk of the police having proof that the man is dead. I am, and always have been, in the closest touch with Scotland Yard, and it would have been next to impossible for me not to have known about it. Besides, the authorities would have been only too glad to make an end out of such a mystery, if only for their own credit."

To convince those who have any doubts on the point, Mr Abberline produced recent documentary evidence which put the ignorance of Scotland Yard as to the perpetrator beyond the shadow of doubt.

"I know," continued the well-known detective, "that it has been stated in certain quarters that Jack the Ripper was a man who died in a lunatic asylum a few years ago, but there is nothing at all of a tangible nature to support such a theory."

He also expressed his doubts about another candidate, evidently Druitt:

"I know all about that story. But what does it amount to? Simply this. Soon after the last murder in Whitechapel the body of a young doctor was found in the Thames, but there is absolutely nothing beyond the fact that he was found at that time to incriminate him. A report was made to the Home Office about the matter, but that it was 'considered final and conclusive' is going altogether beyond the truth…the fact that several months after December 1888, when the student's body was found, the detectives were told to hold themselves in readiness for further investigations seems to point to the conclusion that Scotland Yard did not in any way consider the evidence as final."

He is of course wrong in supposing Druitt to have been a (student) doctor. Might not Druitt's initials, M D, be an explanation for the confusion?

Anderson's Opinion

As his repeated assertions make clear, Sir Robert Anderson, Assistant Commissioner in the Metropolitan Police CID and in charge of the murder investigations from 6 October 1888, was in no doubt as to the murderer's identity. He never names his suspect, but, reading his statements in tandem with Swanson's and Macnaghten's texts, it seems likely that he refers to a man named Kosminski. The Kosminski theory, however, is fraught with problems (see Martin Fido's "David Cohen and the Polish Jew Theory").

Anderson's fullest statement was published in 1910 in the book form of his memoirs, *The Lighter Side of My Official Life*:

> One did not need to be a Sherlock Holmes to discover that the criminal was a sexual maniac of a virulent type; that he was living in the immediate vicinity of the scenes of the murders; and that, if he was not living absolutely alone, his people knew of his guilt, and refused to give him up to justice. During my absence abroad the Police had made a house-to-house search for him, investigating the case of every man in the district whose circumstances were such that he could go and come and get rid of his blood-stains in secret. And the conclusion we came to was that he and his people were certain low-class Polish Jews, for it is a remarkable fact that people of that class in the East End will not give up one of their number to Gentile Justice.
>
> And the result proved that our diagnosis was right on every point. For I may say at once that "undiscovered murders" are rare in London, and the "Jack-the-Ripper" crimes are not in that category. And if the police here had powers such as the French police possess, the murderer would have been brought to justice…In saying that he was a Polish Jew I am merely stating a definitely ascertained fact. And my words are meant to specify

race, not religion. For it would outrage all religious sentiment to talk of the religion of a loathsome creature whose utterly unmentionable vices reduced him to a lower level than that of the brute.

Anderson also embodied into the main text a footnote from the magazine version of his memoirs. This had originally stated that the suspect had been identified by a fellow Jew after being caged in an asylum. Swanson, however, tells us that the identification was made before committal to an asylum, and perhaps he had reminded his old friend of this. It is less clear why Anderson should have omitted the reference to the fellow Jew (who may be Schwartz or Lawende).

I will merely add that the only person who had ever had a good view of the murderer unhesitatingly identified the suspect the instant he was confronted with him, but he refused to give evidence against him.

The Macnaghten Memoranda

In February 1894, Sir Melville Macnaghten, Chief Constable of the CID, Scotland Yard, prepared a refutation of the theory put forward in the *Sun* that Thomas Cutbush, who had carried out a series of assaults on women, was the Whitechapel Murderer. Macnaghten directs our attention to three principal suspects, and tends to consider Druitt the best candidate. Macnaghten's notes, while of the first importance as emanating from a well-informed senior police officer (though not actually with the force at the time of the murders), did not become generally available until Daniel Farson's discovery of a copy in the possession of Macnaghten's daughter, Lady Aberconway, in 1959. The memoranda have been the source of many theories since that time, although information concerning Kosminski, in particular, has proved surprisingly elusive. Macnaghten is mistaken as to the date of Kosminski's admission to an asylum.

The following extract, relating to the suspects, is taken from the Aberconway version. (The notes survive in variant forms.)

A much more rational and *workable* theory, to my way of thinking, is that the "rippers" (*sic*) brain gave way altogether after his awful glut in Miller's Court and that he then committed suicide, or, as a *less* likely alternative, was found to be so helplessly insane by his relatives, that they, suspecting the worst, had him confined in some Lunatic Asylum.

No one ever saw the Whitechapel murderer (unless possibly it was the City PC who was a beat (*sic*) near Mitre Square) and no proof could in any way ever be brought against anyone, although very many homicidal maniacs were at one time, or another, *suspected*. I enumerate the cases of 3 men against whom Police held very reasonable suspicion. Personally, after much careful & deliberate consideration, I am inclined to exonerate the last 2, but I have always held strong opinions regarding *no* 1, and the more I think the matter over, the stronger do these opinions become. The *truth*, however, will never be known, and did indeed, at one time lie at the bottom of the Thames, if my conjections (*sic*) be correct.

No 1 Mr M J Druitt a doctor of about 41 years of age and of fairly good family, who disappeared at the time of the Miller's Court murder, and whose body was found floating in the Thames on 31 December: i.e. 7 weeks after the said murder. The body was said to have been in the water for a month, *or more* – on it was found a season ticket between Blackheath and London. From private information I have little doubt but that his own family suspected this man of being the Whitechapel murderer; it was alleged that he was sexually insane.

No 2 ("Kos") minski, a Polish Jew, who lived in ("the very") heart of the district where the murders were committed. He had become insane owing to many years indulgence in solitary vices. He had a great hatred of women, with strong homicidal tendencies. He was (and I believe still is) detained in a lunatic asylum about March 1889. This man in appearance strongly resembled the individual seen by the City PC near Mitre Square.

No 3 Michael Ostrog, a mad Russian doctor, a convict and unquestionably a homicidal maniac. This man was said to have been habitually cruel to women and for a long time was known to have carried about with him surgical knives and other instruments; his antecedents were of the very worst and his whereabouts at the time of the Whitchapel (*sic*) murders could never be satisfactorily accounted for. He is still alive.

The Swanson Marginalia

Still more data from a respected source has only recently come to light. The following notes were written in a copy of Sir Robert Anderson's memoirs by his friend and associate, Chief Inspector Donald Swanson. Their provenance is impeccable and they are undoubtedly genuine. It is clear that Anderson's text and Swanson's notes refer to the same man, but the information confuses as much as it enlightens. Swanson supplies us with the suspect's name, but who is his witness who is said to have identified Kosminski? If either Schwartz or Lawende is the man in question, both made it clear that they could not make a positive identification of any one person. Nothing which could be referred to as the "Seaside Home" is known to have existed before March, 1890, and the information provided by Swanson does not match any known Kosminski (see Martin Fido's "David Cohen and the Polish Jew Theory"). While Anderson seems to have been satisfied by the identification, it is difficult to avoid the impression that Swanson was unconvinced.

Commenting on Anderson's remark that "the only person who ever saw the murderer unhesitatingly identified the subject the instant he was confronted with him; but he refused to give evidence against him," Swanson notes:

"because the suspect was *also a Jew* and also because his evidence would convict the suspect, and witness would be the means of murderer being hanged, which he did not wish to be left on his mind. D S S."

And he records in the margin: "And after this identification which suspect knew, no other murder of this kind took place in London."

Finally, on the endpaper, he summarizes the suspect's history after identification:

> After the suspect had been identified at the Seaside Home where he had been sent by us with difficulty in order to subject him to identification and he knew he was identified.
>
> On suspect's return to his brother's house in Whitechapel he was watched by police (City CID) by day and night. In a very short time the suspect with his hands tied behind his back he was sent to Stepney Workhouse and then to Colney Hatch and died shortly afterwards – Kosminski was the suspect – D S S.

The "Littlechild Letter"

This letter, dated 23 September 1913, was written by Inspector John Littlechild, head of Special Branch 1883–93, to George Sims, the journalist, and has only recently resurfaced. Evidently the last in a series on crime and, perhaps, specifically on the Whitechapel Murders, it recounts Littlechild's own suspicions of a doctor whom we can now readily identify as Francis Tumblety (see *Other Suspects*).

The relevant extract runs as follows:

> I never heard of a Dr D in connection with the Whitechapel murders, but amongst the suspects, and to my mind a very likely one, was a Dr T (which sounds much like D). He was an American quack named Tumblety and was at one time a frequent visitor to London and on these occasions constantly brought under the notice of police, there being a large dossier concerning him at Scotland Yard. Although a "Sycopathia Sexualis" (*sic*) subject, he was not known as a Sadist (which the murderer unquestionably was) but his feelings towards women were remarkable and bitter in the extreme, a fact on record. Tumblety was arrested at the time of the murders in connection with unnatural offences and charged at Marlborough Street, remanded on bail, jumped his bail, and got away to Boulogne. He shortly left Boulogne and was never heard of afterwards. It

was believed he committed suicide but certain it is that from this time the "Ripper" murders came to an end.

Disputed Texts

Matthew Packer

A Berner Street fruiterer, Matthew Packer's evidence must be regarded with considerable circumspection. His story, first given to the *Evening News* and printed on 4 October 1888, changes repeatedly, so that the "white flower" mentioned in the first account has become, in the light of conflicting evidence to the effect that it was red, "like a geranium white outside and red inside". In the original story, too, the man and the woman ate the grapes as they stood opposite the shop in the rain for half an hour.

By the time Packer made the following statement to Sir Charles Warren in person, there is no mention of the woman's eating the grapes. Whether this has anything to do with the fact that grapeskins and seeds must have shown up in the woman's stomach at the post-mortem, but did not do so, we cannot say. Louis Diemschutz and Eva Harstein both testified that there had been a grapestalk on or near the dead woman's body, but it seems likely that this gave rise to Packer's story rather than corroborating it.

On Sat. night (29 September) about 11.00 pm, a young man from 25–30, about 5 (feet) 7 (inches), with long black coat buttoned up, soft felt hat, kind of Yankee hat, rather broad shoulders, rather quick in speaking, rough voice. I sold him 1 2 pound black grapes, 3d. A woman came up with him from Back Church end (the lower end of street). She was dressed in black frock and jacket, fur round bottom of jacket, a black crape bonnet, she was playing with a flower like a geranium white outside and red inside. I identify the woman at the St George's Mortuary as the one I saw that night.

They passed by as though they were going up (to) Commercial Road, but instead of going up they crossed to the other side of the road to the Board School, and were there for about half an hour till I should say 11.30, talking to one another. I then shut up my shutters. Before they passed over opposite to my shop, they went near to the club for a few minutes apparently listening to the music. I saw no more of them after I shut up my shutters.

I put the man down as a young clerk. He had a frock coat on – no gloves. He was about 1 and a half inches or 2 or 3 inches – a little bit higher than she was.

Unnamed Witness

Testimony reported in the *Star* on the day after the murders of Stride and Eddowes uncovered by Philip Sugden, is an intriguing addition to our knowledge of the "double event", and the description tallies with those given by Marshall, Schwartz and Lawende (*qqv*):

From two different sources we have the story that a man, when passing through Church Lane at about half past one, saw a man sitting on a doorstep and wiping his hands. As everyone is on the lookout for the murderer the man looked at the stranger with a certain amount of suspicion, whereupon he tried to conceal his face. He is described as a man who wore a short jacket and a sailor's hat.

This is a curious, unsubstantiated account of a supposed sighting which first appeared in the *People's Journal* of 26 September 1919, shortly after Sergeant Stephen White's death. Allegedly written by a "Scotland Yard man", it appears to be an embroidered version of a police report made at the time of the murders. If it is genuine, it seems to indicate that

White's meeting with the murderer took place just after the murder of Catharine Eddowes in Mitre Square.

White was active in the Whitechapel enquiries (he is known to have interviewed Matthew Packer but we have no evidence that he was called as a witness at any of the inquests, and we must regard this account with considerable scepticism. The writer appends the comment that Sir Robert Anderson became convinced that the killer was a Jewish medical student, which does not seem to have been true. He also reports that Anderson and White conferred and concluded that two police officers temporarily absented themselves, thus creating an opportunity for the murderer. No other source supports this version of events.

In support of White, the startling resemblance between White's suspect and Montague Druitt should be observed, and Sir Melville Macnaghten, writing of Kosminski, observes cryptically that "this man in appearance strongly resembled the individual seen by the City PC in Mitre Square". White was a Metropolitan policeman, but no other officer has yet been found to fit Macnaghten's bill, so the jury remains out.

For five nights we had been watching a certain alley just behind the Whitechapel Road. It could only be entered from where we had two men posted in hiding, and persons entering the alley were under observation by the two men. It was a bitter cold night when I arrived at the scene to take the report of the two men in hiding. I was turning away when I saw a man coming out of the alley. He was walking quickly but noiselessly, apparently wearing rubber shoes, which were rather rare in those days. I stood aside to let the man pass, and as he came under the wall lamp I got a good look at him.

He was about five feet ten inches in height, and was dressed rather shabbily, though it was obvious that the material of his clothes was good. Evidently a man who had seen better days, I thought, but men who have seen better days are common enough down East, and that of itself was not sufficient to justify me in stopping him. His face was long and thin, nostrils rather delicate, and his hair was jet black. His complexion was inclined to be sallow, and altogether the man was foreign in appearance. The most striking thing about him, however, was the extraordinary brilliance of his eye. They looked like two very luminous glow worms coming through the darkness. The man was slightly bent at the shoulders, though he was obviously quite young – about thirty-three, at the most – and gave one the idea of having been a student or professional man. His hands were snow white, and the fingers long and tapering.

As the man passed me at the lamp I had an uneasy feeling that there was something more than usually sinister about him, and I was strongly moved to find some pretext for detaining him; but the more I thought it over, the more was I forced to the conclusion that it was not in keeping with British police methods that I should do so. My only excuse for interfering with the passage of this man would have been his association with the man we were looking for, and I had no real grounds for connecting him with the murder. It is true I had a sort of intuition that the man was not quite right. Still, if one acted on intuition in the police force, there would be more frequent outcries about interference with the liberty of subject, and at that time the police were criticized enough to make it undesirable to take risks.

The man stumbled a few feet away from me, and I made that an excuse for engaging him in conversation. He turned sharply at the sound of my voice, and scowled at me in surly fashion, but he said "Good-night" and agreed with me that it was cold.

His voice was a surprise to me. It was soft and musical, with just a tinge of melancholy in it, and it was the voice of a man of culture – a voice altogether out of keeping with the squalid surroundings of the East End.

As he turned away, one of the police officers came out of the house he had been in, and walked a few paces into the darkness of the alley. "Hello! what is this?" he cried, and then he called in startled tones to me to come along.

In the East End we are used to shocking sights, but the sight

I saw made the blood in my veins turn to ice. At the end of the
cul-de-sac, huddled against the wall, there was the body of a
woman, and a pool of blood was streaming along the gutter
from her body. It was clearly another of those terrible murders. I
remembered the man I had seen, and I started after him as fast
as I could run, but he was lost to sight in the dark labyrinth of
the East End mean streets.

The letter below, dated 17 September 1888, was discovered in 1988 by
Peter McClelland in a sealed envelope in the Public Record Office. The
hand does not tally with those of the other "Ripper" letters, yet it is
composed almost entirely of phrases taken from the "Dear Boss"
missive and another significant letter. The illiteracy here is strained and
unnatural; "an" for "and" is a phonetic error, familiar to readers of *Just
William*. It is not an error made by a man who writes "forever," for
example, as one word. "Lern" for "learn" and "rite" for "right" are
substitutions which might be expected in a fraud, in that the intended
words are irregularly spelled. Experience indicates, however, that such
irregularities are usually remembered and essayed by genuine
illiterates.

17th Sept 1888

Dear Boss
    So now they say *I am a Yid* when will they lern Dear old Boss!
You an me know the truth dont we. Lusk can look forever hell
never find me but I am rite under his nose all the time. I watch
them looking for me an it gives me fits ha ha I love my work an
I shant stop until I get buckled *and even then* watch out for your
old pal Jacky.
    Catch me if you can
    Jack the Ripper
    Sorry about the blood still messy from the last one. What a
pretty necklace I gave her.

Finally, we have included here for convenience a letter supposed to be
in the same handwriting as the "Dear Boss" missive, and recently

rediscovered. Dated 6 October, it purports to threaten a witness, presumably Israel Schwartz or Joseph Lawende.

> You though your self very clever I reckon when you informed the police. But you made a mistake if you though I dident see you. Now I know you know me and I see your little game, and I mean to finish you and send your ears to your wife if you show this to the police or help them if you do I will finish you. It no use your trying to get out of my way Because I have you when you dont expect it and I keep my word as you soon see and rip you up Yours truly Jack the Ripper.
> (PS) You see I know your address

Current Views

Armed with the basic background and materials, we come to the debate itself, a fascinating collection of diverse opinions reflecting the catholicity of contemporary studies, demonstrating just how many contrary theories there are. The approaches range from the sceptical/historical to the downright eccentric. Each, while unconvincing to one reader, may find an adherent in another. Each adds something to the debate. Some of the candidates are familiar, some surprising; some whose cause we had thought lost reappear, their claims nigh invisibly mended.

Inevitably, in even so comprehensive a book as this, certain old friends and important suspects and the cases for their inclusion are missing. For those unfamiliar with them, or for those who might resent their absence, we have prepared a brief dossier at the end. We have contented ourselves with brief résumés of the more important of those discussed in more detail.

The Real Jack the Ripper

William Beadle

According to the plethora of books about him, Jack the Ripper was, in short order: a midwife, a surgeon, a Russian barber-surgeon, a Polish poisoner, a barrister, a Cambridge don, a slaughterman, an ill-assorted trio of surgeon, painter and cabbie, Queen Victoria's grandson, three Polish nutcases (the Poles may be forgiven for feeling slightly persecuted), a devil worshipper, a Liverpool cotton merchant, a Canadian quack and Mary Kelly's boyfriend. And these are just the suspects who have been taken seriously!

The Ripper can in fact be anyone we want him to be. His crimes took place in the poorest quarter of London, at a time of social unrest. This was a community which resented both immigrants, particularly Jews, and the propertied classes. Hence the murders were blamed on foreign-born Jews or "toffs". Just as a British newspaper once reported "Fog Over Channel – Continent Isolated" so our xenophobic ancestors refused to believe the Ripper could be an Englishman – unless of course he happened to be a dissolute "toff," in which case it was all right!

Echoes of this lingered on for the first three-quarters of this century. Vassiley Konovalov was a homicidally bent Russian and serial poisoner; Severin Klosowski, a Polish immigrant; Dr Stanley, a leading surgeon driven mad by the death of his wayward son; and Montague Druitt, a sexually degenerate barrister.

The suspects of the mid-1970s reflected that era. Stephen Knight's now discredited *Jack the Ripper: The Final Solution* was loudly proclaimed (by its publisher) as "Britain's Watergate". Moving on into the 1990s, we have the celebrated Maybrick diary which unites two classic murder stories – the Ripper and the Maybrick cases – and combines them into a grand soap opera: *Coronation Street* with blood, as I wrote in *Jack the Ripper: Anatomy of a Myth*. It is this soap opera effect which grabs and holds the general public, reflecting our continuing need to be entertained.

The Ripper suspects have to be seen in this light. When we look at them in nitty-gritty terms, and consider whether a hard-headed policeman would have taken them seriously, we find that virtually all of them are flights of fancy.

William Stewart's midwife can be ruled out for the simple reason that all the evidence shows that the Ripper was a man; there is no extant evidence that either Dr Stanley or Konovalov ever existed; Severin Klosowski (aka George Chapman) was a poisoner for gain, not a ripper; Montague Druitt can be dismissed in Inspector Abberline's words: "There is absolutely nothing beyond the fact that he was found (drowned) at that time to incriminate him".

James Kenneth Stephen was roped in for entertainment value; William Gull, Walter Sickert and John Netley were emphatically not Britain's Watergate, more Ripperology's Piltdown Men; Prince Eddy, who was in Yorkshire and Scotland on the dates of the murders, proved an irresistible soap opera lure because he was royalty; and Michael Ostrog has nothing whatever to recommend him.

The police *did* discard Robert Stephenson (aka Roslyn D'Onston), correctly regarding him as a fantasist, and there is no evidence of any nature against Joe Barnett, who was eliminated by the police at the time.

Aaron Kosminski, the second of our mad Poles, was regarded as the Ripper by the Assistant Commissioner, Sir Robert Anderson, and this was seemingly endorsed by Donald Swanson, the policeman in day-to-day charge of the Ripper hunt. But Anderson reflects the insular "He can't be a Brit" mentality. Kosminski was a preconceived notion. In fact that term sums up the police attitude to him throughout. He was "identified" under wholly improper circumstances by a mystery witness; in other words it was arranged to get the result the police wanted. Aside from this, and the fact that Kosminski was a paranoid schizophenic, there is nothing against him. His mental condition was not of the violent type.

The third Pole – at least presumed to be so – Aaron Cohen, is much more interesting in that he probably fits the bill. Why didn't the police notice him at the time? Good question, and there is an answer: Cohen was arrested[1] on 6 December 1888, the same day as Joseph Isaacs, a Polish Jew whom the police wanted to question about the murders (he was speedily eliminated). While their attention was thus diverted the CID allowed Cohen to slip by unnoticed. On circumstantial evidence he is a credible suspect, a violently deranged man who sought the company of prostitutes and was present in the locale. The canonical murders ceased with his incarceration. The problem with Cohen however is that old bug-bear, lack of specific evidence. He is viable but no more.

The same problem arises with Francis Tumblety. Tumblety is an exciting discovery. He was the suspect of Chief Inspector John Littlechild, head of Special Branch in 1888, who described him as a sexual psychopath harbouring great bitterness towards women. My own assessment convinces me that Tumblety was the Ripper suspect mysteriously referred to as also being involved in a plot to assassinate Arthur Balfour[2], and that he was James Monro's preferred candidate.

However there are substantial flaws. The police did not have enough evidence either to charge Tumblety or later extradite him from America. His height and age were quite wrong and on balance the psychological profile tips against him.

Nevertheless, like Cohen, Francis Tumblety is a credible suspect. I am afraid James Maybrick is not. There are simply too many problems, not the least of which is that modern-day pathology reliably puts Mary Kelly's death at much later in the morning, which means that the diarist cannot have been the Ripper.

John Steinbeck wrote: "There are those of us who live in rooms of experience which we can never enter." The Ripper was one such resident; the whole genre of serial killers is a rooming house full of his experiences. In order to understand what he was and how he became it, we need to take the serial murderer apart bit by bit and then reassemble him as Jack the Ripper. When we have fitted the component parts together we shall see that they point clearly to one particular man.

---

1 on unrelated matters.
2 Secretary of State for Ireland in 1888 and Prime Minister 1902–05.

The basic key to anybody's personality is their self-image, built up from earliest memories through into adulthood. It fashions careers, relationships, moods and sexuality. The end product of how we see ourselves is the esteem in which we hold ourselves.

A person of low self-esteem will not thrive in the workplace, no matter how bright they are. They will not be able to forge relationships other than with those they consider as weak and inadequate as themselves. "Glad confident morning" never comes, and their sexuality will be bound up with their own imagined worthlessness. A poor self-image is often accompanied by feelings that sex, and therefore desires and fantasies, is something unclean.

When the self-image dips below normal limits it results in a feeling of utter worthlessness. In women this can lead to the illness known as nymphomania, i.e. addiction to sex with men they despise. Men, the more outwardly aggressive, will tend to become serial rapists or killers. One such man was Jack the Ripper. We shall see how self-image is interwoven with his crimes by examining his successors. So let us wheel on stage John Reginald Christie, Peter Kürten, Ted Bundy, Henry Lee Lucas and William Heirens, plus some supporting players who will wander into our profile from time to time. An abused self-image commences in childhood where our experiences determine what our adult level of esteem will be.

Remembered as the "Rillington Place Strangler" necrophile John Christie murdered seven women and a child with ligatures (his "strangling rope"). Two of the victims, the child and Christie's wife, were killed through expediency. In childhood Christie was dominated by a martinet father and three elder sisters. At the age of fifteen he failed during intercourse and was sneeringly nicknamed "Reggie-no-dick".

Peter Kürten, termed the "Düsseldorf Ripper", confessed to 14 murders before being guillotined in 1931. He was sired by an alcoholic father who raped his mother in front of the children and later went to prison for raping Kürten's sister. At age nine Kürten drowned two smaller boys in the Rhine, and in puberty he masturbated dogs and committed sadistic acts on other animals. He admired Jack the Ripper (his spiritual father) and sent the police a postcard in what he thought was imitation of him.

William Heirens butchered two women and a six year old girl. He was raised by a domineering mother who could be mistaken for Christie's father in drag.

Henry Lee Lucas horrifies us with 200 claimed victims (144 verifiable)[3]. Lucas was beaten to the point of suffering brain damage at the hands of his alcoholic prostitute mother. She became his second victim.

Theodore "Ted" Bundy is not so much the Ripper's love child or disciple as his near identical twin brother. When we look at Bundy, Jack the Ripper confronts us in the mirror. Both even lived with women whom they treated brutally. Bundy grew up a compulsive liar and petty thief which intensified when he learned he was illegitimate. The discovery fragmented his self-image like a broken mirror. Severe traumas can be that simple. A woman I know suffered a devastating blow to her self-image when she was told by the father of her child that she was not the sort of woman men married. This sent her into an 18-month downward spiral in which she slept with any man who wanted her, just as long as they were married. Fortunately she was able to right her self-image and repair her self-esteem by concentrating on the positive things in her life. She is now happily married. Ted Bundy did not recover. His self-image had been misty but after his discovery, despite the facile charm he used to ensnare his victims, his small self-esteem had gone forever.

Childhood events such as these, and the environment from which they spring, produce a thoroughly desensitized adult, already prone to cruelty.

Sexuality warps apace. Ninety five percent of serial killers are sexually motivated. Peter Kürten felt no sympathy for his raped sister; instead he tried to rape her himself. He had been conditioned to believe that sex and violence were one and the same thing. In his entire life he respected only one woman – whom he married – but even with her he could only perform sex by fantasizing about violence. All other women he categorized as husband hunters looking for a man to provide for them. He never understood the emotional need for a mate, or the desire to have children, because his own emotions had long since been destroyed.

3 One source puts it as high as 340.

John Christie was brought up to believe that sex was dirty and loathsome. His victims, he claimed in a pitiful attempt at self justification, had forced themselves on him. Like Christie, William Heirens was imbued with the belief that sex was dirty and abnormal by his mother. Even touching a woman caused him to vomit. Lucas murdered not only his mother but a mentally retarded girl whom he had been sleeping with since she was 13. Bundy's childhood trauma was compounded by his rejection at the hands of a girl he wanted to marry. This unwitting Helen could be said to have launched a thousand corpses! The precise number of Bundy's victims will never be known. Twenty-one is the accepted figure, but some estimates range as high as 36.

We rightly shudder at the thought of such creatures prowling amongst us. Who is safe? Nobody. Heterosexual serial killers murder women, homosexual men and bisexuals alike. Old age is no saviour. Kenneth Erskine, the "Stockwell Strangler", vented his hatred of society on elderly people.

The abnormality of the sexual killer remains carefully hidden from us. We have no way of knowing who they are. Shakespeare's multicidal King, Richard III, was "sealed in thy own nativity" and given a hump to mark his depravity. The pathological killer bears no such blemish. Christie appeared the shipping clerk he was. Kürten looked like everybody's favourite uncle; Bundy was handsome and erudite. Even ugliness misleads. Harvey Glatman was very short with a face that resembled a rabbit caught in a car's headlights. Nobody could possibly have imagined him to be the killer of three women.

The same anonymity haunts the sexual killer in his career. His feelings of worthlessness and inadequacy will prevent him from realizing any potential he has. Heirens was a bright university student but even then he was leading a double life. Bundy obtained a B.Sc. in psychology and afterwards enrolled in law school. He went on to earn high marks as a political aide. During one of his appeals the Judge told Bundy that he would have made a good lawyer. Before embarking on his killing spree he won back the girl who had rejected him by appearing to change his image. He then took his revenge by ditching her. Both incidents clearly signpost Bundy's innate potential. But they also make the point about his self-image. Most men would have realized that they could develop into the facade and would have gained in self-esteem. Bundy could not. His self-image refused to allow him to think it was anything but a facade. Instead it took him down the dark road to serial murder. Ultimately the serial killer reflects his appalling self-image on to his victim. Look at the dreadful photographs of Mary Kelly, and there you will find Jack the Ripper's self-esteem.

The criminal pathologue will kill in the area where he lives and works, and will establish a "safety zone" between his domicile and his crimes, an easily traversible no-man's land between the two. Research has shown that they flee to a different locale when they perceive the existing one has become too hot for them. Ted Bundy provides a classic example. Initially, he murdered in and around Seattle where he slew fourteen times including a ripper-style "double event". Then the murders suddenly ceased there, just as the Ripper's did in the East End at the end of 1888. Bundy had decamped to Salt Lake City. There he started killing again, murdering four victims. Then it was on to Colorado, where the pattern again recommenced and five more innocent lives were sacrificed. Arrested, he escaped to Tallahassee, killing twice more and badly injuring three other girls. Cheryl Thomas, 21, had wanted to be a dancer; Bundy robbed her physically of her balance. On he fled, this time to Jacksonville and Lake City where he carried out a copycat Ripper-type murder, strangling the victim, cutting her throat and mutilating her genitals. Thankfully, Bundy was then rearrested. This time he did not escape.

A significant point is that Bundy could not stop of his own accord. Serial killers cannot even when they want to. Heirens scrawled on a wall above one of his victims: "For heaven's sake catch me before I kill more I cannot control myself." Murder becomes an addictive drug.

Why then did the Ripper not kill again after Miller's Court? Oh, but he did!

Obviously Jack the Ripper caused no alarm bells to ring inside his prostitute victims. He was seen as just another client. Professor David Canter, a renowned expert on criminal psychology, believes that the Ripper would not have been an outgoing man but would have been able to socialize in a limited way. This fits; clearly a prostitute killer does not require social skills. Bundy, on the other hand, did not need to choose his victims from prostitutes and was able to use the adept charm which he honed in his political work. It was his hidden self-image which twinned him with the Ripper.

Just as the Ripper's victims did not suspect him, so neither did his neighbours. They might have if he had lived alone; Joseph Isaacs attracted attention simply by pacing up and down in his room.

The Ripper, as we shall see, had a wife. She also extended his mask of anonymity. When he directed outbursts of violence towards her, neighbours simply treated them as "domestics". This is commonplace. The police actually returned one of Jeffrey Dahmer's victims to him – in fact such domestic violence is often the hallmark of a serial killer. Bundy repeatedly sodomized a woman he lived with and came close to strangling her during dominance sex games. Before graduating to murder Christie wounded with a cricket bat a prostitute he was living with. There are distinct echoes of Jack the Ripper here.

Research establishes that the multitude's homicidal tendencies are released through prolonged intakes of alcohol and drugs. Current investigation suggests that 12,000 violent crimes a week are linked to alcohol. The British Medical Association estimates that 60–70 per cent of murders, 75 per cent of stabbings, 70 per cent of beatings and 50 per cent of domestic violence can be associated in one way or another to drink. Alcohol sheds inhibitions, reduces social control and fuels fantasies.

This can yield positive sexual rewards in a normal coupling, but not where a ruinous self-image correlates with deep and ugly urgings. Alcohol then is the key to unlocking the chamber of horrors. As his crimes progress the pathological homicide becomes more and more dependent on drink. This in turn helps fuel more crimes, a vicious circle with no breaking point. The killer is performing his atrocities in a constant alcoholic haze which step by step erodes all his controls. Most serial killers have drink or drug problems. The Ripper was no exception.

Before unveiling him we should note one final point. This type of murderer traditionally erupts between the ages of 25 and 30. Prior to this they will have engaged in various other forms of crime, the most common being theft. Sometimes this is carried forward into their murders. Examples include Lucas who stole rings from his dead "wife's" body and Gordon Cummins, "the blackout ripper", who invariably robbed his victims.

None of Jack the Ripper's victims were found with any money on them (save for Annie Chapman's measly farthings). Chapman's pocket had been cut away and the murderer had examined the contents. Two rings were stolen from her fingers. According to the press, a ring had also been removed from Polly Nichols's finger. Similar to Chapman, Catharine Eddowes's pockets were cut through and the Ripper had started to empty them. Like Lucas and Cummins, he was a homicidal human magpie who stole his victim's poor little possessions along with their lives.

We have now completed our profile of the man who was Jack the Ripper. So who does it fit?

William Henry Bury was born in Stourbridge, Worcestershire, on 25 May 1859. Previously his tiny distinction in history has been that he was the last person to be hanged in the city of Dundee.

Bury's father, Henry, was a fishmonger, who lived in Hill Street, Stourbridge. It was here that William Henry was born, to Mary Bury, neé Hendy. Selling fish must have kept Henry Bury busy because he did not get around to registering the birth until almost a month later, on 20th June. Or perhaps he didn't really care very much.

One weakness is that we know absolutely nothing about Bury's childhood, or indeed anything much about him up to the age of 28. We know from anecdotal evidence that he had an uncle who lived in Wolverhampton and that Bury apparently stayed with him before moving to London in 1887. There is no reason why he should appear in any records or newspapers. He and his family were wholly unremarkable, more faces among the teeming, anonymous millions. But then serial murderers are generally nondescript figures whom we do not suspect. "The very art of being Gerald the mole," says John Le Carré in *Tinker, Tailor, Soldier, Spy*, "is that he is one of a crowd." The art of being Jack is that he is Jack Who?; nobody notices him as he comes and goes.

According to later investigations by the Metropolitan Police, Bury had been a horsemeat butcher before migrating to London. This is the first point to grab our attention about Bury, and it is a significant one. It was a common belief in 1888 that the Ripper possessed the anatomical knowledge of a butcher or a slaughterman. Dr Thomas Bond, who carried out Mary Kelly's post-mortem, believed that he did not. My unprofessional judgment in *Anatomy of a Myth* was that the murders did not require any anatomical knowledge. On the other hand the case certainly leans towards a suspect who did. Drs Llewellyn, Bagster Phillips and Brown, who conducted the autopsies of Polly Nichols, Annie Chapman and Catharine Eddowes, believed that the killer had a butcher or slaughterman's experience. The belly ripping, the removal of two-thirds of Chapman's bladder and Eddowes's whole left kidney and the cuts to Eddowes's liver are redolent of a butcher cutting up an animal. While the main target was undoubtedly the sexual organs there can be no doubt that the Ripper regarded his victims as little more than animals, i.e. objects that he had previously ripped up with society's approval.

Here also there is an interesting psychological parallel with Charles Avinmain, a French serial killer who cut up his victims' bodies and hurled them into the Seine. Avinmain had been a butcher, a trade in which he was able to indulge his sadistic fantasies to the limit. Not until he was forced to give it up and lost his safety valve did Avinmain start to slaughter humans. William Bury likewise only started to kill after he stopped being a butcher.

Bury arrived in the East End of London in October 1887 and went to work for James Martin, a "general dealer" in Bow. We do not know why he did not seek work in a slaughterhouse. Instead he chose to melt into East London's shadowy backcloth. He found lodgings with the Martins in Quickett Street in Bow and seems to have been employed as a sawdust collector by Martin. But the Quickett Street house was not quite what it seemed, unless we interpret "general dealing" in the widest possible terms. There is an old joke about letting Jack the Ripper loose in a brothel. The Quickett Street house was to all intents and purposes a brothel.

One of the girls who plied her trade there was 32-year-old Ellen

Elliott. In theory Elliott was employed as a "servant", which in the broader sense she was. According to her marriage certificate Ellen's father, George, was a licensed victualler; i.e. a publican. By 1887 she appears to have lost contact with him; it was her sister, Margaret, who supplied the background details about her relationship with William Bury. Possibly Ellen's parents threw her out because of a pregnancy because she told Martin that she had once given birth to a child in a workhouse.

Between October 1887 and the following April a relationship developed between Ellen Elliott and William Bury. It was to prove disastrous for both of them. Bury was a heavy drinker, although there is no evidence that Ellen was. She may well have been drawn to him by the possibility of an escape route into a normal family life. At 32 she was at an age where prostitutes start to long for such things. Bury's interest was in her money. At some point Ellen had inherited some shares worth in excess of £300, in today's values around £20,000. Bury may also have imagined that a prostitute wife would not object to his violent sexual tastes. Here we can see the self-images coming into play.

William Henry Bury was a man of particularly low self-esteem. He was a drunkard, a thief and a man of perverted sexual fantasies – unlocked by alcohol – who had given up a respectable trade to live among the most dubious kind of people. In his choice of work and accommodation – and in particular the woman he had chosen – Bury was reflecting his own self-image and the limitations imposed by it. He wanted money but lacked the capacity to work for it. He hated women and was unable to socialize with them but in Ellen he met somebody whose self-esteem was as low as his and whom even he could court successfully. The self-image manifested itself in his violent attitude towards sex and his drunken despair. This was Jack the Ripper's self-image.

They wed on Easter Monday, 2 April 1888 at Bromley Parish Church. One is tempted to think of two death's heads going down the aisle together, because in a little over a year's time both would have died violently.

Bury's downward spiral into violence may already have commenced. In February a 38-year old woman named Annie Millwood was attacked in Spitalfields and hacked viciously around the legs and genitals. Millwood died of heart failure a month later. Significantly, another potentially deadly assault then took place in Mile End, the parish next to Bow, on 28 March. Ada Wilson, who described herself as a seamstress, was attacked at her home in Maidment Street by a man who demanded money and stabbed her twice in the throat. Wilson was probably a prostitute who took the man home. Wilson's description of her assailant fits the man later seen with the Ripper victims, save for the fact that his features appeared to her to be sunburned, but she may very well have confused this with a complexion flushed by alcohol.

Knife attacks on women were not as common in the East End in 1888 as might be imagined. These assaults stand out. That is why the Ripper murders caused so much panic. There were no murders in Whitechapel in either 1886 or 1887, and one each in 1889 and 1890. These figures point to the sudden explosion of similar murders and attacks in the East End as a whole in 1888 as being the work of one man and not several, as some have suggested. If the same man committed the assaults on Millwood and Wilson, and it is likely, then in all probability it was the Ripper. Serial killers commonly begin with non-fatal attacks and through them work their way up to murder. Peter Sutcliffe is an example.

Mile End was only a few minutes walk from Bow, a much shorter and safer distance for a man on foot than Spitalfields. And in that last week of March, Bury was in need of money; James Martin had just sacked him for theft.

The newly wed couple first took lodgings at Swaton Road, Bow, with an Elizabeth Haynes. On 7 April a highly significant incident occurred. Haynes heard Ellen scream for help. She found Bury kneeling on her and trying to cut her throat. This was not a row which had got out of hand. Ellen discovered that Bury slept with a knife under his pillow. From here on he began to drink very heavily and regularly beat Ellen up.

The attack on Ellen of 7 April is sharply reminiscent of Christie's attack on his prostitute girlfriend. The knife under the pillow is a crucial psychological pointer. The sexual connotation is obvious; Bury shared his bed with both his wife and his knife. Jack the Ripper in effect raped his victims with his knife. That was how he gained his satisfaction. It recalls Peter Kĭrten, who could only have sex with his wife by fantasizing about extreme violence, and the repetitious brutality towards Ellen brings to mind the Ripper's psychological doppelgänger Ted Bundy, who treated his partner in the same way.

Shortly afterwards the Burys moved from Swaton Road, first to 11 Blackthorne Street, Bow, and then finally, staying in Bow, to 3 Spanby Road.

In May Ellen confided to the Martins that not only was Bury knocking her about but that he had also infected her with venereal disease. We don't know whether this was syphilis or gonorrhoea, but Ellen described it as "the bad disorder", suggesting syphilis. This must have been a dreadful blow to this unhappy woman, who had avoided it at the hands of her clients, only to contract it from the man she had married. Bury was using prostitutes. He would therefore be known to them; not a man who would later cause them alarm.

On 7 June Bury conned Ellen into selling two-thirds of her shares. They realized over £194. Earlier on 28 April, she had sold a smaller block for £39. The two sums together amount to approximately £15,000 in today's values. Bury used part of the proceeds to buy a pony and cart, which he stabled in Spanby Road, claiming that he was going to use it to sell sawdust. In reality the enterprise provided a useful cover for his drinking. It also considerably shortened his journey to Whitechapel and Spitalfields, where the main body of prostitutes operated. A safety zone which had been too long and insecure by foot was now easily accessible. He started to stay out very late at night, a fact verified by Ellen to her sister, and later also to a woman in Dundee.

An ideal place to park a pony and cart in Whitechapel was George Yard, which in 1888 was a stable.[4] George Yard was on the doorstep of Martha Tabram's murder, and is central to those of Annie Chapman, Liz Stride, Catharine Eddowes and Mary Kelly. It is such an obvious location that only the lack of a viable suspect to place there has prevented it from being noticed before. That suspect now exists, and George Yard fits right into the heart of the jigsaw.

The normal course of treatment for syphilis in 1888 took around ten weeks. If Bury contracted it in May then the treatment would logically

4 Louis Diemschutz stabled his horse there.

have finished around the first week of August, i.e. August Bank Holiday, which coincides with the murder of Martha Tabram in George Yard Buildings.

Tabram was for many years discarded as a Ripper victim. Recent evaluation, by writers such as myself, Philip Sugden and researcher Jon Ogan, have put her firmly back into the frame. She is not essential to the case against Bury, but on balance I believe she was murdered by the Ripper.

The serial killer does not necessarily mean to start when he does, but sooner or later the final barrier is crossed. Martha Tabram was, I believe, the final barrier. It is easy to see how it happened. Tabram, we know, serviced one client in George Yard Buildings at around midnight and was probably the prostitute who went into George Yard with a soldier at 2 a.m. Bury encountered her as he returned to collect his pony and cart after a heavy Bank Holiday drinking session. Revenge for his recent infection festered inside him, the alcohol unleashed his sadistic fantasies, and he hacked her to death. The reign of the Ripper had begun.

We should note that Bury took Ellen to Wolverhampton for a holiday in August. If he was there on 6 August then either Martha Tabram is not a Ripper victim, or Bury was not the Ripper. No such equivocation is possible if he was in Wolverhampton on the night of 30 August.

If so, he cannot be the Ripper, because Polly Nichols definitely was his victim. In fact we do not know when in August the Burys went to Wolverhampton, nor how long they stayed. He might have wanted to get out of London and come to terms with his first murder until the hue and cry died down.

Polly Nichols was slain in the early hours of 31 August. Her murder was at odds with those of the other canonical victims because the location does not mesh. If Bury was the Ripper, he provides a simple answer. He would have been returning home to Bow along the Whitechapel Road in his pony and cart. Polly, we know, walked up to Whitechapel Station and was touting for business. The scene of Bury coming across her, parking his pony and cart and then taking Polly into Bucks Row fits exactly.

On 8 September the Ripper was out and about in Hanbury Street at 5.30 a.m. Hanbury Street is two minutes' walk from George Yard. Bury, theoretically self-employed and married in name only, could have been out all night or was, ostensibly, peddling sawdust early in the morning. There is always a logical reason for him to be out and about, drinking Ellen's money or allegedly working. Nobody would think it strange; he would be a familiar figure both in the pubs and to the prostitutes. He was simply part and parcel of the surroundings.

We move on to the night of the double murder. Settles Street, where the Ripper was seen in the Bricklayers Arms with Liz Stride, is only a few minutes' walk from George Yard's southern exit. The Ripper, we know, later picked up Catharine Eddowes near Mitre Square and killed her inside the Square. Precisely how he left, via Duke Street or Mitre Street, we will never know, but either would have brought him to Stoney Lane, across Middlesex Street, and then northwards to the top of Goulston Street where the piece of apron was found. At the top of Goulston Street was Wentworth Street. Right here, he could have proceeded along Wentworth Street as it bisects Commercial Street, and he would be back at George Yard where the pony and cart was parked. The Ripper's route from Mitre Square has puzzled Ripperologists for years. William Bury provides the simple answer which makes absolute sense of it.

The "Jack the Ripper" letter, which was published immediately after the double murder, remains a puzzle, a deepening one to following the recent discovery of an earlier "Ripper" letter. In the 25 September letter, the writer talks about "ripping" whores and then goes on to describe it as his "work". In fact "work" peppers the text, appearing no less than six times. A butcher would describe ripping carcasses up as his "work". The police apparently thought that the handwriting in one of the letters was similar to Bury's. This is currently being investigated by handwriting experts.

The pattern of the murders, established in August, was broken in October. Fog descended like a pall. The Ripper did not venture out to kill. A native of the area might have used the fog as a cloak. This suggests that the murderer had quite recently acquired his knowledge of the East End, collecting and delivering sawdust, for example.

Bury's drinking was getting worse. His sister-in-law Margaret's later testimony paints a picture of a man in an alcoholic haze. According to William Smith, his Spanby Road landlord, the only days on which Bury did not drink heavily were Sundays. An important point arises here. Annie Millwood was attacked on a Saturday and Ada Wilson on a Wednesday.

Martha Tabram, Polly Nichols, Annie Chapman, Liz Stride and Cathy Eddowes were attacked in the early hours of Tuesday, Friday, Saturday, and Sunday respectively and Mary Kelly was murdered on a Friday morning. Later, Rose Mylett was strangled on Thursday morning and, according to Bury, he slew Ellen on a Tuesday. What's missing? Sunday evening and the early hours of Monday morning, the one time in the week when Bury was comparatively sober.

The murder of Mary Kelly on 9 November was the ultimate horror. The epithet most commonly applied is "butchered". An attempt had clearly been made to dehumanize Kelly, to reduce her to a butchered animal. This reflected the murderer himself, a dehumanized man, stripped of all his emotions. It may also have reflected his former occupation.

In this context Nick Warren, editor of *Ripperana* and a practising surgeon, after examining the close-range photograph of Kelly's remains, concluded that her left thighbone had been split longitudinally, an injury that could not be inflicted with a knife, but could with a chopper. The police confirmed in February 1891 that a chopper, found at Miller's Court, had been used on Kelly. A butcher's basic tools are a knife and a chopper. Interestingly, Bury attempted to borrow one in Dundee at the time of Ellen's murder.

Miller's Court was no more than a minute's walk from George Yard. Bury sold his pony and cart early in December. In the early hours of the 20th Rose Mylett was found strangled in Clarke's Yard, off Poplar High Street. This was much closer to home for Bury, a few minutes walk from Spanby Road after Whitechapel and Spitalfields had become too dangerous for him because he had disposed of his transport.

Flight followed. Early in January Bury told Ellen's sister that he had a job in Dundee for £2 a week and could get Ellen work for £1. This was a lie. Ellen later entrusted her jewellery to Margaret, fearing that Bury would sell it. To William Smith, Bury lied that he was going to Brisbane, Australia. When Smith asked which dock he was sailing from, Bury answered, "Ah, that's what you want to know, like a lot more". A lot more?

Serial killers flee their locale when it has become too hot for them. They invariably lie about why they are going and where they are going, for obvious reasons. The Burys sailed for Scotland on the *Cambria* on 19 January. Ellen had just seventeen days left to live.

In Dundee they stayed first in Union Street, and then, on the 29th, moved into a basement flat at 113 Princes Street. Here, on 5 February, Bury strangled Ellen with a piece of rope and then ripped her body up, afterwards stuffing it into a trunk.

The murder posed an obvious problem. Bury could hardly dump his wife's body on a street corner. We know from all accounts of the case that he contemplated returning to London and disposing of the trunk in the North Sea. Why didn't he? I think we know the answer.

He also thought of dismembering the corpse and tried, unsuccessfully, to borrow a chopper from his neighbour, Marjory Smith. To Smith he made an interesting remark. Asked jokingly "You're not Jack the Ripper are you?" Bury, who was drunk, replied, "I do not know so much about that".

The days slipped past. On 10 February, Bury visited an acquaintance named David Walker. In Walker's newspaper he came across a tragic story about a couple who had eloped and then committed suicide. Walker was more interested in Jack the Ripper. Bury, he said, became very agitated and "immediately threw down the paper".

That afternoon Bury went to the police with a tale, obviously concocted from the newspaper story, of waking up and finding Ellen dead with a rope around her neck. He said he had stabbed the body (once) and then put it into the trunk.

At Princes Street the police discovered Ellen's body. They also found a forged document transferring the residue of her shares to her husband. And there was more. Behind the door leading down to the tenement they found this message written in chalk: "Jack Ripper is at the back of this door". On the stairway wall was written: "Jack Ripper is in this Seller" [*sic*].

These messages were presumably written by Ellen. Presaging Christie over 60 years later, Bury had strangled his wife with a rope because she knew too much.

Afterwards, drunk, Bury had perpetrated his sexual perversions on Ellen's body. What was another dead prostitute to him?

The medical examination of Ellen Bury's body clearly shows that this was a Ripper crime. Ellen Bury had ten vertical stab wounds ranging from superficial to a deep abdominal rip four and a half inches long, from which 12 inches of intestines were protruding in the manner of the bodies of Chapman and Eddowes. The injuries had been made to the stomach, pubis, vulva and perineum. These wounds were more extensive than those on Nichols, when the Ripper was at the outset of his cycle of ferocity leading up to Mary Kelly. Ellen Bury's murder was clearly indicative of a new cycle commencing.

Leaving aside the injuries to her face and thighs, Cathy Eddowes's wounds were also similar to Ellen Bury's. Of particular importance is the actual design of the attacks. In both cases one major wound in the centre of the body was supplemented with a series of subsidiary rips around it. In Ellen's case the major wound started just above the pubis and ran up the middle, dividing the belly wall and leaving 12 inches of intestine protruding; Cathy was ripped from the pubis to the breastbone, dividing the belly wall and leaving 24 inches protruding. The design is identical. Both women had their genitalia mutilated. Ellen had first been strangled, as were the other Ripper victims.

The only difference was that Ellen Bury's throat had not been cut. But Bury had previously attempted to do so and serial killers often vary their modi operandi slightly, anyway. Peter Sutcliffe did so when he was trying to avoid detection.

Bury claimed that Ellen had committed suicide! Asked why he had not reported her death for five days he replied that he did not want people to think he was Jack the Ripper. He was being disingenuous; the remark is as unveiling as it is evasive.

William Henry Bury was tried on 28 March, convicted, and sentenced to hang on 24 April.

Before he was executed there came a dramatic finale to his story. Scotland Yard detectives investigating the Ripper murders approached

James Berry, the hangman, and asked him to try and obtain a confession while they remained hidden nearby. For the most part the conversation was nondescript but at one point Bury turned to Berry and said: "I suppose you think you are clever to hang me."

Apparently the emphasis was on the "me" because Berry and the listening detectives thought that he actually meant: "I suppose you think you are clever to hang *Jack the Ripper*."

The ambiguity of this remark is similar to Bury's veiled hint to William and Marjory Smith and the Dundee police as well as his behaviour when David Walker wanted to discuss the Ripper. And, if the Metropolitan Police were right, and Bury's handwriting is similar to that in one of the letters, then it resonates this statement in the letter of the 25th: "I have laughed when they look so clever."

But William Bury aka Jack the Ripper was not clever. He was, as a friend so graphically put it to me "one sad bastard who cut up women". That is the image he has left, and it is the Ripper Bury's own self-image.

Since I published my findings on William Bury, some have dismissed him as an imitation murderer. The facts are these:

Bury completely fits the profile of Jack the Ripper. The profile I have established here is similar to the Ripper profiles put forward by Professor David Canter and the FBI's serial killers unit. Bury is the Ripper's psychological photograph.

Bury fits the general physical description of the Ripper who, according to the witnesses who saw him with Chapman, Stride, Eddowes and Kelly, was short and respectably dressed,[5] moustachioed, beardless and between 25 and 35. Bury was short and respectably dressed. He was 29 at the time of the murders and had a moustache. In Dundee he sported a beard and side whiskers, but reports of the Stride inquest, four months earlier, had emphasized the fact that the killer had none. This beardless, whiskerless Ripper had been seen by too many people (ten) that night.

The Ripper was a thief who ransacked his victims' bodies. Bury was a thief and obsessed by money. Stealing and compulsive lying are hallmarks of the pathological killer. Ellen Bury's sister Margaret told the police: "She could never scarce believe a word he said."

5 Testimony of the Dundee witnesses.

Bury resided in the East End throughout the murders. They did not begin until he came to London, and they ended when he left.

He drove a pony and cart during the whole time of the canonical murders. Walter Dew, then a young Detective Constable attached to H Division, confirmed that the police were stopping all pedestrians late at night.

Bury fled London at the beginning of 1889. He lied about where and why he was going.

Ellen Bury and Catharine Eddowes were ripped up in precisely the same way. Ellen Bury, Annie Chapman and Eddowes's sexual organs were identically mutilated. Sexual killers carry out their own individual sexual fantasies.

Jack the Ripper ceased to exist after William Bury's death.

Last, but certainly not least, there are the parallels with other serial killers. I have reserved for this summation a direct comparison between Bury and Fred West. Both were thieves; both appeared respectable. Both had menial occupations; Bury peddled sawdust from a pony and cart, West for a time sold ice cream from a van. Bury married a prostitute from the house he was living in; Rose West serviced clients at Cromwell Street. But the most startling comparison is that Fred West's first wife was also a prostitute before he married her. Afterwards he was consistently violent towards her, culminating in his strangling her to avoid exposure for earlier murders. West then obtained sexual satisfaction from dismembering the body.

Fred West had never heard of William Bury; nor had Peter Kürten, John Christie, or Ted Bundy. William Bury does not imitate Jack the Ripper; other serial killers imitate *William Bury*.

How Jack the Ripper Saved the Whitechapel Murderer

Mark Daniel

I first became involved in Ripperology when, in 1987, I was approached by Penguin Books to write the 'novelization' of a television mini-series, then in production, starring Michael Caine as Inspector Abberline. I was not, therefore, drawn to Ripper study by ghoulishness, nor by the passion for a puzzle, nor, indeed, by any emotion worthy of the name. I was chosen to do the job because I was known as a fast-working and fluent novelist with extensive knowledge of, and interest in, the underworld and its slang.

David Wickes, the producer and writer of the series, had obtained access to Home Office and Scotland Yard files relating to the Whitechapel Murders before they were to be officially released under the 100-year-rule. He furnished me with photocopies of these documents and with the scripts for the series, and gave me carte blanche to tell the story as I would.

This presented me with a problem, because I was thus at once cast in the role of mythmaker and historian. The experience was frankly bizarre, and gave me, I believe, a unique insight into the distinct traditions in Ripper studies which are reflected in the continuing debate, for the script from which I had to work bore little relation to the official documents. There was a great deal of deliberate mystification in the preproduction and in the making of the television series. Quite properly, the film-makers hinted, as part of the hype, that their unprecedented access to source materials would enable them at last to reveal all. They filmed four different endings, identifying four different suspects, and none of us – not I, not Michael Caine, still less the press or the general public – was to know which of these conclusions would be shown as the final solution.

As a professional writer, it was my job to go along with all this taradiddle. I too wrote four endings. I too libelled the much maligned shades of some of the Ripperologists' old favourites: Sir William Withey Gull, the surgeon; John Netley, the depressive royal coachman; Robert James Lees, the spiritualist; Richard Mansfield, the famous American actor; George Akin Lusk, chairman of the Whitechapel Vigilance Committee; and, of course, old collar-and-cuffs himself, His Royal Highness Prince Eddy, Albert Victor, Duke of Clarence and Avondale and heir apparent to the British throne.

As a rational critic, however, I rapidly became aware that none of these was in fact a candidate for the dubious honour of being identified as the Whitechapel Murderer. I had to learn fast, and my reading indicated that there were two different trails, which had confused police investigations at the time and confuse Ripperologists to this day. One is the trail of the Whitechapel Murderer, a convoluted trail, scuffed and further confused by literally thousands of obscure yet feasible suspects. The other is the trail of Jack the Ripper, a legendary figure almost from the coining of the name.

The Whitechapel Murderer does not need a motive comprehensible to the common run. Indeed, subsequent experience of serial killers indicates that he almost certainly had no such motive. The Ripper, however, as a compound of Golem, Gollum and Dracula, with a dash of Robin Hood thrown in, can have been no sick, common man with tortuous inadequacies, but must rather be associated with other legendary attributes. He must have been a magician, of royal blood, an avenging angel, a gentleman or a distinguished surgeon.

The TV series, then, was called *Jack the Ripper* and rightly followed the distinctive and time-honoured trends of that legend. It was an instructive experience at once to contribute to the mythology on the one hand and, on the other, to read the sad, squalid documents of the Whitechapel Murders investigation. It seemed to me then, and seems to me still, that we cannot begin to look for the Whitechapel Murderer until we have first disposed of the legendary elements which at every turn obscure the scent.

Gull was representative of a whole raft of doctors or medics credited with the murders largely on the strength of the discredited assertion of one man, Wynne Edwin Baxter. Given that any unclaimed corpse automatically became the plaything of the medical profession, a surgeon – and certainly a doctor of Gull's distinction – was always an unlikely candidate. One of the more notable characteristics of the Ripper murders is the absence of cruelty. He dispatched his victims rapidly with the minimum of pain, and only then attended to the plundering of the viscera. If murder for murder's sake had been his motive, a doctor might have served as well as any other suspect, but the Ripper's "jollies" came from post-mortem tinkering, which a surgeon could do to his heart's content without fear of censure.

There is a sense, too, that the Ripper, in his ever deeper and more thorough depredations, was seeking something. Polly Nichols was merely slashed open, Annie Chapman had her reproductive organs removed, Catharine Eddowes lost a kidney and the greater part of her womb, while the killer had probed with his knife at the liver, colon, pancreas and spleen. With Mary Jane Kelly, in privacy, the murderer was like a demented child let loose in a toyshop. Such frenzied delving argues ignorance, not the familiarity acquired at the dissecting tables.

The case against Gull depends on a belief in the unreliable Joseph Sickert, and is all tied up with an entirely characteristic web of urban myth, incorporating Lees's visions and the Duke of Clarence's sexual peccadilloes. Unquestionably, Clarence's appetites were catholic and many and the subject of much rumour at the time, but the whole thing is at once too improbable and too horribly obvious. The paranoiac reasoning proceeds thus: there is a mystery concerning an underclass, ergo there is a cover-up, ergo someone with authority over the authorities must be involved, and why settle for a senior policeman or a common earl when we could implicate a wayward heir to the throne itself?

Similar reasoning leads us to Gull. We are looking for a doctor, so it must be the royal physician. The fact that Gull was the son of a bargee somehow, and paradoxically, lends further cause for satisfaction, if no further credence, to the identification of a 72-year-old doctor who had suffered two strokes as the agile and sexually avid Ripper.

The quest for a doctor, or for someone with knowledge of surgery, is not entirely popular wishful thinking, but was, of course, prompted by the extraordinary outburst by Coroner Wynne Baxter at the inquest into Annie Chapman's death. Baxter was a garrulous, tetchy chap with a penchant for headline-grabbing and, it appears, a dislike for the Metropolitan Police. He had various ideas about Chapman's death which no amount of evidence or expert opinion would alter. The police surgeon, Dr George Bagster Phillips, had testified that "there are indications of anatomical knowledge which are only less indicated in consequence of haste".

Baxter, however, after a heart-rending summation of the life of the poor in Whitechapel, announced: "The injuries were made by someone who had considerable anatomical skill and knowledge...The organ was taken out by one who knew where to find it, what difficulties he would have to contend against, and how he should use his knife so as to abstract the organ without injury to it. No unskilled person could have known where to find it or have recognized it when it was found. For instance, no mere slaughterer of animals could have carried out these operations. It must have been someone accustomed to the post-mortem room. The conclusion that the desire was to possess the missing abdominal organ seems overwhelming..."

It did not seem so to the police or to anyone else, but Baxter had made a discovery on his own account. "It has been suggested," he went on, with masterly understatement, "that the criminal is a lunatic with morbid feelings. That may or may not be the case, but the object of the murderer appears palpably shown by the facts, and it is not necessary to assume lunacy, for it is clear that there is a market for the missing organ...Within a few hours of the issue of the morning papers containing a report of the medical evidence given at the last sitting of the Court, I received a communication from one of the officers of our great medical schools. I was informed that some months ago an American had called on him and asked him to produce a number of specimens of the organ that was missing in the deceased. He stated his willingness to give twenty pounds for each specimen. He stated that his object was to issue an actual specimen with each copy of a publication on which he was then engaged... I need hardly say that I at once communicated my information to the Detective Department at Scotland Yard. Of course, I do not know what use has been made of it."

So he hastened to his astonishing conclusion. Linking Chapman's murder with those of "Mary Ann Smith" [*sic*] and "Ann Tabram" [*sic*], he declared, "It is not as if there is no clue to the character of the criminal or the cause of his crime. His object is very clearly divulged. His anatomical knowledge carries him out of the category of a common criminal, for that knowledge can only have been obtained by assisting at post-mortems or by frequenting the post-mortem room. Thus the class in which search must be made, although a large one, is limited."

This is shoddy stuff. Blithely ignoring the fact that, in the cases of Smith, Tabram and Nichols (which he believes to be killings by the same hand), no organs were removed, Baxter gives rise to the enduring myth of the Ripper as surgeon. Even were we to entertain for the merest moment the subsequently discredited notion that the Ripper killed in order to obtain Chapman's uterus, the CID Central Officer's Special Report of 19 October 1888 shows that the killer excised this organ with no great particularity. For good measure, he took away with him "part of belly wall including navel, the upper part of the vagina and greater part of bladder." Hardly a standard hysterectomy.

Drs Sequeira and Saunders were to state that the Ripper evinced no great expertize. Dr Frederick Gordon Brown gave it as his opinion that he possessed knowledge which "might be possessed by someone in the habit of cutting up animals". Dr Phillips was more equivocal. The damage, however, had been done. The public at once responded to Baxter's dictum with approval, favourably comparing the speculative coroner with the more methodical police. The police received a flood of information concerning demented doctors, medical students and midwives. One cannot but wonder how many worthier suspects were disregarded or unreported because they did not have medical training or experience of the post-mortem room. The spirits of Dr Barnardo, Dr Morgan Davies, Dr Pedachenko, D'Onston Stephenson, John Sanders, Druitt, Ostrog and Klosowski owe much (but not all) of their infamy to Wynne Baxter and his discovery.

Unfortunately, even such knowledge as that which Dr Brown supposes does little to limit the class in which the Ripper may be found.

Many soldiers were accustomed to butchery on the march, and the East End was full of feldschers, butchers, slaughtermen, cooks, taxidermists, tanners, hunters and many others accustomed to eviscerating carrion.

Another enduring myth about the Ripper, now largely discounted by students of the Whitechapel Murderer, was that he was left-handed. This is not unexpected in such circumstances, given the majority's tendency to point the finger at the minorities and the enduring assumptions implicit in the word "sinister", the Latin for "left". I rapidly concluded, however, that this too was unlikely to be true. All the victims had bruising about the chin and cheeks, and the doctors rightly supposed that the killer must have held the women's heads. None has been able to explain, however, how the fatal slash could have been delivered or the women persuaded to lie down without sound. Nichols, Chapman, Stride and Eddowes were all killed as they lay on the ground, Kelly again prone on her bed. The assumption, therefore, that the killer was left-handed is founded upon the somewhat ignorant – or innocent – assumption that the killer adopted, as it were, the missionary position before delivering the *coup de grâce*.

Nothing is less likely. It is plain that the Ripper must have propositioned his victims and led them – or been led – to a dark and discreet place for the purpose of coupling. Now, if every tickle-tail in London were to lie down for her every customer, she would in short order be very bedraggled, dusty, muddy and frequently sodden, while the men would be returning home to their wives with inexplicably filthy knees. In an English winter, the streetwalker without business premises could never turn a trick.

The normal position adopted for such a transaction would therefore be a "dog-rig" or "threepenny upright", with the woman bent in front of the man with her back to him, supporting herself on a fence or wall with her hands. In such a position, she would be powerless to defend herself. Then the killer would grasp her chin in his left hand and incapacitate her with his right. This ties in with the fact that all four of his outside victims were found close to walls or fences.

In the case of Chapman, "there were two distinct bruises, each the size of a man's thumb, on the forepart of the top of the chest," in that of Stride "over both shoulders and under the collar-bone...a bluish discolouration which I have watched and *have seen on two occasions since…*", said Phillips. (The italics are my own.) Phillips was present at the examination of Eddowes.

It is my belief that these indicate the killer's method. Firm pressure on the twin pressure points behind the collar bone, cutting off the carotid bloodflow, will induce unconsciousness within seconds. I have not had leisure to find out whether this was common knowledge amongst the criminal fraternity, whether it was taught to soldiers acquiring skills in unarmed combat, whether it was a trick taught by Gurkhas or the Indian Army to all their confrères, or whether it was knowledge exclusive to the medical profession or to Orientals. It is still not – thank God – widespread. I believe, however, that the Ripper possessed this knowledge, and used it.

It has been asserted constantly – though never, save in the case of Chapman, in the official records – that the Ripper's victims were "half-strangled". There is, however, little evidence to that effect. Certainly, if the Ripper had used his hands or a ligature, there must have been massive bruising on the throats of the victims. There was not. He must either, therefore, have used my suggested method, or strangled them with a broad strap or scarf. The evidence does not support this latter supposition.

Once the woman was on the ground and unconscious or semi-conscious, he could readily slash her throat, from either side, with impunity and with no fear of being splashed with excessive blood. That he did thus slash – using the cutting edge of the blade – is in itself significant. It indicates, first, that the Ripper was familiar, be it with pigs, deer or humans, with the process. Anyone unfamiliar with the texture of flesh or wanting confidence in his blade or his skill would, in the Ripper's circumstances, gouge and drag in order to ensure his ends in silence.

Again, this does not reduce our list of suspects much. Anyone who had wielded a sabre would have such knowledge, as would, of course a slaughterman or a butcher. At first, I believed that this very fact – the finesse which the Ripper displayed in his knifework – belied the (admittedly almost certainly spurious) "Jack the Ripper" letters. Jack very specifically did not rip. He honed his knife blades and kept them clean. It then occurred to me that the word "Ripper" was of a piece with the overall tone of masher slang used in the letters, and was intended to convey the meaning of "excellent chap" or, as given in the Oxford English Dictionary of 1870, "one behaving recklessly" rather than referring to the murderer's technique.

The murderer's care for his blades (he must have had at least two, because Kelly's thigh-bone was split, which must have been done with a chopper) is manifest in their consistent sharpness. This raises a host of potentially significant but, so far as I can discover, unasked questions. How did the killer carry these knives? He could hardly carry them loose and clanking, nor could he wander the streets with them exposed.

Hutchinson's account of the "Jewish-looking" man seen with Kelly in Flower and Dean Street (as it was then known) here becomes particularly significant. "He also had a kind of small parcel in his left hand, with a kind of strap around it." Hutchinson subsequently elaborated this description: "He carried a small parcel in his hand about eight inches long, and it had a strap round it. He had it tightly grasped in his left hand. It looked as though it was covered with dark American cloth."

Now I, like all cooks, possess something which could be described as "a small parcel with a strap around it". It is a knife wallet, a length of canvas fitted with pockets for my blades. It can be rolled up and its strap fastened so that it occupies a small space while each knife is kept separate from its fellows and safe from knocks. This is an indispensable piece of kit for anyone whose livelihood depends upon the sharpness of his steels and, incidentally, who wishes to avoid arrest. The journeyman slaughterer or butcher seeking gainful employment must have such an article.

This does not, of course, mean that Hutchinson's masher must have been such a journeyman. It does, however, suggest a potentially rewarding line of enquiry which I am currently pursuing. Knife wallets are to this day made with specific variations for barbers, hairdressers, cooks, carpenters and even sculptors. It may be that, in 1888, each such wallet was hand-made by the owner of the blades, but, if they were manufactured commercially, this dark, American cloth wallet may well have been made for a specific artisan. American cloth, incidentally, is glazed, or, more probably, oilcloth, which suggests a ship's cook, sailor or, again, a soldier.

We find further support for the notion that the Ripper cared for his blades on the night of the double murder. Philip Sugden has uncovered a rarely reprinted account of a sighting of the killer, published in the *Star* the following day: "From two different sources we have the story that a man, when passing through Church Lane at about half past one, saw a man sitting on a doorstep and wiping his hands. As everyone is looking for the murderer the man looked at the stranger with a certain amount of suspicion, whereupon he tried to conceal his face. He is described as a man who wore a short jacket and a sailor's hat."

If this were the Ripper, I do not believe that he was wiping his hands, but his blade, just as the only feasible explanation of the portion of Eddowes's apron found in the doorway of Wentworth Model Dwellings, one hour and 20 minutes later, is that the murderer used the cloth to wipe his blade clean. This insistence on cleaning a blade after an engagement in order to prevent corrosion is a warrior's discipline, and again indicates that the blade was slipped into something habitually used – scabbard or wallet – after use, rather than merely thrust into a pocket or wrapped in a newspaper, for example.

The notion of Lusk as the Ripper, though not to be seriously entertained, was a peculiarly attractive one in that it gave our killer what he almost certainly did not possess – a cogent motive for his crimes. As a radical and inspired reformer, the film-makers surmised, our Ripper engineered a social revolution at the expense of a mere clutch of market dames. He caused Sir Charles Warren to resign as Metropolitan Police Commissioner, he invoked the concern and outrage of Queen Victoria, and, indirectly, he was responsible for the destruction of many a slum rookery and the construction of many a broad, well-lit boulevard. Nobody did more to hasten the demise of gaslight. This was the house that Jack built.

And here was, perhaps, the most startling thing of all about the Ripper murders – the attention which, from the outset, they received from press and public. It is almost as though, on discovering the body of Polly Nichols, it was known that a sensational sequence of slayings had begun. Still stranger, it seems that, within a few days of the death of Mary Jane Kelly, it was widely assumed that the sequence was over.

London in the 1880s had seen a rash of disappearances, particularly in the areas of East and West Ham. Nothing linked them. Children, men and women simply vanished from the London streets, never to be seen again. The extraordinary thing is that many of them seemed to know that something was about to happen, and were torn between terror and fascination. They loitered on street corners, clearly apprehensive. Friends would advise them to go home. They would nod, walk off as though heading homeward, then return to the same point. And vanish.

Eliza Carter was typical. She was patently terrified, but she refused to go home. Her blue dress was later found on East Ham football field. All the buttons had been removed. Eliza was never seen again. For nine years, from 1881 to 1890, several people vanished thus. It was reported that many of the victims, like Eliza, had been seen with "an unprepossessing woman with a long ulster and a black frock". In January, 1890, three girls became the last victims. One, a 15-year-old named Amelia Jeffs, was found strangled in an empty house overlooking West Ham Park. Nothing more was seen of her companions. These girls too had been seen talking to a woman. The coroner plainly knew more than he was prepared to reveal when he delivered his verdict: "Women," he said, "are as susceptible to the lower forms of mania as men".

Here, then, contemporaneous with the Ripper's crimes, we have an unsolved mystery involving tens if not hundreds of respectable victims, yet who now remembers Stanger the baker, Eliza Carter, Charles Wagner the West Ham butcher's son, Amelia Jeffs and her friends or any of the other victims of – of what? White slavers? Cannibals? They have vanished from history as they vanished from their home town, yet Jack the Ripper remains, part folk hero, part bogeyman, and all that he did was execute, then gralloch, a few moribund, drunken trug-moldies.

How did this come about?

In part, it was an accident of history. No less a figure than Caruso acquired enduring fame by being first tenor at La Scala when the phonograph first came onto the market, so the Ripper's reign of terror coincided with the first highpoint of the yellow press. 1888 was also, as it were, the silly season of Victorian England. Nothing much was happening that year. The Empire was at its most prosperous. The Ashanti, the Zulus and the Boers were problems of the past. There are few pages in the chronology with less type on them. The Ripper had a clear field.

Then, of course – and characteristically of calm and prosperous periods – there was social unrest. London was the hub of the world back then, administrative, economic and symbolic capital of the greatest empire in history. Over the previous 30 years, the population of the city had more than trebled. First came the Russians, then Poles, Austrians, Irishmen and Jews from all over the world, in search of labour, easy pickings or merely refuge. Many of these were skilled, many literate, which accounts at once for the success of the popular newspapers and for the rise of socialism.

London expanded westward, but the builders could not keep pace. When the American Civil War ended with the total defeat of the cotton-producing South, an estimated 3,000 Manchester cotton labourers found themselves out of work. Many of them, too, moved south to the capital.

And London absorbed this vast influx, not, as with so many other cities, in sprawling slums and shanty towns, but in its very heart. This is, perhaps, the most extraordinary feature of this extraordinary metropolis. The slums were not sequestered but scattered and in the very shadow of the great palaces and temples of trade. Dark mews and alleyways were mere yards from the broad thoroughfares with their new arc lights. Clare Market, soon to be swept away by the Law Courts, Charing Cross Road and Aldwych, was a seething stew a stone's throw from the great banks. In St Giles's rookery, an area into which no sane man would venture without a police guard, you could hear the carriage wheels from Oxford Street. There were pockets of slum dwellings at the backs of St James's Square, Grosvenor Square, Hanover Square, Queen Square, Covent Garden and many other fashionable and respectable areas. From Ludgate Circus to Charing Cross, over 99 per cent of the houses had been built before 1700 – small, pokey, plaster and lath dwellings and places of trade in the midst of the city.

Much is made of the poverty of Victorian London, and poverty there unquestionably was, but food was cheap and plentiful, and the high incidence of deficiency diseases was due rather to gin and a penchant for "bad" food than to poverty. Mayhew demonstrates the extraordinary abundance of "jobs" which the poor could do in order to earn the threepence a day needed to eat, the fourpence a day needed for a bed. "Pure-finders" collected dog-droppings for the tanning trade, bird-catchers sold goldfinches for a shilling each or larks for half a crown, bone-grubbers and rag-gatherers averaged 6d a day, crossing-sweepers a shilling. The sewer-hunters, though their trade was disgusting and dangerous, earned at least £2 a week. Even, at the very lowest end of the scale, the mudlarks who scavenged in the riverbed at low tide could earn threepence a day. There were street sellers of just about everything imaginable, street musicians, artists and exhibitors of trained animals.

Prostitutes are sentimentally supposed to have been coerced, traduced or compelled into their trade. Before the Lords Committee of 1881–2 on the Protection of Young Girls, Inspector Morgan of the Marylebone and Paddington Division of the Metropolitan CID and formerly an officer in Southwark testified to Lord Salisbury, "I do not remember an instance.

I speak from an experience in town and country, and from a general knowledge of the whole of London, because I was for several years attached to Scotland Yard, and I never met with an instance where a girl was kept in a brothel against her will, where she could not get her liberty." The likes of the Whitechapel Murderer's victims, though doubtless bullied by pimps or prossers, enjoyed still more freedom. Acton, trained at the Female Venereal Hospital in Paris and for some years practising at a public clinic in London, describes the beguiling anarchy and degradation of the lodging-house tart:

> Her company is sought for novelty's sake when she is a newcomer, and her absence or reserve is considered insulting when once she is fairly settled in; so if she had any previous idea of keeping herself to herself, it is very soon dissipated…They are usually during the day…to be found dishevelled, dirty, slipshod and dressing-gowned in this [the lodging house's] kitchen, where the mistress keeps her *table d'hôte*. Stupid from beer, or

fractious from gin, they swear and chatter brainless stuff all day, about men and millinery, their own schemes and adventures, and the faults of others of the sisterhood...In such a household, all the projections of decency, modesty, propriety and conscience must, to preserve harmony and republican equality, be planed down, and the woman hammered out, not by the practice of her profession or the company of men, but by her association with her own sex and class, to the dead level of harlotry.

Acton was no sentimentalist – and it is worth recalling that, having held a post at a public hospital, he was dealing not just with rich "pretty-horsebreakers", flighty "dollymops" or courtesans: "If we compare the prostitute at thirty-five with her sister, who perhaps is the married mother of a family, or has been the toiling slave for years in the over-heated laboratories of fashion, we shall seldom find that the constitutional ravages often thought to be a necessary consequence of prostitution exceed those attributable to the cares of a family and the heart-wearing struggles of virtuous labour."

Prosperity – however relative – widespread education, over-population, a black economy of casual labour threatening the skilled workmen: the conditions demanded socialism, and a host of earnest, well-meaning reformers, many of them Christian, were on hand to tell the people of their rights. In 1885 and 1886, there were riots in Mayfair. On Bloody Sunday, 1887, the organized unemployed marched in pouring rain to Trafalgar Square. They were checked by 300 constables, foot and mounted, and the Foot Guards. Fights broke out. The police fell back.

Charles Warren ordered two squadrons of Life Guards up Whitehall to disperse the crowds. One man died and 150 were injured. These rather unimpressive casualty figures did not prevent the propagandists from giving the day its melodramatic appellation, and, at the time of the Whitechapel murders, the legend "Remember Bloody Sunday" was everywhere to be seen on walls and placards.

The *Star*, one of the newspapers which helped to establish the Ripper legend, was founded in January 1888. The editorial in the first edition clearly declares the proprietor's intentions:

The *Star* will be a radical journal. It will judge all policy – domestic, foreign, social – from the Radical Standpoint…The effect of every policy must first be regarded from the standpoint of the workers of the nation, and of the poorest and the most helpless among them. The charwoman that lives in St Giles, the seamstress that is sweated in Whitechapel, the labourer that stands begging for work outside the dockyard gate in St George's-in-the East – these are the persons by whose condition we will judge the policy of the different political parties…

The House of Lords, the Property vote, the monopoly of parliamentary life by the rich – these all belong to the edifice of Privilege and must be swept away. We hope to help in bringing the day when, as in the United States and in France and in Switzerland, every citizen stands exactly equal before the nation…

Londoners are ruled by one of the worst and most corrupt oligarchy that ever disgraced and robbed a city…Recently, the want of popular control, particularly over the police, has encouraged, on the part of the government and of the police authorities, a system of violent suppression of popular rights which would be impossible in a self-governed city…

It was literally a people-pleasing, rabble-rousing publication, so soon as the Ripper first struck, the radical press was ready to expatiate upon the social evils which gave rise to "social evils", as prostitutes were euphemistically known, to harry the police and to infer that the murderer must be a member of a higher social class, victimizing the poor and vulnerable.

The nature of the murderers' crimes and the inevitable censorship of the details also contributed to his almost instant legendary status. It was known that he did horrible things to his victims, but they were too obscene, according to the standards of the time, to be mentioned in respectable society. The assumption, of course, was that they were too horrible to be mentioned, and there is no horror, as Stevenson demonstrated in *Dr Jekyll and Mr Hyde*, greater than that of the unspeakable.

Perhaps still more remarkable than the Ripper's sudden rise to infamy is the sudden and apparently widespread acceptance that his campaign was over. The last murder took place on the night of 8–9 November 1888. On 26 January 1889, the additional police patrols began to be phased out. By spring of the same year, the Vigilance Committee had been disbanded and police patrols reduced to normal. As early as 12 December 1888, a correspondent to the *Pall Mall Gazette* was starting his letter, "Sir, Although the anxiety to solve the Whitechapel mystery is, for the nonce, allayed, if not extinct..." What had so allayed public fears? After all, 40 days had separated the last two murders, and no one then had assumed that the Ripper's campaign was over.

This inclines one to believe that, rightly or wrongly, the police believed that the Ripper was dead, incarcerated or had sailed for distant parts, and reassured the public accordingly. This ties in with the notion, confirmed by Macnaghten, that certain amongst the police strongly suspected Montague John Druitt and were persuaded by his suicide that they had been right.

It seems that barely a year now passes without a new candidate being positively identified as the Ripper. Final Solutions abound. Many of them concern members of the professional classes or the gentry. Many more posit the Ripper as a VOF or Very Odd Foreigner. Many of the candidates had (or are reputed to have had) medical knowledge or surgical skill.

There is no reason to assume any of these attributes. Their preponderance, therefore, among favoured suspects, must lead us to question their claims. Jack the Ripper may have been an intellectual genius with a motive. He may have been noble or even royal. He may have been a surgeon. All these, however, are unlikely suppositions of the Whitechapel Murderer.

What, then, disregarding the properties of the mythical Jack the Ripper, can we assert or convincingly speculate about the Whitechapel Murderer?

1 He aroused no suspicion in his nocturnal perambulations in the East End. He fitted in, though he did not necessarily belong.

2 He had money, in that his victims willingly accompanied him into the shadows. The whore who is content to be paid cash on delivery has yet to be invented. The fact that he confined his murders to so small an area argues against a rich man. It seems reasonable, however, to assume that he did not have to earn his keep by hard labour during the period of the murders.

3 He was probably sexually inexperienced save with prostitutes, or suffered impotence. The avaricious probing with a knife as a substitute phallus indicates a fascinated enthusiasm incompatible with familiarity. There was no evidence whatsoever of genital contact with any of the victims.

4 He knew how to kill animals at least, before he attended to Polly Nichols.

5 He kept his knives well.

6 He was an inadequate, though proficient in his trade or business, which may have involved bloodshed.

7 He was probably a loner but, again probably, had the protection of a sub culture, afraid of the fury of the mob were he identified.

8 If we are to believe the testimony of all disinterested witnesses, he was shortish (5 feet 2 inches–5 feet 7 inches) and youngish "about 30". Only Elizabeth Long, who saw him from behind, estimated his age at "around 40", and Long's evidence is suspect.

9 If we believe, as we surely have reason to believe, that the "Juwes" legend was the murderer's work (and, possibly the letter accompanying Lusk's kidney) he was literate. Literate or no, it is my view that he was acquainted with the Bible or, at least (for those who seek a Jewish candidate), with the Pentateuch. It is hard to read Chapters 5–7 of Leviticus without recalling the extraordinary scene of Mary Jane Kelly's murder in Dorset Street:

And if a soul sin, and hear the voice of swearing, and is a witness, whether he hath seen or known of it; if he do not utter it, then he shall bear his iniquity.

Or if a soul touch any unclean thing, whether it be a carcase of an unclean beast, or a beast, or a carcase of unclean cattle, or the carcase of unclean creeping things, and if it be hidden from him; he also shall be unclean, and guilty...

Or if he touch the uncleanness of man, whatsoever uncleanness it be that a man shall be defiled withal, and it be hid from him; when he knoweth of it, then he shall be guilty. And he shall bring his trespass offering unto the Lord for his sin which he hath sinned, a female from the flock...for a sin offering...

And he shall bring them unto the priest, who shall offer that which is for the sin offering first, and wring off his head from his neck, but shall not divide it asunder...

And he shall offer the second for a burnt offering, according to the manner: and the priest shall make an atonement for him for his sin which he hath sinned, and it shall be forgiven him.

The prophet goes on to specify the "manner" in which the sinner's sin offering and burnt offering must be prepared:

Command Aaron and his sons, saying, This is the law of the burnt offering: It is the burnt offering, because of the burning upon the altar all night unto the morning, and the fire of the altar shall be burning in it...

In the place where they kill the burnt offering shall they kill the trespass offering: and the blood thereof shall he sprinkle round about upon the altar.

And he shall offer of it all the fat thereof; the rump, and the fat that covereth the inwards.

And the two kidneys, and the fat which is on them, which is by the flanks, and the caul that is above the liver, with the kidneys, it shall he take away:

And the priest shall burn them upon the altar for an offering made by fire unto the Lord: it is a trespass offering.

Every male among the priests shall eat thereof…it is most holy…

And the priest that offereth any man's burnt offering, even the priest shall have to himself the skin of the burnt offering which he hath offered…

His own hand shall bring the offerings of the Lord made by fire, the fat with the breast, it shall he bring, that the breast may be waved for a wave offering before the Lord.

And the priest shall burn the fat upon the altar: but the breast shall be Aaron's and his sons.

And the right shoulder shall ye give unto the priest for an heave offering of the sacrifices of your peace offering…

At last, those who seek ritual in the Murderer's work can find something more credible than those rings and non-existent coins laid at Eddowes's feet. A glance at Thomas Bond's account of Kelly's mutilations indicates that the murderer was, in an admittedly somewhat uncertain and imprecise way, following the instructions in Leviticus.

The fire, we are told, had been blazing in Kelly's room, a claim which has been questioned in recent years in that clothing, the only identifiable fuel in the grate, usually smoulders and smokes. Fat, however, blazes, and it is not unthinkable that the flaps of skin from Kelly's thighs, buttocks and abdomen had been partially stripped of their fat. This association ties in with the Lusk letter, in which the writer claims to have eaten a kidney, though why Lusk should be afforded the status of a priest is unclear.

The causes of uncleanness necessitating such a sacrifice are listed in Leviticus. They are many, and include sodomy, bestiality, incest and having "a running issue out of [one's] flesh". The book promises, however, that a suitable sacrifice can restore cleanliness. We can posit the notion of a young man who has contracted syphilis from, or is merely tormented by guilt following an association with a prostitute or another man, now at once avenging the disease and bidding for a restitution of "cleanness" having heard this text at Sunday school or from a street corner preacher.

10 He had cause to desist from murdering Whitechapel drabs after 9 November 1888. Experience supports the notions of death, incarceration or migration as the reason for this. No other is supported by the literature, theory or history of such "trainee" mass murderers. Glutting is not known with such appetites.

11 He was fit, strong and agile at the time of the murders.

These, I hasten to add, are *my* assumptions about the Whitechapel Murderer. They do not generally match our perceptions of the legendary Jack. Unfortunately, the search for Jack the Ripper, now, as in 1888, confused the trail of the Whitechapel Murderer. Jack the Ripper was just so much more glamorous, so much more intelligent, so much more horrible… The Whitechapel Murderer owes him much.

My Life and Jack the Ripper
A personal perspective on the Ripper story

Stewart P Evans

It was way back in the late 1950s that I first became aware of the name "Jack the Ripper". Little did I know then that it was a name that was to stay with me over the ensuing years. Some time around 1958 (I cannot remember the exact year) my parents took me to Madame Tussaud's waxworks in London where I nervously descended the stone stairs, to the tolling of the Newgate bell, into the claustrophobic depths of the world-famous 'Chamber of Horrors. ' In those days the Chamber of Horrors was an atmospheric and fearful place, with the glassy eyes of notable murderers of the past gazing sightlessly at you. Various tortures were depicted and the chamber was dominated by a guillotine and a gallows. But, despite these fearsome exhibits and tableaux the item that attracted my attention and curiosity the most was a framed Metropolitan Police poster on one of the stone supports. It was the poster showing facsimile reproductions of the letter and post card received by the Central News Agency and requesting any person recognizing the handwriting to communicate with the nearest Police Station. The "Dear Boss" letter and "saucy Jacky" postcard were reproduced in red writing like the originals. I was too young to fully understand the implications of these communications but the content and, more significantly, the signature "Jack the Ripper" fascinated me – a fascination that was to prove to be enduring. I did not know it then but my visit was around the time that author and journalist Donald McCormick was producing his book *The Identity of Jack the Ripper*. Unfortunately McCormick was prone to embellishing his work with his own inventions.

A few years later, around 1961, I first read an account of the Ripper crimes, albeit a not too accurate one. An avid bibliophile I was already collecting books and I obtained a copy of *The Fifty Most Amazing Crimes of the Last 100 Years*, published by Odhams in 1936. This crime anthology included most of the notable murder cases of the past and each story was accompanied by a thumbnail illustration of the villain with the title of the piece at the top of the page. The essay on the Ripper was titled "The Fiend of East London: Jack the Ripper" by F A Beaumont. It consisted of some twelve pages of text plus an illustration of the killer accosting a rather too-good-looking woman under a street lamp.

Although laced with the errors that I was to discover are often found in Ripper writings it did at least give the story of the Whitechapel murders starting with that of Mary Ann Nichols, 30 August 1888 (sic), then including Emma Elizabeth Smith, 2 April 1888 (sic), Martha Turner (Tabram), 8 August 1888 (sic), Annie Chapman, Elizabeth Stride, Catherine Eddowes, and "Marie Jeannette" Kelly. Despite the inaccuracies, in its pages I made the acquaintance of many of the players in the Ripper story for the first time. These included the suspects John Pizer ("Leather Apron") and William Henry Piggott. I also read of the Metropolitan Police Commissioner Sir Charles Warren for the first time, and the story of the infamous correspondence received by the Central News Agency and signed "Jack the Ripper" was also told. Having looked at the murders the writer turned to the vexed question of "Who was this unknown fiend who murdered and mutilated six women, and held all London in terror for more than three months?"

Here the names of the Assistant Commissioner (Crime) Robert Anderson and the criminologist Major Arthur Griffiths were mentioned.

Both, according to the author, thought that the killer was a cunning "homicidal lunatic". Also mentioned was the *Times* religious maniac; Archibald Forbes' monomaniac with medical training and revenge on his mind and coroner Wynne Baxter's idea that the murderer "must have had considerable experience in the post-mortem room of a medical school." Finally the 1929 theory of author Leonard Matters's vengeful deranged surgeon whose son had died as a result of disease caught from Marie Kelly[1] was given as the latest and most likely theory that seemed "to fit the known facts more completely than any other explanation."

By the early 1960s I was versed in the basics of the story and aware of some of the theories as to the killer's identity. The greatest advance for me in these early years came in 1965 with the almost simultaneous publication of two new books on Jack the Ripper, *Autumn of Terror Jack the Ripper: His Crimes and Times* by Tom Cullen[2] and *Jack the Ripper In Fact and Fiction* by Robin Odell[3]. These two excellent books formed the basis for my first real study of the subject. Although well written and well researched both books suffered from the fact that no official papers on the murders had yet been released. Some errors were perpetuated and a few myths created by Donald McCormick were repeated. Although published in 1959 I did not have a copy of McCormick's influential *The Identity of Jack the Ripper*. The importance of the Cullen and Odell books for me was that for the first time I was seeing a wealth of detail, maps, photographs and bibliographies directing me towards books to add to my collection. I had not seen Daniel Farson's television broadcast in November 1959 in his series *Farson's Guide to the British* so I was not aware that he had revealed the initials "MJD" as being those of "Jack the Ripper" which he had discovered in notes belonging to Lady Aberconway.[4] The notes are now famous in Ripper circles as "The Macnaghten Memoranda", written by her father Sir Melville Macnaghten in 1894 and naming the three police suspects M J Druitt, the Polish Jew Kosminski and Michael Ostrog. The importance of Cullen's work was, of course, that he identified "MJD" as the barrister/teacher Montague John Druitt who was now to become the favoured top Ripper suspect for the next twenty three years or more. More mundanely Odell opted for an unknown Jewish ritual

---

1 Matters's theory had been published in *The People* newspaper of Sunday, 26 December 1926, and three years later in a book *The Mystery of Jack the Ripper*, the first full-length English book treatment of the case.

2 Published by The Bodley Head. Cullen was an American author living in London.

3 Published by George G Harrap. Odell's book was accepted by Harrap's editor the well-known crime historian and bibliophile Joe Gaute. It was the start of a long working relationship between the two.

4 Christabel Mary MacLaren, 2nd Baroness Aberconway, was the younger daughter of Sir Melville Macnaghten.

slaughterer, or shochet, as the elusive killer. A named Ripper with an identifiable history did have more appeal, although the Jewish slaughterer idea dated right back to 1888. Needless to say, on balance, I was persuaded by Cullen's theory and Druitt became my preferred suspect. Farson was incensed by Cullen's revelation of Druitt's name and the Macnaghten material. It had been his 'baby' since 1959 and he was planning a Ripper book himself. Farson openly accused Cullen of the theft of his material, even suggesting that Cullen had stolen his folder of notes from a television company office, an accusation that Cullen strenuously denied. Farson's own book on the Druitt theory did not appear until 1972. There were no circles of Ripper enthusiasts (if that's the correct word to use) in those days but some of the Ripper writers and interested amateur criminologists knew each other and discussed their mutual interests. General interest was maintained with the appearance of such films as *A Study in Terror* which pitted Sherlock Holmes against the Ripper in 1965.

By 1966 I had moved from my hometown of Weymouth to the less picturesque surroundings of Ipswich. My interest in the Ripper was still strong and when Robin Odell's book was published in paperback[5] that year I bought it and avidly consumed the new material it contained. This was in the form of an additional chapter "Gentleman Jack" discussing Cullen's Druitt theory. Also included was an appendix quoting material newly found in the London Hospital by Professor Francis Camps, the famous Home Office pathologist and part-time Ripper student. The material, mainly maps and medical sketches relating to the Eddowes inquest, had been found by Camp's assistant Sam Hardy and published in an article, "More About Jack the Ripper", written by Camps in the *London Hospital Gazette*, Vol 1, LXIX, No 1, April 1966. My interest fired by the new material I decided, in August 1967, to make the journey from Ipswich to the City and East End to visit the scenes of the murders. Being a "Ripperologist"[6] in those heady days was a lonely pastime, there were no clubs or groups, no internet and

5 London, Mayflower Dell.
6 "Ripperology" is a term the invention of which claimed by Colin Wilson, see his 1972 introduction to *Jack the Ripper A Bibliography and Review of the Literature* by Alexander Kelly (David Streatfield), London, Association of Assistant Librarians, 1973.

meeting an author was not an easy matter. I travelled down to the City by train and disembarked at Liverpool Street Station. Armed with my trusty Kodak Brownie 127 camera I visited various sites, some little changed since 1888, and took photographs.

After taking several shots of Mitre Square I moved on to Gunthorpe Street, where George Yard Buildings, scene of the Turner/Tabram murder, still stood. In Durward Street, formerly Buck's Row, there were still warehouses standing (as well as the Board School which is still there), Essex Wharf and the row of grimy terraced houses that had silently witnessed the Nichols murder on 31 August 1888. Perhaps most impressive of all I found 29 Hanbury Street in all its shabby glory still standing. I tried the front door, through which the Ripper and Annie Chapman had passed less than 80 years earlier. The door was locked and I scraped some fragments of the peeling pale green paint off the door as a souvenir.[7]

I also went to the London Hospital and entered the library with a view to obtaining a copy of the April 1966 back issues of the *London Hospital Gazette* containing Camp's article. The librarian on duty quizzed me as to why I was seeking the magazine and I, telling a lie, replied, "I am planning to write a book on the Whitechapel murders." I gladly paid 2/6 for the solitary copy that he found in a drawer. In 1968, at a Bournemouth second hand bookshop, I purchased an expensive three-volume set of *Mysteries of Police and Crime* by Major Arthur Griffiths[8] as I knew that it contained an important reference to the Whitechapel murders. The reference was to the three suspects named by Macnaghten, of Druitt, Kosminski and Ostrog, although they weren't named.

Also gaining recognition in the field of Ripper studies at this time was a young City of London Police Constable, Donald Rumbelow, who was also curator of the City of London Police Museum. Rumblelow also made important finds in the dusty old files of the City Police at Old Jewry. As well as a cache of over 300 letters from the public to the City Police at the time of the murders, at Snow Hill Police Station he also discovered a glass plate negative of the external view of Kelly's room at

7 A souvenir now, I fear, lost.
8 London, Cassell, 1903.

Miller's Court, a photograph of Kelly's body on her bed and mortuary photographs of Catharine Eddowes. These had never been seen by the reading public in this country and were a major discovery. All this was unknown to me at the time, but Rumbelow was friendly with other students of the case such as Cullen, Odell, Camps, Farson and Colin Wilson. It was a coterie far removed from my social circles. Rumbelow had shown a great interest in the finds at the London Hospital and, for his part, Camps was delighted with Rumbelow's photographs of the corpses of Eddowes and Kelly. Camps gave Rumbelow the drawings, plans and maps of the Eddowes murder, a City Police crime, for Rumbelow to have framed and displayed at the City Police offices.[9] For his part, Rumbelow gave Camps a set of photographs of the victims. In 1972, Farson finally published his book on Druitt-as-the-Ripper and, in doing so became the first Ripper author to publish the photographs found by Rumbelow.[10] Rumbelow, also an author, was very annoyed at this as Farson had been given the photographs by Camps, who, as we have established, obtained them from Rumbelow.

In September 1969, I had joined the Suffolk Constabulary and, by that time was deeply immersed in another long standing interest of mine – aviation. This interest was shared with my stepfather, Ron Buxton, and together we became involved in early "aviation archaeology", digging up the wrecks of crashed WWII aircraft in the flatlands of East Anglia. The interest became all consuming and my main field of research was the American 8th USAAF and its aircraft based all over the region during the war.

In 1972 I discovered some remaining wreckage of the PB4Y Liberator bomber that had exploded over the hamlet of Hinton in Suffolk in August 1944 while flying on a top secret early guided weapon experiment of the Americans. Taking off from Winfarthing (Fersfield) airfield, near Diss in Norfolk, the bomber was, in effect, a radio-controlled flying bomb from which the two man crew was to bail out over Manston before the remotely controlled aircraft, packed with high explosives, was "dumped" on the German V3 site at Mimoyecques in

9 The framed document was later returned to the London Hospital and is now deposited with the Royal London Hospital Museum archives.

10 *Jack the Ripper* by Daniel Farson, London, Michael Joseph, 1972.

the Pas de Calais area of France. In the event the aircraft had mysteriously exploded in mid-air some 2,000 feet above the Suffolk countryside while the radio remote controls were being tested. The first pilot on board the bomber was none other than Joe Kennedy Jr, son of the American ambassador and elder brother of the future US President John F Kennedy. Both he and his co-pilot, Wilford "Bud" Willy, lost their lives and only fragmented part of bodies were recovered.

News of my discovery of parts of Kennedy's aircraft leaked out to the press, as a result of which I appeared in the international press and appeared on the national and local BBC television news. In 1973, I was one of the co-founders of Friends of the Eighth (FOTE), a group dedicated to the history and research of the 8th Air Force. During this time I met and became friendly with many USAAF WWII veterans. In 1976, I met the movie star James Stewart, himself a Liberator bomber pilot with the 453rd Bomb Group at Tibenham also in Norfolk. It was a great moment, and I spent a good part of the day with, that (then) living legend, who was a wonderful man.

In 1979, I travelled to Memphis, Tennessee, as guest speaker at the reunion of the 390th Bomb Group and established several more friendships. I make this digression, which I hope is of interest, to explain why my interest in Jack the Ripper was largely on the back burner in the 1970s as I didn't advance my researches in that field very far. Indeed, I was actively researching and preparing to write a book on the Third Air Division of the Eighth Air Force (largely Suffolk-based) and my spare time was at a premium.

A result of these other activities was that I missed many of the new Ripper developments during the 1970s, especially the international publicity generated by Dr T E A Stowell's 1970 claim that the Ripper was none other than Prince Albert Victor Christian Edward, Queen Victoria's grandson, albeit he didn't actually name him.[11] He also introduced the name of the Queen's physician, Sir William Withey Gull, to the case. This was to prove a winning formula with the public and film-makers, and the "Royal conspiracy" was now established. In 1972, Michael Harrison published his book *The Life of HRH the Duke of*

11 See *The Criminologist*, November 1979 edited by Nigel Morland.

Clarence and Avondale 1862–1892 Was he Jack the Ripper?[12], which
suggested Prince Albert Victor's Cambridge tutor, J K Stephen as a
suspect. I purchased each new book as it came out. In 1973, new ground
was broken when the BBC screened *Jack the Ripper* with their television
detective team of Barlow (Stratford Johns) and Watt (Frank Windsor)
retrospectively investigating the Ripper crimes over six weekly
episodes.[13] With dramatizations and drawing on official records to
which they had been granted access it was a wonderful series and
certainly inspired new interest. For the first time we became aware of
the eccentric character Joseph Gorman, better known as Joseph
"Sickert", self-alleged illegitimate son of the artist Walter Sickert.
Gorman's tall take built on the Royal conspiracy idea and involving a
Masonic cover-up was aired on the BBC documentary[14] and Ripper
studies were never to be the same again. It also ensured massive general
interest in the subject.

Throughout the 1970s, the Ripper case remained very much a
secondary interest of mine, which was occasionally renewed by the
appearance of a new book or film treatment. A book that was
particularly interesting was *The Ripper File* by Elwyn Jones and John
Lloyd which was based on the fictional BBC TV duo's (Barlow and
Watt) investigation of the case.[15] This book was especially important as
the authors had access to the as yet unreleased Scotland Yard files and
published much new information. The same year, and slightly earlier,
Richard Whittington-Egan published his *Casebook on Jack the Ripper*[16] but
only 700 copies were printed and it had very limited sales exposure and
I did not know of this book at the time. For me the best book of the
decade was the excellent *The Complete Jack the Ripper* by Donald
Rumbelow.[17] A serving police officer, Rumbelow had accessed the
Scotland Yard files and was able to use his own unique collection of
material that he had been gathering since the mid-1960s. With common

12 London, W H Allen, 1972, published in the USA by Drake with the title *Clarence: Was He
  Jack the Ripper?*
13 Screened
14 Gorman appeared in the final episode
15 London, Arthur Barker, 1975.
16 London, Wildy, 1975.
17 London, W H Allen, 1975.

sense it took a varied look at the case, including popular entertainment, and was by far the best book yet published on the subject. In 1976, great Ripper exposure was ensured by the appearance of the book *Jack the Ripper The Final Solution* by Stephen Knight, which was commissioned by Joe Gaute at Harrap. A journalist with the *East London Advertiser*, Knight had been sent to interview Joseph Gorman about his story of Royal/Masonic dark deeds. Knight decided that it was an opportunity not to be missed and wrote a sensational book which was an immediate international best-seller. Many were convinced by the lurid tale of conspiracy and we are still living with its legacy today, the idea of Royal involvement with the Ripper murders still being very popular. However, Knight's book cannot be easily dismissed as complete rubbish as he also included much new material from the official files to which he was given access. Knight realized that there was great mileage in writing exposures of alleged Masonic skulduggery, but such ideas are patent nonsense. More royal fantasy followed with the publication in the US of *Prince Jack: The True Story of Jack the Ripper*.[18] It was far from the true story and was not published in the UK therefore I did not see it at the time.

From the late 1970s up until the mid-1980s, my Ripper interest was very much in the background and was not renewed until the centenary of the murders approached. In 1986 my aviation research ended with the break up of my marriage and was followed by a renewal of my fascination in crime mysteries. One of the most intriguing of these mysteries was the Peasenhall murder of 1902, more especially as it was a local Suffolk case. In 1986 I read in the *East Anglian Daily Times* of two researchers working on a book on the Peasenhall mystery, John Gleeson and Keith Skinner. Skinner, I read, was none other than the grandson of one of the prosecution witnesses in the case, Alphonso Skinner. As a result I contacted Keith and John and met them the same year. I found that Keith was well advanced in the writing of a centenary Ripper book[19] and he was fascinated to hear of my long interest in the Ripper case and to see the photographs I had taken of the murder sites in 1967. It was the start of a long friendship and working relationship with

18 New York, Doubleday, 1978.
19 *The Ripper Legacy*, with Martin Howells, London, Sidgwick & Jackson, 1987.

Keith. We also shared the same year of birth which gave that added understanding and interest that comes when two people have experienced growing up over the same years; Keith said that he too had first visited the Ripper sites in the mid-seventies. In the event Keith did not write the Peasenhall book with John, but with another author – Martin Fido.

The media hype of 1987, as press coverage increased, centred on the seven Ripper books published that year, as each vied to be first into the bookshops. When they did appear, I did not buy them all, I bought only three. They had an unexpected effect on me. I was disillusioned by the "overkill" of Ripper books and made a mistake I later regretted – I sold my Ripper collection, including that treasured copy of the *London Hospital Gazette* bought back in 1967. I was still interested in the Ripper case but my main target was building a collection of crime books centred on the Notable British Trials volumes.[20] It was an expensive hobby and the money from selling the Ripper books helped it on its way. A result of all this was that the Ripper frenzy of 1988 passed me by almost unnoticed.

Of course I caught the publicity brought by the pending release of the TV miniseries *Jack the Ripper* starring Michael Caine and Lewis Collins. The pre-publicity claimed that the identity of the Ripper was going to be disclosed, but I shared the opinion of most Ripper *aficionados* that this was just so much hype and that we should expect another "solution" based on the high-profile Royal/Masonic nonsense. When it did come out I found that my predictions had been proved largely correct, although I found the movie to be an enjoyable piece of hokum. Unbeknown to me a Police History Society conference had been held on 24 September 1988 at the City of London's Wood Street Police Station. It was a starry affair for Ripperologists as amongst those in attendance were many authors both old school and new. The panel of invited speakers included Robin Odell, Donald Rumbelow, Colin Wilson, Paul Begg,[21] Martin Fido and Keith Skinner. It marked the beginning of an influential and enduring research/writing team – Begg,

20 Published by William Hodge, Edinburgh, 1905–1959.
21 The only author producing a true centenary book, *Jack the Ripper The Uncensored Facts*, London, Robson Books, 1988, a useful and well referenced volume.

Fido and Skinner, later aptly dubbed "the Three Musketeers" by Donald Rumbelow. At this time the so-called "Swanson marginalia" had just come into the public domain – discovered by the late Jim Swanson in his grandfather's (Donald Swanson) copy of *The Lighter Side of My Official Life*, by Sir Robert Anderson.[22] As a result of the Swanson material apparently endorsing Anderson's claims that the Ripper was a poor Polish Jew, and with Swanson identifying that Jew as the Macnaghten-named "Kosminski" – a new suspect was gaining a higher profile.

Indeed, Fido's book[23] proposed a Jewish suspect, although not Kosminski whom Fido had identified from asylum records as almost certainly one Aaron Kosminski and who, in his opinion, could not have been the Ripper. Begg's book, although largely a reference work, favoured the word of Anderson and left no doubt that Begg's choice of most likely suspect was Aaron Kosminski. The attendees of the Wood Street conference still voted Druitt in as the most likely Ripper, but the tide was turning and some of the leading authorities of the day were turning to the Polish Jew theory. These intricacies of Ripper reasoning were unknown to me but that was soon to change.

In 1989 Keith began work on a new book with Martin Fido.[24] The book was all about the Peasenhall murder and as I was deemed to be the local "expert" on the case they decided to consult with me. I met Martin Fido when he and Keith visited on their search for the Peasenhall murderer. I already had Martin's 1987 book and for me the ever-expanding collection of theories on the Ripper murders was a bit confusing. Martin and Keith updated me on the latest developments and thinking on the case and, I found, they did not agree what final interpretation to put on the Polish Jew theory. However, it did now seem that the new "preferred suspect" in informed Ripper circles was to be found in the Polish Jew line of reasoning. I learned also of the close working relationship on the Ripper that Messrs Begg, Fido and Skinner shared and of the joint project that was to result, in 1991, in *The Jack the*

---

22 London, Hodder & Stoughton, 1910.

23 *The Crimes Detection & Death of Jack the Ripper*, London, Weidenfeld and Nicolson, 1987.

24 *The Peasenhall Murder* by Martin Fido and Keith Skinner, Stroud, Alan Sutton Publishing, 1990.

Ripper A To Z.[25] My interest in the Ripper case was beginning to grow again and was really fired when I read the *A to Z*. It was unlike any Ripper book previously published – a wonderful touchstone volume.

By the early 1990s I was busily collecting crime books and ephemera, and this included rare items such as letters from murderers and other crime relics. For several years I had been a customer of the "true crime" book dealer Camille Wolff, first based in Lawrence Street, Chelsea, and then in Portobello Road. She knew of my keen interest in crime ephemera. In early 1993 she was contacted by an antiquarian book dealer in Richmond, Eric Barton, who offered her some "Jack the Ripper" related letters. She said that she was not interested but knew a man who was – and that was me! In February 1993, I received a telephone call from Eric offering me, on approval, a few letters relating to Jack the Ripper from the collection of the late George R Sims.[26] A few days later the letters arrived in a jiffy bag. I was amazed to see that one of the letters, typed and three pages long, was signed J G Littlechild. I knew that Littlechild[27] was the Chief Inspector in charge of the Special Branch at Scotland Yard from 1883–1893. As such he would have been one of the department heads in Scotland Yard at the time of the Ripper murders so that anything he had to say about the Ripper would be very relevant.

A quick perusal of the letter revealed a Ripper suspect, Dr Tumblety, that in my previous thirty years plus of Ripper reading I had never heard of. Further to that it also revealed that the journalist generally believed at Scotland Yard to have written the famous "Jack the Ripper" letter and postcard was none other than Tom Bulling, a reporter with the Central News Agency. This was the first discovery of a genuine named police suspect of the time since the publication of the "Macnaghten memoranda". These were very, very important Ripper revelations and I knew then that I would be writing a book about it.

The next few years seemed to be a flurry of activity and research. I had passed details of Tumblety to Keith Skinner who historically

25 London, Headline, 1991.
26 George Robert Sims (1847–1922) author, playwright, poet, journalist and amateur criminologist.
27 John George Littlechild (1847–1923) Metropolitan Police officer, retiring in the rank of Chief Inspector.

identified him and, eventually, trusted friends in Ripper circles shared the information. They were heady days and in 1992 another Ripper sensation was mooted when news of a newly-discovered "diary" began to leak out. As far as I was concerned it couldn't have happened at a worse time. I was planning to write a book on my newly found suspect and the mounting hype on the "diary" increasingly sounded like a hoax being foisted on the reading public. Friends such as the noted "debunker" of hoaxes Melvin Harris,[28] Richard Whittington-Egan[29] and Nick Warren[30] roundly dismissed the hoax – and I had to agree. It wasn't long before the alleged identity of the writer of the "diary", Liverpool cotton merchant James Maybrick,[31] leaked out to the media. My opposition to this hoax resulted in my first Jack the Ripper related TV appearance when I appeared on *London Tonight* with Nick Warren, Martin Fido and Brian Maybrick.

The "diary" saga was to prove enduring as first Shirley Harrison's book[32] and then the video[33] produced by Paul H Feldman, in which I also made a brief appearance, appeared. Keith Skinner was working for Feldman as a researcher and it was through Keith that I met the aggressive and energetic Paul Feldman and for some time worked with him. Paul had suggested that he might "run" Maybrick and my newly found suspect Dr Tumblety (who had Liverpool connections) as a "whodunit".

At this time Martin Fido was also associated with Feldman and the idea was that he should co-author a book on Tumblety with me.[34] However, I was not happy that my perfectly genuine suspect should be "contaminated" by association with this modern "diary" hoax. In the event, about 18 months after buying the Littlechild letter, I began writing my own Ripper book with a journalistic colleague from work,

---

28 Then author of *Jack the Ripper The Bloody Truth*, London, Columbus Books, 1987 and *The Ripper File*, London, W H Allen, 1989.
29 Author of *A Casebook on Jack the Ripper*, London, Wildy & Sons, 1975.
30 Editor of the then only Ripper journal, *Ripperana*.
31 James Maybrick was, of course, a very well known murder victim and his wife, Florence, had been convicted of his murder in 1889.
32 *The Diary of Jack the Ripper*, London, Smith Gryphon, 1993.
33 *The Diary of Jack the Ripper Beyond Reasonable Doubt*, London, MIA (Duocrave), 1993.
34 To this end Martin even produced a proposal.

Paul Gainey. The result was *The Lodger The Arrest and Escape of Jack the Ripper*.[35] During the writing of the book we were fortunate to meet the greatly respected author and historian Philip Sugden[36] who gave us much valuable advice. Although we enjoyed great publicity for this book, selling 15,500 copies in hardback before going into paperback in 1996, it never really fully emerged from the overbearing shadow of the fake "diary". Indeed, with the "diary" being universally declared a hoax, American publication of our book proved difficult to secure.[37] Another important development around this time was the formation of the "The Cloak and Dagger Club" by Mark Galloway[38] which was a group devoted to historical research into the Ripper case and the East End of London.

With publication of my book and the resulting TV documentary based on it[39] came international recognition as an authoritative Ripper author. The year 1996 also saw the first Jack the Ripper conference, organized by my partner (now wife), Rosemarie Howell at the Post House Hotel in Ipswich. It was a great success and resulted in a similar event in Norwich in 1998. My in-depth Ripper research in the early 1990s included purchasing all the Ripper related official Metropolitan Police and Home Office files in hard copy from the Public Record Office[40] at Kew. These I transcribed over the years the final result of which was my largest book *The Ultimate Jack the Ripper Sourcebook*[41] with Keith Skinner. I also co-authored a smaller publication at this time with my good friend, and skilled researcher, Nick Connell. This was, more or less, a biography of Detective Inspector Reid, head of the Whitechapel CID at the time of the Ripper murders, *The Man Who Hunted Jack the Ripper*.[42] With the success of our *Ultimate Sourcebook*, which also went

35 London, Century, 1995.

36 Author of *The Complete History of Jack the Ripper*, London, Robinson, 1994.

37 It was finally published as *Jack the Ripper First American Serial Killer*, New York, Kodansha America, 1996, later going into paperback in the USA also.

38 Now 'The Whitechapel Society.'

39 *The Whitechapel Murders*, made by Just Television for the Channel 4 series *Secret History*, 1996 and presented by David Jessel.

40 Now The National Archives.

41 London, Constable & Robinson, 2000, published simultaneously in the USA, as *The Ultimate Jack the Ripper Companion*, by Carroll & Graf.

42 Cambridge, Rupert Books, 2000.

into paperback, Keith Skinner and I decided on another joint project and *Jack the Ripper Letters From Hell*[43] was born. We realized that the one sizeable official file of Ripper material that had not been properly looked at was that containing the letters allegedly from the murderer and received by the police.[44]

During the writing of this book Keith and I were approached by the Hollywood film directors Albert and Allen Hughes who were planning a major Jack the Ripper movie starring Johnny Depp. It was to be called *From Hell* and was based on the graphic novel of that name by Alan Moore and Eddie Campbell.[45] Keith and I, despite the fact that we did not agree with the theory upon which the movie was based, were taken on by Twentieth Century Fox as historical advisers for *From Hell*. It was a memorable experience and on an initial visit to Greenford Studios I met Sir Nigel Hawthorne who was to play Sir William Gull (the Ripper)[46] impressively dressed in black top hat and cloak with red lining. I also met Heather Graham (Mary Kelly), and Robbie Coltrane (Detective Sergeant Godley), as well as scriptwriter Rafael Yglesias and others. Keith and I also took the Hughes brothers around the actual murder sites in London as well as the actresses playing the victims, Heather Graham (Kelly), Annabelle Apsion (Nichols), Katrin Cartlidge (Chapman), Lesley Sharp (Eddowes) and Susan Lynch (Stride). Rosemarie and I also travelled to Prague to watch some of the filming. The highlight was meeting Johnny Depp, playing Inspector Abberline, whom I discovered was something of a Jack the Ripper aficionado. He told me that he had purchased the first edition of my Tumblety book in London in 1995. We also met most of the other members of the cast including the distinguished Ian Holm playing Gull instead of the ailing Nigel Hawthorne.

I discovered Dr Tumblety over thirty years after first becoming interested in the Ripper crimes. Although he resulted in my first successful Ripper book, it proved to be something of a double-edged

43 Stroud, Sutton Publishing, 2001.

44 Filed under MEPO 3/142.

45 First published in eleven parts Mad Love, The Penny Press, Kitchen Sink Press 1991-1998 and in a collected edition, Australia, Eddie Campbell Comics, November 1999.

46 Shortly afterwards Nigel Hawthorne was taken seriously ill and the part was taken by Ian Holm.

sword. I found myself labelled by some as "the Tumblety man", despite all my efforts to remain objective and factual in my writing. Tumblety was my discovery, he was a genuine and viable contemporary suspect but I knew also that there was no evidence proving that he was actually the Ripper, or even that he was connected with the murders. A book on a given suspect cannot be written without being, to a degree, subjective and selective.

Obviously when choosing which 1888 newspaper reports to use it is necessary to utilize those that refer, or could be interpreted as referring to, the chosen suspect. All I have asked since, is that those looking at Tumblety should do so from the valid perspective that he was a genuine 1888 police suspect for the murders. I expected, as all who write about a chosen suspect should, to receive criticism from those with opposing theories or suspects but I hoped that any such criticism should be informed, valid and factual. Unfortunately it was not. I did not want to stay in a "single suspect rut" and moved on to my subsequent works which were all objective, factual and contained no suspect bias. Of course I kept an eye on research developments with regard to Tumblety and amongst the energetic North American researchers were such names as Roger J Palmer, Wolf Vanderlinden and Joe Chetcuti. They were finding much material.

The catalyst for Ripper research for many years now has been the great internet site, *Casebook: Jack the Ripper* hosted by Stephen P Ryder, so it was easy to keep up with current debate. I had been in touch with Roger Palmer for many years and he had been keeping me updated on his sterling research. Tumblety was an Irish American so the most fruitful area for research on him is obviously the US. I was in the back seat by now as far as Tumblety was concerned and all my research was focused on objective research into the murders. By this time I was contributing articles at various times to the Ripper journals *Ripperologist*[47] in the UK and *Ripper Notes*[48] in the US.

Over the years I had developed a very close friendship with Donald Rumbelow, one of the most respected of Ripper historians. Sitting at home together on one of his visits the idea of a joint Ripper book was

47 Edited by Paul Begg.
48 Edited by Dan Norder.

suggested. I considered it a great honour to be able to write with an author whom I had admired since my early days of Ripper study. We began to write *Jack the Ripper Scotland Yard Investigates*.[49] The book was written from a police perspective and contained much new information and illustrations.

Although having no suspect bias we did present an overview of collective contemporary police opinion and a chapter closely examining the claims of Assistant Commissioner Anderson who was the only senior police officer of the day to make the claim that the identity of the Ripper (a poor Polish Jew) was a definitely ascertained fact. Over recent years certain researchers and writers have accorded Anderson with very great weight and authority. So we presented the first in-depth analysis of Anderson's claims and credibility while adhering to facts and objectivity. The result was that we felt that he really deserved no more attention than some of the other Scotland Yard men. My final conclusion was that if the evidence as to the identity of the Ripper did not exist in 1888 it certainly won't be found today.

Just after the publication of our book Roger J Palmer revealed an incredible find that he had made in the New York press regarding Tumblety. It was a rare discovery of a significant and valuable contemporary newspaper report relating to the Whitechapel murders. It was in the *New York World* of Tuesday 29 January 1889 and it was an interview with Dr Francis Tumblety, described in the piece as "the celebrated Whitechapel suspect". It was odd that Tumblety had not been named in the British press albeit there were at least two references to him in which his name was not disclosed.[50] The *New York World* article is very important for more than one reason.

In developing a viable case against a named suspect it is, as I have indicated, necessary to speculate and hypothesize to a degree and this

---

49 Stroud, Sutton Publishing, 2006.

50 See the *Monmouthshire Merlin and South Wales Advertiser* of Friday, December 7, 1888, front page under the heading "AN AMERICAN JACK THE RIPPER" – "It has been reported by cable from Europe that a certain person whose name is known, has sailed from Havre for New York, who is famous for his hatred of women, and who has repeatedly made threats against females of dissolute character."; also *The Pall Mall Gazette* of Monday, December 31, 1888, page 10, under head "THE SEARCH FOR THE WHITECHAPEL MURDERER Detectives on the Outlook in New York."

requires personal opinion and interpretation of surviving reports. This, of course, makes it easy for critics to attack and often disparage such authors' work. In the case of Tumblety, I had been put into the position of basing much of my case against him on such personal interpretation and opinion. It was therefore nice to see that some of my reasoning was bolstered by Tumblety's own words in this article. In my opinion no evidence will ever emerge that will lead to a positive identification of "Jack the Ripper". It will always be a case of the interested reader assessing all the evidence that has been revealed over the years and deciding for himself which suspect he favours the most. For me the Tumblety interview in this article has greatly enhanced Tumblety's status as a suspect.

First, and perhaps most importantly, Tumblety confirmed that he was actually arrested by the London police as a Whitechapel suspect, rather than for the misdemeanours of gross indecency with which he was finally charged. This is very significant, for it would seem that the Metropolitan Police were sanguine of obtaining some sort of confession from Tumblety, probably the only way in which they could have proved his guilt, if, indeed, he was guilty, for we know there was no witness to any of the actual acts of murder.

It does not matter if a person is suspected of murder, he still cannot be legally held unless there is hard evidence to justify that detention. According to Tumblety, the main reasons for his arrest were that he was an American and that he was wearing a slouch hat.[51] This fitted some of the descriptions that had been circulated in the press that the police had for the alleged murderer, although, undoubtedly, there were other reasons that Tumblety was either not aware of or did not want to mention.

Tumblety had arrived back in New York, from Le Havre, aboard the French liner *La Bretagne* on 3 December 1888. He had immediately gone to ground. As the report described, his name had immediately become a "household word" in the USA in connection with the recent London murders and "from the moment he set foot in New York he was under surveillance". The piece also confirmed that "An English detective,

51 An American style hat with a broad and drooping brim (hence "slouch").

whose stupidity was noticeable even among a class not celebrated for their shrewdness, came over specially to shadow him…" Tumblety was a slippery customer, of that there can be no doubt when reading the accounts about him.

He went directly to the house of a Mrs McNamara at 79 East Tenth Street and remained there under the protective eye of the old Irishwoman who was remarkably loyal to him. According to the World "…it was due to her vigilance that all efforts to see him personally failed. She was able to throw reporters and detectives completely off the scent…"

It is recorded elsewhere that Inspector Andrews of Scotland Yard, who had recently escorted a Canadian prisoner[52] to Toronto, had then moved on to Montreal where he saw the Chief of Police before arriving in New York in an effort to trace Tumblety. The then head of the New York Police Detective Department was Inspector Thomas Byrnes, whose regime was reported to be corrupt and who would have had little sympathy for an English policeman. He would, one suspects, favour a fellow Irish-American who was of wealthy means. Be that as it may, Andrews's attempts to locate Tumblety proved a failure and he soon returned to England empty handed. The American police then "lost interest" in Tumblety. It would have taken some form of solid evidence against Tumblety before Scotland Yard would have ever contemplated a return trip to trace him. Such evidence, I believe, never existed.

So, by the time the *New York World* reporter saw Tumblety at the end of January 1889, the paper was able to report that "The (American) police long since ceased to take any interest in the case, as it became evident that the English authorities had no evidence to hold the doctor." It was true that Tumblety had fled his bail in London, but that was in relation to offences of gross indecency which were misdemeanours and not felonies and thus did not fall under the international extradition laws. Only in Canada would legislation in regard to fugitive offenders for less serious offences and breach of bail be enforceable. Tumblety

52 Roland Israel Gideon Barnett wanted under the Fugitive Offenders Act for bank fraud in Toronto and extradited from England at the Canadians' expense.

could not be touched by the English police while he remained in the US – and he knew it.

The article mentions "pictures that have been published of Dr Tumblety in London and New York give a very good idea of him", and this could mean that there are still some reports yet to be found. The next important point in the article is an updated description of the man himself:

"He is a powerfully built man and stands 6 feet 2 inches in his stockings.[53] His long black moustache has been trimmed close and reaches down in the shape of a thick growth of beard around his chin, which he keeps smooth shaven. His face is ruddy and he has blue eyes."

This confirmed a point that I made years ago that his moustache may not have been so prominent in 1888, for it shows that at that time Tumblety was not sporting the huge "handlebar" appendage of the widely published image, but was wearing a close-cut, droopy moustache that bordered either side of his clean-shaven chin. The description continued with his clothing:

"If he ever dressed sensationally in the past, he does not do so now. Yesterday he wore a dark suit which was by no means new, and a little peaked travelling cap. Altogether he gave the appearance of a prosperous Western farmer. He wore no jewelry."

Again this is fascinating and confirmed what I suggested in 1995 – that Tumblety in 1888 was not dressing flashily or ostentatiously. This was confirmed by Tumblety himself:

"Dr Tumblety talks in a quick, nervous fashion, with a decided English accent, and at times, when describing his treatment by the English police, he would get up from his chair and walk rapidly around the room until he became calm."

"My arrest came about in this way. I had been going over to England for a long time ever since 1869, indeed – and I used to go about the city a great deal until every part of it became familiar to me. I happened to be there when these Whitechapel murders attracted the attention of the whole world, and, in company with thousands of other people, I went

53 Press reports of Tumblety's height vary between 5' 10" and 6' 2" and are, of course, relevant when assessing him against possible contemporary sightings of the Ripper. His exact height is not known.

down to the Whitechapel district. I was not dressed in a way to attract attention, I thought, though it afterwards turned out that I did. I was interested by the excitement and the crowds and the queer scenes and sights, and did not know that all the time I was being followed by English detectives."

"Why did they follow you?"

"My guilt was very plain to the English mind. Someone has said that Jack the Ripper was an American, and everybody believed that statement. Then it is the universal belief among the lower classes that all Americans wear slouch hats; therefore Jack the Ripper must wear a slouch hat. Now, I happened to have on a slouch hat, and this, together with the fact that I was an American, was enough for the police. It established my guilt beyond any question."

Tumblety is surely vilifying the London Police here, but it does show that he felt confident that they could not build a solid case against him. As is well known, the idea of an American Ripper, or an American connection, had been aired in the English press during October 1888. Tumblety was developing the idea that he was a scapegoat. From an inside pocket he produced two magnificent diamonds, one 13 carats and the other 9 carats, together with a superb cluster ring set in diamonds. He felt that his arrest was partly due to the police desiring his diamonds and thinking they could force him to hand them over. Undoubtedly when stopped and searched as a suspect these items would have been found in his pockets if he was carrying them. But it is unlikely that the police would have thought that they could get them off him and keep them. And, in the event, they didn't.

The interviewer then questioned Tumblety as to the length of time he was detained, saying, "How long were you in prison?"

Tumblety replied, "Two or three days; but I don't care to talk about it. When I think of the way I was treated in London it makes me lose all control of myself. It was shameful, horrible."

This is another important point. It supports my contention that Tumblety, after arrest, was not held for over a week until his Police Court appearance of Friday 16 November 1888. What now seems likely is that he was initially taken in on suspicion of involvement in the Whitechapel murders, for which the police could adduce no hard evidence and, a day or two later, was re-arrested on Wednesday 7 November, for the gross indecency offences which they could prove. However, as a misdemeanour a gross indecency charge would mean that Tumblety could not be held for more than a day or so (24 hours) and would qualify for a week's police bail. This too, of course, would tie in with a newspaper report that a warrant was issued for him on Wednesday 14 November. What does seem rather relevant, with hindsight, is the fact that the London police make no mention of Tumblety's arrest on suspicion of the murders, while Tumblety makes no mention of his arrest for, and subsequent charging with, the gross indecency offences.

There is no doubt left by Tumblety as to what he thought of the English police. He was emphatically scathing and abusive about them:

"I think their conduct in this Whitechapel affair is enough to show what they are. Why, they stuff themselves all day with potpies and beef and drink gallons of stale beer, keeping it up until they go to bed late at night, and then wake up the next morning heavy as lead. Why, all the English police have dyspepsia. They can't help it. Then their heads are as thick as the London fogs. You can't drive an idea through their thick skulls with a hammer. I never saw such a stupid set. Look at their treatment of me. There was absolutely not one single scintilla of evidence against me. I had simply been guilty of wearing a slouch hat, and for that I was held, charged[54] with a series of the most horrible crimes ever recorded. Why, if Inspector Byrnes was over in London with some of his men they would have had the Whitechapel fiend long ago. But this is all very unpleasant to me, and I would prefer talking about something else."

In this vicious verbal attack on the London police, Tumblety makes it clear that he knew that they possessed no hard evidence against him for the murders and that he had no confidence in their intelligence. His nod to Inspector Byrnes of the NYPD echoes Byrnes's own words about the Whitechapel murders[55] and, perhaps, is an indicator that the two men had met.

54 There is no reason to think that Tumblety was ever formally charged for the murders, he appears to be using the term here to mean "accused of".
55 See the *Star* of October 4, 1888.

The interviewer had not finished and said, "You are accused of being a woman-hater. What have you to say to that?" Tumblety, in denying the claim, gave a story about meeting a duchess in Torquay and recited a poem she had devoted to Dr Tumblety. "Now, that doesn't look like a woman-hater, does it?" he concluded. However, we know that many press reports at the time alluded to his well known hatred of women, especially 'fallen' women, and Littlechild states in his letter, "...but his feelings towards women were remarkable and bitter in the extreme, a fact on record."

Tumblety then, in his usual style, displayed letters from well-known public figures certifying his character. In doing so he stressed, "I am a frequenter of some of the best London clubs, among others the Carleton Club and the Beefsteak Club. I was the victim of circumstances when this horrible charge was first brought, and since then I have been attacked on all sides and no one has had a good word to say for me. It is strange, too, because I don't remember ever to have done any human being a harm, and I know of a great many whom I have helped." We could almost feel sorry for Dr Tumblety – almost.

So the story of Dr Tumblety is updated. My interest in the case continues unabated. "Jack the Ripper" has had a profound effect on my life. My search for Jack the Ripper may be futile – but it has been a fascinating quest.

David Cohen and the Polish Jew Theory

Martin Fido

I entered the world of Ripper studies in 1985 intending to write a general survey of the case. I did not expect to propose a suspect. I had read every book on the subject since Donald McCormick's *The Identity of Jack the Ripper*, and lurched, like other general readers, from believing one to believing the next, until Donald Rumbelow's masterpiece, *The Complete Jack the Ripper*, appeared, and I accepted his informed agnosticism and the case for Druitt's looking the best of a bad bunch. When Stephen Knight proposed his theory about Sir William Gull and the Freemasons theory appeared in *Jack the Ripper: The Final Solution*, I didn't really want to read another book labouring over the same ground. But I did, and I was well enough informed to be impressed by the dashes of genuine new information it contained, even though I saw at once that the theory torpedoed itself with self-contradictions and bad history. I didn't know about or need Joe Sickert's confession to spot a hoax. I didn't expect anyone thereafter to come up with anything both new and true.

In essence, I thought Druitt the most likely candidate, because he emerged from the opinion of a man who was on the spot at the time (or very soon after) and who obviously had access to information that was now lost. I noted Donald Rumbelow's observation that there was no evidence to support Macnaghten's suspicion, but I knew that was far from ruling Druitt out. Macnaghten might be coy about telling the public what influenced his thinking, but it had to be something more than we now know about Druitt, even though we know enough to correct Macnaghten's mistakes in describing him.

Apart from Knight's, I could not disprove the other theories. But as a trained historian, (albeit a literary historian), I placed little weight on them. They were modern deductions and arguments, often pieced together from a range of disparate and dubious documents. Druitt alone rested foursquare on the opinion of a well-informed contemporary.

Nonetheless all the Ripper books left me with three important unanswered questions which I felt should and could be answered:

1 It was clear that until the arrest of Pizer, the police (and via them, the newspapers and public) had been very confident that "Leather Apron" was the killer. Why didn't we know the reasons for this confidence?

2 Although nobody doubted that Pizer *was* Leather Apron, the prostitutes who had been assaulted by him were said to have refused to identify him. Why?

3 As soon as Emmanuel Violenia's testimony against Pizer collapsed, the whole of the evidence against Leather Apron was swept aside as though it had never been. Again, *why*, given that he had been so strong a suspect from the outset?

As I started work on the Ripper I was aware of the importance of good sources, as all historians always should be. An acceptable theory must come from a reliable person in a position to know, not some armchair detective who "deduced" it 50 years later, as Stowell had done in propounding the Duke of Clarence theory. Not some self-inflating, self-incriminating fantasist with half-baked delusions of grandeur and loony beliefs in magic like Roslyn Donston Stephenson. Not some hard-up hack like Le Queux, with a penchant for exaggerating dubious stories. Not even the great tribe of Victorians, eminent and forgotten, with Walter Sickert and L. Forbes Winslow at their head, who believed that some contemporary's tomcatting or nightwalking showed a mysterious coincidence with murder nights and seemed to be followed by the destruction of some clothes. And since the only reliable contemporary source hitherto cited was Macnaghten, who would hardly have placed self-gratifying fantasies on an official file, Druitt, for all Rumbelow's reasonable reservations, still looked the strongest suspect.

But in researching my *Murder Guide to London* I read for the first time the police memoirs on which so much writing about the Ripper rested, and I made two surprising discoveries. Macnaghten had not been quite so certain that Druitt was the Ripper as Tom Cullen and Daniel Farson would have had us believe (though he was by no means as foggy as Donald Rumbelow and axe-grinding Stephen Knight suggested). And, more important, Dr (not at that time Sir) Robert Anderson, who was in charge of the case, on the spot from the night of the double murders and insistent that the Ripper's identity was known, was emphatically not the empty boaster and liar that Stephen Knight and others maintained. Far from it, he was a bigoted and scrupulous Victorian Christian who wrestled with his soul about telling half-truths to dangerous villains and subversives. So when Anderson said Jack the Ripper's identity was "a positively ascertained fact" he was certainly telling the truth as he saw and remembered it. (Nor, as Philip Sugden would later suggest, was this the hindsighted wishful thinking of a geriatric retired 69-year-old. Anderson was 60 and still in office when he first stated publicly that the Ripper was known to have been incarcerated in an asylum. The published paper is to be found among the HO/44 papers in the Public Record Office, and the words were reproduced again in *On Criminals and Crime* in 1907.)

Anderson, then, said he knew. And he could have known and he wasn't a liar. And he was definite in saying the Ripper could be identified as a "low-class Polish Jew" from "the immediate vicinity of the murders". Nor was it quite accurate, as Donald Rumbelow suggested, that there was no supporting evidence, though the corroboration lay in Anderson's own statement and did not appear to have survived otherwise. Anderson claimed that this man was "unhesitatingly identified" by "the only person who ever had a good view of the murderer".

His remarks further explained why no charges could be brought. The identification took place after the suspect had been certified insane, and the witness refused to swear to his identification on learning that the suspect was "a fellow Jew". An examination of all the theories in 1985 showed that Anderson was unique in both positively identifying his suspect and being in a position to know.

Nor was it true, as Stephen Knight had claimed, that no other policeman gave Anderson's claim any endorsement. Macnaghten's second suspect, "Kosminsky, a Polish Jew & resident of Whitechapel" was, Macnaghten said, "a strong" suspect because of "many circs connected with" him. Thus Macnaghten's version of his notes deposited in Scotland Yard. The version copied by Lady Aberconway instanced one of the circumstances: "This man strongly resembled the individual seen by the City P.C. near Mitre Square." This precise circumstance was puzzling. No such City PC was known to exist: the two constables whose beats touched on the square (the second of whom I discovered myself) missed seeing the Ripper. Nor did I think it likely that there were any Jewish PCs in the City force in 1888, or that any PC whatsoever would dare to refuse a sworn statement on the grounds of sharing the suspect's ethnic background. Macnaghten's witness, then, didn't seem to be Anderson's.

But surely their suspects were the same? Both were local Polish Jews. Both were incarcerated in asylums. Their existence was handed down to us by two almost successive Assistant Commissioners for Crime, one of whom was positive that the Ripper had been correctly identified as the poor Polish Jew, the other of whom offered no positive proof that he wasn't, only citing his own long and careful reflection as deciding him against thinking the Jew to be the Ripper. It seemed safe to conclude that Anderson's Polish Jew *was* Macnaghten's Kosminski, and since both men said he went to an asylum, it should be possible to trace him there. At which point I had no doubt that, on the best historical grounds, we should find the most plausible candidate ever proposed for the Ripper.

But the crossed-hair sight given by my two best primary historical sources was triangulated, and might be fixed or devalued, by the unanswered questions I had already spotted in secondary sources. Pizer was a poor Polish Jew. Leather Apron was a poor Polish Jew. Did this mean the police were obsessively xenophobic about the foreign immigrants in the East End? Or was there a connection?

A little research showed that my questions were very well founded. Questions 1 and 2 were linked. The prostitutes' evidence *was* the principal evidence against Leather Apron. But they had not refused or failed to identify Pizer. *They had never been asked to do so.* Emmanuel Violenia was the only identifying witness, and he had proved a broken reed whom the police believed gave false testimony out of a morbid wish to be shown Annie Chapman's body.

The identification of Pizer as Leather Apron rested on two things only: most importantly, his own statement at Annie's inquest, when the coroner asked if he was Leather Apron and he replied, "Yes." Backing this up was Sergeant Thick's claim at the inquest that whenever anyone in Whitechapel said, "Leather Apron," they meant John Pizer. But both these pieces of testimony were contradicted by the men who gave them. Pizer told the press he had not known that anyone called him Leather Apron until Thick told him so at the time of his arrest. And Thick, two days before the inquest, had been far less certain than he seemed when he confidently rested his testimony on his many years' residence in Whitechapel. Explaining his arrest of Pizer to the papers, he could only say he was *almost* certain Pizer was Leather Apron.

As for his claim that anyone who said Leather Apron meant Pizer, this was roundly denied the following day by Pizer's neighbours, who gave him a hero's welcome home and told the newspapers that he was not known as Leather Apron and did not habitually wear his apron on the street (though Pizer himself agreed that he used to wear it home from work two years previously, since which time he had been unemployed and had not worn it at all).

Pizer was certainly someone who needed to be investigated when the streetwalkers were pointing the finger at an immigrant with a leather apron. Like most shoemakers (and butchers and carpenters), he owned one. And, as I would later discover when working with Paul Begg and Keith Skinner, he had been sent to prison the previous year for attacking a rival shoemaker with a knife. More striking still, he had been charged with indecent assault shortly before the outbreak of Ripper killings, though as often happened when East End women complained of some offence against the person, the case was dismissed, probably because the complainant didn't show up at court. If his innocence hadn't been so conclusively proved by the police themselves at Annie Chapman's inquest, I might be thinking to this day that John Pizer looked as likely a suspect as any other.

And given that he wasn't Leather Apron or – as I now think probable – given that Leather Apron as described by the press combined various features of several sinister and maybe half-mad men (possibly including Pizer) who frightened prostitutes with threats that differed from the usual bullies' efforts to rob them, then it seemed to me that one of these men was probably Anderson's suspect and the Ripper. And he was probably Jewish; probably a shoemaker; probably living in Whitechapel; probably called Kosminski.

There was evidence that the police had been at some pains to suppress any suggestion that they were interested in a Jewish suspect after the original Leather Apron scare had given rise to threats of anti-Semitic violence. Commissioner Warren's public announcement that the word "Juwes" did not mean Jews in any known language gratified the Chief Rabbi, though neither man can seriously have imagined that the Goulston Street graffito-writer meant anything else. Witness Hutchinson's account to the police of a "Jewish-looking" punter going to Dorset Street with Mary Kelly was retained on police files, but altered for press consumption to "foreign-looking".

Anderson's memoirs, however, confirmed that this did not represent a CID conviction that no Jew was involved. Quite the contrary, after studying the statements already taken when he returned from the continent after the double murder, he and his colleagues concluded that the murderer was a Polish Jew enjoying the security that his fellow countrymen would not be inclined to turn him over to the police. And every contemporary report indicates that this must mean the original prostitutes' accusations against Leather Apron were still seen as the most reliable evidence, even though Pizer's clearance had supposedly closed that line of enquiry.

Nor had the prostitutes changed their tune. Even after Pizer had been identified and taken to the inquest, they continued to tell police and newspapers that they suspected a man who had been on the streets threatening them. "Pearly Poll", Eliza Cooper (who fought with Annie Chapman shortly before her death) and Elizabeth Allen all stayed at one time or another at Crossingham's lodging house, whose deputy, Timothy Donovan, knew Leather Apron by sight and had thrown him out for threatening a woman. Donovan was the one named local source reporting that Leather Apron wore a two-peaked cap. He attended Annie Chapman's inquest, yet he was never asked to confirm that Pizer was the man he knew as Leather Apron.

At the time of Martha Tabram's death the three women told the police they suspected a man who lived somewhere near Buck's Row, and according to the *Echo*, this man was still suspected by some of the police as late as 20 September, two weeks after the exoneration of Pizer. Yet the phrase the police had insisted on whenever Pizer or Leather Apron was discussed prior to Annie Chapman's inquest came up again. There was "only suspicion against him".

And, as I learned later, Philip Loftus's account of the (now lost) set of brief Macnaghten notes that he had been shown by Macnaghten's grandson named three suspects: Druitt; "a feeble-minded man...who followed young girls and stabbed them with nail-scissors"; and "a Polish Jew cobbler nicknamed Leather Apron". If Loftus remembered correctly what he had seen (and there is no apparent reason to doubt him), then at one point at least, Macnaghten had definitely believed that his "very strong suspect" Kosminski really was the original suspect Leather Apron, just as I had surmised.

Leather Apron as Anderson's suspect and the probable Ripper might be a bridge too far for those who believed the official claim that Leather Apron was Pizer together with Don Rumbelow's ingenious speculation that Violenia was Anderson's witness (though that speculation in itself implied that Anderson's suspect really was Leather Apron). But in 1985 I was frankly astonished that nobody had seen the obvious connection between Macnaghten's Kosminski and Anderson's Poor Polish Jew and amazed that nobody had taken the trouble to check Anderson's credentials and realize that, from a historian's point of view, his claim was the most promising line of enquiry in the Hunt the Ripper game. Unbeknownst, I misjudged my contemporaries. Martin Howells had spotted the link, but, already a committed Druittite, he decided that Donald Rumbelow's solution made a better way of cutting the Gordian knot. Paul Begg, starting like me from the published memoirs and assessing the validity of each as a source, had come to exactly the same conclusion I had: Anderson's was the most reliable historical claim to identify the Ripper. His suspect must be Macnaghten's Kosminski, and a search of asylum records should bring him to light and identify the probable killer. Paul had employed professional researchers to comb the records for him, but they had drawn a blank.

I could not afford professional researchers, and had no intention of looking for Kosminski. It was my publisher's insistence that my arguments were manifestly sound and I must go and find him that sent me scurrying beyond memoirs and newspaper reports to infirmary and asylum registers.

On the way, however, the newspaper reports and memoirs had thrown up another nugget that cleared the way for Kosminski the Polish Jew. All commentators hitherto had stated that Inspector Abberline was in charge of the case, and that if anyone knew who the Ripper was, he did, and he definitely did not endorse any of Macnaghten's suspects. But I soon saw that Abberline was *not* in charge of the case.

He made several of the arrests of suspects, and was usually responsible for transporting them between police stations. He was quoted by reporters as saying he was in charge of the case at one of the inquests – and that might mean as much or as little as Abberline and the reporter chose. In fact, Walter Dew, who might be assumed to remember which officers he worked with, recorded that Chief Inspector Swanson at Scotland Yard was *in charge*; Abberline was only *important* because of his profound knowledge of Whitechapel and its underworld. Macnaghten, too, cited Swanson as a most able officer who worked on the case. And if Abberline was quoted correctly at the time of Annie Chapman's inquest, he told reporters that he did not know the nature of her injuries: something that would be out of the question if he were the man "in charge".

It transpired that all those from Donald McCormick onwards who used Abberline's 1903 interviews with the *Pall Mall Gazette* were culpably selective. Abberline indeed pooh-poohed the idea that the Ripper was either a young doctor who drowned in the Thames (presumably Druitt) or a man who died in an asylum a few years previous to 1903 (presumably the Polish Jew or the Russian doctor, both of whom Macnaghten believed to have gone to asylums). He said he was in touch with Scotland Yard and knew all about those theories, but the reporter could take it from him there was nothing in them. But he also gave a set of specious arguments to support the claim that the Ripper might have been Severin Klosowski, recently executed as George Chapman. The arguments that a man who was "capable" of the manic butchery of strangers was equally "capable" of the calculated poisoning of unwanted wives hardly answered the observation that Chapman's crimes were very unlike the Ripper's. And subsequent research has shown that Abberline was quite wrong in thinking Chapman lived in Whitechapel at the times of the murders, and quite wrong in believing that Ripper-type murders took place in New York when he went there. The interview tells us much about Abberline's confidence in his own judgment, and warns us that it could be seriously misplaced.

It was certainly very misplaced when he pontificated that "we knew the motives for those murders", and trotted out the hoary old canard about a doctor offering money for wombs and inspiring a revival of burking. My own work showed that the *British Medical Journal* had authoritatively refuted this back in 1888, something of which Abberline remained sublimely unaware 15 years later. Robert Anderson and Melville Macnaghten were obviously better judges when they took it for granted that they were looking at the work of a sex maniac.

And so I went to the archives to look for Jack the Ripper. I was told at once that asylum records were closed for 100 years, so it seemed impossible to find data there about a man who, according to Macnaghten, was incarcerated in or about March 1889. But Stephen Knight offered the useful hint that poor lunatics were normally dispatched to asylums from their local workhouse infirmaries, whose records were open. I hastened to examine Whitechapel's, looking for a Kosminski admitted between 1888 and 1890. I found none.

But I did find Nathan Kaminsky. He was a 23-year-old bootmaker living at 15 Black Lion Yard in March 1888; a bachelor with no known relatives who had fulfilled the necessary year's residence for treatment in the parish infirmary; a man who was treated for syphilis in a ward which later research indicated was almost certainly used for out-patients and ambulant cases.

Kaminsky was quite the wrong age for Leather Apron, stated by all the newspapers to be about 40 (Pizer was 38), but in other respects he looked a very strong suspect indeed. His surname was near enough to Kosminsky for inaccurate Anglo-Saxon gentiles. Indeed, it was proposed by Dan Farson as one possible form of the name on a damaged corner of the Macnaghten memoranda he had seen. His occupation was exactly right. His address was absolutely in the heart of the five Ripper murders, and making for home by the most direct route would have carried him safely off the beats of the two policemen who failed to see the murderer escaping from Polly Nichols's murder site. Going straight home from Mitre Square would also have taken him past the Goulston Street doorway where the piece of Catharine Eddowes's apron was found: indeed, it would have been the first open doorway he would have passed if he crossed Goulston Street diagonally as soon as he reached it. (And I had long noted that the location of that piece of cloth, indicating the direction in which the Ripper travelled, and the sudden ending of the murders, indicating that something happened to the killer not long after 9 November 1888, are the only two cast-iron clues remaining today.) As for Kaminsky's age, the police were taking seriously accounts by at least three witnesses – including one by Joseph Lawende, the only person we can confidently say saw Jack the Ripper – who estimated the ages of the men they had seen with victims shortly before the murders as 30 or under.

Kaminsky's ailment was another possible pointer to his guilt. Several policemen suspected that the Ripper might have suffered from a venereal disease and sought vengeance on the women who infected him. This was a common motive for assault in the nineteenth century, and for Joseph Connor's notorious murder of Mary Brothers (aka Anne Tape) in 1845. Moreover, Kaminsky's treatment started four days before the unsolved murderous attack on Ada Wilson in Mile End, a little distance from Buck's Row. I had already noticed that this crime bore several circumstantial features suggesting that it might have been an early and unskilled assault by the Ripper in the same district as his first known murders (such as subsequent psychological profiling by the FBI and Professor David Canter suggested must have taken place). The assailant's description matched Mr Lawende's description of the Ripper. Miss Wilson's given occupation of sempstress was one of the commonest self-descriptions used by prostitutes asked by officialdom for their occupation. The motive she alleged – robbery – would serve to distance any investigation from anything dubious in her own life. (This last deduction should be treated with caution as a good example of a second speculation built upon a first.)

Altogether I was extremely excited by the discovery of Nathan Kaminsky. Had I found him proceeding smoothly into a lunatic asylum shortly after the murders stopped, and dying there not long afterwards, I have no doubt most sensible people today would agree that he was certainly the man to whom Anderson referred, and that Anderson was very likely right. It was at this time that I first made contact with fellow Ripper researcher Richard Whittington-Egan and enjoyed his generous encouragement to pursue this suspect vigorously. He saw immediately the promise of the central Black Lion Yard address, and he had always felt that the police were far from stupid in having their doubts about the vast local population of deprived and sometimes criminal immigrants.

And so began my long and exhaustive hunt for Kaminskys. I called every one in the London telephone directory, irritating a couple of Polish gentile throwbacks who proved disturbingly annoyed at being approached in a search for a Jew. I checked all the England and Wales death registers down to 1960, and took in Kosminskis on the way, for good measure. I examined all the quarterly dockets of poor pauper lunatics returned by the parish vestries from 1888 to 1900. I checked the other workhouse infirmary records in London to see whether Kaminsky had moved parishes before being finally incarcerated. I checked ordinary workhouses to see whether Kaminsky had ever been sheltered as a pauper. I found two Nathan Kaminskys whose ages fell within ten years of the man I was hunting, and traced their descendants to learn conclusively that they were definitely not the same.

And I found nothing else. Nathan Kaminsky, of too lowly a status to seem likely to have gentilized his name or re-emigrated, simply disappeared. He must have died. But it wasn't recorded. A Nathan Karnsky who died in Colney Hatch in 1908 looked the nearest possibility. He seemed too young, but Bethnal Green Board of Guardians were hazy about his age, changing it from quarter to quarter in their returns. The best possible projected date of birth to link him with the Ripper crimes was 1870. At any rate, he pretty certainly wasn't Nathan Kaminsky the bootmaker. The authorities were hazy about his name, too.

His mother and sister were discovered shortly after he had been incarcerated and registered as Karnsky. They proved that the real name was Arginsky, but nobody ever bothered to correct Nathan's surname on the records. And since he was not incarcerated until 1899, it seemed out of the question that he could be Jack the Ripper. Nobody except dippy Donstonians or alternative-motive Barnettians has ever seriously imagined that the ferocious maniac who mangled Mary Jane Kelly would thereafter have calmed down, his sadistic appetite sated, and survived without incarceration throughout the next ten years.

I seemed at an impasse. I had the names and destinations of every Jewish lunatic to pass through a London parish infirmary between 1888 and 1890, and there wasn't a single K-anything-sky among them. Good fortune was with me, however. The staff at the Greater London Archives had watched my laborious searches, and they told me that, as a serious scholar, I should probably find the asylum records open to me if I approached the right health authorities. Most were stored on the outskirts of London, and when I finally had the roster of permissions complete, I was so close to the deadline for submitting my manuscript that I had to content myself with hearing archivists read me the entries over the telephone. They confirmed the correctness of my previous research, but the succession of senile imbeciles and harmless hallucinators didn't give a hint of anyone who might be Jack the Ripper. And quite certainly none was bootmaker Nathan Kaminsky.

But one set of records was lodged at the Greater London Archives in Clerkenwell. And that one was the most important: Colney Hatch, where the overwhelming majority of pauper lunatics from north of the Thames were held. The Men's Day Book contained the fullest records, and the volume including 1888 ran to 1890, quite long enough to ensure that the Ripper must be within its covers if he had actually wound up in the Hatch. I checked every entry over the two-year period, paying most attention to Jewish inmates from Whitechapel admitted after 9 November 1888. The first of these, a young and hair-raisingly violent tailor called David Cohen, was already in my notebooks from his passage through Whitechapel Infirmary at the beginning of December. His name was wrong for the man I sought. His occupation was wrong. His address in Leman Street was just outside rather than centrally inside the Ripper's territory. I passed on swiftly, and devoted much earnest thought to a savage wife-murderer from Spitalfields. But he clearly didn't fit either.

And suddenly I noticed three things about David Cohen. His year of birth made him exactly the same age as Nathan Kaminsky. Like Kaminsky he had no known relatives. And he had been brought to the infirmary as a lunatic at large and unable to care for himself by the Metropolitan Police themselves.

Added to that, he was far and away the most violent lunatic to enter the asylum in the two-year period: dangerous to himself and others. He was said to have attempted suicide. He attacked other patients if he was allowed near them. He tried to damage the infirmary ward. He refused food and spat it out. He had to be put under restraint (presumably a straitjacket or tied hands) for transfer to the asylum, where he threw himself on the floor on arrival. He continued to threaten other patients and refuse food. He had to be force fed. He was "spiteful and mischievous" (i.e. threatened to do them a mischief) if allowed near other patients. His habits were dirty. He tore his clothes if not watched, and had to be segregated and put in special clothing. He spoke little but German (presumably Yiddish). And after an attempt to build up his wasted constitution with the addition of two daily eggs to his diet, the hospital watched him go into a decline until he died of "exhaustion of mania and pulmonary phthisis" (congested lungs) in October 1889.

No other Jewish patient over the two-year period so perfectly fitted the description "sadistic maniac". And this man came from Whitechapel. He was the only one whose incarceration would explain the sudden ending of the murders. Indeed, in the whole of London he was the most probable suspect if one assumed the murders really stopped because the murderer was "safely caged in an asylum," as Anderson said. He was the same age and race and parish as the vanished Nathan Kaminsky. Surely, I thought, this was Jack the Ripper. Surely he was the lost Kaminsky?

But what about his name and address and occupation? The occupation was open to very plausible explanation. If I was right about this man, he should have been Leather Apron the cobbler or bootmaker. I already knew that a House of Lords Select Committee on Immigration in the summer of 1888 had discovered that the Jewish community, concerned to preserve the right to immigration, was at pains to see that none of its members became a charge on the rates. (I knew they succeeded. The workhouse records listed inmates' creeds and occupations. Jews and nonconformists hardly ever showed up among paupers or prostitutes, who were almost invariably Catholic or Anglican.) If completely unskilled Jewish immigrants landed and could not be found labouring jobs, the elders of the community placed them in one of two types of sweatshop, whence their clumsy workmanship could be sold cheaply in the street markets. The two trades were shoemaking and tailoring. Leather Apron (not being Pizer) had disappeared completely not long after the search for him began. It seemed likely that he would need to abandon the cobbler's apron that gave him his nickname. If he was Jewish and had no other skill, he would have become a sweated tailor. This might explain Cohen's recorded occupation if he really were Kaminsky or Leather Apron or both.

The address in Leman Street – No. 86 – was even more mysterious. It housed the Whittington Chambers with Whittington Protestant Boys' Club and Blue Riband Shoeblacks' Refuge (heirs to the former East London Industrial School at the same address). It seemed obvious to me that no 23-year-old Jewish tailor, sane or insane, would be living there. I speculated that a slip of the pen had led this number to be recorded instead of the house next door, No 84, which held the Temporary Shelter for Poor Homeless Jews. There were only two other houses between these two institutions and Leman Street police station, the headquarters for the local Ripper investigations, which led me to speculate furiously (and, let it be said at once, totally inconclusively) about the possibility of the police leaving the address of a responsible institution which would ensure that an insane suspect they wanted watched would be returned to their vicinity if he was discharged as cured. But since that time two things have rendered Cohen's address still more puzzling. Jewish authorities consulted by Paul Begg have observed that the Temporary Shelter was for recently landed immigrants, and only accommodated them for two weeks, so if David Cohen really was identified as living there, he could not have been the Ripper. And conversely, the Whittington Boys' Club, while its quota of bootblacks and management were all gentiles, actually had a nightwatchman called Henry Cohen. He was three years younger than David, being 23 when he was recorded as staying there on the night of the 1891 census. Unlike David, described in the records as being foreign, he was born in Whitechapel. But could a tribe of Cohens have had access to the Whittington Chambers to shelter a distant relative, refraining to come forward when he was arrested as a lunatic? Or refusing, as Anderson claimed, to give him up as a suspected murderer?

It was and is an unsolved puzzle, just as it remains strange that the name, age and occupation of anyone quite so mad as Cohen could have been recorded confidently without any witness prior to his incarceration having apparently made any statement about him.

And what about that name? Not obviously similar to "Kaminsky", though a nasally sounded madman's "Nathan" might have been misheard as "David". If he had at one time used the name "Kaminsky" this might explain Macnaghten's ultimately giving the name as the similar-sounding "Kosminsky". This particular difficulty led Richard Whittington-Egan to despair of the Cohen/Kaminsky solution. "I like it," he wrote to me. "I *want* to believe it. But I can't."

But at that time I did not know, as I learned later from informants in London, New York and even Vienna, that gentile authorities confronted with unpronounceable Jewish names were inclined simply to label them "Cohen". This, too, has been denied by the Jewish authorities consulted by Paul Begg, who assured him that officialdom was at pains to make sure it got the names of immigrants right. But I know from my own research that this was not true in the case of "Nathan Karnsky" and several other listed lunatics and paupers whose names were never correctly established in the records. And I have it on the authority of at least one Miss Cohen that her family know very well that they were given their present surname by immigration officials who could not be bothered to transcribe the difficult Polish original.

Paul Begg's subsequent research, too, established beyond doubt that the police themselves were not sure or careful about Cohen's forenames. When they took him to the magistrates' court in the morning as a wandering lunatic to be sent to the infirmary on the bench's authority, they called him Aaron Davis Cohen. But they handed him over to the parish in the evening as plain David Cohen, which he remained.

My own re-examination of the magistrates' court records traced by Paul showed that Cohen's case was minuted with a madam and two of her girls who had been arrested in a raid on a brothel. For all four to have their cases listed in the same minute indicated that Cohen had been arrested at the same time. There is the tiniest suggestion of support on the Home Office files for a suspect living in a brothel. HO/144/220/A49301.C/8 includes a memo that "a brothel keeper who will not give her address or name writes to say that a man living in her house was seen with blood on him on the morning of the murder. She described his appearance and said where he might be seen – when detectives came near him he bolted and got away and there is no clue to the writer of the letter." But the procuress's suspicions were of the same insubstantial kind as Walter Sickert's landlord's, and her address would certainly not be 84 or 86 Leman Street.

The key to suspecting David Cohen is very simple and straightforward. Anderson said the Ripper was identified after he had been sent to an asylum, and he was a poor Polish Jew from the vicinity. ("Polish" was likely to be a very loose descriptive term amounting to little more than "central European immigrant" – one police report calls the Russian gentile Ostrog "a Polish Jew" – but Anderson's suspect's Jewishness was positively attested by the Jewish witness's refusal to swear to his co-religionist's identity.) And of all the lunatics in London, *only* David Cohen both fits Anderson's meagre description *and* (on general grounds such as the time of his incarceration and the nature of his madness) could have been Jack the Ripper. Forget about Macnaghten and his Kosminsky. If my survey of the sources was right (and, though I didn't know it, it was supported by Paul Begg, the only other person to have made a similar historian's careful reassessment) then Anderson's suspect was the most probable Ripper to be identified. And Anderson's suspect could only be David Cohen.

So it was a shock to me when, four months after I'd submitted my confident manuscript, I found Kosminski (spelled thus). By a production error, my publishers found themselves with 20 pages to spare, and asked me if I'd like to add an appendix, so I decided to include everything I could find about David Cohen, and sent for the Colney Hatch Admissions and Discharge book, which might (though it was unlikely) include some fragment of information missing from the Men's Day Book. The Admissions book including 1888 started later than the Day Book and ran to 1894. And there was Aaron Kosminski, foreign Jewish hairdresser of Sion Square – I misread it as Lion Square, and was not corrected until Keith Skinner examined the book – incarcerated in 1891. And exactly the same age as David Cohen and Nathan Kaminsky. I had missed him in Colney Hatch because he was incarcerated too late. I had missed his passage through Mile End Infirmary in 1890 because his name was so misspelled that, like Charles Nevin of the *Daily Telegraph* later, I failed to identify it, and it would not be detected until Keith Skinner's trawl through the Workhouse Creed Book. I had ignored him on my list of deceased Kosminskys because he had been removed from Colney Hatch to Leavesden Asylum for imbeciles, where he didn't die until 1919. I had less than a week to send for the Colney Hatch Day Book for fuller details and rewrite everything that needed to be rewritten in a manuscript that had confidently (and correctly) asserted that there was no Kosminsky in any asylum between 1888 and 1890 and deduced that Macnaghten really meant David Cohen who had probably been using the name Kaminsky in March 1888. And I should have to pay for the resetting.

The Day Book showed that, however Kosminski came into the equation, it was certainly not as an alternative Jack the Ripper. He was positively harmless: of no danger to himself or others, even though it was thought he had once taken up a knife and threatened to kill his sister, hardly unusual behaviour in overcrowded slumland. He was a highly visible East End lunatic, who used to go around the streets picking up bread from the gutter to eat. He thought he heard voices that told him what other people were thinking. He refused to wash, and indeed, his only moment of mild violence after his incarceration was when he attacked Leavesden Asylum staff with a chair as they came with the intention of bathing him.

He was certainly not Leather Apron. Unlike Kaminsky and Cohen, he was positively identified by a loving family who themselves took him to the infirmary and seem to have taken responsibility for his treatment, since he did not show up on the quarterly returns of pauper lunatics in the care of their parishes. Macnaghten was shown to be positively wrong about the date of his incarceration, which he set in March 1889. That in itself had suggested a surprisingly long period at liberty for a maniac who showed every sign of uncontrollable murderous impulses. The two years Kosminski spent picking up bread from the gutters without attacking any streetwalkers cleared him of suspicion.

Three forensic psychologists invited later, without briefing, to compare the case notes of Cohen and Kosminski and to suggest which might be the Ripper, all agreed that Kosminski did not look likely, but that Cohen looked impossible, because his manic state would have disabled him from escaping arrest. But this must be offset against the opinion of Professor Luigi Cancrini of Bologna who had heard of neither Cohen nor Kosminski when he prepared a psychological profile of the Ripper in which he concluded that the murderer's crescendo of sadistic violence would have turned against himself in the end, and he probably committed suicide. On seeing Cohen's case notes he agreed immediately that this man, believed to have attempted suicide, could very well have been the Ripper, impelled into a final disabling mania by the frustration of a heavily policed Whitechapel which impeded his continuing murders.

But Kosminski's name popped up again within a few months. When my book was reviewed in the *Daily Telegraph*, Chief Inspector Swanson's grandson made renewed efforts to publish his grandfather's notes on the case which had come into his hands some years earlier and been accepted, but never printed, by the *News of the World*. Released from what he felt to be a commitment of honour to the paper which had paid him £75 for the information it had not used, Mr Swanson now sent the notes to the *Telegraph*, which consulted Donald Rumbelow, and learned from him that mine was the only book showing any knowledge of what they were talking about. For Swanson's notes were a pencilled marginal gloss in his copy of Anderson's memoirs, confirming and expanding his chief's description of the suspect.

Only they did not confirm the earlier account Anderson had given when his memoirs were serialized in *Blackwood's Magazine*. They contradicted it in part. For Anderson, who made small alterations to this part of his book before its appearance in volume form, had said explicitly in *Blackwood's* that the suspect was identified "when (he) was caged in an an asylum": a phrase he omitted in the revisions (which seem to have been a response to Major Smith of the City Police who accused him of reckless anti-Semitism).

Swanson stated that the identification took place at the "Seaside Home", after which he was returned to his brother's house, from which he was later taken, "with his hands tied behind his back" to "Stepney Workhouse and then to Colney Hatch" where he died shortly afterwards. And unlike Anderson, Swanson named the suspect. Kosminski.

Alerted by the *Telegraph*, I had a long meeting with Donald Rumbelow, and we both puzzled over a document that simply didn't fit the facts as we knew them. The "Seaside Home", in police jargon, is the Police Convalescent Home in Hove. But that did not open until 1890 (positively ruling out David Cohen, who died the previous year). On the other hand, as I later discovered, the Convalescent Home Fund had been the most popular police charity since 1887, and it sent officers to ad hoc homes on the south coast until the building at Hove was purchased. Swanson also said the suspect was taken to the Home "with difficulty" by the Met, which seemed to mean difficulty with officialdom. But as Don remarked (and he was a serving policeman at that time), in a case this notorious they could have taken any suspect to the moon if they wanted!

Swanson said the suspect was returned to his brother's house in Whitechapel (which, indeed, was the address given for Kosminski by Colney Hatch), where he was watched by the City Police CID, until his family hospitalized him. The "wrong" force gave Don no problems. In a case of this notoriety either force would covertly trespass on the other's patch if it meant solving it. But neither of us could imagine why Swanson wrote that Kosminski died soon after transfer to Colney Hatch. In 1910, when Anderson's book came out, Kosminski was still alive and had another nine years to live. There was supporting evidence that the police thought their insane suspect had died: Abberline referred to a man who died in an asylum some years before 1903. But no policeman I've ever spoken to has thought it likely that they would take their eyes off an incarcerated suspect in a case of this magnitude, and, as has been suggested, casually assume he was dead when in fact he had been transferred to another institution. Nor could the identifying witness be, as Macnaghten had claimed, a City policeman. But then, Macnaghten had been hopelessly inaccurate about the age and profession of his chosen suspect, Druitt.

Since Swanson's evidence, unlike Anderson's, contradicts a definite historical fact (the time of Kosminski's death), the historian has a positive duty to offer some hypothetical explanation of Swanson's error if he proposes to make use of him as strong corroboration. And after sleeping on the problem and digesting the professional police information I had acquired from Don, I saw a possible answer. Basically Swanson said six verifiable things about the suspect which went beyond Anderson's statement that he was a mad Polish Jew from Whitechapel who wound up in an asylum.

1 He named the workhouse he went through as Stepney, which was technically untrue of both Kosminski and Cohen, but given the ever-increasing size of Stepney Borough by 1910 could easily be a slip of the memory for either.

2 He named the asylum to which he was taken as Colney Hatch: true of both men.

3 He said he was taken to the infirmary with his hands tied behind his back, which was untrue of Kosminski, but compatible with the recorded fact that Cohen was taken from the infirmary to Colney Hatch under restraint.

4 He said he died shortly after transfer to Colney Hatch: true of Cohen, who was the only Jewish patient to die prematurely between 1888 and 1892: glaringly untrue of Kosminski.

5 He said he lived at his brother's home in Whitechapel: true of Kosminski; untrue of Cohen. (Without further evidence I would not accept any suggestion that Whitechapel-born Henry Cohen of 86 Leman Street was the younger brother to the German- or Yiddish-speaking David.)

6 He said his name was Kosminski.

There it is: facts 1 and 2 applying equally to both men, facts 3 and 4 applying to Cohen but not Kosminski; facts 5 and 6 applying to Kosminski but not to Cohen. Bearing in mind that these two men were both European Jewish immigrants, of the same age, resident in the same parish, and sent to the same asylum, one conclusion seemed certain. They had been confused with each other. Swanson thought the two men were one and the same and so created a composite portrait with details drawn from each. But why?

The probable answer, it seemed to me, lay in Swanson's remark about the City CID and Don's explanation of it. We knew that the Met were uncertain about Cohen's forenames, and he had been incarcerated under the surname often given to Jews by officials who were similarly uncertain. Since Anderson, Swanson, Macnaghten and Abberline were the only people to mention this suspect in any way, and Abberline's reference was more than sketchy, while Macnaghten's was clearly wrong in calling the identifying witness a City policeman, it seemed that information about this positive identification had been rather closely guarded on a "need to know" basis. This dovetailed with the manifest senior police anxiety about anti-Semitism being fostered if it were known they believed the Ripper was a Jew. Not many people, then, even in the Met, would have known for sure that the presumptive Ripper was dead by the end of 1889. If, as seemed most likely, the Met's witness was Mr Lawende, who saw the Ripper in the City, then the City Police should have been informed, for he was a City Police witness (not as Macnaghten thought a City policeman witnessing). But if the City could covertly keep watch on Kosminski on Metropolitan territory, why should not the Met covertly use a City witness, suppressing the fact when they found they could not even get a sworn statement from him to confirm to the Home Office that the case was now closed? Might this not explain the "difficulty" in taking the suspect for the identification that Swanson mentioned?

And then, when the City Police saw their suspect taken to the asylum in 1891, their need for close secrecy about the covert watch would end. And somebody might have let slip the name Kosminski. As Don had remarked, they could be quite certain about that name, since they knew of his sane family. A few Metropolitan policemen knew that the Ripper was thought to be a Whitechapel Polish Jew of uncertain name, born in 1865 and dying in Colney Hatch. Might they have concluded that the Whitechapel Polish Jew, born in 1865, whom some City policeman now said they had seen taken to Colney Hatch, was the same person? Might they have accepted the City's positive identification of the name, never bothering to check further since the man they believed to have been thus identified was dead? Especially if they had an inkling that their "Cohen" was suspiciously similar to Nathan Kaminsky? (For which inkling, let me say at once, there is not a shred of evidence.)

That explanation, at any rate, covers all the known facts except Swanson's puzzling and implausible account of the suspect's being released after an identification at some Seaside Home. Let it be noted, this string of speculations is not offered as proof that David Cohen was Jack the Ripper: only as a hypothetical explanation of the problems posed by Swanson's (and Macnaghten's) erroneous remarks. Despite suggestions that any valid explanation must be simpler, no one has ever managed to postulate one, except the blanket suggestion that "Anderson was wrong" – which does not address the real problem of Swanson's errors.

The case for Cohen as the Ripper rests foursquare on: Anderson's demonstrable integrity and, wherever he can be tested, unique accuracy and certainty in his accounts of the Ripper case; and on Cohen's unique fit with both Anderson's account and the psychological profile of the

Ripper. All subsequent attempts to disprove it, except for the citation of Littlechild's doubt about Anderson's certainty, have rested either on inadequate attempts to undermine Anderson's probity, or on the acceptance of supposedly "better" evidence, ranging from an insistence on disregarding Swanson's demonstrable errors and giving him the highest priority, through allegedly deliberate anagrams, to pretty obvious falsehoods or forgeries. I believe, though I cannot prove, that "David Cohen" was probably Nathan Kaminsky. I think he was almost certainly Jack the Ripper. I am sure he is more likely to have been than anyone else who has ever been suggested.

Catch Me When You Can

Paul Harrison

I am often asked what first intrigued me about the series of murders which occurred in Whitechapel in London in 1888. Today, after 13 years' hard research into the subject matter I am still at a loss to explain why the almost futile search for the anonymous killer of four (some say five) London prostitutes still captures our imagination. Some of the greatest investigative minds of our time have voiced opinions upon just about everything connected with the case, yet not one individual has provided conclusive evidence to the satisfaction of other theorists or historians.

To this writer's mind, the universal search for the identity of the Whitechapel Murderer has somehow lost its way. Far too many theories have been expounded which are far too complicated, far-fetched, or plain farcical. Personal opinion does fill the numerous voids between the known facts of the case. As a crime historian and police officer I have researched or practically investigated a great number of murder cases, but I can think of no such instance where the motive was so complicated as to cause consternation among the investigating authorities.

Murder is not an intelligent act. Indeed, it is an extremely foolish reaction to some mental deficiency deep within the killer's mind. Jealousy or avarice are perhaps the two main reasons for such acts of violence. It is without doubt that murders which occurred back in 1888 were as basic as they are today. The miscreant known as Jack the Ripper was no genius, but an insecure, somewhat pathetic individual who yearned for nothing more than the security of a woman's love.

Ultimately this quest turned into an irrational hatred of women – not all women, just those of the type which surrounded him, the common prostitute.

To point an accusing finger at any one of the actors in this drama requires no more than a little imagination. Many theories are based upon nothing more than supposition and poor reporting of known facts. It is difficult, if not virtually impossible for any serious researcher to look at the crimes without harbouring some initial thought as to a possible suspect. Those theories which are incredulous can be eliminated, such as HRH Duke of Clarence (royal diaries prove him to have been elsewhere on more than one occasion), Masonic conspiracy (how could so many maintain such secrecy for so long in what is as complicated a theory as any fiction writer could create?), Thomas Neill Cream (imprisoned elsewhere during part of the Ripper's reign), Frederick Bayley Deeming (also imprisoned elsewhere). The majority of suspects proffered as the miscreant carry little weight in the factual stakes, the facts being manipulated to fit the suspect. The grim reality is that there are possibly just four suspects worthy of research: the three identified by Sir Melville MacNaughten (Kosminski, Druitt and Ostrog), and one other man who was arrested immediately after the Ripper's final known murder, thus identifying him as more of a leading suspect than any other, Joseph Barnett.

These individuals are of note because of basic evidence. MacNaughten may well have heard of his three suspects from police officers involved in the Ripper investigation. He had no first-hand knowledge of the crimes, thus much of what he noted in his now infamous "memoranda" is supposition based upon hearsay evidence. Even then he leaves any reader of the memoranda ill at ease, as he fails to follow up his opinions with any supporting evidence. Joseph Barnett, meanwhile, has to be a suspect. It is unanimously believed that by the time of the Kelly murder the police must have had their suspicions as to a possible identification of the killer. Immediately after the discovery of Mary Kelly's remains it was Joseph Barnett who was held for questioning, but, as so often has been stated, was released, after some claim, "satisfying the police of his innocence". This is not altogether accurate, as will be discussed later.

Jack the Ripper possessed a thorough geographical knowledge of Whitechapel and its surrounding streets, since we know that he escaped capture from all four murder sites, namely Bucks Row, Hanbury Street, Mitre Square and Millers Court – Dorset Street. The killer must have been able to blend in with his surroundings, and was perhaps someone well known locally, someone whom the prostitute community would feel comfortable with. Doctors carrying Gladstone bags, strangers bearing gifts or outsiders would draw attention to themselves, if not by the police then by the local community. Vigilante committees were patrolling the streets on the look-out for strangers who might fit their own opinion of what Jack the Ripper was like.

My own research into the case led me to Barnett by a process of elimination. Investigation into his lifestyle is virtually impossible, since everyday people lead everyday lives, mundane and perhaps ordinary. There is not one crime historian who can tell us what any one suspect was really like, as nobody can provide first-hand information upon these individuals. Even police or medical records depict a minuscule insight into the persona. Sadly, this is where any objective investigation into the case falls apart. Any writer who proposes a suspect achieves only theories.

Today it is not a matter of who Jack the Ripper was, it is more a case of destroying other writers' theories in order to proffer one's own as being the most suitable. The average reader must find it bewildering, assessing the thousands of printed pages of ephemeral data, none of which could be used as direct evidence in a court of law. The solitary disillusionary fact which encompasses every facet of the case is that Jack the Ripper did exist and was never brought to justice, and 110 years later we face fewer facts and ultimately less qualified investigations and investigators. Is it really possible to name him after all this time? Only common sense will answer that mystery.

It is my opinion that where financial gain is viewed as a reward then objectivity may become secondary. The police officers of the era, like those of today, were provided with a basic income, with nothing further to gain other than the removal of a criminal from the streets. Today, the quest for the identity of Jack the Ripper has become a commercial industry.

In my work, *Jack the Ripper: The Mystery Solved* (1991), I stated: "I am man enough to stand up and be counted," with regard to my research and understanding of the topic as being as accurate as I believed it could be. If errors were made then they were genuine mistakes, not fabrications of the truth, nor extension of the known facts. I have been criticized for my endeavours in this field, but stand by my firm belief that suspect Joseph Barnett is the most likely person to have been the Ripper. It has subsequently been revealed that at least two different Joseph Barnetts existed in the area at the time, but it matters little for the main theory remains intact. It is now irrefutable that more suppositional evidence exists against this individual than any other yet proffered. He was a nobody who became a somebody.

Fish porter Joseph Barnett made a chance meeting on Good Friday, 8 April 1887 while in Commercial Street, Whitechapel. There he met with a common prostitute known as Mary Jane Kelly; well versed in the unwritten law of the streets, worldly wise, devious, and without principle, she was without doubt experienced in the way of sexual activity. Whether she saw Barnett as "another punter" or approached him for a different reason is not known; of course it may well be that Barnett approached her, we can never be certain. The couple struck up conversation, which resulted in them arranging a further meeting the following day.

There can be no doubt that the fish porter found his new-found companion compelling company. She was in her mid-twenties, perhaps a more attractive woman than many of her contemporaries, albeit from sketches of the era she can hardly be described as a raving beauty. The common prostitutes of that era in Whitechapel were at virtually desperation stakes. By virtue of their occupation and the manner in which they flaunted it they cannot have possessed a great deal of self-respect; despite what has been said before, Mary Kelly was no different from any other prostitute operating in the district. She needed a pittance to survive in the squalor of the Whitechapel lodging houses, for her life offered few opportunities.

When the pair met the following day, it was agreed that they should live together. A brief encounter had resulted in a situation which was to irrevocably alter their lives. Barnett must have viewed the situation in a positive manner in order to take the risk of offering himself as an individual to the prostitute. Kelly told him of her previous encounters in life, a brief sojourn to France where she socialized with "gentlemen", a relationship with a Welsh miner which ended because of his untimely death in a colliery accident. It must have been a typical tale of ill fortune falling upon a sweet innocent woman who deserved so much more than Whitechapel could currently offer. Barnett believed everything. Much of what was indicated to him revealed a woman who wanted to be loved, a woman who had once mixed and been loved by gentlemen, a woman who had lost her dignity after the unpleasant death of her partner, a woman whom he could love and receive reciprocal devotion in return.

The couple took a room in lodgings, Barnett continuing to earn funds by working locally. He had lost his job at Billingsgate fish market for some form of serious breach of regulation. It has been deduced that this was for theft, but there is no evidence to confirm such speculation. All that is known is that he lost his licence for a period stretching well into the twentieth century. As a man devoted to making a relationship work, Barnett must have strived for security; he would not wish his partner to act as a common prostitute, thus he made every effort to raise funds to keep them both. This would often mean long hours at work allowing Mary the freedom to lead her own life.

Over the weeks that followed it is known that the stronger of the two personalities began to take control of the relationship. Barnett was introduced to many of Mary's prostitute colleagues as visits to the local public houses became more and more frequent. A move of lodgings to Little Paternoster Row, a small dwelling area off Dorset Street, deep in the heart of slumland took place. In order to maintain the continuity of the relationship, Barnett was forced out to work more and more frequently. He must have known deep in his own spirit that he had to provide for Mary if he was to be successful in keeping her off the streets and satisfied with his sole attention.

Despite his best efforts, Barnett found it difficult to gain any control over Kelly. He was by this stage totally obsessed with her. Perhaps the challenge of reforming her had replaced the initial emotion he had felt. The one thing that is certain is that by this stage he had grown accustomed and devoted to his partner's companionship. The last thing he wanted was to lose her.

It was not too long before disaster struck. Barnett himself had been dragged into the depths of depravity and neglect. He failed to find regular income and found himself spending more and more time with Kelly, a situation which may well have pleased him as he could monitor her comings and goings with greater ease if he was with her. The rent on the Little Paternoster Row accommodation had not been paid for some time. Irresponsibly the pair found it easier to hide from the basic responsibilities of life through alcohol. Early one morning, the landlord of the accommodation arrived at their door in order to recover overdue rent money. To his ultimate surprise he found both Kelly and Barnett so drunk that he could get no sense out of them. Worse still, both showed complete disregard for the debt and hurled abuse at the man. Quite naturally he resorted to the only option available to him, and Kelly and Barnett were evicted. There could have been no greater disgrace than eviction from lodgings in Dorset Street, which has been described as the most immoral street in London at the time. It cost prostitutes just a couple of pennies to find accommodation there, yet Barnett and Kelly were being evicted.

The grim realization that things could not get any worse may have caused the change of attitude in Barnett. Perhaps Kelly threatened to go back on the streets in order to find rent money? He returned to his hardworking ways, relying on the trust that Mary was maintaining her integrity and being faithful to him. Eventually a room was found at 13 Miller's Court, another small yard off Dorset Street, and Mary Kelly's final home. As time progressed, the relationship began to become more and more strained. Barnett's absence from home again provided Mary with the opportunity to hawk her wares. It would not be beyond the realms of probability that both Mary Kelly and Joseph Barnett knew and associated with other prostitutes in the area, particularly the known canonical victims of Jack the Ripper: Mary Ann Nichols, Eliza Ann Chapman and Catharine Eddowes. After all, each one of these had at one time or another lodged in Dorset Street, drank in the same pubs, and walked the same streets. It was a close-knit community, where lodging-house people became familiar quickly. Furthermore, Eddowes often used an alias, Mary Ann Kelly, which has to be far too great a coincidence for her not to know of the existence of another prostitute in the area with an almost identical name.

The relationship between Barnett and Kelly deteriorated. Kelly fraternized more and more with members of the prostitute community. Barnett had lost control. No matter how hard he tried, the pull of the streets was too great a temptation for Mary Kelly to resist. She openly returned to prostitution, abusing the initial trust her paramour had placed in her. This must have been a most disturbing time for Barnett. One can only imagine how depressed and desperate he must have felt. The object of his desire had spurned him. The dreams he must have harboured for their future together had been obliterated. Although the couple continued to live together the devotion appears to have been a one-sided affair, Kelly doing little more than taking from him, giving nothing in return. Despite the psychological turmoil he must have suffered, Barnett refused to believe that it was over. He clung on to his dream in the hope that something would change Mary's mind.

That something may well have arrived in the early-morning editions of the press, which reported the murder of a prostitute in George Yard Buildings, Whitechapel. It was an unusual murder in as much as the victim, Martha Tabram/Turner had suffered greatly, sustaining 39 individual knife wounds to her body. This led to a press inference that the killer must be some kind of maniac. Barnett must have innocently related the news to Kelly, perhaps voicing his genuine concern for her safety. The impact of the crime seems to have sent shock waves throughout the prostitute community, including Kelly, as personal security and self-awareness became of paramount importance. For a short period, the fear of meeting Tabram's killer instilled fear into the Whitechapel prostitutes but time is a great healer, and soon the whole affair was just about forgotten, the George Yard Buildings murder being judged as a singular event unlikely to occur again. Thus Mary Kelly returned to the streets. Joseph Barnett had again served his useful purpose.

Desperate situations call for desperate measures, and Barnett was no doubt a desperate man. Mary was being generous with her affection, particularly while absent from Miller's Court. She would never return home with a client as this would mean confrontation with Barnett and the probable loss of trade. To add to his troubles, the rent arrears at Miller's Court were rising by 4 shillings per week.

As a desperate man, he was now faced with the greatest dilemma of his life, yet quite innocently, a solution to the problems facing Joseph Barnett had been presented to him with the sad demise of Martha Tabram. For a short time he verbally intimidated Mary Kelly, reminding her of the perils of prostitution and how the murder which took place in George Yard Buildings could, in fact, have occurred to any Whitechapel prostitute. The ferocity of the Tabram murder – 39 independent stab wounds – indicated that her killer must have been in an absolute fury in order to inflict so many wounds. This was, more than the death itself, a serious point of concern. Tabram's killer must have held some deep-rooted hatred of her, or perhaps, as Barnett may have put it, of the prostitute community.

The personal stress created by his predicament meant that Barnett was now thinking irrationally. The more Mary Kelly remained absent from his company and the Miller's Court room, the more intense the pressure became. It is difficult to assess just when Barnett elected to take the only option he could see to remedy his problem, but it is without doubt that the seeds had been sown since the aftermath of the Tabram crime. The murder of just one more Whitechapel prostitute may just force Kelly back into his arms and once and for all put an end to her whoring.

Barnett had to be selective of his victim. He required someone whose death would make a great impact upon the life of Mary Kelly, thus Mary Ann (Polly) Nichols met her demise on the morning of 31 August 1888. In order to promote his handiwork, Barnett, himself now a hater of the prostitute community, disembowelled his victim, since it was the use and existence of the female sexual organs which was causing his loved one to leave him behind. The crime scene at Buck's Row was not specially selected. It was a simple matter of seeking out a familiar whore and inflicting as much bodily damage as was possible in order to create a sensation. To Barnett's mind, it would be as simple as gutting a fish. These women were, to him, worthless, hardly worth the full cost of a piece of fresh fish at Billingsgate Market. The authorities would make no special effort to find the killer of a "tuppenny whore". Newspaper columns were often filled with reports of how the area had to be sanitized. What he was doing was of actual assistance, not only to himself, but to the area in general.

Unfortunately for Barnett, the crime did not initially create the impact he had anticipated. The police were quickly on scene, but a delay in the identification of the body and a serious flaw in the initial medical examination resulted in the authorities being somewhat resentful of admitting the entire facts. The fact that Dr Llewellyn, who certified death at the scene of the Polly Nichols murder, had failed to observe that the corpse had in fact been disembowelled (he initially stated that the body had sustained injuries to the neck only), indicates a somewhat lackadaisical attitude and causes concern about the professional standards of some of the Victorian authorities.

News of the murder did spread through the community, but the full details of the crime would not be revealed in their entirety until the inquest, with the police at a total loss for a motive for the crime. They requested a further period of time to procure evidence, which ultimately they failed to do. Indeed, by the time of the final inquest, 22 September 1888, no further evidence or information had come to light, resulting in the Coroner chastising the authorities for their apparent ineptitude. To his own mind, Barnett's first murder had made little impact. He may have judged it as a failure, though, as he had assumed, he had escaped detection. The only course available to him was to kill a second prostitute, Eliza Ann Chapman.

The body of Annie Chapman was found in the rear yard of 29 Hanbury Street at 5.45 am on the morning of 8 September 1888. Once again foul mutilations had occurred to the disembowelled body (the uterus had been cut from the body and removed from the scene). On this occasion, the police revealed that the killer had left a number of clues at the murder scene, "which would be easily followed up". In one police Inspector's opinion, "it was only a matter of time before the killer was caught". Annie Chapman favoured a lodging house at 35 Dorset Street, the same street where Barnett and Kelly lived. It is without doubt that Kelly must have known Chapman, hence the impact her death would have upon the object of Barnett's desire would be severe.

The latest murder ensured that Mary Kelly refrained from prostitution for a period of time. She was forced back into the arms of Joseph Barnett, who appreciated the attention she once again showed him. Barnett, it is known, would read reports of the Whitechapel atrocities to Mary Kelly to reinforce the horror of the situation and confirm the obvious dangers to which a Whitechapel whore would be exposed if she chose to walk the streets. Why the uterus was removed from Annie Chapman's body can never truly be known. However, it is claimed that Mary Kelly herself was with child. Could it be that Barnett was unsure of the identity of the father? His contempt for the female reproductive organs may have driven him to insatiable anger, the removal of the uterus being a souvenir of his success in placating this rage. If correct it does indicate his frenzied state of mind when committing the crimes, and his disguised nurturing hatred for the way in which Mary Kelly had treated him.

With such confused emotions running through his mind, Barnett might well have turned into something of a recluse in order to escape from the reality of his situation. Certainly, his relationship with Kelly was anything but stable. His feelings towards her associates, whom he may have blamed for their downfall and for leading her astray, would be obvious should he maintain constant contact with them. It made sense for him to maintain a low profile, forever attempting to keep Mary Kelly by his side.

It is possible that in order to keep the pressure on he sent out letters to the press, identifying himself as none other than "Jack the Ripper". He was known at Billingsgate fish market as "Jack" and this pseudonym would allow him the curious self-satisfaction of identifying himself and his handiwork. It would further strike fear into Mary Kelly that some evil lunatic was at large in the community.

On 30 September 1888, the body of Catharine Eddowes was found in Mitre Square. Once again severe injuries had been caused to the body, more severe than any previously inflicted. The throat had been severed, intestines were drawn from the torso, some being strewn over the woman's right shoulder, and these were smeared with some feculent matter. A piece of the intestine had been detached from the body and lay between the torso and the left arm. The lobe and auricle of the right ear were cut obliquely through, the eyelids had been vertically slit, and the tip of the nose removed, ensuring that the remains provided a ghastly sight. Blood had been smeared on the arms and thighs, almost as though the killer had wiped his hands of the blood which must have dripped from them. There was no sign of sexual interference.

Police officers at the scene carried out thorough searches of the area. It has been further claimed by one senior official at the scene that in pursuance of the offender police had located a blood-stained sink off Dorset Street, down which bloody water had run. The blood was claimed to be fresh and it was further speculated that this was the very spot where the murderer had stopped to rinse his hands.

Should this evidence be deduced as being accurate, and despite everything else, no one today can positively disprove it, once again we have a clear indication that the killer headed back to the Dorset Street area. Certainly, one irrefutable fact is that a piece of Catharine Eddowes's apron, cut from the clothing she wore at the time of her murder, was found in a doorway of the Wentworth Dwellings, and it was covered in blood and faecal matter. The killer then, was certainly heading in the direction of Dorset Street, where curiously, Joseph Barnett lived.

The police were adamant that on this occasion they had been provided with a good description of the man they now actively sought. Detective Stephen White later revealed the following information, the location of which is deemed by most commentators to be Mitre Square:

For five nights we had been watching a certain alley just behind Whitechapel Road. It could only be entered from where we had two men posted in hiding, and persons entering the alley were under observation by the two men. It was a bitter cold night when I arrived at the scene to take the report of the two men in hiding. I was turning away when I saw a man coming out of the alley wearing rubber shoes, which were rather rare in those days. I stood aside to let the man pass, as he came under the wall lamp I got a good look at him. He was about five feet ten inches in height, and was dressed rather shabbily, though it was obvious that the material of his clothes was good. Evidently a man who had seen better days, I thought, but men who have seen better days are common enough down East, and that in itself was not sufficient to justify me stopping him. His face was long and thin, nostrils rather delicate and his hair was jet black. His complexion was inclined to be sallow and altogether the man was foreign in appearance. The most striking thing about him, however, was the extraordinary brilliance of his eyes. They looked like two very luminous glow worms coming through the darkness. The man was slightly bent at the shoulders, though he was obviously quite young – about thirty-three at the most and gave one the idea of having been a student or professional man. His hands were snow white and the fingers long and tapering.

This was an incredible description bearing in mind the fact that such a meeting would occur within the space of just a few seconds, in dim light! White's report of this incident was not revealed for some time after the event, and while it would be easy for anyone to compare the description of the individual to any respective suspect, it has to be said that the details should be treated with some suspicion. It would be virtually impossible to take in so much of a description with such a fleeting encounter.

It is curious to note that White claims that the man wore rubber shoes; many of the men associated with the Whitechapel Vigilance Committee were provided with such shoes in order that they could sneak around the streets with the minimum of noise. I was once told by an ex-curator of Scotland Yard's Black Museum, who openly stated that "no one knows as much about Jack the Ripper as I", that Joseph Barnett was in fact a member of the same Whitechapel Vigilance Committee. Should this assertion be correct, then Barnett would have been presented with the perfect disguise, a distressed man assisting his fellows in tracking down the Ripper. Such a position would allow him information as to how the local community intended to hunt down the killer, and perhaps the odd piece of police intelligence.

On 16 October 1888, George Lusk, the head of the Whitechapel Vigilance Committee, and a well-to-do businessman received at his Alderney Road home address, a package in the form of a cardboard

box. Within the box was what appeared to be a human kidney and a
missive:

> From Hell.
> Mr Lusk,
>   Sor, I send you half the Kidne I took from one women,
> prasarved it for you, tother piece I fried and ate it, it was very
> nise, I may send you the bloody knif that took it out if you only
> wate a whil longer.
>   Signed.
>   Catch Me When You Can Mishter Lusk.

This package and letter had to be sent to Lusk by someone who clearly
knew him and what he apparently stood for, as well as his personal
address. Members of the Vigilance Committee would be aware of such
details, which further provides evidence which can be used against
Barnett. Only members of the local community would deem Lusk
important enough to receive such a communication, knowing full well
that he would communicate with the press, the official authorities, and
just about everyone in Whitechapel. It was a clever ploy to further
advertise the horrors of the murders.

Other letters were submitted to the press in the full knowledge that
these would be published in the columns of the newspapers. The
Ripper desperately required publicity to drive home his self-believed
power. What could be the motive behind such actions other than to
strike fear into the community – or in Barnett's case, into one
individual, Mary Jane Kelly?

Over the weeks that followed, Mary Kelly became more
disenchanted with her association with Barnett, until finally on 28
October 1888 she announced that it was her immediate intention to
move a fellow prostitute into the room. The reason behind this is
unclear. Some have speculated that Kelly may have held lesbian
tendencies. More simply, it could have been that she held some deep-
rooted fear for her immediate safety, and felt that either Barnett could
no longer provide that safety (in fact he could well have posed a threat)
or that by moving another prostitute in, then Barnett would have no

option but to move out. There is some suggestion that Kelly was in fact in fear of some individual(s) and that she was greatly worried by the Ripper crimes, to such an extent that she considered leaving London.

This is not indiscriminate fear, which must have been held by most of the prostitutes of the region, but a real personal terror. To relate this to the scenario that she moved a fellow prostitute into her room infers that she wanted Barnett out without further discussion. Fear for her own safety would be eased if she was not alone with him. This is the more likely reason for the introduction of a colleague into her home life.

Arguments between Barnett and Kelly had occurred. On one such occasion, a small window had been broken. The atmosphere in the tiny room must have been a volatile one. Eventually, two days after the fellow prostitute had moved into 13 Miller's Court (30 September 1888), Barnett moved out, taking up new accommodation with Mr Buller at 24–5 New Street. This departure brings us to a further salient point of the Ripper investigation, which, to this very day, causes a great deal of controversy amongst commentators of the crimes.

The room key to 13 Miller's Court had somehow been lost, creating problems for securing the room when it was to be left empty. The breakage of a window allowed Barnett or Kelly access to the inside of the front door if they put an arm through the broken pane to lock or unlock the door latch as and when necessary. This information would be known to just a few, yet it becomes more evident as we progress.

On the morning of 9 November 1888, the remains of Mary Jane Kelly were found within 13 Miller's Court. Thomas Bowyer, assistant to Kelly's landlord, first sighted the body through the muslin-curtained window of the room through which he peered, having received no reply to his knocks at the door. The remains are best described as gruesome. Much of the body had been skinned, the breasts and other other organs had been removed and placed on a bedside table, and intestines were strewn around the blood-splattered room. The police attended and attempted to gain entry and eventually, as a sketch of the era reproduces, forced the door open with a pick axe.

By virtue of this evidence we are left to wonder how the door was locked? If Jack the Ripper had been a complete stranger to Mary Kelly, then how would he know to secure the door on his departure, through the broken window? However, if one considers that Joseph Barnett was the same miscreant then he would possess such first-hand detail, and would perhaps carry out such a task automatically and without further thought. At the inquest of Mary Kelly, Inspector Abberline confirmed to the hearing that the key to the room was lost and had been so for some time thus confirming the fact that Barnett must have been one of the few people who knew of the routine with the broken window.

Inspector Abberline made routine enquiries at the scene of the Kelly murder and demanded that Joseph Barnett be brought to Miller's Court, initially to identify the body. Barnett did this, although the remains were so hideous that to make a definite identification would have proved most difficult for anyone. A search of the inside of 13 Miller's Court revealed a number of items, including ginger beer bottles and a man's clay pipe.

The infamous "Dear Boss" letter received by the Central News Agency in September 1888 contained the following detail: "I saved some of the proper red stuff in a ginger beer bottle over the last job to write with but it went thick like glue and I cant use it." The locating of ginger beer bottles within 13 Miller's Court is yet another association with Barnett which cannot truly be dismissed. Similarly, Barnett claimed that he left Kelly and 13 Miller's Court to live elsewhere on 30 October, but he was, by his own admission, a man of very little means. Some nine days later, his clay pipe was found there, not tucked away in some dark corner, but on top of the fireplace! For some inexplicable reason the police missed these facts.

Despite the suggestion that the investigating authorities were little more than incompetent, it must be said that the entire course of the investigation was determined by the press, politicians and the higher social classes in general. These people were determined to prove that the Ripper had to be someone with a markedly higher intelligence than those generally found in the East End of London at that time. The police hierarchy were all too pleased to promote this aspect, since they had proved their inability to catch the miscreant. It was an easy option to disguise their own incompetence with a belief that the killer was not of average intelligence but some form of superhuman who drifted into the area, killed and left before they had been alerted to a crime occurring.

Despite this fact, the officers who worked the area held different beliefs. They clearly believed that the Ripper was a local man. Too many local arrests were made for this assumption not to be correct. It is now commonly accepted that the local police, by the time of the Kelly murder, held suspicions about a number of suspects. Immediately after the murder of Mary Kelly the first man held and questioned was none other than Joseph Barnett. It has been claimed (quite recklessly) by some authors, that the police questioning of Barnett must have satisfactorily been concluded with the suspect providing evidence of his innocence. There is not one available piece of evidence to dictate this fact. In fact Barnett's only alibi was that he had been playing cards in his lodgings and he had retired to bed.

Joseph Barnett visited Mary Kelly just a few hours prior to her death. We do not know the reason for this visit. He claimed that he was still on good terms with the woman, yet he had not been so when she brought another prostitute into their home. Indeed, a witness at Kelly's inquest told how Barnett would not allow Kelly to go out on the streets as a prostitute and how he often spoke of detesting her from acting in this way.

Barnett himself confessed to the fact that he would read the newspaper reports of the murders to Mary Kelly, which again indicates how his mind operated at the time. There can be little doubt that when Barnett and Kelly split, as with any relationship with one party deeply hurt and offended, that animosity existed. Barnett had suffered the ultimate humiliation. The love of his life had scorned him and all but forced him from the room they had found as a couple. All of a sudden he was an outsider, an alien in her life. He would hardly be likely to accept her actions at face value and move on as though their relationship had never occurred.

We will never truly know why Barnett returned to Miller's Court to visit Kelly that evening. However it is a curious coincidence and it is quite unbelievable to accept that he returned to give her money and wish her well. It is far more likely that he returned to her in the hope that he could persuade her to have him back. She refused, hence he took the last option available to him. If he could not have her, then no one else ever would.

The mutilations to Mary Kelly's body were far greater than those inflicted on any of the previous three victims. (I discount Liz Stride as a Ripper victim.) Her looks were totally destroyed, making her form something to repulse every human being who gazed upon it, something which ultimately pleased Barnett, if only he had been able to achieve this while she was alive. His final and perhaps most incriminating act was as ghastly as the mutilations themselves. Before leaving Mary Kelly for the last time he took away with him something he had yearned for during the previous 18 months. He stole Mary Kelly's heart.

The theory is but a basic one. No cover-ups, no political inferences, just plain old life at its simplest. Today, a high percentage of domestic murders are committed by a partner or ex-partner of the victim. Perhaps this explains why Inspector Abberline identified Joseph Barnett as his immediate suspect after the Kelly murder. Added to the other evidence, this achieves a good deal of doubt as to Barnett's innocence. He lived at the epicentre of the crimes, knew at least one of the victims personally, possessed skills with a knife, and had a thorough geographical knowledge of the district. Joseph Barnett had to be Jack the Ripper.

The Diary of Jack the Ripper

Shirley Harrison

I was a newcomer to the world of the true-crime enthusiast. The centenary of Jack the Ripper in 1988 had passed me by. A good Agatha Christie film in the cinema was the limit of my interest in detective stories and I had never heard of the trial of Florence Maybrick. My previous books concerned an exploration of religous cults, a history of the English Channel, a study of new approaches to cancer and the story of Father Christmas. What's more, I had never been to Liverpool.

Then something happened to change all that.

In the spring of 1992 former Liverpool scrap-metal dealer Michael Barrett came to London, bringing with him the Diary which was to cause such widespread havoc and to fragment the Ripper world. He claimed it was the Diary of Jack the Ripper. We met in the office of my literary agent, Doreen Montgomery of Rupert Crew Ltd. Doreen was naturally suspicious and had asked me to "sit in" on the meeting.

On first sight the Diary was unexceptional. It was written in a black, leather-bound album of which the first 64 pages had been roughly removed. Flicking through the remaining 144 pages I noticed how the writing changed erratically from controlled schoolboard neatness to sprawling angry violence punctuated with vicious slashes and blots. Its contents were sickeningly gruesome and there was a macabre obsession with cannibalism. But not till the final words did the full significance of what I was reading hit home. The writer signed himself starkly: "Yours truly Jack the Ripper Dated this third day of May 1889".

I learned later that this was also the year in which a pretty 26-year-old, Florence Maybrick, became the first American woman to be tried for murder in Britain. Her 50-year-old husband, James, an outwardly respectable Liverpudlian cotton merchant, had died in mysterious circumstances on 11 May 1889, apparently poisoned. He was addicted to arsenic and strychnine and had a secret mistress who had borne him several children.

In August 1889, Florie was condemned to death for her husband's murder. Hers was an outrageous trial, today accepted as one of the most famous of all miscarriages of British justice. Information was suppressed, the judge was on the edge of insanity and the jury was incompetent. There was no evidence to connect Florie with the crime and the sentence was commuted. Nevertheless, she spent 15 terrible years in gaol. Her autobiography *My Fifteen Lost Years*, published in 1905, tells only of the agony of her trial, of prison life and the worldwide efforts for her release. The secrets of her unhappy marriage she guarded. When she died, a broken recluse in her homeland in 1942, they were lost, probably forever.

The tragic truth of what had really happened in the Maybrick household was never established. Certainly no connection was ever made at the time with the Ripper killings the year before.

At first the identity of the diarist was not obvious. The clue lay in a sentence on page two where he writes, "Tonight I shall return to Battlecrease." The names "Bobo" and "Gladys" are also mentioned. Michael Barrett discovered that the tenant of Battlecrease House, in Riversdale Road, Liverpool in 1888–9 was none other than James Maybrick. His children were called Gladys and Bobo and "my darling Bunny" was Maybrick's pet name for his wife Florence. His brother Michael, who plays a key role in the Diary, was the internationally famous Victorian singer/composer Stephen Adams who later wrote the bestselling hymn "The Holy City".

The writer also catalogues the five Whitechapel murders in bloodcurdling detail, recording with chilling insight the agony of a man being destroyed by simultaneous feelings of love and hatred for himself and for his family. It follows his disintegration step by step through 1888 and ending on 3 May, the very day that James Maybrick is known to have visited his office for the last time. Moreover it suggests a motive for the killings in the East End: Maybrick knew that, trapped in a miserable marriage, Florie had herself been unfaithful. In a male-orientated Victorian society this was unforgivable.

The Diary clearly means that James Maybrick was Jack the Ripper. Here was a new and utterly unexpected suspect.

I knew that I was holding either a fascinating forgery or a unique historic document. The challenge was irresistible.

Even the thrill of the chase did not prepare me for what was to follow. I did not realize at that time that the murderous campaign of Jack the Ripper, who butchered five women in Whitechapel, had since spawned a specialist industry of books, films, articles and television programmes. I had no idea that there were thousands of men and women all round the world passionately engrossed in trying to solve the mystery; I was unaware that clubs and magazines with such names as *Ripperana* and *Ripperologist* were devoted to the topic. Their members knew every twist and turn of the streets of Whitechapel; they followed in the footsteps of the "unfortunates" who were slaughtered. Almost to a man (there were very few women), they were to rise against the Diary. They were each defensive of their own well established "suspects". In addition to the three best known police suspects (Kosminski, Montague John Druitt, Ostrog), Queen Victoria's grandson (Prince Albert Victor, Duke of Clarence) has been the subject of books and films. So too has Dr Francis Tumbelty, an American "quack" doctor, David Cohen, Dr Roslyn D'Onston, the Queen's physician Sir William Gull, Dr Barnardo and even Lewis Carroll are also on the list.

Then came the Diary, the latest and most intriguing of three Ripper-related artefacts to have emerged since 1888. "Jack the Ripper's knife" is now owned by former policeman Donald Rumbelow, author of *The Complete Jack the Ripper*. "Catharine Eddowes's shawl" is in the possession of Sue and Andy Parlour, who published their own book *The Jack the Ripper Whitechapel Murders* in 1997.

Michael Barrett told us he had been given the Diary by a dying friend in 1991. At that stage he too had no appreciation of the impact it would make. He dreamed only of buying a greenhouse. If only things had been so simple!

I knew that it was essential first for me to establish the Diary's provenance. Michael Barrett's story was hardly reliable and many people would understandably be convinced (and still are) that he wrote it himself.

Before coming to London, Michael Barrett had made a determined effort to conduct his own research into the background of his new possession. It was after all, he who originally recognized the name "Battlecrease" and made the first connection between Jack the Ripper and Maybrick. He took pages and pages of notes in the local library, which his wife, Anne, had carefully transferred to the word processor for him. These notes are very revealing. They show his enthusiasm and hard work but they also effectively demolish any theory of Michael Barrett "the great forger". For instance:

There is mention in the Diary of a cartoon which appeared in *Punch* in 1888 in which great play is made of the word "May". Michael records his efforts to find this in the library: "check for copy of *Punch* around Sept 1888 onwards. Nothing to date…"

James Maybrick worked in Knowsley Buildings, Liverpool. Michael notes: "Where was Knowsley Buildings? To date cannot find."

"Question. Who else other than the Ripper would have known that he was almost caught? Answer: Not sure, but if the diary is genuine and written at that time these facts could have only been possibly known by the Ripper."

These are not the notes of a man who knows; they are the genuine queries of a man seeking answers. This is the work of someone eager to understand, puzzled and sometimes confused by what he reads. They are not the words of a man creating a literary hoax. Michael Barrett is no fool; he certainly needed money. But Michael Barrett could not have written the diary. So who did? And when?

Serious research needs financial backing and as a writer the only way I knew to find sufficient resources was through the interest of a publisher. A publisher's advance (deducted later from royalties) would be a start.

In 1992, some preliminary ink tests and a visit to the British Museum suggested that there was no conclusive evidence to preclude the Diary from having been written in the late nineteenth century. I decided that it was safe for me to conduct full-scale research. Michael Barrett, Anne Barrett and I signed a collaboration agreement and he and I a contract with publishers Smith Gryphon. We agreed to share all expenses and resulting income. My investigations would explore:

1 The historical accuracy of the Diary. Was there anything in the content that could not be gleaned from other sources? Was any detail clearly wrong?

2 The ink and paper. What is each made of and when were the two brought together?

3 The handwriting. How did it compare with that of Maybrick and the generally accepted "Dear Boss" letters which were received by the Yard and of which the Diary writer claims authorship?

4 How does the personality of the Diarist match that of a serial killer?

5 The language of the Diary. Is it Victorian?

6 Is there anyone in Liverpool who could have composed the Diary as part of a modern conspiracy?

7 If not, where has the Diary been in the years between 3 May 1889 and the day it was handed to Michael Barrett in Anfield in Liverpool?

Working with my research partner, Sally Evemy, I enlisted the help of the three authors of *The Jack the Ripper A–Z*, Paul Begg, Martin Fido and Keith Skinner, as advisers.

The journey was to take me from the Star Wars world of some of Britain's best forensic laboratories, to museums, auction rooms, art galleries and universities. I explored the superficially glittering, confident and duplicitous world of the Victorian middle class as well as the rubbish-rotten streets of London's Whitechapel. Drugs and sex were currency common to both.

The Diary described its writer's double life. I needed to establish whether this unknown, apparently respectable Liverpool cotton merchant was indeed familiar with the seamy surroundings of the East

End 200 miles away, and whether evidence existed to prove he could not possibly have been in the capital during the autumn of terror. Was Maybrick a reasonable suspect as Jack the Ripper?

I first read the only three published books on Florence Maybrick: *This Friendless Lady* by Nigel Morland (1957); *Etched in Arsenic* by Trevor L. Christie (1968); and *The Poisoned Life of Mrs Maybrick* by Bernard Ryan and Sir Michael Havers (1977). I also obtained two mammoth tomes: *Treatise on the Maybrick Case*, a 600-page analysis and comment by the Scottish lawyer Alexander MacDougall (1891), and J. H. Levy's less emotional *The Necessity for Criminal Appeal* (1899). From America I was sent *My Fifteen Lost Years*, and I studied the complex *Toxicological Study of the Maybrick Case* (1891) by the doctors C. N. Tidy and R. Macnamara. I then trawled through yard upon yard of newsprint to see what newspapers everywhere were saying about both the Maybricks. All this convinced me that, despite the outpouring of words, there was still a great deal that was unexplained about the hidden character and secret life of James Maybrick.

Where better to begin than the little known Maybrick files, stored among the Public Record Office archives at Kew in Surrey? There we found boxes and files, packed with papers and tied with tape, which had been classified information, not available to the public until 1985. We were among the first to unwrap and read their secrets.

They contained the Maybrick trial reports, associated correspondence and affidavits. There were letters from the family, from Florie's lawyers, from the doctors attending Maybrick and later from Florie's mother, who kept up a relentless campaign to free her. Many American supporters also lobbied for her release. But for reasons we do not yet know Queen Victoria was adamant. In 1889 she had replied to the Home Secretary, Henry Matthews on his recommendation for a commutation of Florie's sentence: "the only regret she feels is that so wicked a woman should escape by a mere legal quibble..."

We were also given access to a delightful collection of memories by an elderly lady – Florence Aunspaugh – donated to the University of Wyoming by author, Trevor L. Christie. Florence had spent the summer of 1888 as a boisterous eight-year-old, at Battlecrease House. Her cotton merchant father was a business associate of Maybrick.

From this rich source of information we accumulated a great deal of material. More importantly, we found many new leads towards the untold story behind the events at Battlecrease House in the last year of Maybrick's downward-spiralling life.

James Maybrick was born in 1838, the second of five brothers. William, Michael, Thomas and Edwin. As a young man he was apprenticed in 1860 in London; by 1871 he was back in Liverpool where he later established Maybrick and Co., cotton merchants. Before long he had also opened a branch in Norfolk, Virginia. It was on the SS *Baltic*, returning from America in 1880 that he met 17-year-old Florence Chandler. She was from a wealthy, well-connected Southern family. He was 24 years older. They were married in 1881 at the fashionable St James's Church, Piccadilly, London.

Two weeks before the wedding, Maybrick was granted a somewhat pretentious Coat of Arms from the ancient college of Heralds in London. It cost him £76. 10 shillings (the equivalent today of over £3,200). On it, a bird of prey sits above a full flowering may tree and three golden bricks. The legend it bears is chilling: *"Tempus Omnia Revelat"* – Time Reveals All.

Florie, of course, was unaware that her husband already had a mistress who was possibly his wife. Maybrick's other life was mentioned briefly by Alexander MacDougall and we went on to discover, what had been so far unknown, that he had lived with her in London as man and wife – on the fringes of Whitechapel – in the 1860s! According to MacDougall, her family believed they were married. It was in this very area that James Maybrick's ancestors had settled when they first came to London from the West Country many years before. The Maybricks were very familiar with Whitechapel.

Not only was James Maybrick an adulterer and possibly a bigamist but he had also been addicted to arsenic and strychnine for years. At Florie's trial and in later correspondence and affidavits there were numerous observations by friends and business colleagues about his "habit", which led to many of the symptoms so clearly described in the Diary. For example: "As usual my hands are cold, my heart I do believe is colder still." He was a hypochondriac, obsessed with his own health:

"Fuller (his doctor in London) believes there is very little the matter with me. Strange, the thoughts he placed into my mind. I could not strike. I believe I am mad, completely mad."

Between late June and September 1888 his visits to the doctor increased dramatically. He saw the family physician in Liverpool, Dr Hopper, on about 20 occasions. During November and early December he also made five appointments with a Dr Drysdale, telling him that for three months he had suffered from acute pains in his head, numbness and an eruption of the skin on his hands. The Doctor was not impressed, "I should say he was hypochondriacal," he said at Florie's trial.

From the outset we had been constantly on the look-out for mistakes in the Diary. Surely from the known dates of these surgery visits we would find evidence which proved Maybrick could not have been in London at the time of the killings? Yet none of the appointments matched the dates of any of the killings. Of course, this did not prove that Maybrick was, indeed, in London when the murders were committed. We knew that he was familiar with Whitechapel as a young man, but was this the case in 1888? Could he have produced convincing cover for visits to London? The Diary speaks of its author taking a room in Middlesex Street (better known as Petticoat Lane) and we established that Maybrick's partner, Gustavus Witt, had an office in Cullum Street, on the edge of the City of London, only a stone's throw from Middlesex Street. Maybrick travelled frequently between the two. Another coincidence?

Moreover, Maybrick had a second bolt-hole. Brother Michael lived in a smart apartment in St John's Wood. They shared the same doctor, Dr Fuller. In the Diary, James describes one terrible evening at Michael's flat. "If it were not for Michael insisting that we take dinner I would have tried my hand that very night. I cursed my brother as I have never cursed him before…The pain that night has burnt into my mind. I vaguly (*sic*) recall putting a handkerchief in my mouth to stop my cries. I believe I vomited several times…"

Like many people at the time, we became increasingly suspicious of the high-flying bachelor, Michael Maybrick, with his elevated connections and rather shadowy life. How could he deny at Florence's trial, despite evidence from friends and doctors, that his brother took drugs? Why did he lie? Why did he conceal evidence, and what was his hold over James and their younger brother, Edwin? Edwin's daughter, Amy, said many years later that her father would not tie his shoelaces without consulting Michael. At the time of Florie's trial, many love letters from Edwin to Florie were discovered in a drawer, and Charles Aunspaugh wrote that Edwin was "deep in the mire". The letters were destroyed.

After James's death, Michael conveniently and quietly married his long-term housekeeper, a butcher's daughter, inexplicably left the two Maybrick children, aged seven and four, in the care of the childless, middle-aged Dr and Mrs Fuller and retired from the concert platform. He built up a new life, camouflaged respectably as the Mayor of Ryde in the Isle of Wight. Edwin, too, married (probably at Michael's instigation) although his daughter, Amy, declared that her father never enjoyed the company of women and was very cold.

Little by little, we were developing a tantalizing glimpse through the dark curtains of Battlecrease House, which hid the sinister truth about the Maybricks and their entourage.

At the same time, it was essential that I also became acquainted with the basic facts of the Whitechapel Murders. I was never attracted in the same way to this aspect of the story, not least because I felt that the Ripper evidence was unreliable. If the Diary was genuine it could rewrite the story and we felt we all had a unique opportunity to examine the murders, for the first time, through the Ripper's eyes. I presumed that mistakes might have been made in the contemporary recording of events and that it was even possible that the Diary's interpretation could be correct. Philip Sugden has said, in his erudite book *The Complete History of Jack the Ripper*, that eyewitnesses were notoriously unsafe and even the police evidence conflicted.

The arguments ranging around the Ripper content of the Diary are mainly centred on five separate issues: the "Dear Boss" letters which were signed "Jack the Ripper" and which do not match the handwriting of the Diary or James Maybrick's alleged will; the envelope, coins and rings; the "Tin match box, empty"; the writing on Mary Kelly's wall; and Mary Kelly's missing heart.

The "Dear Boss" Letters and the Problem of Handwriting

On 29 September 1888, Scotland Yard was sent the now notorious letter signed, for the first time, "Jack the Ripper". This was to be followed by hundreds more, very few of which are generally accepted as genuinely penned by the Ripper. But even these are controversial and many specialists believe they were in fact all the work of a hoaxer – maybe a journalist. However, the Diary claims responsibility for the original inspirational use of the name "Jack the Ripper". If that first letter *is* a hoax, it follows that the Diary is also forged. On the other hand, if it is genuine, why does the Diary's handwriting not resemble them more closely?

Handwriting analysis is a controversial science. Graphology concerns the art of character-reading through letter formations, whereas document analysis is the science of deciphering the differences between one person's handwriting and another's. Both are used in police work.

At this stage, film producer Paul Feldman arrived on the scene. He had bought the video rights to our book and an option on a film and had become passionate about the project. Paul invited internationally respected graphologist Anna Koren to look at the Diary. Anna is Director of the Graphology Center in Haifa, a member of the American Association of Graphologists and a forensic document examiner for the Israeli Minister of Justice.

She had not heard of the Ripper and had not seen the Diary. She did not know what to expect. After 20 minutes, during which she did not read the words themselves but scrutinized their formation, her off-the-cuff assessment was astounding. The man she described was James Maybrick: "Unstable...inner conflicts...inferiority...hypochondriac... brutal...a distorted image of his masculinity...deep-rooted loneliness... exhibitionism...a tendency for his behaviour to be repeated in cycles..." She later responded forcefully to the suggestion that this was contrived handwriting: "Impossible."

Document analyst Sue Iremonger believes: "Handwriting is as revealing as fingerprints...the components of every individual's handwriting remain consistent." She could see no link between the letters she examined, Maybrick's will or the Diary.

I am uneasy about too great a reliance on handwriting as evidence. Paul Feldman has developed an argument to support his certainty that James Maybrick's will was itself forged by his brothers and thrust before James for signature as he lay dying. Even Sue Iremonger agrees that Michael and James had "remarkably similar" hands. Over the years we have collected a vast amount of documentation and have noted how, for instance, Florence's handwriting at the time of her trial was forward-leaning and spidery, whereas by the time of her death, it was rounded and upright.

In the last few years a hitherto unpublished "Dear Boss" letter from Galashiels in Scotland has been unearthed. It is signed "The Ripper" and refers to the writer being on his way to the Innerliethen tweed factories. Cotton merchants from Liverpool were regular visitors to that area. Moreover the writing on this is curiously similar to that of a letter written by Maybrick aboard the SS *Baltic* in 1881. The problem of the handwriting became all the more interesting when we discovered from private, unpublished papers, that James Maybrick's favourite pet name for himself was "Sir Jim". There was no way that a forger could, at any time, have known this, yet whoever wrote this Diary is acutely aware of the inner conflict about the name to use when writing to the police:

"Before I am finished all of England will know the name I have given...Perhaps her gracious Majesty will become acquainted with it. I wonder if she will honour me with a knighthood...I can now rise Sir Jim...All whores will feel the edge of Sir Jim's shining knife. I regret I did not give myself that name, curse it, I prefer it much more than the one I have given."

The Envelope, the Farthings and the Rings

It is generally agreed that, after the second murder, a piece of coarse muslin, a small tooth comb and a pocket comb were left beside Annie Chapman's body. There was also a scrap of envelope. But were there any farthings? And where were her rings?

The Diary provides its own answers to these questions, answers that add a slightly different interpretation of events:

~~Letter M it's true~~
Along with M ha ha
Will catch clever Jim

According to the authors of *The Jack the Ripper A–Z*, the envelope bore the crest of the Sussex Regiment and a letter "M" in a man's handwriting. Philip Sugden adds that there was also an "Sp", assumed to be part of the address – Spitalfields.

When Paul Feldman acquired the private papers belonging to the late Stephen Knight, author of *Jack the Ripper: The Final Solution* he found a document transcribed in Knight's handwriting from the original by Inspector Chandler, written after his visit to the Sussex Regiment at Farnborough in Hampshire. It said "Enquiries were made amongst the men but none could be found who corresponded with anyone living in Spitalfields or with any person whose address commencing (*sic*) with 'J'…"

But in Inspector Chandler's original report a figure "2" is formed in exactly the same way as the "J". The envelope has consequently been dismissed as irrelevant, despite the fact that the Inspector's report speaks unequivocally of "letters" and makes no reference to "numbers".

Controversy also surrounds the brass rings which Annie's friends claimed she had been wearing and which were missing when the body was found. Inspector Abberline, in charge of local investigations, said they had been forcibly removed. According to the Diary there were two rings and they were removed for very good reason:

"Begin with the rings, one ring, two rings, bitch, it took me a while before I could wrench them off. Should have stuffed them down the whore's throat. I wish to God I could have taken the head. Hated her for wearing them, reminds me too much of the whore (his wife Florie)."

The press at the time reported that "a pile of rings and coins" had been found beside the body. Later this became "two new farthings". These were not mentioned at Annie Chapman's inquest. Author Martin Fido wrote to me: "It is my speculation that the initial silence on these coins was police strategy to hold back information that would only be known to a guilty subject." Other Ripper historians do not believe in the farthings and Philip Sugden does not mention them at all in *The Complete History of Jack the Ripper*.

But sure enough, the Diary does:

> One ring, two rings,
> a farthing one and two
> ~~Sir Jim will do true~~
> ~~Letter M its true~~
> Along with M ha ha
> Will catch clever Jim
> Its true…

At the inquest of Alice McKenzie, in 1889, Inspector John Reid, who was head of Whitechapel CID at the time of Jack the Ripper, confirmed the existence of the farthings when he said that "coins under her body were similar to those in Annie Chapman's case".

The Tin Box

This innocuous-sounding item, found by the body of the fourth victim, Catharine Eddowes, has, surprisingly, been the focus of more comment than almost anything else. "I showed no fright, and indeed no light, Damn it, the tin box was empty…"

It appears as "one Tin Match Box, empty" in the police list of Catharine's possessions but which was never published in full. It lay unnoticed until Donald Rumbelow and Martin Fido mentioned it in their respective books published in 1987. In 1888 no one but the murderer himself could have known of the tin box. This fact alone seemed to confirm that the Diary is either a modern forgery or it is genuine.

The Writing on the Wall

Perhaps the most macabre evidence of all was confirmed by modern techniques when Paul Feldman arranged for computer enhancement of a photograph which had first appeared in a French magazine in 1890.

This was the now famous picture of Mary Kelly's butchered body which was reproduced in Stephen Knight's book *Jack the Ripper: The Final Solution* in 1976. In 1988 researcher Simon Wood noted an initial on the wall of her room. Enlarged, this writing becomes more clearly identifiable as an F and an M – the initials of Maybrick's wife.

The ferocity of this, the final murder, is almost beyond belief. And yet, even here, within the Diary it is described by a man suffering the torments of hell. Even here there is poetic imagery alongside unspeakable bestiality.

The Heart

The last words in the inquest report on Mary Kelly by police surgeon Dr Thomas Bond were: "The Pericardium was open below and the Heart absent." There never was a reliable explanation of where the heart might have been. Certainly Dr Phillips and Dr Roderick Macdonald, the district coroner, returned to Mary Kelly's room to sift through the ashes in her fireplace in search of burned human remains.

The Diary does not refer to the heart at the time of the murder. Only towards the end of his life and in total despair does Maybrick utter the words which could have been applied equally to Mary Kelly or to the wife he believes deceived him. "I do not have the courage to take my life. I pray each night I will find the strength to do so but the courage alludes (*sic*) me. I pray constantly all will forgive. I deeply regret striking her, I have found it in my heart to forgive her for her lovers.

"I believe I will tell her all, ask her to forgive me as I have forgiven her. I pray to God she will understand what she has done to me. Tonight I will pray for the women I have slaughtered. May God forgive me for the deeds I committed on Kelly, no heart no heart…"

Mary Kelly is the only victim mentioned by name in the Diary.

In July 1993, prior to publication in Britain and America, the *Washington Post* cast doubts on the authenticity of the Diary. The American publisher Warner Books ordered a last-minute examination by a committee of experts headed by Kenneth Rendell, an antiquarian bookseller who had been involved with the unmasking of the Hitler

Diaries. Samples of ink were taken and a facsimile version left for further study by a handwriting expert and a historian. The initial scientific tests concurred that there was nothing in the ink to conflict with a date of 1888–9. An additional examination of ion migration which aimed to pinpoint more exactly when the ink went on the paper suggested a median date of 1921, "give or take 12 years". After less than two weeks, the handwriting specialists produced a lengthy report. Its main criticisms were:

1 *The handwriting is not Victorian.*
However, the British Museum had already assured us that "by the late nineteenth century Victorian handwriting becomes difficult to define. From that time a wide variety of hands, some quite modern in appearance, can be found."

2 *The Diary is not written in a standard Victorian diary book.*
This is a strange statement from a man used to dealing in such books. Diaries were written in all manner of books. I have myself seen a Victorian album, almost identical to the Maybrick Diary, which belonged to a prosperous middle-class family and was which used not only for letters, photos and postcards but also diary notes.

3 *The handwriting of the Diary bears no relationship to that of James Maybrick's will.*
This is true – but hasty. Over the next four years independent research revealed evidence that the will in Somerset House, London, may indeed, not be in Maybrick's hand either. Or, could it not be, as Anna Koren suggested, that the Diary writing is natural and spontaneous, whereas the "Dear Boss" letters are artificial and the will is formal?

4 *The Diary contains phrases not in use in the late nineteenth century and language that does not fit a respectable cotton merchant.*
Another hasty judgment. Editors at the Oxford English Dictionary and Websters have confirmed that the date of the appearance of particular colloquial phrases in a dictionary does not always correspond to their vernacular use. One such controversial phrase was "one-off"; said by

the dictionary to have originated in 1925, I found it myself among the records of a Kent builder dated 1862.

As a result of this report Warner rescinded their contract, although fortunately for us a new publisher, Hyperion, emerged within hours to foster our troublesome child. In London the *Sunday Times* produced their own team of "experts" who undertook no forensic tests and whose handwriting expert saw the Diary for a matter of minutes. They declared in a circulation-boosting two-page spread that the Diary was a modern forgery written within two years of its appearance in London. No evidence was offered and no suspects named and yet they were to deposit their papers with New Scotland Yard and so initiate a full police enquiry.

When, eventually, my own book *The Diary of Jack the Ripper* appeared in October 1993, the Ripperologists (the phrase coined by author Colin Wilson for students of the Whitechapel Murders) mostly joined forces with the *Washington Post* and the *Sunday Times* and declared the Diary a fake. At the same time a "Committee for Integrity" was formed by writer Melvin Harris, whose own book on the Ripper was due for publication. The Committee was based on the assumption that we knew the Diary was a forgery and that we were cynically promoting it for financial gain. His aim, initially, was to orchestrate the opposition to my book and to block any film contract "in the public interest".

These were tumultuous times. In our long professional lifetimes neither my agent, my publisher, nor I had experienced anything like it.

So we were not best pleased when, in August 1993, Smith Gryphon's Managing Director Robert Smith took a phone call. The accent at the other end was unmistakably Liverpudlian. The caller said, "I have got James Maybrick's watch." We had been anxious that artefacts might arise from nowhere, "discovered" by people anxious to jump on the bandwagon. But something about this particular call made us feel we should not dismiss it out of hand.

This was a wise decision. The caller proved to be Albert Johnson, an honourable, family man, semi-retired from his college security job. He had, he said, bought the Verity lady's watch for £225 in 1992 from a jewellery shop in Wallasey. He had intended to keep it as an investment for his grandaughter, Daisy. Mr and Mrs Murphy, who own the shop, said that they had acquired the watch when Mrs Murphy's father gave up his antiques business in Lancaster about 18 years before. It did not work and had lain in a drawer with other items until 1992, when they finally decided to have it repaired.

Not long after he bought the watch, Albert was discussing the television programme, *The Antiques Roadshow*, with some pals at work. They were arguing about the existence of 18-carat gold in the nineteenth century. Albert took his watch to the college where the men noticed, for the first time, some scratches on the inside back of the case. Under a microscope these showed up as "J Maybrick. I am Jack". Round the edges were five sets of initials. All this meant nothing. But when an article about the Diary appeared in the local paper Albert made the connection and realized that his watch might be important.

In July 1993, he decided to pay for the scratches to be examined by Dr Turgoose of the Corrosion Protection Centre of the University of Manchester Institute of Science and Technology (UMIST). He then contacted Robert Smith. The result of that examination was very exciting for us all. In summary it said "It is clear that the engravings predate the vast majority of superficial surface scratch marks (all of those examined). The wear apparent on many of the engravings, evidenced by the rounded edges of the markings and 'polishing out' in places, would indicate a substantial age for the engravings…"

In 1994, this time at my expense, the watch was sent for a second opinion at the Interface Analysis Centre in Bristol. The results were better than we dared hope. Like Dr Turgoose at UMIST, Dr Robert Wild at Bristol photographed slivers of blackened brass embedded within the scratch marks. Emphasizing the need for further tests Dr Wild said:

"Provided the watch has remained in a normal environment, it would seem likely that the engravings were at least of several tens of years' age…in my opinion it is unlikely that anyone would have sufficient expertise to implant aged brass particles into the base of the engravings…" Even this did not satisfy the critics. Martin Fido wrote "while recognising the impressive two concurring lab. reports on the watch I do not think they have proved the watch to be genuine; in fact, without having any easy explanation....I think it is most probably a modern forgery and inspired by the diary."

That was four years ago. A great deal has happened since. Every year new evidence arises to reshape our thinking and improve our understanding.

Despite repeated allegations, the Diary has *not* been proved to be a forgery and those of us who have spent so much time examining its pedigree have never abandoned our belief in its historic status. It has survived possibly the most rigorous investigation of any manuscript this century.

A website was eventually launched on the Internet, as a vehicle for informed debate. But the debate sank to such a low level of vitriolic abuse, based mainly on wild speculation and misinformed comment, that its potential research value was destroyed. I have been accused not only of knowingly perpetrating a fraud for commercial gain, but also of lying and of being an accessory to murder; private detectives have been employed to prove such fictions.

In Liverpool and in London this Diary has wreaked havoc within many of the families whose lives it touched. Michael and Anne Barrett divorced and at one point, unable to cope, Michael claimed that he had forged the Diary, a "confession" which was leaped upon with glee by our critics, ignoring the tragic circumstances in which it was made. A huge amount of money has been spent on lawyers, forensic scientists and specialist experts in many fields. We have made no fortunes.

In 1994, a new provenance for the Diary arose from the most unexpected, and unwelcome, source. Michael Barrett's former wife, Anne, made a taped confession. What she told us did not demolish Michael's original story at all. She had not lied. She had simply not told the whole truth. She said that Michael had, indeed, been given the Diary by Tony Devereux, but it was she who had given it to Tony. The Diary had been in her family, at least since 1942. She told us that her great-grandmother, Elizabeth Formby, had been a friend of one of the maids at Battlecrease House and attended the trial with her. Granny Formby could neither read nor write and she died in 1939. In 1943, Anne's father, Billy Graham, returned on leave from the war and recalled seeing the Diary in a black metal trunk with some white letters on it.

He had not the slightest interest in Jack the Ripper and so the Diary was stacked away with a lot of military paraphernalia and bric-a-brac and forgotten. At Christmas 1950, around the time that Anne was born, Billy's stepmother Edith Formby (Elizabeth's daughter) gave him the trunk and said, "Your granny left this for you." Billy was unimpressed and he forgot all about it.

Anne first saw the Diary in about 1968, when she was just 18. It was still in the trunk, at the back of a big, dark, walk-in cupboard that had always terrified her. The trunk was full of gas masks and tropical gear. "We were moving at the time because my mother had died and my dad was remarrying and so I packed the Diary to take with us. But my dad wasn't at all bothered and as he couldn't tell me anything about it I just stuffed it into a wardrobe."

In 1969, Anne emigrated to Australia as a nurse. When she returned, in 1976, she met and married the youthful and very persistent suitor, Michael Barrett. The family were against the marriage, partly because Michael had had a bad accident and could not work; it was doubtful if he would have children. However, Caroline, his pride and joy, was born in 1980. "Michael was a brilliant Dad," Anne says.

Not till her father was dying, did he give the Diary to her. She hated it and hid it. But in 1991, when Michael was out of work and drinking too much, she hatched a plan. Michael had always nursed the dream that he would like to write a book, so Anne decided to give the Diary to him so that he could use it as the basis of a novel. But, to avoid him pestering her sick father with questions, she wrapped the book in brown paper and took it to Michael's friend, Tony Devereux. She asked Tony to pass it on to Michael without saying where it had come from, a plan that was to cause untold damage.

Just before he died, in 1993, Billy recorded an interview with Paul Feldman. His words were typically forthright: "Blimey, if I'd known what it was worth I'd have cashed it years ago. I wouldn't have been slaving away in Dunlop's on dirty big tyres!"

All through 1993, as the police homed in on Liverpool, interviewing everyone concerned with the Diary, Anne kept quiet. In London, while we were ourselves researching every possible angle to resolve the Diary's authenticity, Anne said nothing. Eventually, in July 1994, largely because of the pressure from Paul Feldman, she recorded a defensive and apologetic message to myself, Doreen Montgomery and Robert Smith.

The rest is history.

"I wanted to feel proud of Michael again," she explains. "But when he said he was taking the Diary to London I really thought he would be sent packing. I never dreamed things would escalate as they did." In August 1991, Tony Devereux died. By the time that the paperback publication of my book was due, in 1994, Billy Graham too, was terminally ill. I never met him – he died soon afterwards. Anne made her confession (with his approval) and with him died our last key witness.

Of course, just as the Ripperologists did not believe in the Diary, or the watch, so they did not believe Anne's story. At first I did not believe her myself. It was hard to accept that anyone could be so uninterested that they could leave such a Diary at the bottom of a trunk for so many years. It was even harder to believe that anyone could have so deceived those of us who trusted her and were her partners.

Anne's story may provide us with an all too convenient provenance, but I would ask those who still do not believe to consider this. She lives in a modest housing association house; she has no car, she does not have holidays; she lives very simply. There have been no cash inducements for her confession. Anne has since explained her actions. In long hours sitting in her living room we have talked through the events that have rocked her life. She is a very private, devoted mother, not given to sharing her thoughts or feelings.

From the time the publishing and collaboration contracts were signed, she says, quite truthfully, that she had little or no contact with us. Michael was the link with London. She hardly knew us and certainly did not (at that stage) think of us as friends. She was unaware, she says, of the terrible trials we too were facing or the financial distress caused by legal fees incurred through the activities of *The Sunday Times*. She was still not interested in the Diary. Her own life was in turmoil. She had no thought for outsiders. Her father was dying, her marriage was at an end (she is Catholic) and she could not share her problems with anyone, least of all us. Only after intolerable intrusion into the lives of relatives and friends did she know she had to put a stop to it.

Her confession was too much for Michael Barrett. He cracked. He had been distraught to lose his daughter and now felt cheated of his Diary too. At one stage he "confessed" that he had written the Diary himself to "get back at Anne". But since he later also claimed that he was a member of MI5 who had single-handedly brought about the IRA ceasefire, then that he had disinterred Maybrick from his grave and been told that he was the Ripper, we could not now rely on anything he said.

The conclusion? This Diary is *not* a crude modern hoax. It has not been "cobbled together" by a nest of forgers in Liverpool. The consensus, particularly among those who deal professionally in the world of the criminally insane, is that it is unlikely to be a work of a calculating forger. David Canter, Professor of Psychology at Liverpool University and an internationally respected criminal psychologist, works closely with the police. He agreed to write the preface for a new and fully updated edition of my book, which was published in September 1998, because he finds the Diary a remarkably sophisticated and fascinating document.

The violence described in the Diary could perhaps, on its own, be an expression of a sick writer's prurient pleasure and gratification. Maybe, as if depicting literary scenes of explicit sex, he could have had an eye on commercial opportunity. But the Diary is different in the way such violent acts are laced together with underlying emotional sensitivity. Time and again there are gratuitous references to feelings that are quite clearly genuine and events that are recounted nowhere else. Additional material – such as the "trial" murder in Manchester, or the hatred of Maybrick for his young clerk Lowry – could have been extremely risky inclusions for a forger and might have easily been exposed.

There is no reference material from which the Diary's intensely perceptive understanding of James Maybrick can be gleaned: his jealousy of his brother Michael, affection for the weaker brother Edwin, loneliness, confusion. Its complex content and psychological insight are those of a man who understands and who has suffered the agony he describes, those of a man who adores his young son and daughter but who can write of fears that he could kill them; of a tormented man who loves his wife but speaks of cutting her up and serving her to the children, a cannibal who begs forgiveness and longs to join his dead parents.

"I took some of it away with me. It is in front of me. I intend to fry it and eat it later *ha ha*. The very thought works up my appetite. I cannot stop the thrill of writing. I ripped open my God I will have to stop thinking of the children they distract me so I ripped open...

"I miss Edwin. I have received but one letter from him since his arrival in the whores country...I visited my mother and fathers grave. I long to be reunited with them...

"I have received several letters from Michael. In all he enquires about my health and asked in one if my sleepwalking has resumed. Poor Michael he is so easily fooled. I have informed him it has not. My hands still remain cold. I shall be dining tonight. I hope kidneys are on the menu...

"At this moment I have no feeling in my body, none at all. I keep assuring myself I have done no wrong. It is the whore who has done so, not I. Will peace of mind ever come? I have visited Hopper too often this month. I will have to stop, for I fear he may begin to suspect. I talk to him like no other."

Bruce Robinson, Oscar nominee for his script of *The Killing Fields*, has said, "If this Diary is a forgery – which I do not believe it is – and if I had written it, I should consider it to be the summit of my literary achievement."

The mountain of material which has been gathered, both for and against the Diary, has left many people baffled. There are a number of problems still unresolved. Research continues. Since the original uproar, we have consistently tried to pursue the scientific investigations into the ink, in particular, using some of the country's most sophisticated equipment. But this has been a confusing experience and the results often contradictory. Most infuriating of all has been our tussle over a little known chemical preservative, chloroacetamide. I looked into the background of chloroacetamide and discovered that it was a very complex substance, first cited in the Merck Index in 1857 and used since in the production of, among other things, woollen goods and probably paper.

It was said by Melvin Harris that it was only used commercially on a very small scale in ink production from 1972. Most importantly it was used by Diamine Ltd, a Liverpool manufacturer who specializes in "Victorian" manuscript inks. Mr Harris arranged for samples taken from the Diary in America to be brought to England in sealed capsules and tested for chloroacetamide. Analysis for Industry conducted the tests and found that indeed there was a minute amount of the substance. For the critics of the Diary this was proof positive.

But I was unhappy, both that the samples tested had come from America and that the amount shown was so small. I decided to ask Leeds University to take their own samples, directly from the Diary and, like Analysis for Industry, to test then for chloroacetamide. On a first test, they too found a minuscule amount of the chemical, but on a second examination there was none and they concluded that the first result was because of contamination. I also invited Analysis For Industry to test the paper of the Diary for chloroacetamide in case it had bled into the ink from that source. There was none.

At the end of the day I was totally confused. I wrote for help to ICI, at the Wilton Research Centre, Manchester, which houses the finest equipment in Europe for examining ink. Dr David Briggs replied: "All this amounts to several days' work at the cost of £1,000 a day. I have to stress once again that this is not a simple standard test, far from it…Given the uncertainties, I do not therefore recommend that you pursue this approach." What more could I do?

The Diary is an enigmatic, endlessly fascinating discovery. Once handled, it is insidious, impossible to forget. Some say it is evil.

The circumstantial evidence largely supports those who believe it to be, at the very least, a historic document of, so far, uncertain date. As such it should be studied seriously and this is the route I hope we can now pursue. I was greatly encouraged by the approach from the Department of Psychology at Liverpool University to participate in the September 1998 seminar with Professor David Canter and Keith Skinner to discuss the Diary's psychological content. This is exactly the standard of reasoned debate I would like to see in future.

Meanwhile, the watch is still ticking away loudly, reminding us all, critics and believers, of that legend on James Maybrick's crest: "Time reveals all."

The Facts Speak for Themselves

Bruce Paley

To best appreciate how a stammering, unemployed 30-year-old fish porter named Joseph Barnett turned into a fearsome and monstrous serial killer, it is necessary to consider both the brutal and impoverished environment from whence he came, and the circumstances that led to his donning the mantle of Jack the Ripper.

There have been worse slums than the East End of London in the latter half of the nineteenth century, but few ever existed in such blatant contrast to the tremendous wealth and prosperity that characterized Victorian Britain. At the time of Barnett's birth in 1858, London was arguably the greatest city on earth, regarded by many as the centre of culture and civilization, while Britain was unchallenged as the world's wealthiest nation.

Yet in the very heart of the capital, people were literally starving, and forced to exist in deplorable conditions of hardship and want. In the East End, the poverty rate was close to 50 per cent and it was here, in Whitechapel, that Barnett was born and raised, in the very same streets that 30 years later, Jack the Ripper would terrorize.

The East End in the latter half of the nineteenth century was a teeming labyrinth of narrow closes, alleyways, passages, yards and courts, crammed with tenement buildings populated largely by labourers and their families. In the early part of the century, it had been largely farmland and pastures, but with the advent of the Industrial Revolution, the area became a favoured site for factories and industry. The promise of employment brought an influx of immigrant workers to the area, many of them Irish or Eastern European Jews, seeking to escape the poverty and persecution they suffered in their native lands. So great was this migration, that the East End quickly became overcrowded, and soon there were far more workers than there were available jobs. At the docks, for example, then a thriving concern, 10,000 people would show up in the predawn hours each morning in the hope of getting a day's work, although jobs only existed for about half that number, and in some instances, as many as 20 men might compete for a single position.

One result of such terrific job competition was that employers were able to keep wages down to an absolute minimum. At the same time, inadequate housing forced labourers and working-class families to move to less savoury areas, where they mingled with the criminal element. But at least rents were affordable, and labourers could be close to their workplaces. This was often a necessity: casual dock workers, for example, would begin queuing for jobs at around 3.00 am, while market porters, costermongers, and others also had to show up for work in the early morning hours. Many women, who did piecemeal work from home, needed to be near to their employers as well in order to pick up and drop off their work.

Such jobs, in the so-called "sweated" trades, were one of a limited number of options available to unmarried, abandoned, or widowed women who were forced to fend for themselves. In Victorian England, most girls were raised solely to become housewives, and received little in the way of proper education or job training beyond the skills required to keep house.

The majority of working women found employment as domestic servants, while those who could took positions as teachers, shop attendants, clerks and bookkeepers. But for those unqualified or unsuited for such work, the only legitimate alternative was menial factory work, light industrial jobs or employment in the sweated trades. Almost without exception, the work was long and tedious, and conditions were often unhealthy and unhygienic, if not downright dangerous.

Payment was determined solely by production, and even with the help of children, if there were any, earnings were extremely low. In many cases women had to buy their own tools or equipment, while employers offered no compensation for slack periods or time lost because of illness or incapacitation.

It's no surprise then, that many otherwise respectable women turned to prostitution simply to survive. Although earnings on the streets were erratic, because of the often fierce competition, a woman could sometimes earn as much in a night as she could in an entire week toiling in a sweatshop. Henry Mayhew, in his pioneering survey of London's working class and poor (*London Labour and the London Poor*, first published in 1851), found that as many as one out of every four workers in the sweated trades also worked as prostitutes. The Metropolitan Police estimated that there were some 1,200 prostitutes in Whitechapel alone, while William Booth, the founder of the Salvation Army, declared that there were between 60,000 and 80,000 full- or part-time prostitutes in London in the 1880s. Although Booth may have exaggerated his figures, there is no question that prostitution in London, and particularly in the East End, was rife.

But while it may have provided a lifeline for some, prostitution was hardly an attractive option, and most women turned to it only out of desperation. Besides the undependable income, women were vulnerable to physical danger and the ever present threat of venereal disease, not to mention the social stigma, shame and likelihood of estrangement from family and friends. Nevertheless, many women felt that they had little choice: as Booth put it, "Sin or starve" was the order of the day.

Many prostitutes and casual labourers, as well as thieves and beggars and others who existed on an irregular wage and lived from day to day, could only afford accommodation in one of the so-called "doss houses", or common lodging houses, that proliferated throughout the East End. In 1888 there were 149 such registered hostels in Whitechapel alone, and countless unlicensed ones as well. In such establishments, a bed could be had for fourpence per night, in a room with perhaps 70 others. For twice as much, a more private bed could be found, and families often stayed in the same doss house for years at a time.

Four of the five victims of Jack the Ripper were living in such places at the time of their deaths; two of them had just been out on the streets when they encountered the Whitechapel Murderer (as the Ripper was initially known) because they had been turned from their regular doss houses as they lacked even the few pence necessary for a night's bed.

It was into this environment then that Joseph Barnett was born on 25 May, 1858, the fourth child of four sons and a daughter born to John and Catherine Barnett, both Irish immigrants. John was 41 at the time of Joseph's birth and worked as a dock labourer and a fish porter at Billingsgate Market, while Catherine, presumably, kept house.

Come summertime, and the Barnetts and thousands of other local families would go on an annual sojourn to the Kent countryside to pick hops, an East End institution that survived well into the twentieth century, when mechanization took over. Although the hours were long and living conditions tended to be inadequate, the work was relatively easy, with the added advantage that the entire family could participate. Even the children pitched in. For many of them, the trip to the countryside served as a holiday and a welcome respite from the deadly smog and pollution of London, where respiratory ailments were then the single greatest cause of death. John Barnett and three of his sons, including Joseph, would all eventually die of lung-related ailments.

At the time, working-class families like the Barnetts tended to move frequently as their fortunes fluctuated. By the time of John Barnett's premature death from pleurisy in 1864, the family had moved house several times, though they always stayed in the East End.

In the wake of John's death, it fell to his widow Catherine to provide for the family, as their eldest son, Denis, was then only 14. But sometime within the next seven years, however, Catherine Barnett inexplicably and mysteriously disappeared, apparently having abandoned her family.

Coupled with the death of her husband, Catherine's disappearance seemed to have a profound and traumatic affect on Joseph, who developed a stammer, and would later display symptoms of a little-known psychological disorder known today as echolalia, in which a person repeats certain words or phrases spoken by another. Common to autistics, echolalia may also be symptomatic of schizophrenia, and can occur as a personality mannerism, or at times of great stress or anxiety.

With both parents gone, Denis Barnett would have had to assume the mantle of family breadwinner, a position he probably held until his marriage in 1869, at which point the next eldest brother, Daniel, then 18, took over.

Like his father before him, Daniel worked as a fish porter at Billingsgate Market, though his struggles to support his three siblings were such that a couple of years later the family was living in one of the worst areas of the East End, in a small, overcrowded street a mile north from where Joseph had been born, that would soon be condemned by the Medical Officer for Health as being unfit for human habitation.

Despite the hardships they faced, Daniel saw to it that his two younger brothers, Joseph and John, remained in school, while their sister Catherine, 17, probably oversaw domestic chores until her marriage in 1871 to a local carman, or driver, named Joseph Beer.

Catherine and Joseph Beer moved out of the East End, but their attempts to raise a family were marred by the deaths of at least four of their infant children, a high mortality rate even for Victorian England, where one of every four infants were to die within a year of their births. At that time, diseases such as scarlet fever, measles, whooping cough, diphtheria, dysentery, tubercular meningitis and phthisis were all major causes of death, as was premature birth.

By 1878, all four Barnett brothers were working as fish porters at Billingsgate Market. Portering, which consisted mainly of unloading and transporting fish, was hard strenuous work that required considerable physical strength. Fish would be packed in large trunks weighing about 6.5 stones each, which porters carried about balanced on their heads. To facilitate this they wore specially designed hats, called bobbins, though these did not prevent porters from going prematurely bald, a common job affliction caused by constant weight and pressure on the scalp.

The porter's work day began at 5.00 am, and generally lasted four hours, although porters who were permanently employed by a market shop generally stayed on for another four or five hours cleaning and packing fish. As Joseph would work at Billingsgate for at least ten years, and considered himself to be "in good work", it is likely that at some point he held such a position.

Like pieceworkers, porters were paid by the amount of work they did, and different tenants often paid different rates, so wages varied, but a steady, diligent worker could earn as much as £3 per week, a considerable sum for a labourer at that time, and one that would put him at the top of his class.

Barnett was still working at Billingsgate Market in April 1887 when he met the young prostitute Mary Jane Kelly, who would end up as the final victim of Jack the Ripper. Twenty-two or twenty-three years old at the time, Kelly was by all accounts an attractive woman, who stood 5 feet 7 inches tall, (the same height as Barnett) and was fresh-faced with blue eyes and a full, fine head of waist length hair.

It was Kelly's youth and freshness that set her apart from many of her fellow prostitutes. The East End at the time was full of middle-aged, often alcoholic women, widowed or separated or abandoned by their husbands, for whom life was little more than a daily struggle for survival, an unbroken quest for the next drink and a bed in a doss house at the end of the day. All of the Ripper victims except for Kelly herself fell into this category.

Despite her youth, however, Kelly had already fallen far. Born in Ireland, she had come from a large, stable family that relocated to Wales. At 16, Kelly is said to have married a local collier who was tragically killed in a mining accident a year or two later. She then went to stay with a cousin in Cardiff, who introduced her to prostitution, and probably to alcohol as well, as Kelly soon became a heavy drinker.

Around 1884, Kelly arrived in London, where she worked out of a brothel for a time, before drifting over to the squalid East End, her rapid decline evidently hastened by alcohol. In the East End, Kelly first got involved with a man named Morganstone, before taking up with Joseph Fleming, a mason's plasterer. The couple apparently planned to marry, but split up instead, although the couple remained close, and Fleming would visit Kelly and give her money when he could, even after she was living with Joseph Barnett.

Although Joseph Barnett disapproved of prostitutes, it appears that he first met Kelly as a customer, and they set up house together the very next day. To Barnett, still single at 29 and suffering from a speech impediment, the young, fresh and pretty Kelly must have seemed like a terrific catch, and he seems to have become quite smitten with her, to the point of sexual obsession.

To Mary Kelly, Barnett may have seemed a welcome change from the sort of men she was probably used to. Barnett had had some education, was fairly articulate, could read and write, and even seemed to fancy himself as something of a toff. Sketches of Barnett testifying at Kelly's inquest show an elegant, dapper-looking man in a waistcoat and cravat with neatly combed hair and moustache, who favoured a top hat, hardly the typical attire of a Billingsgate fish porter, a breed infamous for their coarseness and vulgarity.

All things considered, however, Kelly's interest in Barnett seemed to be based more on convenience than it was on romance, and if she had been initially impressed with him, she later grew to despise him. But given her circumstances and their environment, the value of a good, steady earner like Barnett was not to be underestimated, and not only did he secure them a regular room, and provide for them well, but Barnett also kept Kelly off the streets, something that was very important to him. He was also quite kind to Kelly, spoiling her with gifts, and giving her money when he could, and for some time at least things seemed to go well for the couple.

Barnett and Kelly lived in three different East End locales before settling into a tiny room at 13 Miller's Court, 26 Dorset Street, one of the very worst streets in the East End, widely known as a centre for crime, gambling and prostitution. So bad was its reputation that it was said that even the police were wary of entering it.

Although only about 150 yards long, with a pub at each end and several nearby, the narrow thoroughfare housed 1,500 people, most of whom lived in one of its 13 registered doss houses. One such hostel was Crossingham's Lodging House at 35 Dorset Street, which was situated almost directly opposite Miller's Court.

For 4 shillings and six pence per week, Barnett and Kelly got a shabby and unkempt 12-foot-square room that contained little more than a couple of small tables and a narrow bed. The room had its own entrance, as it had been partitioned off from a storage shed known to be a favoured refuge of homeless women.

Barnett, who was either guilty of self-delusion or of creating a false facade, claimed that he and Kelly lived together comfortably, but in fact their relationship came to be punctuated by frequent, even violent rows that were triggered by Kelly's drinking, as she was the kind of alcoholic who underwent a drastic personality change when drunk. Those who knew Kelly described her as a nice, quiet, decent and likeable woman who inevitably became quarrelsome and abusive when drunk, which, by all accounts, was quite often. "I have frequently seen (Kelly) the worse for drink," a close friend later testified, "but when she was cross, Joe Barnett would go out and leave her to quarrel alone."

In April 1888, when Barnett and Kelly had been together for a year, there occurred a precursor to the Jack the Ripper murders, when Emma Smith, a 45-year-old local prostitute, was brutally murdered. This was followed a few months later by the fatal stabbing of a second prostitute, both of whom, coincidentally, had lived on the same street as Barnett and Kelly once had, perhaps even at the same time.

Despite its well-deserved reputation as a nefarious and violent place, murder was actually an extremely rare occurrence in the East End. In the two years prior, not a single homicide had taken place in Whitechapel, so the brutal murders of two prostitutes created quite a stir in the community. The killings would have held particular significance to Mary Kelly, who may have known the two women personally; if not, then she at least would have known who they were, as all three women were hard-drinking local prostitutes, who had not only once lived on the very same street, but in all likelihood worked the same areas and frequented the same pubs. Kelly could not have helped but to have felt a strong identification with them, and it may have been her fearful reaction to their deaths that initially inspired Barnett to kill.

Around the time of the second murder, when Barnett and Kelly had been together for about 15 months, an incident occurred that would set in motion a sequence of events that would culminate with the death of Mary Kelly herself at the hands of Jack the Ripper: after over ten years working at Billingsgate Market, Joseph Barnett inexplicably lost his job. Although there is no record of any reason for his dismissal, it's very likely that he was caught stealing, an offence that automatically carried the maximum penalty. Barnett seemed very eager to please Kelly and sought to buy her favour with frequent gifts "such as meat and *other things*" (as he later put it), referring perhaps to the fish he may have been smuggling out of the market as a treat for Kelly.

The loss of Barnett's job changed everything, particularly the nature and balance of his relationship with Kelly. Although he managed to find some work at the docks and fruit markets, Barnett would never again be able to support Kelly in the style to which she had become accustomed. The average casual dock worker took home only about one-ninth of what Barnett was earning at Billingsgate Market and, given the prevailing economic conditions, it would be impossible for him to find another job that paid even nearly as well. It thus fell to Kelly to supplement Barnett's meagre earnings, the only way she could. As the *Daily Telegraph* would observe, "(Barnett and Kelly) seemed to pay their way honourably; but earnings were often irregular and then it is to be feared that the woman resorted to the streets."

With the loss of his job, Barnett had relinquished his greatest asset, and he knew that without his steady income he would be of little use to Kelly. If she had tolerated him before, or had even felt some affection for Barnett, it had long since faded. As Kelly would confide to her friend Julia Venturney, she could no longer bear to be with Barnett, and regretted having split from Joseph Fleming.

Barnett knew that he was running out of time, and if he was going to prevent Kelly from leaving him, then drastic measures were called for. Driven by his unrequited love and sexual obsession with Kelly – a twisted and overpowering emotion responsible for countless homicides to this day – Joseph Barnett concocted a desperate plan in which he would *frighten* Mary Kelly off the streets by murdering and mutilating a series of prostitutes, leaving their disembowelled bodies lying out in the open as a warning for all to see. At the same time, it must be pointed out that Barnett was equally driven by whatever psychological compulsions and disorders that a person capable of committing such atrocities invariably possessed. Research into the subject has revealed that serial killers have been known to take jobs as butchers or hospital or mortuary attendants in which they can vicariously experience their morbid, destructive, fantasies. For Joseph Barnett, it was no great leap from gutting fish to mutilating women. Certainly he had the dexterity with a knife and the practice in using it that the Ripper demonstrated.

Where several physicians were of the opinion that the murderer had some surgical skill, Dr D. G. Halstead, who was stationed at London Hospital at the time and had spent time in the North Sea, recorded in his memoirs that "the great surgical skill which (Jack the Ripper) used to apply to his female victims could easily have been picked up by a man accustomed to boning and filleting fish".

And for a while Barnett's ploy worked: at the height of the Ripper's reign of terror, nary a prostitute could be found on the East London streets after the pubs closed, and for a couple of months longer, at any rate, he and Kelly remained together. If nothing else, Barnett had bought himself some time.

The Whitechapel Murderer first struck in the early hours of 31 August 1888, shortly after Barnett lost his job. His victim was Mary Ann "Polly" Nichols, a 43-year-old alcoholic prostitute who had resided at lodging houses a couple of minutes' walk from Dorset Street, where Barnett and Kelly were then living. Turned out of one of her regular haunts because she lacked the four pence necessary for a bed, Nichols was found a few hours later lying in the road near the Whitechapel train station, not far from a busy thoroughfare. Her throat had been slit, and she had been cut so severely that her bowels were protruding from her abdomen. The press erroneously linked the killing to the previous two, and an atmosphere of panic and terror began to take root in the East End.

Eight days later the still unnamed killer claimed his second victim. The mutilated remains of "Dark" Annie Chapman, a prostitute in her late 40s, were found in the backyard of a local tenement building. Her abdomen was ripped open and a portion of her intestines had been strewn over her shoulder, while her throat had been cut so deeply that the police surgeon speculated that the killer may have been trying to sever Chapman's head.

In the months prior to her death, Chapman had been staying at Crossingham's Lodging House, at 35 Dorset Street, opposite Miller's Court. Prior to that, she had been a habitué of the doss house at 30 Dorset Street, two doors away from Barnett and Kelly, while one newspaper would later report that Chapman had been a friend of Kelly's.

The press sensationally played up the latest killing, and the climate of fear that had taken root in the East End now erupted into outright mayhem. Anxious, agitated crowds in their thousands gathered around the latest murder site, while mobs attacked "suspicious" passers-by and besieged the police stations. Bizarre rumours circulated, such as the one that claimed that the killer had scrawled a message saying he would kill several more women. As one paper noted, the "butchery" of Annie Chapman had driven the inhabitants of Whitechapel nearly crazy, and had left them "paralysed with fear".

Much out of character, the locals turned to the police for help, but despite employing the tried-and-true detection methods of meticulously combing the neighbourhood for clues and interviewing countless people, the police were unable to track down the unseen killer who struck at random and seemingly without motive, and left behind no useful clues or evidence.

At that time, the effectiveness of fingerprinting had yet to be demonstrated, while forensic science – including the practice of psychological profiling – was in its nascent stages. Yet if they did sometimes act foolish, and were guilty of being inflexible in their methods, the police nonetheless fared no worse than many of their modern counterparts. Even with the advantage of modern sophisticated detection methods, many modern-day serial killers have killed far more people and over a much greater length of time than did Jack the Ripper.

Three weeks after the Chapman killing things were beginning to die down somewhat when the Whitechapel Murderer struck again, this time in the most spectacular fashion yet. In the early hours of 30 September, he killed twice in the same night, each time barely escaping discovery.

The night's first victim, 44-year-old "Long" Liz Stride (who stood only 5 feet 5 inches tall but had a long face) was killed in a dark courtyard adjoining a Jewish Socialist club. While the inhabitants of the building sang songs, the killer slit Stride's throat, and was probably about to begin his ritual mutilations when the unmistakable sounds of an approaching pony and cart forced him to flee, only a minute or so before the driver, a club member, arrived on the scene.

In the years preceding her death, the heavy-drinking Stride had been living at the lodging house at 38 Dorset Street, only a couple of dozen yards from Barnett and Kelly, while the night's second victim, 46-year-old Catharine Eddowes, was known to have sheltered in the abandoned shed favoured by homeless women located at 26 Dorset Street, the very same address where Barnett and Kelly lived. In fact, Barnett and Kelly's room actually adjoined the shed, and it's hard to imagine that Eddowes and Barnett would not have encountered one another. At the very least, they would have known one another by sight.

This was probably the case with all of the victims. As someone who had spent his entire life living and working on the same East End streets as they did, Barnett was a familiar local figure, and as Kelly's boyfriend he was probably known to her peers. Barnett may have even been personally acquainted with some of, if not all of the murdered women, as three of the first four victims had been living in Dorset Street at the time of their deaths, while the other, Polly Nichols, lived only a few short minutes' walk away. In any case, Barnett's familiarity alone would have enabled him to approach his victims in the early morning hours without causing alarm, even during the height of Jack the Ripper's reign of terror. This allowed Barnett to get the jump on them, as all the victims had been taken by surprise.

About 45 minutes after he murdered Liz Stride, Barnett resurfaced 1,000 yards south of the scene of the first crime, having taken a circuitous route through the familiar streets he grew up in, to avoid detection.

Knowing that the neighbourhood would soon be aswarm with police, Barnett may have been heading for the Orange Market that adjoined Mitre Square, the second murder site, on the pretext of seeking work. Vendors were already gearing up for the next day's business, and as Barnett had recently been working as an orange hawker – perhaps even in that very same market – it would have provided him with a perfectly logical reason to have been on the streets at that hour.

But just as he arrived there, Barnett unexpectedly encountered the intoxicated Catharine Eddowes, and as his sadistic craving had gone unsatiated (and, as will be seen, he had been unable to keep a promise he made to the police), Barnett probably found her too tempting a target to resist. Perhaps this is why he sacrificed his customary caution and risked being seen, as a passer-by noticed a woman whom he later identified as Eddowes (by her distinctive clothing) talking to a man who matched the description of Joseph Barnett. The couple were standing near the entrance to Mitre Square, where Eddowes would be found dead and mutilated less than ten minutes later. Although there would be other "eyewitness" reports – some of which fit Barnett's description, some of which didn't – this account in particular was given credence by Major Henry Smith, the acting Commissioner of the City Police, under whose jurisdiction Eddowes's murder had fallen.

Unlike his peers in the CID, Smith never sought to save face by ludicrously claiming that he had had some secret knowledge of the Ripper's identity; rather, he admitted that the killer had completely outfoxed and outsmarted him. But after personally interviewing the witness, a cigarette trader named Joseph Lawende, Smith became absolutely convinced that the man was telling the truth. For one thing, unlike so many other so-called "witnesses", Lawende wasn't seeking the infamy or notoriety that came with an involvement in the sensational drama then unfolding – in fact he neither knew nor cared very much about it. Instead, he had been ferreted out by the police during a subsequent house-to-house search of the neighbourhood. Smith was further impressed by the fact that he was unable to sway Lawende from his story with trick questions, and later recorded in his memoirs that "without doubt" Lawende had seen Jack the Ripper with one of his victims.

For the second time that night, the Whitechapel Murderer was almost caught with one of his victims when the distinct sound of boots clomping against the pavement alerted Barnett to the approach of a police constable. He quickly fled, though not before he had slit Eddowes's throat, sliced open her abdomen and removed her kidneys. He also disfigured her face, and managed to slice off part of her right ear, which in his haste got lost among the folds of her clothing.

Barnett's escape was once again facilitated by his intimate knowledge of the myriad nooks and crannies of the Whitechapel streets, but this time he left a trail behind him in the form of a piece of blood-stained cloth torn from Eddowes's apron, which led Major Smith to a bloody sink in Dorset Street, where, of course, Barnett lived (although as Mary Kelly was still alive, this would have had no significance at the time). Although Smith never gave the precise location of the sink, there was a water tap in Miller's Court, just outside Barnett and Kelly's room.

In fact, not only did Barnett live very close to all of his victims, but he also lived within a few minutes' walk of all of the murder sites. Were imaginary circles to be drawn around the scenes of all the murders, the victim's addresses at the time of their death and Joseph Barnett's 11 known addresses up to that time, then the three circles would overlap considerably, with Dorset Street the centre of activity. This equates with what Britain's leading psychological criminal profiler Professor David Canter calls the "circle hypothesis", wherein a criminal is often found to be living within an area circumscribed by his crimes. Canter also found that a large percentage of serial killers live within a few minutes' walk of their crimes.

The double murder had already sent the East End into a frenzy, whence came the startling revelation that the Central News Agency had received a letter and follow-up postcard purported to have been written by the killer, who called himself Jack the Ripper, the first use of that chilling nom de plume.

The letter read as follows:

Dear Boss
I keep on hearing the police
have caught me but they wont fix
me just yet. I have laughed when
they look so clever and talk about
being on the *right* track. That joke
about Leather Apron gave me real
fits. I am down on whores and
I shant quit ripping them till I
do get buckled. Grand work the last
job was. I gave the lady no time to
squeal. How can they catch me now.
I love my work and want to start

again. You will soon hear of me
with my funny little games.
I saved some of the proper *red* stuff in
a ginger beer bottle over the last job
to write with but it went thick
like glue and I cant use it. Red
ink is fit enough I hope *ha. ha.*
The next job I do I shall clip
the ladys ears off and send to the
police officers just for jolly wouldnt
you. Keep this letter back till I
do a bit more work then give
it out straight. My knife's so nice
and sharp I want to get to work
right away if I get a chance.
Good luck.
Yours truly
Jack the Ripper
Dont mind me giving the trade name.
wasnt good enough
to post this before
I got all the red
ink off my hands curse it.
No luck yet. They
say I'm a doctor
now. *ha ha*

The postcard, smeared with ink and undated, read as follows:

I wasnt codding
dear old Boss when
I gave you the tip.
youll hear about
saucy Jackys work
tomorrow, double
event this time

number one squealed
a bit couldnt
finish straight
off. had not time
to get ears for
police thanks for
keeping last letter
back till I got
to work again.
Jack the Ripper

The letter was postmarked 27 September, which means it was sent two days before the double murder. The postcard was franked 1 October, the day after the murders.

Both were initially generally regarded as a joke, or a hoax, but the name caught on, and, bizarrely, the press and police were soon deluged with thousands of copycat letters signed "Jack the Ripper". One even contained a portion of a kidney that may or may not have come from Catharine Eddowes's body.

In any case the first letter and postcard were undoubtedly genuine. For one thing, they accurately predicted the next murder. Previous killings, including the first two unrelated murders, had occurred at random intervals, so there was no way for anyone other than the killer to have known when the murderer would next strike, yet the writer is smug and confident enough to suggest that his letter be held back in order for him to show that he is indeed the killer. Had the double murder not followed so closely on its heels, then the letter would have been rendered meaningless and insignificant and would have been quickly forgotten. Had it not been for the unexpected flood of copycat letters, then there probably would have been further communications from Jack the Ripper himself.

Secondly, there was no way for anyone other than the killer himself to have guessed that he would have tried to do anything so bizarre as to slice off the victim's ears, something that had not been done before. But the attempt had been made; as Dr Frederick Gordon Brown, the City Police surgeon later observed at her inquest, Eddowes's right ear had been sliced through, and as he was examining her body, "the missing piece of ear dropped out of (her) clothing". As the killer explained, he "had not the time to get ears for police". As the existence of the letter had been kept from the public as requested, at that time only the killer would have known that not only had the promise been made, but also that it had not been kept. (Nor is there any doubt that the letter and postcard were written by the same hand, given the references in the letter to the former, the similarity of the handwriting, and the use of phrases common to both.)

It's curious too that the writer noted that "Number one (Stride) squealed a bit", when no one in the vicinity had reported to have heard any sound at all. But why say it unless it was true? As only the killer would have known, Elizabeth Stride must have managed a brief stifled cry that was drowned out by the sounds of singing coming from the Jewish socialist club.

If the letter and postcard were indeed genuine, then it's obvious by their macabre contents and devilish tone that their intent was to terrify. And their words were intended specifically for Mary Kelly's ears.

"I am down on *whores*", the killer wrote, singling out his targets, "and I shant quit ripping them until I do get buckled (caught)... I love my work and want to start again... You will soon hear of me with my funny little games... My knifes so nice and sharp..."

And Barnett knew that his gruesome message would reach Kelly, because, in a stroke of perverted genius, it would be Barnett himself who would personally deliver it to her. As he later explained at her inquest, Kelly's fear of the Ripper was such that she would have Barnett go out and buy the newspapers so that he could read to her the latest news about the killer.

This is why the letter and postcard were sent to the press, rather than to the police. And by sending it to the Central News Agency, instead of to a specific newspaper, Barnett knew that his message would get the widest possible exposure, as it would be carried by every single London newspaper.

At the same time, the letter provided an outlet for the killer to gloat about his cleverness. Barnett had been born and raised in poverty and despite his affectations and apparent intelligence, toiled away in anonymity and frustration, held back, perhaps, as much by his stammer as by his class and the economic realities of the East End. But as the Whitechapel Murderer he had suddenly become the most talked-about and feared person in the country. He had outwitted the police and authorities, his deeds filled the newspapers day after day and his name was on everybody's lips in every pub and at every street corner. Now, through the letter and postcard, Barnett could at last celebrate his newly found infamy.

As intended, the back-to-back impact of the double murder and the Jack the Ripper letter virtually emptied the East End streets of prostitutes, who were nowhere to be seen after closing time. This included Mary Kelly. As *The Times* later reported, a police sergeant making enquiries into Kelly's death discovered that she had stopped frequenting her local pub, where she used to go nightly, since around the time of the double murder, and it was about this time as well that Kelly and Barnett stopped paying their rent, further indication that Kelly was no longer soliciting.

Not surprisingly, there then followed the longest gap without a killing since the Ripper had first struck, an interlude that would end with the most shocking and brutal death of all, that of Mary Kelly herself.

After a few weeks of being forced to stay in a tiny room with the suffocating presence of a man she could not bear, Mary Kelly disregarded Barnett's objections and took in a prostitute friend, Julia (possibly Julia Venturney), to stay with her and Barnett. This was a great affront to Barnett. Not only did this mean that the three of them would have to co-exist in a tiny, cramped room that contained only one narrow bed, but Barnett also feared that Julia's presence might influence Kelly to return to prostitution.

But Kelly would have welcomed the presence of a friend in whom she could confide, and who would also provide a distraction from Barnett, for no sooner did Julia move out than Kelly took in a second friend to stay with them, Maria Harvey.

This proved to be more than Barnett could take, and he gave Kelly an ultimatum: she must choose between either Mrs Harvey or himself. But if this was meant to be a show of bravado, Barnett had misread the situation, and Kelly called his bluff. At 5.00 pm or 6.00 pm on the evening of 1 October, Kelly and Barnett engaged in a violent row in which objects were thrown and two window panes were broken. The outcome saw Barnett move into a nearby lodging house, promising to return once Mrs Harvey had left. (If there had been any question as to who was the dominant one in the relationship, Barnett's departure left no doubt, and despite the fact that he had long been the breadwinner, their room had actually been rented in Kelly's name.)

It was also around this time that the key to Kelly's room disappeared, something that would eventually take on considerable significance.

Without Barnett's income, however meagre it may have been, Mary Kelly now had no choice but to risk the danger and return to the streets simply to survive – if she had not already done so. As Barnett told Inspector Abberline, only hours after Kelly's death, "in consequence of (my) not earning enough money to give her, and her resorting to prostitution, I resolved on leaving her".

But Barnett quickly changed his story. In a statement given to the Central News Agency published two days later, Barnett stated that "Marie (as he called her) never went on the streets when she lived with me. She would never have gone wrong again and I should never have left if it had not been for the prostitutes stopping in the house." Testifying at Kelly's inquest three days later, Barnett again put the onus for his departure on Kelly's friends, rather than on himself. "My being out of work had nothing to do with it," he insisted, blatantly contradicting what he had told Inspector Abberline only three days earlier. Yet Abberline, who was present at the inquest, either didn't notice the curious discrepancy in Barnett's remarks, or thought it to be of no significance.

In any case, Barnett and Kelly were soon back on good terms. Whatever animosity she may have felt towards Barnett may have eased with his departure, and Kelly couldn't deny that he had been kind to her, and had kept her off the streets and had provided well for them. Nor was she in any position to refuse any help he might offer her.

Barnett first visited Kelly the day after he moved out, and he stopped by almost daily thereafter, giving Kelly money when he could, and biding his time until Mrs Harvey left, at which time, as he had promised, he would move back in.

Or so Barnett believed.

If Mary Kelly was glad to be free of Barnett, she was nevertheless worse off now than she had ever been. For a young and attractive woman from a stable family background, she had fallen extremely far. Still only 24 or 25 years old, Kelly was now an alcoholic and a low-class prostitute with no money to speak of and no prospects for the future. She was living in a tiny, squalid room in one of the sleaziest and most disreputable streets in the East End, and unless she could somehow come up with the six weeks' back rent that she owed, she would soon be homeless – a frightening prospect with winter fast approaching and the spectre of Jack the Ripper still haunting the East End streets. (On top of everything else, there has been considerable speculation that Kelly was pregnant, which would have further complicated her already precarious situation.)

Not surprisingly, Kelly's friends found her very despondent at this time, given to despair and even contemplating suicide. "About the last thing she said to me", Kelly's friend Lizzie Albrook told the press, "was 'whatever you do, don't go wrong and turn out as I have'…She told me, too", Albrook continued, "(that) she was heartily sick of the life she was leading and wished she had money enough to go back to Ireland where her people lived". Another friend called Margaret saw Kelly on the last night of her life. "She told me she had no money and intended to make away with herself," Margaret said.

On the evening of 8 November, Barnett visited Kelly in her room. He later said that he told her that he was out of work, and was sorry that he couldn't give her any money.

Barnett did not say what else they talked about in the hour or so that they were together, but as Mrs Harvey had moved out a couple of days earlier, Barnett would have been expecting to move back in with Kelly, as he had promised to do once Mrs Harvey had left.

But Kelly didn't want him back. However poor her circumstances, her options were greater and her life less complicated without Barnett.

Precisely what passed between them during their first meeting that night can never of course be known. Perhaps Kelly tried to reason with

Barnett, explaining that even if they didn't live together they could still be friends, or it may have been that alcohol got the better of Kelly, as it often did, and she bluntly told Barnett what she thought of him. Whatever the case, Barnett was apparently so distraught that his brother Daniel went to see Kelly later that night, probably to plead Barnett's case for him.

Kelly appears to have been affected by the meeting as well, for she later went out and got extremely drunk, and apparently took two different men back to her room before retiring for the night.

But it was not to be. Some time in the early hours of the morning, Joseph Barnett let himself back into Kelly's room by reaching through one of the broken window panes and manipulating the catch, a method of entry that he and Kelly had devised after the key to the room had disappeared.

Once again precisely what passed between the couple can never be known, but it was probably something of a replay of their session earlier that evening in which Barnett argued and pleaded with Kelly to take him back, and she refused to do so. But whatever the exact form of the exchange, what passed between them was enough to pitch Barnett into a frenzied rage during which he first thrust a sheet over Kelly's head before slitting her throat and then spending several hours mutilating her corpse. Among other atrocities, he disfigured Kelly's face beyond recognition, cut off her breasts, cut her flesh down to the bone, and removed her heart, liver, spleen, uterus, kidneys and a large portion of her intestines.

And in his final ghoulish act, Barnett took Kelly's heart with him when he left.

As it turned out, two neighbours heard a faint cry of "Murder!" at around 3.00 am, but such was the nature of life in the East End that neither of them paid it any attention.

Kelly's body was discovered the next morning when the landlord sent someone round to try to collect some of the back rent that Kelly owed. He saw the corpse when he peered through one of the broken window panes. The police were immediately sent for, and Barnett himself soon arrived on the scene.

As the door to the room was locked, Barnett identified the body by looking through the window, and then was taken to the local police station, where he was questioned for a number of hours by Inspector Abberline, before being released. No record of the interview exists, other than a few remarks made by Barnett and Abberline.

Meanwhile, the landlord broke the door down himself to allow the authorities to enter the room.

It was at Kelly's inquest a few days later that the press noted Barnett's stammer, along with his curious habit of his echolalia. But Barnett's extreme anxiety and nervousness were taken for grief rather than guilt, and his contradictory statements went unnoticed or ignored. Nor did anyone seem to recall that Major Smith claimed to have tracked the killer to Dorset Street on the night of the double murder. In any case, Joseph Barnett was never seriously suspected of being Jack the Ripper, until I presented the case against him myself in an article in the April 1982 issue of *True Crime* Magazine.

Mary Kelly was buried on 19 November 1888, in Leytonstone Cemetery, East London.

Joseph Barnett returned to the anonymity from whence he came, and new information that has just come to light shows that he raised a family before he died on 29 November, 1926, at the age of 68, taking his great secret with him to the grave.

Jack the Ripper meanwhile, was never heard from again.

The puzzle of the locked door and missing key to Mary Kelly's room represents one of the most significant pieces of evidence of all, yet it has been downplayed or altogether ignored by everyone who has written about the case. But the fact is that the door to the room was locked, and the police had the landlord break it down in order to gain entry. This means that the last person to leave the room – the murderer – locked the door behind him.

In other words, Jack the Ripper had somehow come into possession of the key to Kelly's room.

But how could this be? Barnett explained to Inspector Abberline that the key had been missing for some time, and that he and Kelly would enter the room by reaching through the broken window pane and moving back the catch. "It is quite simple," Abberline told the press. But this method of entry only became valid once the window panes had been broken, which means that the key to the room had disappeared on or since the night Barnett moved out. The most likely explanation is that Barnett simply took the key with him when he left, knowing that its possession assured him access to Kelly, if need be. The couple had parted on acrimonious terms following a heated row, but so long as he had the key, Barnett would be able to enter Kelly's room by the alternate means of entry they had devised at any time.

And after having butchered Kelly's body in a frenzied rage, Barnett simply locked the room behind him when he left, hoping perhaps to buy himself a few hours, or even a few days' time before the body was found.

A Summary of the Main Points of the Case Against Joseph Barnett
Joseph Barnett precisely fits the contemporary mould of Jack the Ripper

1 Jack the Ripper knew the East End streets extremely well, as demonstrated by his ability to avoid detection, especially given his two narrow escapes on the night of the double murder.

Joseph Barnett was born and raised in the very same East End streets, and by 1888, had lived close to all of the murder sites.

2 Jack the Ripper was probably known to his victims, given the ease with which he was able to approach them without causing them alarm, even after the first few murders had made prostitutes wary of whom they went with. All the Ripper victims were taken by surprise, and died without putting up a struggle.

As a lifelong East Ender, Joseph Barnett was a familiar local figure, and as Mary Kelly's boyfriend, was probably known to her fellow prostitutes. He may have even been personally acquainted with some, if not all, of the murdered women, as three of the first four victims had lived in Dorset Street at the time of their deaths, while the other lived only a couple of minutes walk away. One of the murdered women, Annie Chapman, was even reported to have been a friend of Kelly's while Catharine Eddowes, victim number four, had sometimes stayed in the shed that adjoined Barnett and Kelly's room.

3 Jack the Ripper was physically strong, proficient with a knife, and had some sort of anatomical knowledge.

Joseph Barnett's job as a fish porter required considerable physical strength, while years of cleaning fish made him handy with a blade. As one local doctor observed, the so-called surgical skill which the Ripper possessed "could easily have been picked up by a man accustomed to boning and filleting fish".

4 An eyewitness report that the acting Commissioner of the City Police Major Henry Smith was convinced was absolutely accurate described Jack the Ripper as being 30 years old, 5 feet 7 inches or 5 feet 8 inches tall, of medium build, with a fair complexion, and a moustache.

Joseph Barnett was 30 years old at the time of the murders, stood 5 feet 7 inches or 5 feet 7.5 inches tall, and was of medium build, with a fair complexion, and a moustache.

5 On the night of the double murder, Major Smith tracked the killer to Dorset Street. Joseph Barnett lived on Dorset Street at the time.

6 Somehow, Jack the Ripper had come into possession of the key to Mary Kelly's room, and used it to lock the door behind him when he left.

The key to Kelly's room disappeared around the time Barnett moved out following a violent row with Kelly. The likelihood is that Barnett took it with him when he left, knowing that its possession guaranteed him access to Kelly's room, if need be, whenever he desired.

7 All of the Ripper victims, (with the possible exception of Catharine Eddowes, who may have only appeared to be one), were known prostitutes. Jack the Ripper singled out prostitutes as his intended targets in the first Jack the Ripper letter.

Barnett strongly disliked prostitutes, blaming them for what he called Mary Kelly's "downfall" and the fact that she had "gone wrong".

8 The obvious intent of the initial, genuine Jack the Ripper letter and postcard was to terrify, and the killer singled out "whores" as his

intended targets. Its author had been to school, as evidenced by the letter's neat and largely grammatically correct (if unpunctuated) hand, written in the copperplate style taught in the schools of the day. Ginger beer bottles were mentioned in the letter.

Mary Kelly lived in fear of Jack the Ripper, and would have Barnett buy the daily newspapers so he could read to her about the latest developments of the case. In that way, Barnett knew that Kelly would hear about the letters, which had been written with her in mind. Barnett had also been to school, and could read and write. Ginger beer bottles were found in the room he and Kelly had shared.

Further points of evidence against Joseph Barnett

1 Testifying at Mary Kelly's inquest, Joseph Barnett blatantly contradicted what he had told the police three days earlier as to why he had left Mary Kelly, though apparently this went unnoticed. The press noted Barnett's nervousness and anxiety in the witness box, although this was seen as symptomatic of grief rather than of guilt.

2 Catharine Eddowes was killed next to an orange market, where Barnett, an orange seller, may have worked. Barnett might have even been heading there, when he unexpectedly ran into Eddowes, who had lived next door to him in Dorset Street. As a known market porter and labourer, Barnett could justify his presence on the streets in the early morning hours if need be, as workers often had to report for such jobs in the middle of the night.

3 When Kelly took in two successive prostitute friends to share their room, Barnett moved out following a violent row, promising to move back in once the women had left. But after they had gone, Barnett never moved back in, even after the women had gone, presumably because Kelly wouldn't have him. Barnett then apparently sent his brother to plead his case, but when Kelly still wouldn't have him back, he murdered her in a fit of rage.

4 After Kelly's death, Jack the Ripper was never heard from again.

Joseph Barnett precisely fits the mould of the modern day serial killer

The former FBI agent and instructor Robert K. Ressler is the world's foremost expert on serial killers. It was he who coined the term "serial killer" and before his retirement Ressler had become the FBI's top criminologist, and most experienced practitioner of criminal psychological profiling, the science he himself helped develop and refine.

In an attempt to gain much needed insight into the mind of the serial killer, Ressler interviewed more multiple murderers than anyone else, before or since, and as a result of his studies, was able to isolate certain fundamental characteristics common to the large majority of serial killers, as outlined in his book *Whoever Fights Monsters* (Simon & Schuster, 1993).

In hindsight, Joseph Barnett *precisely* fits Ressler's profile of the typical serial killer, particularly in the five key points listed below:

1 Most serial killers are white males in their 20s and 30s; most sexual killers are under 35.

Joseph Barnett was 30 years old at the time of the Ripper murders (which fall under the category of sexual murders, even though no physical sexual act took place).

2 Most serial killers come from dysfunctional families, marked by cold, distant and unloving mothers, and absentee fathers. According to Ressler, "potential murderers became solidified in their loneliness first during the age period of eight to 12; such isolation is considered the single most important aspect of their psychological make-up. Many factors go into fashioning this isolation. *Among the most important is the absence of a father* (my italics)."

Joseph Barnett was 6 years old when his father died, and his mother had disappeared by the time he was 13, seemingly having abandoned her family.

3 Many serial killers are intelligent men, often employed in menial jobs far below their true intellectual capabilities.

Unlike many of his peers, Joseph Barnett had been to school, was well spoken, and appears to have been fairly intelligent; he certainly seemed capable of doing something more than the tedious backbreaking labour required of a fish porter.

4 Many serial killers suffer from physical ailments or disabilities.

Joseph Barnett had a speech impediment. He also exhibited signs of echolalia, the psychological disorder that can be symptomatic of schizophrenia, and common to autistics.

5 The initial murderous impulse is often triggered by some sort of stress before the crime, such as the loss of job, the break-up of a relationship, money problems, etc.

The Jack the Ripper murders began shortly after Joseph Barnett lost his long-term, well-paying job, which forced Mary Kelly to return to prostitution, against Barnett's wishes.

6 Professor David Canter has surmised that serial killers often live within an area circumscribed by their crimes, and that knowledge and familiarity with the area is often a prerequisite for violent criminals, many of whom live within a few minutes walk of their crimes.

Joseph Barnett lived within such an area. He had been born and raised in the same East End streets where the Jack the Ripper murders took place, while Dorset Street, where he lived at the time of the murders, was but a few minutes walk from each of the murder sites.

The Ripper Project

The aim of the Ripper Project was to find a solution to the Jack the Ripper murders through the application of modern scientific detection techniques. Among the various experts in forensics and other relevant fields was Supervisory Special Agent of the FBI John E Douglas, a former protégé of Robert Ressler, who adapted the latest FBI techniques to compose a psychological profile of Jack the Ripper.

As was the case with Ressler's studies, the main "perpetrator characteristics", as determined by Douglas, precisely fit Joseph Barnett, in this instance to such an extraordinary degree as to pinpoint specific characteristics unique to Barnett, such as his speech impediment. This can be said of no other Ripper suspect. Douglas's findings were as follows:

1 Jack the Ripper was a white male, aged 28–36, who lived or worked in the Whitechapel area.

Joseph Barnett was 30 years old at the time of the Ripper murders, and had lived and worked his entire life in and around the Whitechapel area.

2 Jack the Ripper would have come from a family with a weak, passive, or absent father.

Joseph Barnett was 6 years old when his father died.

3 Jack the Ripper would have sought a job where he could vicariously experience his destructive fantasies, such as a butcher, mortician's helper, medical examiner's assistant, or hospital attendant.

Joseph Barnett's job cleaning and gutting fish provided the necessary atmosphere wherein he could indulge in his morbid fantasies.

4 Jack the Ripper would probably have had "some type of physical abnormality that, although not severe, he would perceive as psychologically crippling (such as) *a speech impediment* (my italics)".

Joseph Barnett had a speech impediment.

5 Jack the Ripper would have been interviewed during the course of the investigations, but would have been overlooked, and/or eliminated as a suspect, in part because his ordinary appearance would not have fit the preconceived notion that both the police and local populace held of Jack the Ripper as being an odd or "ghoulish"-looking man.

After Mary Kelly's murder Joseph Barnett was interviewed by Inspector Abberline for several hours before being cleared. He did not look out of the ordinary, and was not of an odd or "ghoulish" appearance.

6 Jack the Ripper "would be perceived as being quiet, a loner, shy, slightly withdrawn, obedient, and neat and orderly in appearance. He would drink at the local pubs."

Joseph Barnett was described by one source as looking "very respectable for one of his class", and was in fact a well-dressed man, who took obvious pride in his appearance. The impression is that Barnett was indeed quiet, shy, and somewhat withdrawn, as described above, as people with speech impediments often are. The room Barnett shared with Kelly was rented in her name, even though he paid the rent, and when the couple parted, it was Barnett who left. Following Kelly's death, he was found by a reporter in a local pub.

7 "Jack the Ripper would not have committed suicide after his last homicide. Generally, crimes such as these cease because the perpetrator has come close to being identified, has been interviewed by the police or has been arrested for some other offence. We would be surprised if Jack the Ripper simply would suddenly stop, except for one of these reasons."

The police took Barnett in for questioning after Mary Kelly's murder, and the fact that they held him for up to four hours suggests that they might have initially suspected him of being the murderer. After Kelly's death, Jack the Ripper was never heard from again; Joseph Barnett lived for another 38 years.

8 "Jack the Ripper believed that the homicides were justified – that he was only eliminating garbage."

Joseph Barnett had a strong dislike of prostitutes, and blamed them for Mary Kelly's "downfall" and the fact that she had "gone wrong".

As for the other theories, there are too many to address individually. Suffice to say that those that haven't been discredited by others essentially disprove themselves, and none holds up to close inspection or makes any real sense. Most simply "feel" wrong, and are based on weak and flimsy premises, on top of which they offer dubious circumstantial evidence at best and precious little genuine evidence of any sort.

Many theories seem to operate on a principle that is akin to trying to fit the wrong piece into a slot in a jigsaw puzzle, and bending and forcing it into the hole until it somehow goes in. In such a way are circumstances stretched to accommodate the suspect into the parameters of the crimes, and if contradictions still arise, then these are dealt with by adjusting the parameters. For example, if a suspect was known to be elsewhere at the time of a murder, then rather than accepting the logical conclusion that the suspect could not therefore have been Jack the Ripper, the devisers of such theories would instead have us believe that someone else must have committed that particular murder, and a case is then assembled to prove the point.

Many theories also make the mistake of looking for complex and convoluted solutions that stretch logic and rationale.

But most important of all is the simple but significant fact that in not one of the other theories is a direct and indisputable connection actually proven between the suspect and any of the victims. Nor have any other suspects been reliably placed at or near any of the scenes of the crimes. It is not enough that the suspect was in London, or even in the East End at the time; a connection must be made between suspect and victim(s), and suspect and the scene(s) of the crime(s). These are the basic premises upon which any theory must be founded, and until such a link is established, no theory can be taken seriously.

Only Joseph Barnett both perfectly fits the contemporary mould of Jack the Ripper, while also fitting to an extraordinary degree the complex mould of the modern-day serial killer, as based upon the FBI's latest criminal psychological profiling techniques and their overall knowledge of the makings of a serial killer.

No other theory can make such a claim.

The facts speak for themselves: Joseph Barnett was Jack the Ripper.

This article is essentially a condensation of my book *Jack the Ripper: The Simple Truth* (Headline 1995). For detailed source notes, readers are referred to the book.

The Case of William Bury

Euan Macpherson

When we look at the Jack the Ripper murders, more than one hundred years after the event, the most important fact to consider may well be the sudden cessation of the murders. It is not in the nature of serial-killers to stop; usually, they behave as if they are addicted to the thrill of the chase and cannot stop but go on until they are caught.

That suggests that we have two main lines of enquiry when hunting the Ripper. The first is to assume that something happened to make the Ripper stop in November 1888. Perhaps he died; perhaps he was incarcerated in prison for a relatively minor crime with no one knowing who he was. The second line of enquiry is to assume that he did not stop. We know there were no more "Ripper" murders in London after 1888 but could there have been murders elsewhere? What if, at the height of the investigation, Jack the Ripper simply moved out of London and stalked another British city for his next victim?

This means that, if we are to look for Jack the Ripper, there is a logical line of enquiry we can follow. We can look for a killer who murdered women in the style of Jack the Ripper and who was also living in the East End of London during the second half of 1888. Such a man does, in fact, exist. His name was William Henry Bury and he first became a suspect for the Whitechapel atrocities when he walked into the Central Police Office, Dundee, at 6.50 pm on Sunday, 10 February 1889.

Bury asked for an interview with the officer on duty and was taken into a private room where he came out with a peculiar story. He said that he lived in an apartment at 113 Princes Street, Dundee, and that he and his wife had been at home drinking heavily on the night of 4 February and that he did not know at what time he went to bed. He awoke next morning at about 10 am and was surprised to find that his wife was not in bed with him. On looking around the apartment, he saw her lying on the floor. He called to her but got no response.

Getting up and going over to her, Bury discovered that she was lying dead on the floor with a rope around her neck. He was then seized with a mad impulse; after looking at her dead body for a minute to two, he picked up a knife and plunged it several times into her abdomen. He then packed the woman's body into a box.

Bury was asked, if this had happened on 4 February, why did it take him till 10 February to contact the police? He replied that he was afraid he would be arrested as "Jack the Ripper." It is clearly not logical that a man whose wife had committed suicide in Dundee should be suspected of the crimes of Jack the Ripper in London. However, Bury was not asked to explain this. Instead, he was detained at the police station while his basement flat was searched by candlelight.

The apartment was bare with very little furniture. Police officers quickly spotted a large wooden box, or trunk. When they took the lid off, they found themselves looking at a woman's body. Her intestines were seen poking through the stab wounds in her abdomen and her right leg had been broken to make it fit into the box. They did not examine the body, leaving that task to the police surgeon. On continuing their search, they found a knife with blood, flesh and hair on it and a rope. They also found a woman's ulster, or jacket, which was heavily bloodstained and had large rips in it indicating that the knife had been plunged into it with considerable force. But another, more intriguing, discovery was also made that night. Written on chalk on a door were the words "Jack Ripper is at the back of this door." On going through the door, more writing was found on a wall, viz: "Jack Ripper is in this seller" (sic).

In the deadhouse, or mortuary, Dr Templeman examined the victim's injuries and concluded that it would have been impossible for her to have inflicted these injuries upon herself. He believed that she had been strangled from behind and scratches on William Bury's right wrist indicated that she had scratched him as she fought for her life.

William Bury was arrested and charged with murder. The date of his trial was fixed for 28 March. Meanwhile, people were not slow to spot the similarity between the murder in Dundee and the recent murders in Whitechapel. This, allied to the fact that the accused had recently been living in the East End of London, led to rumours spreading through the streets that Jack the Ripper had come to Dundee.

So who was this man who had recently turned up in Dundee? Was he none other than Jack the Ripper himself? Or was he merely a copycat killer? Not much is known about William Bury's early life. He had been born in 1859, the third child of a fishmonger in Stourbridge. By the time he was one year old, his father had died and his mother had been incarcerated in Worcester County and City Lunatic Asylum. By the time he was five years old, both his parents were dead.

He was brought up by an aunt in Wolverhampton but was described as having an irritating and quarrelsome nature and lacking in the principles which tend towards success in life. He could not hold down a job. His first job was in a warehouse in Horseley Fields, Wolverhampton. Whether he walked out or got the sack is unclear. His next job was with a locksmith in Lord Street, Wolverhampton. Once again, he lost his job. By the summer of 1887, Bury was selling lead pencils in the street at Snow Hill, Birmingham.

In October 1887, he moved to London and took up employment with James Martin of 80 Quickett Street, Bow. Martin was a brothel-keeper who also ran a sawdust business. Bury was employed to collect sawdust from sawdust mills and take it by pony and cart to public houses and butcher shops, where it was scattered on the floor. No doubt Martin's sawdust business ran at a profit but it was also a convenient cover for the brothel, allowing him to declare income from the brothel as the proceeds of his sawdust business.

One of the perks of working for James Martin was that he allowed his sawdust salesmen who had spent all their wages on drink to sleep in his stables. Bury regularly slept in the stables and it was during this time that he came into contact with a prostitute in Martin's employment called Ellen Elliot.

Ellen was a sickly woman whose poor health had resulted in her missing much of her education. She could not read or write. However, she had recently inherited £300 from an aunt of hers and had used the money to purchase shares in The Union Bank of London. She intended to use the dividends as a supplement to the income she received from prostitution. Perhaps motivated by the fact that Ellen had money, Bury courted her and married her on Easter Monday, 1888. It is from his marriage to Ellen that evidence of his violent nature emerges.

While Ellen was working for James Martin, she rented a room from 50-year-old Elizabeth Haynes on Swaton Road, Campbell Road, Bow. Mrs Haynes described Ellen as a "quiet, respectable woman". When she married Bury, he moved in with her and Mrs Haynes later said that she was obliged to evict them both because of William Bury's "violence and bad language."

The worst example given by Haynes of Bury's violence came late at night on 7 April 1888, when she was wakened by Ellen Bury screaming. She went upstairs to the Burys' room and pushed open the door to find William Bury kneeling on top of his wife and holding a bread knife to her throat. It was only when Mrs Haynes threatened to fetch a policeman that William Bury put down the knife. The next day, Ellen gave Mrs Haynes a key to her room and told Haynes that she was afraid William would lock her in her room and kill her. For this to occur less than a week after the couple were married, when they should have still been hopelessly in love with each other, is astonishing. It is not an ordinary example of domestic violence.

After they were evicted by Mrs Haynes, the Burys took lodgings with William Smith of 3 Spanby Road. Smith later testified that William Bury was always drinking "with the exception of Sundays" and that he (i.e. Smith) was always having to intervene to stop Bury assaulting his wife. His evidence is corroborated by Mrs Margaret Corney, sister of Ellen, who visited her at Spanby Road on one occasion. Ellen told her that William had hit her on the nose and mouth the previous day. Margaret noticed blood on the walls of the passage and guessed that that was where the attack had taken place.

But perhaps the most interesting piece of evidence about Bury's violence comes from James Martin, who also testified that Bury was a drunkard who was violent towards his wife. Martin said that he was in a public house between half past five and six o'clock one morning when

Ellen came in to look for her husband. She told Martin that she had not seen him for three days. Coincidentally, Martin looked out of a window and saw William Bury walking down the street. He said to Ellen, "There is Bill." Ellen went to the door of the public house. As Bury came in, he hit her three times on the face until she fell down.

Not only was William Bury violent towards women but this evidence also shows that he was in the habit of disappearing for two or three days at a time. Whoever Jack the Ripper was, he had to have the ability to disappear. Unless he lived alone, he could not have returned home with blood on his clothes on the nights of the murders. We know that there were nights when William Bury did not return home. It is also interesting to note that the second victim, Annie Chapman, was killed at 5.30 in the morning and that William Bury was wandering the streets at that hour. None of these facts make William Bury the Whitechapel murderer but neither do they allow us to eliminate him from our enquiries.

The picture we have of Bury is of a hard-drinking, violent and inconsiderate man. He does not seem to have had one redeeming quality. When he was sacked by James Martin, he used Ellen's money to buy a pony and cart and set himself up in business as a sawdust merchant in direct competition with James Martin. However, Bury did not have the discipline to run a business by himself; he would spend his time drinking in the public houses he was supposed to be selling sawdust to.

Nor did Bury know anything about horses, even though he was sleeping in James Martin's stables and presumably transporting sawdust by horse and cart while employed by him. The first pony bought by Bury fell ill with the glanders and his wife was forced to give him the money to buy another.

Between April and January, when Bury was supposedly self-employed, he was actually living on his wife's inheritance. We know this because, on 28 April, she visited the Union Bank of London to sell one-sixth of her shareholding and was paid 39 pounds, seven shillings and sixpence. Then, on 7 June, Ellen sold the rest of her share holding and received £194 and seven shillings. On both occasions, she was chaperoned by her husband. She was already living in fear of him and we can assume that he now had access to the whole of her money.

In January 1889, Bury told his wife he had received an offer of employment from a jute firm in Dundee called "Malcolm, Ogilvy & Co". Consequently, they left for Dundee by boat on 19 January and arrived there the following day. Bury's story about having received an offer of employment was a lie and how he explained this to his wife when they arrived in Dundee is not known. Neither do we know Bury's reasons for wanting to go to Dundee.

At his trial, the prosecution alleged that he believed Scotland to be the place depicted in the novels of Sir Walter Scott where wild men ran about wearing kilts and brandishing swords. He may have believed that a man could commit murder in this barbarous country without anyone taking any notice. More likely, however, is the simple fact that he had decided to murder his wife and knew he could not do so in London where there were too many witnesses of his violent treatment of his wife. He may have hoped, by getting her away from London, that the police would accept whatever story he told them and would not go to the length of interviewing witnesses down in London. If that was his thinking, he was badly mistaken.

The most frustrating aspect of the Bury case is the fact that he was put on trial for murder but that no one asked him about the Jack the Ripper murders. The Dundee Police prosecuted him for the murder he committed in Dundee and, for obvious legal reasons, the evidence given at his trial was restricted to the murder that took place in Dundee. However, there must have been contact between the Dundee and London police forces because the Dundee police must have telegraphed London to ask them for information about the dead woman. Sadly, no correspondence has survived which makes it impossible to know if telegrams were exchanged discussing Bury's links with the Jack the Ripper murders.

The other frustrating aspect of the case is the fact that Bury chose not to give evidence at his trial. If he had given evidence from the dock, we might have been able to learn a bit more about his character. As it was, much of the trial became concerned with establishing whether or not it was possible for Bury's version of events to have occurred. The prosecution brought forth doctors who stated that the case was clearly one of homicidal strangulation while the defence claimed that Ellen Bury had committed suicide. In the end, the jury accepted the prosecution's version of events. Bury was found guilty and hanged on 24 April 1889.

But was Jack the Ripper hanged in Dundee while the police were still scouring the City of London for him? There was one man who thought so; James Berry, public hangman from 1884 to 1891. If Jack the Ripper died on the scaffold then it is reasonable to conclude that Berry was the man who hanged him. And James Berry certainly held the view that he had hanged Jack the Ripper in Dundee on 24 April 1889.

How or why James Berry held this view is not known. He certainly would have spent some time with William Bury prior to his execution. The two men may have spoken to each other though nothing has been recorded. This leaves us with a frustrating dead end. The public hangman believed that William Bury was Jack the Ripper but on what did he base this conclusion? We do not know.

Stronger evidence comes from the injuries received by the victims of Jack the Ripper which are very similar to the injuries received by Ellen Bury. The generally accepted modus operandi for Jack the Ripper is that he strangled his victims first and then mutilated their bodies with a knife after death. This is based on the fact that none of the victims were heard screaming, indicating they could not scream, and on the fact that there would have been more blood at the scenes of the crimes if the heart had still been pumping when the victims' bodies were lacerated. In the case of Annie Chapman, the second victim, the coroner specifically stated that her breathing had been interfered with before death.

If we look at the injuries received by the victims, a clear pattern emerges. Polly Nichols's throat was cut and her abdomen was cut open. Annie Chapman was strangled, her throat was cut and her abdomen was cut open. Elizabeth Stride's throat was cut only; she had no other injuries. Catharine Eddowes's throat was cut, her abdomen was cut open and her face was mutilated. Like the others, Mary Jane Kelly's throat was cut and her abdomen was cut open. Her face was also mutilated and there were horrific injuries to her torso. In all cases, we can say that the cause of death was strangulation but that the evidence of this was destroyed when the killer cut the throats of his victims. In Eddowes's case, it is generally accepted that there were no further injuries because the killer was interrupted in his work.

Therefore, we can say that the modus operandi of Jack the Ripper was as follows; death was caused by strangulation and then followed by the cutting of the throat and the mutilation of the body, particularly the abdomen. Ellen Bury was strangled and her killer mutilated her abdomen afterwards. Thus, the pattern of strangulation followed by mutilation of the body is repeated.

The only significant difference is that Ellen Bury's throat was not cut but, even here, the pattern remains very similar to that of Jack the Ripper. Like Jack the Ripper, William Bury attacked the neck and abdomen of his victim. Like Jack the Ripper, he strangled his victim and then leaned over her prostrated body to slide a knife into her and rip open her abdomen.

As to why Bury did not cut his wife's throat, there are two possible reasons. The first is that he could not, if he intended to tell the police that she had committed suicide by hanging or strangling herself. The second is that Jack the Ripper was working in the streets where a policeman on the beat might have come upon him at any time; he could not allow his victims to cry out. Hence, the cutting of the throat after strangulation ensures that the victim cannot cry out. In his basement flat in Dundee which never received any visitors, Bury was more confident that he had time to do his work. If his victim, after strangulation, showed signs of a recovery of consciousness, he had time to re-apply pressure to her neck. He was not having to look over his shoulder for passers-by coming along the street or, in Kelly's case, clients knocking on her door.

We know that William Bury was living in the East End of London from October 1887, because that was the date he entered James Martin's employment. Martin sacked Bury in March but, on 2 April 1888, Bury married Ellen Elliot in Bromley Church. By May 1888, Ellen complained that she had got "the venereal disease very bad" and that she had got it from him. This suggests that William Bury was already in the habit of having intercourse with the prostitutes of London's East End.

I do not wish to move too much into the realm of speculation but it is worth noting that the Whitechapel murders begin about two months after William Bury had contracted a venereal disease. Was he taking revenge on the women who had given him the disease? We shall never know.

However, we can say that William Bury was a hard-drinking man who was in the habit of consorting with prostitutes. He was repeatedly violent towards his wife and is known to have held a knife to her throat on one occasion. Before we go any further, let us stop to ask ourselves how much – if anything – we know about Jack the Ripper? Polly Nichols was last seen alive at 2.30 am on Friday, 31 August, on Whitechapel Road. One and a half hours later, her dead body was found in Bucks Row. No witnesses ever came forward to say they saw her with her killer. However, the second victim, Annie Chapman, was seen with her killer. A woman called Elizabeth Long was walking down Hanbury Street, on her way to Spitalfields Market, at 5.30 am. She was certain of the time because a clock had newly struck. Long saw a man standing on the pavement, outside Number 29, talking to Chapman. The man said "Will you?" and Chapman replied "Yes." According to Long, the man had dark hair, wore a deerstalker hat and spoke with a foreign accent.

At 5.32 am, Albert Cadosch passed through the yard at 27 Hanbury Street and heard something fall against the fence that separated Number 27 from Number 29. He had been in the yard moments earlier, and had heard a woman's voice say "No!" At 5.45 am, John Davis found Chapman's dead body in the yard at Number 29. We can be very confident that the man seen with Chapman by Elizabeth Long was Jack the Ripper. There simply was not time for Chapman to leave the man and then find another client before being murdered at 5.32 am. What Cadosch must have heard was Chapman's body falling against the fence as she lost consciousness.

So we can say that Jack the Ripper had dark hair, wore a deerstalker hat and spoke with a foreign accent. In the Victorian era, a "foreigner" was someone who was not local. We know how the word is used today, exclusively meaning someone who was born in another country and probably speaking a different language. In 1888, "foreigner" was a term used to describe an outsider. Emily Brontë uses the word in this way in

Wuthering Heights when an Englishman is described as a "foreigner" because he does not belong to the local community (see *Wuthering Heights*, Volume 1, Chapter 6). Thus William Bury, with his Midlands accent, would have fitted the description "foreigner" as it was used in 1888. What this tells us is that Jack the Ripper, whoever he was, did not speak like a native Londoner. All suspects who did must be eliminated.

Elizabeth Long's description of a man seen with the murdered woman is important because it occurred only two minutes before the murder. Other sightings of the murdered women with men who might have been the killer are not so close to the time of the murder. For example, James Brown saw a man with Elizabeth Stride about ten minutes before her murder.

The problem here is that prostitutes working the streets would be going from one man to another and that men might come along the streets of Whitechapel fairly frequently even in the early hours of the morning. Thus, even in ten minutes, a woman might have the time to leave one man and approach another. For us to be confident that a witness saw the dead woman with her killer, the sighting would have to take place very close to the time of the murder. Elizabeth Long's sighting of a man is probably the only one which was close enough to the time of the murder for us to be confident that the man was definitely Jack the Ripper.

A very detailed description was made of a man seen with Mary Kelly, the fifth victim, by George Hutchinson. Hutchinson saw Kelly at 2.00 am and stated that the man followed her to her room and was still there at 3.00 am. The problem with Hutchinson's evidence is the rather obvious fact that Kelly's dead body was not discovered till 10.45 am. There was plenty time for the man seen by Hutchinson to have left and for Kelly to have found another client. And as a prostitute working the streets, this is not improbable.

It was not till 1.30 pm that Dr Phillips examined the body and declared that she had been dead for five or six hours. This put the estimated time of death at something like 8.00 am which leaves five hours unaccounted for, between 3.00 am and 8.00 am. It also gives Kelly plenty of time to get rid of the man seen by Hutchinson and find another client.

There is simply too much time from the sighting by Hutchinson to the discovery of the body for us to confidently identify this man as Jack the Ripper.

A "short, dark man" was seen with Kelly by Caroline Maxwell between 8.00 am and 8.30 am. This evidence has been disputed by some researchers who have taken the view that Kelly may have made a mistake about the day and time of her sighting. However, it is interesting to note that William Bury was 5 feet three and a half inches tall and had dark hair which means the description given by Maxwell does not allow us to eliminate him. Whether or not the "short, dark man" was her killer is unknown but it must be considered a possibility.

This brings us onto another aspect of Bury's suitability for the crimes. As a self-employed sawdust merchant with his own pony and cart, he had the freedom to wander the East End of London more or less at will. Nichols was killed between three and four o'clock in the morning; Chapman at 5:30 am. Stride was killed at about 1.00 am and Eddowes at about 1.30 am. If Caroline Maxwell was correct in her identification of Kelly, then Kelly was killed between 8.00 am and 10.00 am. If Maxwell was mistaken, then Kelly may have been killed earlier – perhaps as early as 4.00 am.

It is clear that Jack the Ripper had to have the ability to wander the streets at night. So what kind of job was the man doing during the day? Manual workers at this time were beginning work at 6.00 am and working till 6.00 pm. It is undisputed that Jack the Ripper killed Annie Chapman at 5.30 am. If he was out on the streets looking for victims at that time in the morning, he was clearly not getting ready to go to work.

Bury, being a self-employed man who did not pay attention to his business, had the ability to wander the streets at night. He had no supervisors which meant no one would be asking where he was or why he had failed to turn up for work on a particular morning. He could drink through the evening, wander the streets at night and sleep through the day if he wanted to. This means that he had the opportunity to commit the murders.

Thus, in William Bury we have a brutal wife-killer whom we know also had the opportunity to commit the Whitechapel murders. It is consistent with what we know about Bury's personality to suggest that he was responsible for the Jack the Ripper murders but is it *only* coincidence that the murders began after he arrived in the East End of London and ceased when he left?

While in London, he was able to wander the East End at all hours of the day and would be absent from home without explanation for two or three days at a time. He left a confession written in chalk in his basement flat in Dundee, viz: "Jack Ripper is at the back of this door" and "Jack Ripper is in this seller" (sic). When he was in the custody of Dundee Police, he told Lieutenant Parr that he was afraid he would be arrested as Jack the Ripper. And, finally, the hangman who hanged Bury strongly believed that he had hanged Jack the Ripper.

He arrived in London in October 1887, and left in January 1889. After he left, there were no more "Ripper" murders in London but there was a murder in Dundee. The one thing which, above all, makes William Bury a strong suspect for the Whitechapel murders is the fact that we know he committed a murder in the style of Jack the Ripper less than one month after he left London and only three months after the murder of Mary Kelly. Was he Jack the Ripper? He was living in the East End of London at the right time and everything we know about his nature tells us that he had the ability to commit these kinds of crimes.

The Mad Doctor

Gary Rowlands

Born in Dublin on 4 July 1845, Thomas John Barnardo could not have arrived at a more inopportune moment. Earlier that same day his father, John Michaelis Barnardo, a Jewish immigrant originally from Havelberg in Germany had lost a small fortune following the collapse of the Wicklow and Wexford Railway Company. No sooner had news of the hitherto highly successful businessman's failed investment filtered through than the possibility of an even bigger crisis threatened to engulf the entire Barnardo family.

Abigail, John Michaelis's second wife, was experiencing complications during childbirth. Having lost his first wife Elizabeth – Abigail's older sister – in similar circumstances (she died while giving birth to their seventh child), John Michaelis was understandably deeply concerned for Abigail's well-being. Fortunately, though considerably weakened from her ordeal, Abigail gave birth to her fifth child, a boy, whom they named Thomas John Barnardo. Alas, the new addition to the ever expanding Barnardo family was small and extremely frail and was not expected to survive. Moreover, as Abigail was too weak to nurse him, the poor mite was placed in the care of a local wet nurse. Thus, crucially, mother and child were prevented from "bonding" in the normal way.

Though apparently too weak to care for her newborn son, Abigail quickly fell pregnant once more and was packed off to the country to be cared for by relatives. During her absence, Thomas and his nurse moved into the family home on Dame Street, where she continued to look after him until he was approaching his first birthday. Meanwhile,

Abigail had given birth to a baby girl who tragically died within a few hours of being born.

However, she soon fell pregnant yet again and the following year gave birth to a son, Henry Lionel. Unfortunately for Thomas, whereas he was a short, rather unattractive child, Henry was an absolute cherub and the apple of his mother's eye. Thus, he was frequently summoned to the drawing room by his doting parents and shown off to family and friends, whilst poor Thomas was cruelly kept hidden away in the nursery.

Not surprisingly, this cruel and insensitive treatment left Thomas feeling completely unloved and unwanted and so he would frequently throw a tantrum in a desperate attempt to gain his parents' attention and thus receive the love and affection he craved. Such parental neglect and total lack of display of affection can of course leave a child emotionally scarred for life and, as we shall see, have far-reaching consequences.

In the early 1970s, FBI agent and pioneer of psychological profiling, Robert K. Ressler, set about interviewing 36 convicted murderers, in order "to know what made these people tick, to better understand the mind of the murderer". Aware of the myth that murderers come from broken, impoverished homes, his research "showed that this wasn't really true. Many of the murderers started life in a family that was not desperately poor, where the mother and father lived together with their son". However, his study revealed that "all the murderers – every single one – were subjected to serious emotional abuse during their childhoods".

Moreover, he discovered that "relationships between our subjects and their mothers were uniformly cool, distant, unloving, neglectful. There was very little touching, emotional warmth, or training in the ways in which normal human beings cherish one another and demonstrate their affection and interdependence. These children were deprived of something more than money – love."

We can see at once just how much Ressler's survey mirrors Barnardo's own childhood. Like the 36 murderers interviewed, he too, was an "emotionally abused" child. Moreover, his mother could arguably be described as being "cool, distant, unloving and neglectful" towards him. She certainly deprived him of love. Thus, there can be little doubt that Barnardo's loveless upbringing instilled in him the potential to become a serial killer.

As he grew older, his behavioural problems continued. From the age of ten, he attended St John's Parochial School in Fishamble Street and then left to attend St Patrick's Grammar School at 112 Stephen's Green: "He disliked both and shone at neither. Whenever there was trouble in either school Barnardo was usually involved; and he was reprimanded almost daily for carelessness or untidiness."

Upon leaving school, Barnardo secured employment in a clerical capacity at a local wine merchant's. However, far more importantly, the previously irreligious teenager had now found God and within the space of a few weeks had joined the Open Plymouth Brethren, the Young Men's Christian Association and various other Christian Organizations.

So dramatic was the effect of his new-found faith on him that the previously self-centred adolescent spent much of his free time spreading the word of God in Dublin's ragged schools and as a Sunday School teacher at Merrion Hall, a focal point of Brethrenism, built by the wealthy solicitor William Fry.

Despite his demanding schedule, Barnardo grew restless and was keen to acquire a room in order to hold his own prayer meetings. He obtained a room in Augier Street and the meetings began in earnest in the summer of 1863. Yet, despite the participation of several influential guest speakers from the Brethren movement, the venture was not particularly successful. Given that revivalism was at its height in Dublin at this time, Barnardo's motives for holding his own prayer meetings are certainly questionable and probably had more to do with his dominant personality and consequent desire for power, rather than any perceived need on his part for additional spiritual enlightenment for the masses. Noting this aspect of his personality, biographer Gillian Wagner wrote: "Although a convinced and sincere Christian, Barnardo never found it easy to subdue his need to assert himself, to dominate others and to impose his will on those around him."

Significantly, it is now widely recognized that sexual serial murders are not in fact motivated by the perpetrator's desire for sex, but rather by his compulsive urge to exert his power and dominance over his victim. Renowned Ripperologist Colin Wilson has suggested that serial killers such as the Ripper, belong to the "dominant 5 per cent" of the male population. With his autocratic attitude, Barnardo patently belongs in this grouping.

Although his own prayer meetings had proved no great success, Barnardo's enthusiasm for the revival was undiminished and he continued to attend prayer meetings and Bible classes at Merrion Hall and elsewhere. It was at one such meeting that he first learned of the terrible famine in China. Hudson Taylor, founder of the China Inland Mission, was visiting Dublin in search of volunteers. Though only a little over 5 feet in height, Taylor was a powerful and gifted orator and he deliberately set out to shock his captive audience by informing them of "a million a month dying in China without knowing Christ". Not surprisingly, Taylor's emotive words had a profound affect upon his audience. Barnardo and several others approached Taylor and pleaded to be allowed to go to China as missionaries.

Thus, in April 1866, Barnardo, much against his father's wishes, left his native Dublin for London in order to begin his training as a missionary. However, no sooner had he arrived than Taylor began to have serious misgivings as to his suitability for China. Typically, the root of the problem was Barnardo's overbearing and superior posture. Believing he knew and could do best, he was openly critical of the way in which the Mission was being run. Thus, when Taylor and his band of volunteers set sail for China in May, aboard the *Lammermuir*, Barnardo was not among them.

Although extremely disappointed, Barnardo decided to study medicine in the mistaken belief that this would ultimately help him achieve his burning desire of going to China and he registered as a student at the London Hospital in Whitechapel in November of the following year. Perhaps not surprisingly, Barnardo took an especially keen interest in anatomy and spent most of his time in the dissecting room. In a letter about his studies to Hudson Taylor's Chief Administrator, W.T. Berger, he wrote somewhat enthusiastically that thus far "with God's help I have worked hard, having up to this (3 January) been enabled to dissect two complete subjects".

Of particular interest however, is the attitude of Barnardo's fellow students towards him. He was not at all liked by them. First and foremost, they felt he was a religious fanatic, particularly as, during a cholera epidemic in which several thousands people had lost their lives, "he was found in one of the streets standing on a crate preaching the Gospel to the despondent masses". They also took exception to the fact that he was not the least bit sociable, preferring his own company to theirs. Moreover, his peers despised his decidedly superior attitude. Deemed a weirdo, he was effectively ostracized by them. Indeed, Barnardo had few, if any, true friends throughout his life and was in effect, a loner.

Significantly, a 1980 FBI report on lust killers such as the Ripper states: "The disorganized asocial lust murderer exhibits primary characteristics of social aversion. This individual prefers his own company to that of others and would be typified as a loner."

During his spare time Barnardo helped out at a little ragged school in Ernest Street, where he taught Bible classes and basic literacy skills. However, he was forced to resign after the committee learnt that he had misleadingly used the school's name to appeal for funds in the religious journal *The Revival*, when in reality he had intended to use the money to start his own facility for the irreligious urchins of the East End. Here, yet again, is a prime example of Barnardo's autocratic behaviour.

Having resigned his post at the school, he eagerly set about acquiring suitable premises in order to start his own juvenile mission. After quite a struggle, he succeeded in raising more than £90 towards the cost of the venture, when out of the blue came an offer of the use of the assembly rooms at the King's Arms at the corner of the Mile End Road and Beaumont Square. Seeing this as the answer to his prayers, he celebrated his good fortune by holding a massive tea party for the poverty-stricken youths of Stepney and the surrounding area. However, shortly afterwards the King's Arms changed hands and unfortunately the new owner did not possess the same charitable disposition as his predecessor and immediately cancelled the agreement to let the rooms. The news so devastated Barnardo, particularly as he had spent the entire £90 getting the venture up and running, that he had a nervous breakdown.

This, the first of several breakdowns, all occurring at particularly stressful periods in his life, is especially interesting as a report by the FBI Behavioural Science Unit in 1985 states that "86 percent of all serial killers have experienced some form of mental health problem".

It was the best part of three months before Barnardo felt sufficiently recovered to continue his work. He immediately set about developing his own mission centre with renewed vigour. Thus, on 2 March 1868, the forerunner of the Barnardo's organization, the East End Juvenile Mission, was formed. So successful were his efforts that by November 1870 he finally abandoned his dream of going to China in order to concentrate fully on managing his ever expanding mission centre.

Having decided against China, Barnardo no longer saw any point in continuing with his medical studies, so he ceased to attend the London Hospital, a decision he would live to regret. Although he had passed the first professional examinations in anatomy and physiology at the Royal College of Surgeons in England in 1869, he was not, as his detractors pointed out, fully qualified and therefore not entitled to assume the title of doctor, which he had been doing for quite some time.

Realizing that by falsely adopting the title of Doctor of Medicine he had left himself open to attack, Barnardo resumed his medical studies in order to silence his critics. He finally qualified as a licentiate of the Royal College of Surgeons in Edinburgh. Curiously, he also gained a certificate as an accredited accoucheur. Considering he had no intention of ever practising medicine and had only resumed his studies so that he could legally describe himself as a Doctor of Medicine, one is puzzled by the reason for the acquisition of this additional qualification and can only conclude that Barnardo had a morbid fascination with female genitalia.

Barnardo's surgical skill is particularly significant when we recall the comments of coroner Wynne Baxter regarding the removal of Annie Chapman's uterus: "No mere slaughterer of animals could have carried out these operations. It must have been someone accustomed to the post-mortem room." This opinion was endorsed by police surgeon Dr George Bagster Philips who asserted: "Obviously the work was that of an expert – of one at least, who had such knowledge of anatomical or pathological examinations as to be enabled to secure the pelvic organs with one sweep of the knife." On this evidence there can be no doubt that, like Barnardo, the Ripper possessed considerable anatomical knowledge and surgical skill.

Down on Whores

Of all the people suspected at one time or another of being Jack the Ripper, none have had more cause to despise the Whitechapel harlots than Barnardo. Not only did they constantly undermine his efforts to rescue innocent young girls from a life of immorality, but one of them had come perilously close to destroying his reputation and all that he had worked for.

Having forsaken his missionary aspirations in favour of rescuing the destitute mites of London's East End, Barnardo quickly began to make a name for himself as a philanthropist. He set about expanding the East End Juvenile Mission and also opened his first home for destitute boys. However, prompted by the realization that most of the boys in his care had come from broken homes and that in most cases drink had been the cause of the family breakup, he launched his own temperance campaign.

In an audacious move, he held nightly prayer meetings in a large mission tent right outside the Edinburgh Castle, a notorious and extremely popular drinking den famed for its lewd variety entertainment. Throughout the summer of 1872, Barnardo and the proprietor of the Castle fought a desperate battle for the patronage of local tipplers. By the autumn, Barnardo had emerged the victor as the decline had forced the publican to put the "Citadel of Sin" up for sale. Although this was Barnardo's most notable success thus far, he was not content to rest on his laurels and in an inspired move he proceeded to buy the Castle and turned it into a mission church and coffee palace.

However, not everyone was anxious to share in Barnardo's success. One man in particular, a Baptist minister, the Reverend George Reynolds, a former railway porter, was furious when the congregation of his small church "The Cave of Adullam" in Mile End Road, had flocked to Barnardo's new Peoples Mission Church. The consequence of their desertion spelled disaster for Reynolds as he was dependent upon the donations of his flock for his livelihood. Thus, seeing starvation staring him in the face, the aggrieved Baptist minister set about ruining Barnardo.

In the summer of 1874, Mrs Johnson, a neighbour of Reynolds and former landlady of Barnardo's, provided the Reverend with the ammunition he needed. After a little prompting, she admitted to Reynolds that she and Barnardo had been lovers when he had lodged in her house in Bromley Street during his days as a medical student. Reynolds seized this opportunity to damage his rival's credibility and discreetly circulated details of Barnardo's alleged indiscretion throughout the East End.

Barnardo was livid upon hearing of the scandalous rumour. Not only was he being accused of having had sexual relations with a married woman, he was also being charged with fornicating with a prostitute. As Reynolds was all too aware, that had become Mrs Johnson's sad fate following the collapse of her marriage.

Despite Barnardo's vehement denial of the "wicked woman's" claims, there was no refuting that he had ample opportunity to indulge in extramarital activities with the "unfortunate" woman, as he had been her lodger for the best part of two years, during which time her husband, a sailor, was often away at sea. Thus, the wretched woman's allegations had to be taken seriously and so Barnardo's deacons at the Peoples Mission Church were forced to act. They interrogated Mrs Johnson in the presence of her mother and a doctor, and faced with the choice of taking the word of a harlot over that of their esteemed pastor, they not surprisingly dismissed her claims as the ramblings of a woman "suffering from a form of sexual hysteria".

Undeterred, Reynolds continued to attack Barnardo at every opportunity. In the spring of 1875, he enlisted the help of Frederick Charrington in his campaign to discredit Barnardo. Like Barnardo, Charrington was a philanthropist and important temperance worker and at one time the two men had been friends. However, they had quarrelled over a piece of land in Mile End Road. Charrington claimed to have been planning to build a mission church and coffee palace there, when he heard via the philanthropical grapevine that Barnardo was intending to build a second mission church and coffee palace, the

Dublin Castle, on virtually the same spot. Charrington requested a meeting with his philanthropical rival and, after informing him of his own plans for the site, requested that Barnardo withdraw from the area. This Barnardo stubbornly refused to do, claiming that building work had already begun and thus he was legally obliged to see the project through. Charrington was furious at Barnardo's intransigence and in extremely vengeful mood.

Reynolds, having heard of the dispute between the two men, approached Charrington and informed him of his own grievances against Barnardo, and the two of them joined forces against their bitter rival.

The opening salvo in their war of words, was in the form of a letter sent to Barnardo's wife, Syrie, accusing her husband of having had an immoral relationship with Mrs Johnson and adding that "on many occasions since his marriage he had been seen walking the streets arm in arm with prostitutes and then entering their homes". Barnardo was livid at the accusations and wrote a strongly worded letter to Charrington demanding an apology.

However, Charrington and Reynolds were unrepentant and increased the pressure on Barnardo by circulating reports of the alleged affair. Once again Barnardo wrote demanding an apology, whereupon Charrington denied any involvement in the report and, in a clever move, dared Barnardo to take him to court, knowing full well, that as a Plymouth Brother, Barnardo was prohibited from entering into litigation.

Thus, powerless to act, Barnardo had to sit back as the feud escalated to the letters column of the local press. Finally, after three years of constant sniping and innuendo, Reynolds boldly discarded his cloak of anonymity and launched an all out attack on Barnardo in a 62-page booklet entitled *Dr Barnardo's Homes: Startling Revelations*. The revelations certainly proved startling and were readily snapped up by the public at a shilling a copy. According to Reynolds, the children in Barnardo's care were malnourished, physically abused and frequently locked up in a coal shed for several days at a time for the most trivial offences. He also suggested that medical and sanitary arrangements at the homes were non-existent, resulting in a prevalence of disease and death. The booklet also saw the resurgence of the Mrs Johnson affair under the provocative heading "The Very Wicked Woman And Her Story".

Not surprisingly, the constant feuding between the three men was doing untold damage to the evangelical movement and so they were persuaded to take the matter to a court of arbitration. The arbitrators found in favour of Barnardo and he was exonerated of practically all of the charges.

Though finally vindicated, Barnardo had paid a heavy price. His personal and professional reputation had been severely damaged and this was reflected in the drastic reduction in donations received by the homes. Moreover the constant strain and stress he had endured during the past three years had taken its toll and he was on the verge of yet another nervous breakdown. Small wonder then, that Barnardo was "Down on Whores", given that it had been a prostitute, Mrs Johnson, whose allegations against him had been the initial and indeed dominant factor of Reynolds's campaign.

Incredibly, Barnardo is almost certainly unique amongst Ripper suspects, in that he possessed not one but two equally powerful motives for wanting to rid the streets of the Whitechapel "daughters of joy". With contraception being virtually non-existent, many of the East End harlots fell pregnant. To these wretched creatures, pregnancy was simply seen as an occupational hazard. Their unfortunate offspring were neither loved nor wanted, and often abandoned in favour of the gin bottle (several of the Ripper's victims were habitual drunkards who had forsaken their own children).

Furthermore, those prostitutes that kept their children frequently sent them out on to the streets to beg, borrow or steal the money to pay for their drink. Indeed, so desperate and depraved were some of these gin-sodden creatures that they even forced their own daughters, often of tender years, into a life of prostitution in order to finance their inebriated existence.

Barnardo was all too painfully aware of this fact, which was reflected in the case histories of some of the young girls in his care: "Exposed, day by day, to the influence of common prostitutes' society" was an all too familiar entry against the names of the young girls listed in his records. Particularly sickening was the entry concerning a girl of only eight: "Father dead. Given up by her abandoned mother to the keeping of a prostitute, whom the girl was in the habit of accompanying at night and in whose room and bed she has slept, it is said, in company with men who were brought home."

Initially, Barnardo had tried to help the local prostitutes and had for several years held special evening surgeries of a deeply religious tone for their exclusive benefit. However, his attitude towards them (no doubt prompted by the Mrs Johnson affair) had begun to change and by the mid-1880s had developed into an almost pathological hatred of them and their kind. And he was now blaming their vile influence for the high levels of child prostitution in the area: "In the vilest haunts of women of shameful lives, in 'furnished rooms' where decency and virtue are disregarded, if not mocked at, in those low lodging houses which are the hot-beds of immorality and vice, are to be found many virtually unshielded girls of tender years whose dangers cannot be thought of without a shudder." Barnardo's own words clearly demonstrate his contempt and hatred for these women, women such as Martha Tabram, Mary Ann Nichols, Annie Chapman, Elizabeth Stride, Catharine Eddowes and Mary Jane Kelly.

Barnardo tried to solve the problem by opening a home for girls in "imminent moral danger". So desperate was he to save young girls from a life of debauchery that he readily admitted to breaking the law in order to rescue children "from circumstances the most dangerous, morally, that it is possible to conceive". Although the home proved a success it did little to curb the problem as a whole. He finally realized that far more drastic action was needed if young girls were to be saved from being led into a life of immorality. And in the autumn of 1888, I believe that Barnardo took that action.

An Enterprising Journalist

According to Sir Robert Anderson and Sir Melville Macnaghten the "Dear Boss" correspondence was penned by a journalist. Recent research has offered up two main candidates as the likely authors of the "gruesome stuff".

The first, a freelance journalist called Best who claimed to have worked as a penny-a-liner on the *Star* newspaper during the murders, is reputed to have claimed responsibility for the Ripper missives "to keep the business alive". This claim is easily refuted, as we may recall that the author of the first letter specifically requested that it be held back "till I do a bit more work". Thus, if Best really was the correspondent, how could he hope to sustain interest in the case by asking for the letter to be held back until the next murder?! By this time the ensuing publicity from any such atrocity would have eliminated the need for the bogus missives anyway!

The second press man allegedly responsible for writing the missives was an employee of the Central News Agency and would appear to be the same journalist that both Anderson and Macnaghten suspected of penning the "enterprising" copy, but were reluctant to name. Fortunately, his identity is divulged by Chief Inspector George Littlechild in the "Littlechild Letter", discovered by Stewart P Evans:

> With regard to the term "Jack the Ripper" it was generally believed at the yard that Tom Bullen of the Central News was the originator but it is probable Moore, who was his Chief, was the inventor. It was a smart piece of journalistic work. No journalist of my time got such privileges from Scotland Yard as Bullen. Mr James Munro when Assistant Commissioner, and afterwards commissioner, relied on his integrity. Poor Bullen occasionally took too much to drink, and I fail to see how he could help it knocking about so many hours and seeking favours from so many people to procure copy. One night when Bullen had taken a "few too many" he got early information on the death of Prince Bismarck and instead of going to the office to report it sent a laconic telegram "Bloody Bismarck is dead". On this I believe Mr Charles Moore fired him out.

Regrettably, there is not a single scrap of hard evidence to support Littlechild's claim. Admittedly Bullen had the means and the opportunity to pen the letters, as he was of course, an employee of the recipient of the correspondence and was also privy to confidential police information. However, he had absolutely no motive whatsoever for writing the offensive material.

The suggestion that he wrote the letters to heighten public interest in the murders and thus create a boom for the press is sheer nonsense and can be seen to be such, when we examine a third, less well-known "Dear Boss" missive. Addressed once again to the Central News Agency and in a similar hand and style as the two previous communications, it read:

5 Oct. 1888

Dear Friend

In the name of God hear me I swear I did not kill the female whose body was found at Whitehall. If she was an honest woman I will hunt down and destroy her murderer. If she was a whore God will bless the hand that slew her, for the women of Moab and Midian shall die and their blood shall mingle with the dust. I never harm any others or the Divine power that protects and helps me in my grand work would quit for ever. Do as I do and the light of glory shall shine upon you. I must get to work tomorrow treble event this time yes yes three must be ripped. Will send you a bit of face by post I promise this dear old Boss. The police now reckon my work a practical joke well well Jacky's a very practical joker ha ha ha keep this back till three are wiped out and you can show the cold meat.

　　Yours truly

　　Jack the Ripper

The murder referred to in this communication was that of an unknown woman whose limbless, headless torso had been discovered on 2 October (two days after the "double event") in the cellars of New Scotland Yard.

If Littlechild is to be believed, and Bullen did in fact write the missives, supposedly with the intention of increasing newspaper sales, then why on earth did he deny carrying out this latest murder? Common sense tells us that he would have leaped at the chance of adding this latest, horribly mutilated victim to his cast of carnage, particularly as the poor woman's body had been found at no less a place than New Scotland Yard itself! Such a claim, coming so soon after the "double event", would have sent newspaper sales through the roof.

Moreover, if Bullen had indeed written the correspondence, why, on all three occasions, was the address incomplete and thus rather vague? The sender omitted to include both the number and name of the street (5 New Bridge Street) and also the postal district (Ludgate Circus),which one would have expected Bullen to have known and used. After all, he did work there.

That the correspondence was written by a journalist there can be very little doubt. However, I believe that the journalist responsible for penning the "gruesome stuff" was none other than Barnardo.

Although a doctor of medicine, Barnardo had in fact earned a living for several years prior to the murders, as a journalist. He would have known precisely where to send the missives (the Central News Agency) to gain the maximum publicity. Moreover, during a visit to the United States in 1884, he spent some time with detectives studying the underworld in New York, Chicago and Boston, and so he would have been exposed to the Americanisms such as "Boss" contained in the communications, as they were in everyday use in this particular environment. Furthermore, Barnardo's editorial offices at 279 Strand were close to the location where the first letter was posted.

Barnardo's motives for sending the letters were threefold. Firstly, as a committed philanthropist, he obviously wanted to draw attention to the appalling poverty and immoral way of life that many of the children in the East End slums were forced to endure.

Secondly, and more sinisterly, the communications and the violent threats contained in them were intended to intensify the sheer terror already being felt by the Whitechapel prostitutes and thus drive them off the streets (also his motive for committing the murders). That his plan was an unequivocal success is confirmed by newspaper reports following the sending of the missives and subsequent double murder: "From the deserted condition of the streets there is no doubt that the state of panic into which the frequenters of the streets by night in this neighbourhood have been thrown continues undiminished," noted the *Echo*. Indeed, such was their panic that the *Daily Chronicle* reported: "It is not too much to say that the unfortunate creatures who ply their wretched vocation in the streets are paralysed with fear." And it was not only the Whitechapel strumpets that were terrified of bumping into Jack on a dark night. Respectable women were equally wary, as observed by the *Star*: "Miles of streets in the neighbourhood of Whitechapel may now be traversed at night without ever meeting a female."

Barnardo's third motive for sending the correspondence involved a cunning ploy to avert suspicion away from the medical profession. It was common knowledge that, following the murder of Annie Chapman because of the degree of surgical skill employed by the perpetrator, the police had begun to focus their attention in the direction of a medical man and had thus begun making enquiries into the movements of all the physicians residing in the area.

Thus, in a clever attempt to shift suspicion away from the medical profession he ended the first letter with the mocking remark: "They say I'm a doctor now ha ha." It was also because of the belief that the killer was a doctor or surgeon that considerably less surgical skill was used in later murders in order to throw the police off the trail.

Catch Me When You Can

Robert Anderson's appointment as the Assistant Commissioner of the Metropolitan CID was a huge stroke of luck for Barnardo. Not only had he known the man now entrusted with his capture for the best part of twenty years, but he had also for most of that time enjoyed a close working relationship with his new-found adversary.

For Anderson had served on the management committee of Barnardo's East End Juvenile Mission since its inception in 1878, and in that time had proven himself to be a most valuable and loyal servant. Thus, ironically, Anderson's new status as head of CID enabled Barnardo, the very man that he was unwittingly charged with capturing, to become privy to confidential police information that he was later able to use to avoid detection while continuing his murderous activities. Although Anderson had succeeded James Monro as head of CID at the end of August, he claimed to be suffering from exhaustion and so after only one week in his new post left for a month's holiday in Switzerland. It was not until his return on 6 October 1888 that he took a full and active role in the investigation.

However as soon as he took over the inquiry there was a sudden cessation of the murders. Moreover, when the Ripper finally resumed his killing spree he had seen fit to change his modus operandi. Whereas up to that point all five of the Ripper's victims had been ruthlessly struck down and hacked to pieces on the blood-drenched cobblestones of Whitechapel, his final victim Mary Kelly was murdered indoors. It is far too much of a coincidence to accept that these sudden changes, coinciding as they did with Anderson's return to duty, were totally unconnected. Unquestionably, the evidence suggests that Barnardo discussed the murders with Anderson shortly after his return to Scotland Yard, and that it was from his unsuspecting, high-powered colleague that Barnardo learned all about the latest police efforts to apprehend the murderer.

Moreover, it was this information, particularly the news that a large number of plain-clothes officers (including some disguised as women) were now being deployed on the streets of Whitechapel, that prompted him to put a halt to the murders for almost six weeks, and, when he eventually resumed his murderous campaign to alter his modus operandi, to his final victim, Mary Kelly, behind the relative safety of closed doors.

After having been made aware by Anderson's loose tongue, of the huge risks he was running, Barnardo realized that he could not hope to get away with his homicidal deeds much longer. He resolved to bring an end to his abominable activities in the most horrific fashion imaginable. Of particular significance in this, his final murder, was his choice of victim. She epitomized everything Barnardo most despised. Not only was Mary Kelly an habitual drunkard and a shameless whore, she was also, unlike the previous victims, a Roman Catholic, belonging to a religion that Barnardo found particularly abhorrent, "amounting almost to paranoia". Such was his pathological hatred of followers of "Romish doctrines" that he sought to publicly attack and humiliate them and their church whenever the opportunity arose.

One such occasion presented itself the year preceding the murders.

In 1887, after having begun corresponding with Cardinal Manning, supposedly with the intention of coming to some sort of agreement over the large number of destitute Roman Catholic children in the East End, Barnardo, in a second letter to the Cardinal, deliberately goaded him into an angry and seemingly uncaring response. He then cunningly proceeded to publish the correspondence under the provocative title of *The Cardinal's Conscience*, leaving the public to judge the rights and wrongs for themselves.

Not surprisingly, Barnardo presented himself as the injured party to his readers, claiming that he, the good doctor, had received little or no help from the harsh and uncaring Catholic Church in his efforts to rescue Roman Catholic children from a life of poverty and degradation. Moreover, in an attempt to reassure his readers that he had no desire to proselytize these foundlings he added:

> Frequently when a child of Roman Catholic parents had been brought to me for admission, I have expostulated with the poor relative who has pleaded on its behalf, and urged that application ought to be made in the first instance to his or her own religious adviser, in the person of the priest...for strongly as I was and am opposed to Romish doctrines and to the Romish Church, it was infinitely better, I felt, that the children of Romanists should even become attached to the doctrinal errors of that Church in homes and schools under priestly influences, than be allowed to remain in and grow up among the impurity, degradation, and suffering in which I found them. Well I knew that the hand of Our Lord was able to reach them...and save them, even amidst the thick darkness of Romanism.

Unfortunately, Barnardo's claim that he had no wish to proselytize, was a complete falsehood and also made a mockery of his proud claim "No Destitute Child Ever Refused Admission'. It was a very real condition of admittance to the homes that Barnardo be allowed to educate the child as a Protestant regardless of its hitherto religious upbringing. Thus Roman Catholic parents who had fallen on hard times through illness or unemployment were faced with a stark choice: having their beloved children dragged off to the workhouse, or admitted to the relative comfort of Barnardo's Homes. They reluctantly signed an agreement granting Barnardo this power.

Contrary to his claim that he had no wish to proselytize, Barnardo's hatred of Catholics was so strong that he was prepared to go to any lengths, including breaking the law, to prevent any child under his care from being raised as a Catholic. At the height of the murders, Barnardo admitted three young Catholic children, Harry Gossage, Martha Tye and John James Roddy into the homes on the understanding that they be educated as Protestants. However, only a few weeks later, Barnardo was contacted by representatives of the children's parents, who requested that the children be allowed to leave the homes, so that they may transfer to more suitable Catholic institutions. Barnardo's reaction was not all together unexpected, given his deep hatred of Catholics. According to biographer Gillian Wagner: "Barnardo's response was typically high-handed; two were immediately bundled out of the country in such a way that they could not be traced, and Barnardo applied to the courts to support his claim for the custody of John James Roddy."

Barnardo's desperate actions in this matter confirm that his earlier assurance to Cardinal Manning that he had no wish to proselytize was an utter lie. He attempted to justify his behaviour in allowing Harry Gossage and Mary Tye to be taken out of the country by pointing out that both children had been severely mistreated by their parents and that he had merely acted in their best interests. However, he failed to anticipate the reaction of the public, whom, despite having being made aware of the abuse meted out to the children, were as Gillian Wagner points out: "alarmed at the idea that a private individual should attempt to act according to his own interpretation of the law, in opposition to the law of the land, no matter how much 'moral' right there was on his side." And so he was virulently condemned by the press and public alike.

That Barnardo fully deserved the bitter criticism aimed at him is evident when we examine the comments made by Gillian Wagner on the matter. Despite Barnardo's claim that he was merely preventing the children from being returned to their cruel and neglectful parents,

Wagner reveals the real reasons behind his actions: "Without doubt, in all three cases he was fighting to retain custody not principally to prevent children returning to cruel and neglectful parents, but to prevent their being brought up as Roman Catholics." Moreover, Wagner, who at the time of publishing her book in 1979 was Chairman of the Barnardo Council, and thus whose opinion commands the fullest respect, also makes the poignant and telling remark: "One cannot help regretting that instead of concentrating on the obvious evil of child neglect and abuse he should have chosen to fight on such a narrow front and to give sectarian religious considerations priority over glaring social wrongs." It was this intense hatred of Roman Catholics (confirmed by an esteemed member of the Barnardo Council) that goes some way to explaining his choice of victim for his frenzied finale and also the grotesque carnage that ensued at 13 Miller's Court on that fateful day.

Moreover, the date of Mary Kelly's murder was no coincidence, as 9 November 1888 also happened to be the date of the Lord Mayor's Show. This centuries-old procession, full of pomp and pageantry, was completely overshadowed by the news of the savagery that had taken place earlier that same day. All eyes were now focused on the East End. The killer, a "first-class publicist", had finally succeeded in grabbing the attention of the middle and upper classes, many of whom were only now being alerted to the terrible poverty and living conditions in the dilapidated East End.

It had taken six dreadful murders, each one more brutal than the last, before the money to commence a much needed rebuilding programme was finally made available, an irony that was not lost on George Bernard Shaw: "Whilst we conventional Social Democrats were wasting our time on education, agitation and organization, some independent genius has taken the matter in hand..." That genius was Barnardo!

Of that there can no longer be any doubt. In addition to the damning evidence against him, Barnardo, as we shall see, also matches the description of the killer as furnished by two key witnesses.

According to Mrs Elizabeth Long (Darrell), the man seen with Annie Chapman was over 40, of foreign appearance (which according to *The*

Jack The Ripper A–Z was "usually a euphemism for Jewish") and a little taller than his soon-to-be victim. Mrs Long's description although not particularly detailed, is still nevertheless a remarkably accurate portrait of Barnardo. He was over forty (Barnardo was 43) and more importantly he was half-Jewish and hence could quite easily be mistaken for a "foreigner". Moreover, he was only 5 feet 3 inches and so was indeed only a little taller than Chapman who was just over 5 feet tall.

These same physical characteristics were also observed by George Hutchinson, who is generally accepted by most Ripperologists as being the witness most likely to have seen the Ripper. In his statement to the police Hutchinson confirmed the suspect's Jewish appearance and small stature. He also noted that Kelly's assailant had a "slight moustache curled up at the ends". Photographs taken of Barnardo around the time of the murders, confirm that he also had a "slight moustache curled up at the ends". Significantly, Hutchinson's "detailed description" effectively rules out the likes of Joseph Barnett, Montague Druitt and Dr Tumblety as suspects as, unlike Dr Barnardo, none of the aforementioned were of Jewish appearance.

One noticeable aspect of the numerous descriptions furnished by the various witnesses concerns the Ripper's mode of dress. He was depicted as being everything from "rather rough and shabby", to "shabby genteel", right through to "respectable" and even "affluent". This has prompted John Douglas of the FBI Behavioural Science Unit to speculate that the murderer may have deliberately dressed up to fool his intended victims into thinking he was well-off and thus relieve himself of the task of initiating contact with them.

Though Mr Douglas's theory has some merit, it should be remembered that, prior to their deaths, virtually all of the victims had been drinking and were in fact intoxicated (which was one of the reasons why they were targeted in the first place). In their drunken state, the victims would be far less inhibited and have little sense of danger. There would have been no reason for the Ripper to "dress up" as a means of impressing his chosen victims and thus gaining their confidence, as they were evidently far too inebriated to have noticed what he was wearing or to even have cared. Nevertheless, Mr Douglas was right in suggesting that the Ripper "dressed up" but for the wrong reasons.

The true purpose of the Ripper's (Barnardo's) dressing up (and down) was to disguise himself. He was, after all, well known throughout the East End, particularly by his intended victims the prostitutes, whom he frequently came into contact with when rescuing neglected and abused children from the common lodging houses and brothels. Adopting the art of disguise was a skill Barnardo had mastered several years earlier. During a reconnaissance visit to a common lodging house he disguised himself as a tramp by donning ragged clothes and smearing his face with soot.

Moreover, not only was he adept at disguising himself, but his intimate knowledge of the locale was second to none. He had worked in Whitechapel for a number of years, while a medical student at the London Hospital and, more importantly, for the best part of 20 years searching night after night for destitute and abandoned children throughout the East End. Significantly, his nocturnal forays took him to Whitechapel and Spitalfields, so he knew every nook and cranny of the entire area and was aware of literally dozens of hiding places, unknown to the police, where children desperate to avoid the dreaded workhouse, had prior to their rescue, sheltered from the cold.

Furthermore, Barnardo's midnight ramblings had frequently brought him into contact with the policemen whose assistance he had occasionally called upon when attempting to remove an underage child from a brothel. Consequently he had come to know many of the police officers by name and was also familiar with the times and routes of their patrols.

Armed with his unique knowledge of secret hiding places and his awareness of the times and routes of the various police patrols, is it any wonder that he was seemingly able to "vanish into thin air" after each murder?

Yet, at the same time, his presence on the streets, even on the night of a murder, would have gone largely unnoticed by the police anyway. He had spent twenty years searching most nights for homeless children, and was obviously a familiar sight to the police. He was able to come and go without fear of being stopped and searched.

It has been argued, not least by John Douglas of the FBI Behavioural Science Unit, that, because all the murders were carried out at such a late hour (between midnight and 6.00 am), the killer was single and thus free from family accountability.

Despite being married with children, Barnardo was also seemingly free from family accountability. His schedule had become so hectic that "sometimes it was not certain where he would be sleeping". Often he might be found burning the midnight oil at the homes' Stepney headquarters, before he eventually retired to his private suite for the night. Other times he might be visiting his Girls' Village Home at Ilford, or, often as not, out roaming the East End streets searching for destitute children until the early hours.

By now, even the most sceptical of readers must surely agree that the case again Barnardo is fairly conclusive. However there is still one question that remains to be answered. Why did the killings stop?

Barnardo had of course learned from Anderson of the large number of plain-clothes police officers (including some disguised as women) now being deployed on the streets of Whitechapel and the surrounding area. Although this information prompted him to put a halt to his murderous campaign throughout October, it ultimately failed to act as a sufficient deterrent and he soon returned to his killing ways.

It was Sir Melville Macnaghten who first came up with the theory that "the 'Ripper's' brain gave way altogether after his awful glut in Miller's Court and that he then committed suicide". Although Macnaghten was obviously referring to his prime suspect, Montague Druitt, the idea that the murderer took his own life after killing Kelly is still regarded by many latter-day students of the case as the most likely explanation for the cessation of the murders. While Barnardo clearly did not kill himself, the events at Miller's Court certainly seem to have affected him, as following Mary Kelly's murder he was off sick from work for several days.

Other popular suggestions for the Ripper's retirement include him being caged in an asylum after being found to be hopelessly insane, or alternatively being imprisoned for an unrelated offence or even for him to have emigrated so that he may continue his murderous career elsewhere.

The real reason for the cessation of the murders is far simpler. Shortly after his return to work following Kelly's murder, Barnardo had an accident while diving into a swimming pool. He seriously impaired his hearing, rendering him almost totally deaf. Thus, no longer able to listen out for sounds such as the clatter of an approaching horse and cart (Diemschutz) or the heavy footsteps of a patrolling policeman, the Ripper was thankfully forced into early retirement. Until now, well over 100 years later, he has remained undetected.

The Way To Hell

M J Trow

I have dined out on Jack the Ripper for years. Over a century on, Jack still holds a fascination for us, reaching parts other murderers cannot. Since 1888 a whole variety of experts – retired policemen, journalists, psychiatrists, sociologists – have put forward their pet theories, some silly, some likely, some impossible, all fascinating. And where there is no named individual, these experts have come up with a "type" so beloved of the late Victorians – the railway policeman, the mad doctor, the bungling midwife. Of all of these, my favourite is the deranged social worker.

It was the Victorian period – and specifically the Victorian slum – that gave rise to the man and the occupation. Dictionaries of the 1890s use the term "social worker" for the first time, yet like many others working in the field of poverty, alienation and social deprivation, he was an amateur. In the appalling poverty of Jack London's "Abyss", the area less than a square mile that encompassed Whitechapel and Spitalfields, both of the grimmest social problems of the age were concertinaed with ghastly concentration – drink and prostitution.

In 1888 London was still the biggest city in the world, a place where people became lost in a terrifying new world of steam, noise and the pursuit of money. Those who could, coped. Those who couldn't, went to the wall, or more accurately, to the bottom of the Abyss. The year after the Ripper struck, Charles Booth, owner of a successful steamship company and leather business, wrote *Life and Labour of the People in London*, a gigantic sociological survey of the poor, a subject which Henry Mayhew had touched on back in 1862 and which Seebohm

Rowntree was to tackle in the city of York in 1903. Its pages make depressing reading, underlining the abject poverty of Whitechapel's half million, condemned to short, sad lives of violence, crime and drunkeness.

In September 1888, *Punch* produced its famous ghoul, floating like a phantom on the slum's foul air, "The Nemesis of Neglect":

Look at these walls; they reek with dirt and damp,
But in their shadows crouched, the homeless tramp
May huddle undisturbed the black night through.
These narrow winding courts – in thought – pursue.
No light there breaks upon the bludgeoned wife,
No flash of day arrests the lifted knife,
There shrieks arouse not, nor do groans afright.
These are but normal noises of the night…
…Must it be
That the black slum shall furnish sanctuary
To all light-shunning creatures of the slime,
Vermin of vice, carnivora of crime?

Jack London, an itinerant American journalist, finding himself in the capital of Empire in the summer of 1902, became forever caught up in the horrors of the sights he saw there:

"To pound one's wife to a jelly and break a few of her ribs is a trivial offence compared with sleeping out under the naked stars because one has not the price of a doss. They become indecent and bestial. When they kill, they kill with their hands… They gouge a mate with a dull knife… They wear remarkable boots of brass and iron, and when they have polished off the mother of their children with a black eye…they knock her down and proceed to trample her."

Most people in the Queen-Empress's capital didn't give a damn about the extraordinary people of the Abyss: "It is, then, to the East End," wrote novelist Guy Thorne in 1912, "and to a series of incidents so rich in drama, a time so breathlessly exciting and *at all times so strangely seen in a light which is not of this world*, that readers of this memoir are coming with me."

This was an age before the powerful trade unions, the Labour Party and the nanny state. It was still the era of self-help. And if the East End did not choose to help itself, what did it matter? Whitechapel was teeming with harlots, vagabonds, drunks and Jews, the flotsam and jetsam of a great city, people beyond the pale. In this city of endless toil, however, a trio of men were starting to make a difference.

One was the Irish doctor, Thomas Barnardo, who trained at the London Hospital, a few hundred yards from the Ripper murder sites, and who talked to Liz Stride on the last night of her life. Appalled by the street urchins running barefoot and grimy-faced through the grease-covered courts and alleys of the Abyss, Barnardo set up a home for them in Stepney Causeway. By 1905, the year in which he died of overwork, Barnardo had built 102 schools, convalescent homes and training centres and had saved the lives of thousands of children.

In cellar, in garret, in alley and court,
They weep and they suffer and pine,
And the wolves of the city are prowling near,
Back, wolves. For the children are mine.

Another was "General" William Booth, whose wild white hair and beard were as familiar as the penny gaffs he detested along Mile End Road. A fiery evangelist and brimstone preacher, Booth promised "Heaven in East London for everyone" from his open-air pulpit on the Mile End Waste. His bread, his soup and his tambourines were little rays of sunshine in a naughty world, and all of them saved lives. Out of the aptly named Angel Alley, Booth's Salvation Army girls brought food and hope to the insatiable half million, sharing their hardships with them, dying young.

But the third – and least well known today – of the three, was the strangest: Frederick Nicholas Charrington, aka Jack the Ripper. In his late teens, he witnessed a sight which led to a deep and lasting religious conversion. Outside one of the innumerable East End pubs to which his father's company supplied beer, he saw a wife being beaten to a pulp by her drunken husband: "I looked up and saw my own name in high gilt letters... and it suddenly flooded into my mind that that was only one case of dreadful misery and fiendish brutality in one of the several hundred public houses that our firm possessed."

"Master Fred" was born on 4 February 1850 at Bow Road, Stepney, a stone's throw from the great brewery owned by his father in Mile End. Guy Thorne, Charrington's only biographer, described it as:

> a huge pile of almost goblin masonry, with its colossal ladders, towers and vast receptacles for malt... It hits the eye like a blow, with its vastness, its suggestion of mighty, vested interests, solidity and wealth... From the mighty portals...day by day throughout the year, a never-ending flood of alcohol is pouring and in these enormous vats who shall say how many souls have been dissolved?

The little boy was brought up in what was in effect a schizoid household, doing untold damage to his psyche. His mother, an evangelical Anglican, went about performing good works and his father too was a decent man. Unfortunately, he was a decent man who provided the very alcohol that caused much of the East End's problem. While Mrs Charrington was giving non-alcoholic cordial, home-brewed of course, to her down-and-outs, her other half was getting them roaring drunk. Today we see heavy drinking as an attempted solution to the historical problem of poverty; in Charrington's day, drink was seen as an evil in itself. Charrington Senior refused to accept responsibility just because some men could not hold their liquor.

Typical of middle-class sons of far more than average wealth, Fred Charrington was sent to board at Marlborough, the public school in Wiltshire which still dominates one whole end of the town in a cluster of red-brick Victoriana. An unspecified fever cut his time there short and, for reasons which are unclear, he went next to Brighton College. Rather belatedly, in 1867 he went on the Grand Tour. By this time, the Tour was somewhat obsolete, but perhaps the Charringtons sought respectability in the same way Benjamin Disraeli had a generation earlier, and the boy visited Switzerland, Italy and the Paris Exposition. Traditionally, the Tour was a veneer of culture, soaking up the classical, literary and poetic sights of Europe; beneath the veneer, it was an organized pub and brothel crawl, a chance for a young man to sow a few wild oats before the respectable drudgery of marriage and career. We do not know the exact tenor of Charrington's Tour, but bearing in mind his companions were fellow brewer J H Buxton and the Reverend Thomas Scott, it is likely that the schizophrenia of the young man's life continued.

On his return, Charrington served as apprentice manager of the firm of Neville, Read and Company, brewers to the Queen at Windsor. He was due to join his father's firm in Mile End Road, but in carrying out good works with a Mr Peters, nephew of the great Cunard shipping magnate, he stumbled on the brutal wife-beating incident outside the Rising Sun and, after a showdown with his father, left the brewing business forever. Charrington was consciously throwing away a fortune. His personal inheritance of £1.25 million – the equivalent of £140 a day in the early 1870s – vanished at a stroke.

Beginning in a hayloft that served as a ragged school, Charrington's name spread quickly along the Mile End Road as a philanthropist. He used his family friends – the most distinguished was the Earl of Shaftesbury – to provide money to build a technical workshop for boys at Hertford Place and another for girls at Heath Street, Stepney. The "Mile End Gang" and the "Kate Street Gang" from Whitechapel, intent on a punch-up, with sticks hidden up their sleeves, became quietly converted by Charrington and joined his meetings. Over a thousand street urchins had reason to be grateful to him. He set up workshops, savings banks and work placements among the fishing smacks of Great Yarmouth.

In the mid 1870s he moved to 41 Stepney Green, still within sight of his father's brewery. He practised "self-denial with an almost monkish enthusiasm". He chose celibacy "like other workers for God" and owned one table, two chairs and a bed and no carpet. Even his housekeeper was called Mrs Pilgrim! Friends, who called frequently, referred to No. 41 as the monastery. His usual diet was bread and cheese and he had a fondness for animals, owning a pet monkey.

Charrington's determination to bring the word of God and teetotalism to the people of the Abyss knew no bounds. He held open-air meetings along with General Booth on the Mile End Waste and in his halls at Carlton Square, Twig Folly in Bonner Lane and Oxford Street (in the East End). In May 1876 he erected a huge tent in White Horse Lane and soldiers from West End barracks marched the ten miles there and back to hear and sometimes to preach the gospel. "These splendid, scarlet-coated men" accompanied Charrington on his wanderings through the Abyss, "Charrington's Bodyguard" as they were known. He erected huge hoardings covered with uplifting scriptural texts. Even the police noticed: "The guardians of law and order on their solitary beats at night turned the light of their lanterns upon the hoardings and in the darkness and the silence of the night read the story of Christ's love for them."

Much of Charrington's work was muscular Christianity aimed at the demon drink. With his cranky homespun preachers, he descended on the breweries and the pubs like an avenging angel. "Hellfire Tom", drunken engine driver turned evangelist; Henry Holloway the burglar, who had survived seven years in the rotting Gibraltar hulks; and Harvey Teasdale, the "chief man monkey of London" who entertained the crowds leaping around the balconies of the Sadler's Wells Theatre: all of them hit the Liquor Lords where it hurt, signing hundreds, perhaps thousands to the pledge. Charrington built the biggest temperance hall in the world, the Great Assembly Hall in Mile End Road. Its vast windows and orange and brown interiors provided a chapel, a coffee palace and a book saloon where only wholesome literature could be read and club rooms for both the YMCA and YWCA. The initial cost was £8,000 and the Hall held 5,000 people. Impressive and influential as this was, it was not – and could not be – a total success. Carried away, no doubt, with patriotic fervour, the 2nd Tower Hamlets Rifle Volunteers went on the rampage in 1887 to honour the Golden Jubilee of the Queen. Beer was thoughtfully provided by Spencer Charrington MP, controller of the brewery, and it prompted Frederick to write a letter of disgust to Victoria, especially as the "People's Palace" had been used to sell beer. A reply from the Queen's private secretary, Henry Ponsonby, settled the matter. The Trustees of the People's Palace would not allow "intoxicating liquor" on the premises again, so the "drunken six hundred" had had their last drink on Frederick Charrington.

The huge rally he organized in Hyde Park, at which an estimated 200,000 people attended, was probably the biggest ever held. And the posters went up and the temperance tracts multiplied:

Who fills his pockets with the sale
Of porter, beer and generous ale,
Which crowd the workhouse and the gaol?
My Brewer.

Who fills our slums with waifs and strays?
Who havoc with our nation plays,
And brings disgrace on all our ways?
My Brewer.

Charrington set up "The Blue Ring of Total Abstinence", a medal struck in enamel and gold worn by all those who had taken the pledge. By his own estimation, over 50 per cent of those who signed stayed on the wagon forever. At Osea Island, off the Essex coast, he set up a temperance haven. The land, with its bracing sea air, its heron, tuke and bar-goose colonies, could be reached by a road – "The Hard" – at low tide, and Charrington had his own steam packet to get there when the tide was in full flood. The island's village hall provided concerts, billiards, badminton and roller skating and the "temperance island" was a breath of Heaven itself after the foul, death-laden tenements of the Abyss.

Drink runs like a river of blood through the Ripper case. Polly Nichols staggered from the Frying Pan on the night of her death, merrily drunk and showing off her new bonnet. Frederick Stevens, a fellow lodger at Crossingham's doss house, drank a pint of beer with Dark Annie Chapman five hours before she met Jack. Long Liz Stride was drinking in the Queen's Head, where she had often been drunk and disorderly, on the night of the double event. Kate Eddowes was locked into a cell at Bishopsgate police station by Constable 31 Louis Robinson of the City Force, who had found her dead drunk on the pavement in Aldgate High Street. Hours later she wandered westward into Mitre Square and a kind of immortality. Mary Kelly, the last to meet Jack, visited the Britannia and the Horn of Plenty on the last night of her life. She was still tipsily singing "Only a Violet I Plucked From My Mother's Grave" as she went into her room at 13, Miller's Court for one last time.

In 1887, Frederick Charrington's crusading zeal took a different turn. We do not know why. Perhaps it was the death of his close friend Ion Keith-Falconer, a fellow missionary who died in Aden that year. Perhaps it was altogether a more sinister building of tension that had been growing in Charrington for years. Whatever the trigger, he turned his blue light on prostitution in the Abyss.

To be fair, he had always had a fascination with the subject. In his celebrated Battle of the Halls, which he fought on and off for over ten years, Charrington targetted the music halls (which he called "hells") and stood defiantly outside the brashest of them: Lusby's, the Mahogany Bar at Wilton's in the Ratcliffe Highway, Paddy's Goose, the Gun Boat, the Jolly Sailor and the Kettledrum. It was not only drink that was the problem here, but open prostitution. They were centres of "vice, drunkeness and crime, tenanted by fiends in human form". Charrington himself hardly ever ventured inside, but his teetotal missionary friends did, men like "Mr Charrington's grocer" of the London County Council, who reported the most lewd and lascivious activities going on in the theatre boxes in the glow of the naphtha flares: "You can go to the theatre", Charrington wrote, "and your eyes can gaze upon the indecent dance, and there you can hear the filthy song."

In February 1885, Messrs Crowder and Payne, proprietors of Lusby's, took Charrington to Chancery, accusing him of stopping innocent customers from entering their premises and so damaging their business. His testimony, backed by missionaries, evangelists and reformed harlots, lasted a marathon four and a half hours: "Since 1880 I have, amongst other things… endeavoured to rescue prostitutes from their evil courses."

Charrington stood outside halls like Lusby's from 11.00 pm until 1.00 am most nights, watching, waiting… He kept a little black book and noted down the madams and their girls and their clients – the "mashers" and "swells" from the West End who slummed it in the Abyss; the drunken sailors who staggered ashore, looking for a girl in every port; Becky Hunt, who kept a house of ill repute in Canal Road; a couple who did the same in Cleveland Street; a fat procuress named Fraser. Sometimes Charrington followed the girls' cabs to the fashionable West End brothels of the Haymarket and Duke Street, haranguing embarrassed clients. "Her house", he would shout, "is the way to Hell, going down to the chambers of death." The judge was impressed. Crowder and Payne lost their case.

Charrington was less lucky when he tackled the Variety Theatre in Leicester Square with its indecent ballet, *A Dream of Wealth*. It was as though the cosmopolitan West End, with its money and its power, was too much for the simple Valiant- For-Good who was out of his depth. Like a former-day Mary Whitehouse, he found himself a laughing stock among the sophisticates of London. The *Scots Observer* criticized Charrington for not actually going into the halls he despised. And his "Grocer", the evangelistic member of the London County Council who did, was further ridiculed because he recognized prostitutes by the fact that they walked in pairs and didn't look at him because he wasn't sufficiently "swell"! These "chieftains of the fig-leaf" became, in the hands of the journalists of *The Sporting Truth*, "the Peeping Toms, the Paul Prys, the key-hole listeners, the dirty-minded, leprous beings". But the British public was not in one of its periodic fits of morality, and Charrington lost that one.

So he targeted the brothels of the East End. "He came", writes Thorne, "as an avenger of Christ in the first instance. He came to reprove the blackest evil – he came with a sword in his hand to destroy it. And destroy it he did." The brothel-keepers "feared Frederick Charrington as they feared no policeman, no inspector, no other living being". A Mrs Rose, whose name was in Charrington's black book, saw him approaching her house with his customary furled umbrella. She rushed inside, locking the door and keeled over, dead from a heart attack.

"It must have been an august and terrible thing", sermonized Guy Thorne in 1912, "for a man to know that, filled with the power of the Holy Ghost, he was the medium of so sudden and awful a death." With the help of H Division, Frederick Charrington closed down over 200 East End brothels.

What is the evidence against the brewer-turned-avenger? Let's begin with his appearance. In 1912, when Charrington was 62, Guy Thorne described him as:

> a tall, though not a very tall man. He is broad shouldered, but slender… His hair, of a dark brown, grows thickly. He wears moustaches and a very small imperial (beard). The eyes are of a deep, steadfast blue, and have an extraordinary power of penetration…the eyes of a man who has nothing to conceal. The nose is straight and Grecian, the lips tender and humorous – a singularly handsome man, in short.

At the time of the Ripper killings, Charrington was 38 and the best known photograph of him, in profile, was probably taken ten years before this. He has a centre parting, a drooping moustache and no imperial. The adjective that springs to mind is ordinary, rather than singularly handsome. In his public wanderings round the East End, Charrington usually carried a furled umbrella. Without it, he would attract less attention. The eyewitness accounts of men seen talking to Jack's victims shortly before they died differ quite considerably and we are obviously talking about witnesses whose memories were impaired, whose eyesight was poor, whose glimpses were brief and in bad light. It is also clear that we are talking about more than one man. Even so, some of the witnesses could have been describing Charrington. One of two men with Liz Stride on the night of the double event was 5 feet 11 inches tall by Israel Schwartz's reckoning. He was 35 and had a fresh complexion and light brown hair. The man seen by Joseph Lawende talking to Kate Eddowes later the same night could also have been Charrington. He was between 5 feet 7 inches and 5 feet 9 inches tall (but again we are dealing with the appallingly lit Church Passage that led into Mitre Square) and he had a fair complexion and moustache.

If the Ripper was Charrington, why did no one recognize him? The answer is they did, and this explains the ease with which he lulled them into a false sense of security. For all that Charrington was the *bête noire* of the brothel keepers, his known contacts with their girls was always friendly. On one occasion, he paid for a breakfast for 20 of them who had been turned out of a brothel; on another, a gang of a dozen, snarling and spitting like the Furies, saved him from a severe beating by West End "swells". Suddenly, given Charrington's deep religious convictions, the line to Liz Stride in Berner Street – "you would say anything but your prayers" – takes on a new meaning. Why didn't Frederick Charrington actually go into the music halls and brothels he so despised? Was it because he was afraid he'd be recognized from those four nights when his wanderings were not so innocent? And when Polly Nichols, Annie Chapman, Liz Stride, Kate Eddowes and Mary Kelly, came face to face with their killer, they wouldn't scream or cry out because it was just Mr Charrington. The most they had to fear from him was a sermon.

The Abyss proper – that square half mile that included Whitechapel, Spitalfields, Aldgate and all the murder sites – was not actually Charrington's stamping ground. But it was his back yard. Have we been looking too closely for a man who lived in that tight labyrinth of courts and alleys? Should we cast our net wider? He was born in Bow Road and lived for most of the period at 41 Stepney Green. His various temperance halls were built along Mile End Road. Half a mile to the west lay Buck's Row where Polly Nichols died and half a mile beyond that the other murder sites. The furthest Charrington would have had to walk, to Mitre Square, was a mile and a half. He would have known the area well, but he would not draw too much attention to himself by killing on the Mile End Waste itself. Similarly, Charrington didn't target "girls" in their brothels, where there'd be witnesses and where he'd be recognized (his photograph was pinned on the wall of some of these premises). Neither did he kill in the music halls, because the chance of his detection would be enormous. Better to pick on the singletons, women who "carried the banner" in somebody else's manor, broken down-and-outs who were the next social level down from the working girls who frequented the halls.

What other evidence is there? Experts on serial killers today – and Jack was undeniably the first recorded example of this type – agree that there is in such men a childhood "triad"; three habits which are warning signs. We have no idea whether Frederick Charrington wet the bed as a small boy or showed sadistic urges from the age of seven or eight, but we do know of an incident that took place when he was nine. At his father's house in Wimbledon, "Master Fred" threw a bundle of bank notes on the fire because "he wanted to see a blaze". Guy Thorne, in the psychological innocence of 1912, tells this story proudly, as it shows Charrington's contempt for money and all things material at an early age. Many serial killers are fascinated by fire and experiment with arson for years before, during and after they take to murder. It is interesting that in the case of Charrington *vs* Crowder and Payne, the evangelist's evidence was that he regularly watched Lusby's music hall "from 1880 up to the time of the fire". Fires in the East End, especially in dockland, were common (there was one on the night of Polly Nichols's murder), but for Charrington to use this as a landmark in time is very telling.

What of his private life? Celibacy, self-denial, the spartan rituals of his home at the "Monastery" – all these form a definite, if circumstantial pattern. Charrington lived alone, in a separate part of the house from his housekeeper, Mrs Pilgrim. In that sense he could come and go as he pleased, in any range of drab East End clothing that suited him. We know nothing of Mrs Pilgrim, but we can be sure she was used to his nightly wanderings (on his own evidence in court he was often out until the early hours) and he would not be remotely suspicious if he came in late. And if she was up and noticed blood on his clothes? Well, it was that brave, reckless Mr Charrington standing up for good again and taking a beating at the hands of harlots' "bullies" or the West End "swells".

His relationship with the police is fascinating. On numerous occasions he had to be rescued by them from a hostile mob; on others he saved a patrolling constable from a beating. Generally, though, he saw too much of their corruption and negative attitude to speak well of them. He wrote letters to the press complaining of their drunkenness and would harangue a tipsy copper in the street. There were times when they abandoned him to his fate and during the Chancery proceedings of 1885, when asked for police testimony of the behaviour of prostitutes in the Theatre of Varieties, he said, "We know all about the police. We do not want any evidence from them." Is this an honest man unimpressed by a police force that habitually took back-handers and turned blind eyes? Or is it a guilty man who wanted to stay as far away from the law as he could?

What do we know of Charrington's sexual history? Almost nothing, but in Victorian England that is hardly strange. The subject was taboo, spoken of in hushed whispers in polite circles, if at all. We know that Charrington was celibate, and this by choice. His biographer says nothing of any relationships he may have had, but then Guy Thorne, for all he warns against authors who gush about their subjects, is guilty of such sycophancy. Reading *The Great Acceptance* we have a nauseating two- dimensional picture of the man, larded over with Victorian schmaltz. It is noticeable that Charrington was "an observer", which our more cynical age might read as "voyeur". And of course the East End, with its illicit couplings in courts and alleyways, was a voyeur's paradise.

When the crusading journalist W T Stead began to research material for his exposé of the child prostitution racket – "The Maiden Tribute of Modern Babylon" (1885) – who should he turn to but Frederick Charrington? In turn, the evangelist passed him on to a reformed brothel-keeper, but Charrington was clearly regarded as an expert on sordid and taboo subjects, a man in the know.

What can we gauge of Charrington's motives? He was, in modern psychological jargon, a mission-oriented killer. We know that the famous Ripper letter – "I am down on whores" – was a forgery, but Jack shared the sentiments absolutely. Charrington was not so much down on whores as down on the society that made them. By 1888 he had spent nearly 20 years fighting the liquor lords, the indifference of the wealthy and the hypocrisy of the church-going West End, who nightly slummed it with the girls of the Abyss. He had had successes, certainly, but they were limited. In modern American parlance, you can't fight City Hall forever. But what if something appalling were to happen in the East End? Not in the Mile End Road or Stepney Green, because that was too close to home. What about the Ghetto, the Abyss, Whitechapel and Spitalfields? And it would have to be appalling, in that den of dreadful violence, for the world to sit up and take notice. And appalling it was. Charrington struck five times, each time (except the third, when he was interrupted) becoming more vicious so that the world could not close its eyes any more.

He knew the Abyss like the back of his hand. His face was well enough known for no one to find it odd that he was there. He knew the police patrols, the streets they walked and those they missed. The victims were random; he was probably spoiled for choice. And luck, of course was on his side. No one reported Mr Charrington talking to any of the five. No one saw him slipping unseen out of Buck's Row or Hanbury Street or Dutfield's Yard or Mitre Square or the wretched little room rented by Mary Kelly, the room, incidentally, in which Frederick Charrington couldn't resist lighting a large, fierce fire in the tiny grate.

The fire he lit in the Abyss in the Autumn of Terror spread with terrifying speed to the West End; to Britain at large; to the world. American newspapers wrote of Jack the Ripper, so did French, so did Russian. And when Guy Thorne spoke of the 1880s in 1912 he wrote of a time that had already vanished. By our standards, of course, there was still poverty in the East End, but, comparing 1888 with the post-Edwardian world, a minor miracle had occurred. It was not just the 200 brothels that Charrington himself had closed down, but the Four Percent Building Company and the Rothschild tenements that transformed the whole area. The world was horrified by the killings in the Abyss and slowly, but with grim determination, the world began to put it right.

When Peter Sutcliffe, the Yorkshire Ripper, was arrested for his crimes, he saw himself as "the street cleaner": "The women I killed were filth – bastard prostitutes who were littering the streets. I was just cleaning the place up a bit".

Frederick Charrington was the street cleaner in 1888 and in that sense Guy Thorne is quite right when he says that his hero began a furious, God-inspired onslaught upon the dens of East London". As he cut the throats of Polly Nichols, Annie Chapman, Liz Stride, Kate Eddowes and Mary Kelly, it was more furious than Thorne could imagine. "We must do something," Charrington wrote to a friend about the curse of the demon drink. "We must get a gang of men armed with cudgels and go and smash the fronts of the public houses. We shall never do anything 'till we call attention to it."

He carried out the same resolve against prostitution, not with a gang of men, but alone; not with cudgels, but a knife. And Guy Thorne is writing about someone else, whose name he does not give us, but it might as well be Charrington:

> His open life was kindly, polished, cultured and blameless. He *was* kindly and cultured. But beneath it all, as very few people ever knew, as very few people will ever know, this man lived a life of such black shame that one can only hope and pray that his stained soul has not gone to swell the red quadrilles of Hell.

There – you fell for it. Or at least, I hope you did. I want to apologize publicly to Frederick Nicholas Charrington, because he was a good man doing a difficult job in a difficult time, and because he was no more Jack the Ripper than I am.

But isn't it easy – frighteningly easy – to put a man in the frame? To take the random jottings of a life – any life; it might be yours or mine – and build them into a sinister framework of guilt and complicity? That, in essence, is what we've done for a hundred years in the case of the Whitechapel murderer. Isn't enough enough?

Was James Kelly "Jack the Ripper"?

James Tully

What *is* it about the "Ripper" murders that they should continue to fascinate successive generations? There have, after all, been other series of killings before and since which involved equally savage mutilations, and in which the perpetrators were never caught, so what is perceived to be different about these? Of course, the fact that "Jack" was never apprehended is a major factor, but that is by no means the be all and end all of it.

To my mind, the legend which maintains the interest began at the inquest of what I consider to be the third victim, Annie Chapman. It was then that the police surgeon declared that the manner in which certain parts of the body had been removed denoted an expert or one who, at least, had anatomical knowledge. That started the hare of the "mad doctor" running and, even though other medical men involved in the investigations did not agree, it runs to this day.

Then, as theories involving "toffs" came along, the evening dress aspect was added until the popular conception of a *Phantom of the Opera*-type figure, complete with scarlet-lined cape, top hat and Gladstone bag, emerged. Never mind that such a figure might have been just a little conspicuous in the labyrinths of stinking alleys, nor that he might have aroused some apprehension in potential victims at the height of the "Ripper" scare – he is here to stay.

Combine such a "romantic" figure with Victorian buildings, foggy gas lit cobbled streets, the supposed screams of the victims, the blowing of policemen's whistles and, not least, the letters, and a scenario was created to live on down the years.

So, who *was* "Jack the Ripper"?

Everyone "knows" – and yet nobody does.

Those with little or no interest in the mystery "know" that he – for I think we may take it for granted that he *was* a man – was a mad high society doctor or a "Royal", and that, almost certainly, the Freemasons were involved.

If pressed, they are hard put to say from whence such "knowledge" was acquired, and that is hardly surprising for it is an amalgamation of theories based upon tenuous evidence, completely fictitious films and highly imaginative East End folk lore.

Then there are the "experts" who will tell you quite definitely who "Jack" was, and are usually blinkered to all other possibilities. Even were a video recording available of someone other than their candidates actually committing the murders, they would not believe it.

However, among those who fall into neither category, there would seem to be a general wish for an objective look at the few known facts, with nothing omitted or altered, in order to accommodate a particular theory.

That, though, is easier said than done for the average "Ripperist", for few have the time or inclination – or are prepared or able to spend the money – to go back to source documents, and nothing else, in an effort to separate the factual wheat from the fictitious chaff of over a century.

I have studied these killings, on and off, for almost 40 years now. It has taken me most of that time to effect such a separation, and to light upon a suspect whom I consider to be the most likely candidate to date.

It will be noticed that I have not stated dogmatically that he *is* the "Ripper", and my book was called *The Secret of Prisoner 1167: Was This Man Jack the Ripper?* to reflect my opinion that we shall never know for certain who he was. Nevertheless, James Kelly *is*, in my opinion, the most believable suspect yet.

"Well, he *would* say that, wouldn't he?" I hear some declare and, having written a lengthy book about him, I suppose that I should expect to be accused of having a vested interest in promoting his candidature. That, however – and you have only my word for it – is far from being the case.

Over the years I have examined in detail every major theory ever put forward, but somehow I was never convinced, and I viewed some writers' lack of objectivity with dismay. In fact I so despaired of what was being published that the idea was born to write my own book, but the circumstances were not right and so I placed the whole mystery to one side for a time and concentrated upon other things.

All the time, though, I had a gut feeling – if such a term is permissible in connection with the "Ripper" – that, as I have written elsewhere, these atrocities were nothing more than a series of sordid murders perpetrated in a particularly sordid area by, almost certainly, the sort of sordid nondescript portrayed in modern psychological profiles. I pictured an apparently inoffensive little man who lived and worked in the area, a faceless being so ordinary that he aroused no interest or suspicion and was able, therefore, to pass freely. Such a man would probably have been known by sight at least to his victims, and so he would have been perfectly acceptable to them as a client, even when the panic was at its highest.

In my book I have described how James Kelly was brought to my attention by contemporary press reports, and how I was persuaded to investigate him. I began to examine his background with great reluctance, and I fear that I would have been even more half-hearted had I known that I was embarking upon nine long years of research and frustrations. Ironically though, the frustrations which attended my initial enquiries at the Home Office and Broadmoor were what whetted my appetite and gave me the determination to continue that I might otherwise have lacked.

Eventually, but only through the good offices of two Secretaries of State, I was granted access to two confidential files hitherto unseen by any other "Ripper" researcher, and I was allowed to visit Broadmoor.

The Home Office file is closed to the public until the year 2030 and the Broadmoor one in perpetuity. Some documents have been removed officially from the former, despite an injunction on the cover that "This file should never be destroyed" and others are missing. Material has also disappeared from the Broadmoor dossier over the years, but the two files complement each other to a great extent. Together with other information which I unearthed, they revealed a fascinating story.

Obviously it is impossible to set out the contents of a book of almost 400 pages within the confines of this article, but the bare bones of the tale are as follows:

James Kelly was born illegitimately in 1860 of an illiterate 15-year-old Liverpudlian working-class girl, Sarah Kelly, whose family included at least one member who had been certified as insane.

As a result of the stigma attached to unmarried mothers in those days – there were no "love children" then – Sarah abandoned James, leaving her own mother to bring him up as her own son, and she never saw him again. In 1870, Sarah married quite well. Her husband was John Allan, a master mariner with a share in his ship. He died in 1874 leaving everything to his widow, but she died only 11 weeks later. She left a will in which she at last acknowledged her "natural son" and bequeathed him most of her estate – which amounted to around £26,000 by present-day values – to be held in trust until he was 25.

Because of legal delays, James was not told of his mother's death and the contents of her will until early in 1875, and only then did he learn of the circumstances surrounding his birth. The revelations came as a terrible shock to him and were to affect him for the whole of his life. He had been reared in a religious household and was already deeply religious himself, but suddenly his entire world was turned upside down. The woman whom he had always thought to be his mother was actually his grandmother, while his true mother, who had abandoned him at birth, was regarded as having been of loose morals. As recent case studies have confirmed, it was an upset that could have disturbed the mind of a normal lad but, probably because of the insanity in his mother's family, it affected him more than most. Such was his confusion that thereafter he was always known in Liverpool as "Jim Kelly" or "Jim Allan", but when away he preferred to adopt his father's name of John Miller.

Kelly had left school at 13 and had been apprenticed to a firm of upholsterers in Liverpool. He enjoyed the work thoroughly but, as money was now available from his mother's will for his further education, his apprenticeship was terminated and, without being consulted, he was packed off to a business school across the River

Mersey. He was at the school for over two years. Although he seems to have been a good pupil, it was a lonely, bewildering and miserable time for him.

When he was 17, and again without any consideration of how he might have felt about it, a position was found for him with a Liverpool pawnbroker and he was placed in lodgings nearby. Lonely and friendless, he became more and more dissatisfied with his situation and gradually symptoms of mental instability began to appear. His work was unreliable, and any minor incident was sufficient to send him into a rage. He became filled with an obsession to leave Liverpool and everyone who knew of his background and had taunted him about it. Therefore, after only 18 months with the pawnbroker, he had a meeting with the solicitor acting for the trustee of his mother's estate. The outcome was that it was agreed that money would be made available to him to enable him to go to London and resume his trade as an upholsterer.

Once in London, Kelly registered with the East London Upholsterers' Trade Society as an "improver". Its lodge was at the Horse and Groom pub which was, and indeed still is, in Curtain Road, Shoreditch, and less than 300 yards from Commercial Street. Regular employment in the upholstery trade was scarce, and every morning Kelly went to the Horse and Groom to see whether any casual work was available.

Sometimes it was, but on the many occasions when it was not he took whatever unskilled jobs he could find elsewhere. That took him all over the East End and he began to know the area intimately, especially Spitalfields, Whitechapel and Bethnal Green. For a time he is believed to have lodged with the Lamb family at 37 Collingwood Street, Bethnal Green, which was less than 200 yards from where Polly Nichols's body was later discovered in Buck's Row.

Forbidden by his faith to have sexual intercourse outside of marriage, and disliking and distrusting most women, James Kelly had had no girlfriends or sexual experiences in Liverpool. All that changed shortly after his arrival in London.

With money in his pockets, and nothing else to do at nights, he began to drink heavily and became a target for the many prostitutes and "enthusiastic amateurs". Hardly surprisingly, therefore, it was not long before he lost his virginity to one. Despite the remorse which he was to feel after every such encounter, he continued to patronize them. For a young man in his circumstances, the use of their impersonal services was part of the answer to his problems with women. It was possible to obtain instant sexual gratification without being involved emotionally, and afterwards he could dismiss them with contempt. The only trouble was that his religious conscience bothered him, and also he found that his money was disappearing fast.

It may well have been the realization that he could not continue upon such a path of self-destruction that eventually, when he was 19, drove him away from London to, for some reason unknown, Brighton. We have only the briefest details about what he did there. All that is known comes from some papers from Clerkenwell Prison which state that Kelly was "for some time in lodgings in Brighton – does not know street. Then in an American man-of-war."

There is no explanation of why he was on board an American warship, nor of where he went in it, but two years later he was back in the East End, stronger physically and more mature, but still mentally unstable.

He resumed contact with his trade society in Curtain Road, and obtained casual work all over the East End and other parts of London. As before, he turned his hand to whatever else was available between upholstery jobs and, using the knowledge acquired on the American warship, no doubt, he appears to have secured casual employment on some of the many boats which made regular trips to and from the Continent, as well as working in and around the docks. That, therefore, was another district which he came to know very well, and where he made some good friends who were to stand by him in the perilous years ahead.

By then Kelly was drinking more heavily. The indications are that he was patronizing prostitutes on a regular basis again, until he met 20-year-old Sarah Brider, known within her family as "Titty". There must have been something exceptional about that young lady because soon he was courting her and then he moved in with her family as a lodger at their home at 21 Cottage Lane, just off City Road.

Sarah's mother always extolled her daughter's virtue, and certainly no intimacy took place between the young couple for over a year, during which time Kelly continued to enjoy the favours of the East End demi-monde. Then he began to experience severe pains in his head, which were accompanied by nasty discharges from both ears. His work began to suffer and he became more moody. It was at that time that, to add to his misery, he discovered that he had contracted a venereal disease during one of his casual encounters and that added hatred to his contempt for such women. Kelly did not consult a doctor about any of his maladies, preferring instead to treat himself. The result was that his head pains became worse and he was sacked from his first permanent job because, as his employer wrote: "He was obviously not right in the head."

Despite that, James Kelly and Sarah Brider were wed on 4 June 1883, but the marriage was to last less than three weeks. Kelly began to row violently with his wife, accusing her of being a prostitute and inveigling him into marriage for his money. In his madness he even alleged that it was she who had infected him with venereal disease. Only a fortnight after they were married he threatened her with a large carving knife and then, on 21 June, the last act took place. In the middle of yet another row, he suddenly put his arm around her neck, dragged her head down to the floor, stabbed her below the left ear and began digging away with the penknife as if bent upon further damage.

He was interrupted by his mother-in-law, who ran into the street screaming for help. Subsequently Sarah was taken to St Bartholomew's Hospital and Kelly to Old Street police station. He told the PC who arrested him, "I don't know what I am about. I must be mad."

Sarah died on 24 June 1883, and on 1 August Kelly was in the dock at the Old Bailey charged with murder. The jury found him guilty, but added a recommendation of mercy.

When asked if he had anything to say before sentence was pronounced, Kelly launched into a lengthy tirade during which he declared that he was sure that God had already forgiven him, and that he would like to live in order to serve Him.

He was allowed his say in full, but then he was sentenced to death, with the judge adding that what Kelly had said during his address to the court was likely to affect the jury's recommendation. Still ranting, Kelly had to be removed from the dock forcibly and was then taken to the condemned cell in Newgate Prison.

An appeal was lodged, but the Home Secretary refused to commute the sentence to life imprisonment and the date of execution was arranged for 20 August. Nevertheless Kelly continued to assert that he would not be hanged. He maintained that God would save him because He had a mission for him – and, to his mind, he was proved right.

On 7 August the Superintendent of Broadmoor reported to the Home Office that he had been part of a team which had examined Kelly. He stated that: "Our examination has afforded us sufficient evidence to show that the prisoner is a man of defective mental capacity: and although tranquil at the present time yet that he has always been of unstable mind and a person whom one would expect to become actively insane from a comparatively minor cause."

That report saved Kelly. Only three days before he was due to be hanged, he was certified insane and removed from Newgate back to Clerkenwell Prison. On 24 August he was admitted to Broadmoor, firmly convinced that he had been saved by divine intervention. He was housed in the block which held "the quite mad, but quietly so, and the suicidal", and was found to be paranoid, deeply depressed and exhibiting signs of religious mania.

For three years Kelly was withdrawn, brooding over his festering grievances against women. He blamed his mother for being of loose morals, the circumstances of his birth and for abandoning him; his grandmother for deceiving him; prostitutes for giving him venereal disease; and his wife and mother-in-law for tricking him into marriage and the many other deceptions which he thought they had practised upon him. During that period he was quite incapable of coherent speech and was left to his own devices by staff and inmates alike.

Then, around the middle of 1886, subtle changes began to take place in his condition which the doctors were unable to explain. In the following year those changes became more noticeable. A Broadmoor report states that he was "more contented and cheerful", but again the doctors did not know why, and they had no idea of what he was thinking and feeling.

The only clues to his secret thoughts lie in his subsequent statements and actions. All along he had remained convinced that there was a divine plan for him, and he had not been able to understand why it was taking so long for his destiny to be fulfilled. Almost daily he had expected a sign, and had suffered bouts of depression when it did not come.

In the event there were two events that could have been construed as signs and Kelly and an accomplice ended up making duplicate keys for the outside door of their block. Then, on the night of 23 January 1888, Kelly – with what he described as "Devine (*sic*) Help" – went over the wall on his own, leaving the keys for his partner to use on another occasion.

It took Kelly over three days to walk to his destination, which was a particular lodging house in the East End docks where he had friends. When he arrived he was, in his own words, so "knocked out" by the privations which he had endured in getting there that he was forced to lie up for a whole week. He recuperated, and regained his strength. Then he "got a little money from friends" and made for Liverpool, taking casual work in the Midlands en route. In Liverpool he "got some more money off friends" and then he walked to Harwich where he managed to secure a berth in a ship with a view to working his passage to the Continent. We are not told how long all that took him, but he must have been well pleased with his progress and even more convinced that God was aiding him.

However his luck, or whatever, almost ran out at Harwich. His ship was tied up alongside, and one day while he was working on deck an observant bobby recognized him from the description which had been issued and went on board to arrest him.

He escaped by the skin of his teeth and, with little money and nowhere else to go, he slogged his way back to London and reappeared in the East End at some time during the first half of 1888. There he "stayed with friends" for a time, who may or may not have been the Lambs in Collingwood Street, until he had recovered and felt that the hunt for him had died down. All that he could do during those first weeks was to husband his money and avoid going out during daylight hours.

Kelly was always reticent about where precisely in the East End he lived, and what he did, for the next five or six months. Two facts which are indisputable, however, are that Martha Tabram was murdered in the early hours of 7 August 1888, and that James Kelly fled precipitately and almost penniless to France immediately after the killing of Mary Kelly on 9 November.

Martha Tabram is not generally accepted by the "experts" as having been one of the "Ripper's" victims, despite the opinions of several highly placed policemen of the time that she was. For my part, I have little doubt that she was, and I think it more likely than not that James Kelly killed her and that the subsequent murders exhibited the classic symptoms of escalating violence associated with serial killers as he perfected his technique.

One of the reasons why some consider that Martha was not a "Ripper" victim is that her throat was not *sliced* from ear to ear, as in the later cases, but *stabbed* with an ordinary penknife. If, however, Kelly was the "Ripper", those stab wounds to the throat – and with a pocket knife at that – bear a remarkable similarity to the injuries which he inflicted upon his wife. The other wounds that Martha suffered had sexual connotations which one would expect after the years that Kelly had spent alone in Broadmoor fantasizing over what more he could have done to Sarah had he not been interrupted.

So the murders began. Although James Monro, the Assistant Commissioner (CID) of the Metropolitan Police, had been in correspondence with Broadmoor about Kelly less than six months before – three letters in three weeks – and despite the fact that Kelly's narrow squeak at Harwich had been reported upon far more recently, the penny did not drop at Scotland Yard until immediately after Mary Kelly's death. That, as we know, was on 9 November. On the very next day the "Detective Police" raided James Kelly's former home in Cottage Lane and gave his mother-in-law such a rough time that she had her solicitor write a letter of protest. Part of that letter states that "so severely was she questioned, and so rudely was she treated, that she is now in a state of ill-health consequent upon this treatment."

Then, and very coincidentally, on 12 November "CET" at the Home Office dusted down James Kelly's file, after eight months, and wrote a minute to "CM" which reads: "Would it not be well to make inquiry as to what steps have been taken to recapture this man? It is not likely he is the Whitechapel murderer; but his offence was cutting his wife's throat, and he escaped last January, it would be well to know what has become of him."

"CM" then wrote to Broadmoor and received a reply from the Superintendent stating that: "No tidings have reached us of James Kelly since his escape. My impression was and is that he may possibly have gone abroad."

He was, of course, completely right. After the killing in Miller's Court, Kelly walked the 80 miles to Dover and managed to work his passage to Dieppe on a cross-Channel steamer. In his usual way, when anything which he may have said could have incriminated him or others, Kelly was to draw a veil over what exactly he did next. All that we know is that, for whatever reason, he hugged the coastline of northern France, between Dieppe and Boulogne, during the ensuing months. In that period, during which there is reason to believe that Kelly sometimes worked on cross-Channel boats, Alice McKenzie and Frances Coles were murdered, but then, in an abrupt change of direction, Kelly walked to Paris.

Life was not easy for him there and so he slogged back to the Channel coast and, with the aid of a sovereign loaned to him by a clergyman's son, he was back in England at the end of January 1892. By the spring of that year he had acquired sufficient money to buy a ticket for America, via Rotterdam, and he sailed to New York on a German steamer named the *Zaandam*. He was in the United States for 18 months, but at the end of that time he had had enough of the country. The change of climate and the mosquitoes caused him to become very ill, and he longed to get back to England.

In 1895 there was a rumour that he had been seen in Liverpool, and that may have been true because soon after that he worked his way back to the States. By a combination of walking and "stealing rides on trains", he made his way through California, Arizona and New Mexico to El Paso and Dallas.

He found regular work in Dallas for a while and used the opportunity to rest before undertaking the next leg of his travels which took him to Louisiana and New Orleans. It was there that he again decided that he had had enough of America and that he wanted to go home, and so, on 27 January 1896, he walked into the British Consulate and surrendered himself to the Vice-Consul. He made a long statement recounting his history to date, but omitted all mention of his return to London in 1893.

The British Consul, a Mr C L St John, forwarded that statement to the Foreign Secretary, who passed it to the Home Office which, in turn, sought the opinion of Dr Nicholson, then Superintendent of Broadmoor. Nicholson replied that "he ought certainly to come back to Broadmoor again", but still the Home Office dithered and so, after four weeks of kicking his heels and hearing nothing, Kelly took matters into his own hands.

He told Mr St John that he would "see the thing through" himself, and work his passage home, if the Consul would use his influence to secure him a berth. That was done, and Kelly was escorted to the steamer SS *Capella* which was bound for Liverpool. He signed on in his father's name – "John Miller".

The Foreign Office informed the Home Office of what had been organized, and when the *Capella* was due to dock, and they in turn told Broadmoor and Scotland Yard. It was arranged that a party of attendants from the asylum would meet the ship in, but the Liverpool police were asked to have an escort on hand at the docks in case the Broadmoor contingent was "unexpectedly delayed". In the event, however, neither party was present when the *Capella* docked, so Kelly changed his mind about surrendering, crossed over the Mersey to Birkenhead and laid low until whatever hue and cry which may have been mounted had died down. He then walked all the way back to the East End of London.

During the following years Kelly was to make the return trip across the Atlantic at least five more times. In 1901, though, he was homesick again and therefore he tried once more to give himself up to the authorities. He went to the British Consul in Vancouver and told his story. The Consul notified London. Just as before, however, no reply was received and so, after waiting for three whole months, Kelly again worked his passage back to Liverpool.

It was a long voyage, giving him an opportunity to consider fully the implications of his decision, and once again he had a change of mind about surrendering. Therefore, and contrary to what he had intended, he did not loiter in Liverpool when the ship docked, but made straight for London. Over the next few years Kelly worked in London and various other places as an upholsterer or coach trimmer, and it is possible that he made some of his other trips to the United States during that period. However the next time that he came to the attention of the authorities was by way of an anonymous letter.

Contained in a small envelope marked "Important" and bearing a penny stamp, the letter had been posted in Liverpool on 25 January 1906. It was addressed to "Detective Sergeant Pierpoint, Dale St, Liverpool", and reads:

I see by Liverpool Exchange on the escape of Liverpool murderer (22.1.06).

All that I can say is that the authorities haven't looked much for him as he is and has been for some time in London living on the Caledonian Road under the name of John Miller and following his trade when he can of an upholsterer.

Two months ago he was seen for a dead certainty in East Ham.

He is a bicycle rider and still at that time had his bicycle.

That is the truth and can be proved in 2 or 3 months time from now, but before that you ought to find him. You will find him still crazy and dangerous and mad as a hatter on certain points and better off under lock and key than he is now.

He had his violin until this last few years, perhaps he has one now for all I know. He has rooms furnished by himself.

For a man in your position he is as easy to find as St Georges Hall in Liverpool or Cleopatras Needle on the Embankment and still haunts the neighbourhood of his crime.

Several Liverpool people that know him from early days noticed that account in the papers, although he was called James Kelly in the *Echo*, recognized him as Jim Allen and now John Miller living on or off the Caledonian Market.

The letter was sent to the Home Office and the contents were relayed to Broadmoor and Scotland Yard, but the latter, in marked contrast to all its excitement about Kelly in 1888, displayed little interest in trying to apprehend the fugitive. It issued a circular which omitted many of the facts contained in the letter, and ended with the remarkable instruction that Kelly was "Not to be arrested but, if traced, immediate inf. to this office".

In the files is a report attached to that circular. It is unsigned and there is no addressee, but it is headed "Criminal Investigation Department, New Scotland Yard", and is dated 6 February 1906. It gives a few facts about Kelly and may have formed the basis for a long, undated report signed by "Chas. Arrow, Chief Inspector", and countersigned and recommended by "A. Hare, Superintendent". This document states that "these papers" had been sent out for the information of Superintendents G, K & Y Divisions and ends:

> Police have no photograph of this man and, as he was last in the hands of the police 23 years ago, there is scarcely likely to be an officer serving who could recognize him.
>
> I respectfully submit that, considering the meagre (?) and unreliable information given, there is little chance of tracing this man by enquiry in the neighbourhood of the Caledonian Road or East Ham and suggest that a special enquiry might be called for; upholsterers, description of the man etc. for what it is worth.

These are extraordinary documents.

The last report states that in 1896 Kelly had worked his passage from New Orleans under the name of "John Miller", but the circular does not mention that nor Kelly's other known aliases. Also, none of the papers included the clues that would have been invaluable to a bobby familiar with his beat, i.e. that Kelly (a) was living in the "*Market*" area of Caledonian Road; (b) rode a bicycle; and (c) played the violin.

One positive statement that Arrow *did* make was that the Metropolitan Police had no photograph of Kelly but, unless they had lost them, that was untrue because two photographs of him were sent to the Commissioner on 30 January 1888. In any event, no inquiries were made to see whether Broadmoor had one – and they did. Arrow also wrote that there was "scarcely likely to be an officer serving who could recognize him", but no effort was made to find out if that was so, nor to attempt to trace any retired officers who might have known him.

There is an air of defeatism about Arrow's report that is summed up in his phrase "for what it is worth" and that seems to reflect the whole attitude of Scotland Yard. It appears to have been a case of "It's doubtful whether Kelly can be traced, but if you do happen to trip over him, despite our having withheld vital information from you, don't arrest him, just tell us and we'll allow him to escape again." The impression given is that Scotland Yard did not want Kelly caught.

Needless to say, he was *not* apprehended, and in 1907 Broadmoor disowned him formally. In the "Notice of Discharge", they stated that: "As this patient has not been recaptured, he has been written off the Asylum's books."

During the years that followed Kelly went back and forth to America. In between trips he found work as an upholsterer or coach trimmer in London and other places, one job which he held being only eight miles from Broadmoor. However his hearing had been failing for some years, and in 1917 he became totally deaf. His deafness, together with his periodic episodes of unusual behaviour, made him the target of much abuse, and sometimes he was treated quite brutally by his fellow workers. Then, in 1924, his general physical health began to deteriorate and he was no longer able to command the good wages which he had enjoyed.

By that time his trade society had merged with the Amalgamated Union of Upholsterers, but he was still registered as a member – under the name of "John Miller" – and he was found less demanding work, in Luton. However the pay was very much lower, and he was treated even more poorly by his new workmates. He was convinced that "sinister influences" were working against him, and he became even more peculiar in his ways. That notwithstanding, he continued to work and was able to support himself until about August 1925, when he became unemployable in his trade.

Kelly was then 65, and for the next 18 months he struggled to survive. He had returned to the East End and although he was sometimes forced to walk the streets at night – with all the memories which they might have held for him – he managed to exist by earning a few pence here and there from odd jobs. However, even after all the years that had elapsed since 1888, he, in his own words, lived in "constant fear" that he "might be pounced upon" by any passing policeman.

Eventually, feeling that old age was closing in, and that "the struggle was hopeless", he took a decision which he had been considering for some time, and set out for Broadmoor.

He appeared at the main gate on the afternoon of 11 February 1927, "a wizened little man with grey hair and wrinkled face, footsore and half-starved" as the *News of the World* described him and pleaded for shelter.

The attendant on the gate listened incredulously to Kelly's long rambling tale, made worse by his inability to hear any questions, and then summoned the Superintendent, Dr Foulerton. Kelly was interviewed at length, but then, pending identification, the Wokingham police were telephoned and asked to remove a lunatic!

Next day he appeared before the local magistrates charged with being "a mentally deranged person wandering abroad". In the meantime, however, and in complete contrast with the lethargy displayed by Scotland Yard, the Superintendent had instituted inquiries and had found two retired attendants who had known Kelly. They identified him instantly, and Dr Foulerton therefore informed the Home Office and requested instructions.

The reply came by telegram. He was told that Kelly should be readmitted to Broadmoor, and that a report should be submitted on his mental condition and his history since 1888. That "Medical Report" was sent on 14 February, and the Superintendent gave his opinion that "Broadmoor ought not to be regarded as an alms house or place where criminal lunatics may return to spend the waning years of life." He went on to state that "Kelly seems more suitable for a workhouse infirmary than for Broadmoor Asylum, he would not be certifiable as insane". An accompanying letter devoted only three lines to Kelly's history since his escape.

Dr Foulerton's views were ignored. He was instructed to do as he had been asked and submit a more detailed report on Kelly's movements since 1888. Also, and unusually, he was ordered to make regular reports on the patient's mental condition. However something significant must have taken place at the Home Office in the interim because, only three days later, without any of its officials having even seen the patient and in direct contradiction of the Superintendent's professional opinion, he was told flatly that Kelly was "now insane" and should be kept in Broadmoor!

Kelly's mental condition deteriorated rapidly from that moment on, and within a year he was complaining that he was being "dosed in order to make him an idiot".

By May 1928, he was described as being "delusioned and mentally enfeebled" and in December of that year his bodily condition was said to be "weak". He was diagnosed as being paranoid and showing signs of senile degeneration.

He could not have been *that* senile, though, because in 1929 he decided that he did not like what was being done for – or to – him and he made several efforts to escape again. However he had always been kept under close supervision. In addition, the boundary wall had been raised to 16 feet in 1892, thus presenting an obstacle which would have been formidable even to the young and fit James Kelly of 40 years before.

His health continued to worsen and eventually he gave up the ghost, dying peacefully on 17 September 1929. The subsequent post-mortem examination report stated that he had died of double lobar pneumonia and, at an inquest held on 19 September, the coroner recorded a verdict of "natural causes". Kelly was slipped quietly into his grave at Broadmoor the next day, taking all his secrets with him.

Those, then, are the bare bones of the James Kelly story. There is much, much more in my book, but I feel that there is sufficient here to cause an objective reader to wonder why Kelly has never been taken seriously as a candidate for the "Ripper" title.

Let us consider the facts.

1 Kelly is the only suspect ever named officially as possibly being the "Whitechapel Murderer".

2 Kelly was the only convicted insane woman-killer at large in the East End during the period of the killings.

3 Kelly was young, active and strong, and fits virtually every psychological profile of a serial lust killer, although some will object to that, saying that serial killers do not stop their activities voluntarily and therefore Kelly cannot have been one.

That is not completely true, though, but also we do not know whether Kelly, if he *was* the "Ripper", continued his activities in America, and I do not know how one would find out. It would entail writing to every sheriff of every county of every state in the United States, and assumes that they all kept records in those Wild West days, and those records had been preserved.

4 Kelly inflicted injuries to his wife's throat similar to those to Martha Tabram's.

5 Kelly hated women generally, but prostitutes in particular.

6 Kelly was sought actively by the police immediately after the death of Mary Kelly.

7 Kelly had an excellent knowledge of the East End, especially the area in which the murders took place.

8 Kelly had sharp knives and ripping chisels as tools of his trade.

In addition, there are many, many correlations between Kelly and the "Ripper". Just a few of those points mentioned in my book, albeit minor in themselves, when taken together and combined with the points set out above, make up what I consider to be an overwhelming circumstantial case against Kelly.

a Kelly's handwriting is very similar to that in the two original "Ripper" letters, and his margins were observed just as meticulously – as befits one who attended a business academy.

b He had a connection to account for the Americanisms in those letters.

c More than any other suspect, he had every reason for giving "Jack the Ripper" as his *trade* name. Just consider: Kelly used the alias "John Miller" most of the time, and that was the name under which he worked and was registered with his *trade* society. "Jack" is a common diminutive of "John", and one of the tools which he would have used most often as an improver upholsterer involved in renovation work was a ripping chisel – hence "Jack the Ripper"? Is it not possible, also, that the mysterious instrument which broke Martha Tabram's sternum was just such a tool?

As I have said, there are many, many more correlations, including the fact that something like seven "Kellys" are mentioned in connection with these murders. To my mind, there are far *too* many coincidences between James Kelly and the activities of "Jack the Ripper" for them to be merely that.

On top of all of that, we should also consider the, to say the least, peculiar attitudes adopted by the Home Office and Scotland Yard towards Kelly. Now I know that tales of official cover-ups abound in the "Jack the Ripper" saga, but what *are* we supposed to think of James Kelly's case?

Let us recapitulate the facts.

Here was an insane woman-killer whose escape from Broadmoor was known not only to a department of Scotland Yard – the Convict Office – but also to James Monro, the then Assistant Commissioner of police (CID). It is true that Monro did not have an official role in the "Ripper" investigation, but there is no doubt that he was very active behind the scenes.

Monro is reputed to have been an excellent detective, and if that is true it is highly unlikely that he had no thoughts at all about the throat-cutting Kelly when Martha Tabram, Polly Nichols and Annie Chapman were all murdered in similar fashion within a month. He had, after all, written the last of his several letters about James Kelly only just over five months before Martha was killed, and the escape of a murderer from Broadmoor, of all places, was not exactly an everyday occurence. I think we may take it, therefore, that Monro at least had considered the

possibility of Kelly being the murderer and, as he was very close to the
Home Secretary, Henry Matthews, it is likely that he mentioned them to
him. That likelihood is increased by the fact that Matthews told his
private secretary, Evelyn Ruggles-Brise, that "Monro might be willing
to give a hint to the CID people if necessary".

However, when one considers all the facts, including the internal
politics of Scotland Yard at the time, it appears unlikely that Monro did
mention Kelly to the CID, especially as there are no records of the hunt
for him having been revived until after the murder of Mary Kelly some
nine weeks later.

The likelihood is that Monro simply sat on his hands, and all
thoughts of Kelly were forgotten until Mary's death, when either one of
two sets of circumstances arose:

1 The police discovered something in 13, Miller's Court that pointed
directly to James Kelly and caused them to hasten to Cottage Lane.
Their find, and the subsequent fruitless interview with Mrs Brider, was
reported to the Home Office, where Matthews immediately recalled any
mention of Kelly that Monro may have made. He then decided that
Broadmoor should be asked if, by chance, they had any idea where
Kelly might be, but ordered that the inquiry should be couched in
casual terms in order to avoid suspicion that Kelly really might be the
killer.

2 The murder of another "Kelly" revived Home office memories of the
Broadmoor escape, and their note to the Asylum of 12 November was
coincidental with, and independent of, any police find.

Where at all possible, I tend to discount coincidences, and therefore I
plump for the first alternative. However, should I be correct in doing so,
I must say that it was rather remiss of the Home Office not to have told
Dr Nicholson that the police had already enquired at Cottage Lane. Had
they done so, he would not have incurred the wrath of Mrs Brider and
her solicitor.

Of even more interest (and yet another coincidence?), on the
evening of 10 November, i.e. of the same day that the police harassed

Mrs Brider, the *Star* newspaper published an article in which it was stated that: "It is believed by people who pass among their neighbours as sensible folk that the Government do not want the murderer to be convicted, that they are interested in concealing his identity, that in fact, they know it, and will not divulge it." Had someone spoken out of turn?

First thoughts must be that if both the Home Office and the police knew that Kelly was the murderer they would have lost no time in publicizing the fact. It is only when one considers all the possible consequences of such an act that the possibility of a cover-up arises.

Supposing they had revealed that they had been aware, all the time, that a named homicidal maniac was on the loose and yet not only had they done nothing to apprehend him but he *still* eluded capture? Even worse, what if it had become known that, even though the Home Office and James Monro had been aware of Kelly's escape, nobody had had the wit to connect him with the killings? Heads would have rolled, and both the Home Office and Scotland Yard would have been laughing-stocks once the anger had subsided. Even the government could have come under threat.

No, once the James Kelly/"Jack the Ripper" penny had dropped, far from being made public, the main concern would have been to keep it secret.

That could have been done only if most of the policemen actively involved in the investigation had not known that the killer had been identified, because it would have been impossible to silence them all. Who among them, therefore, would have known of any possible Kelly "Ripper" link? Well, it may well be that *none* of them did or, at the most, only a few, but that would depend upon the nature of whatever clue may have been found in Miller's Court.

Had it been something minor, the subsequent report about the Cottage Lane raid could have been pooh-poohed by Monro and the Home Office, with whom alarm bells would have been ringing. On the other hand, a major find would have been followed up by only the most senior of the detectives, and they could easily have been sworn, or bullied, to silence because of the traditions of their department. That would explain why some of them never discussed the case thereafter, while others, constrained to silence about the murderer's true identity, were nevertheless unable to resist the temptation of hinting that they knew more than they could say.

There were some, just as eager to boost their public image, who achieved their joint objectives of secrecy and bolstering their vanity by actually naming possible suspects but not, of course, officially. They merely added to the confusion caused by those who knew nothing but still put forward their wild inventions, thus creating red herrings which continue to deceive some, and obscure the trail, to this very day.

It is also possible that Monro did his utmost to preserve secrecy by ensuring that any investigations involving Kelly or 21, Cottage Lane, were conducted by his own Section D men.

Despite the foregoing, it may well be that there are some readers who still remain to be convinced that there was, and is, a cover-up. Of those I would ask these questions:

1 Why is James Kelly's Home Office file still in the category of "sensitive subjects"?

2 Why does no report of the appearance of detectives at Cottage Lane appear in any *known* file?

3 Why is it that the Home Office file does not contain the original of their enquiry to Broadmoor about the possibility of Kelly being "the Whitechapel Murderer"? Broadmoor itself had no reason to be involved in any cover-up and so, yet again, we find a document in *their* file without which we should not know that the official finger of suspicion had been pointed at James Kelly.

4 Why, in 1906, did Scotland Yard state that they had no photograph of Kelly when we know that they were supplied with two when he escaped? Why did they not ask Broadmoor for one if the originals had been mislaid?

5 As we have seen, there were many communications to and from Scotland Yard about Kelly between 1888 and 1906; what, then, happened to *its* file on him which has, apparently, disappeared? The

Metropolitan Police told me that all their papers, "that have survived" (!), are held for permanent preservation at the Public Record Office at Kew, but that they are unable to trace anything about Kelly. Is that not peculiar? The Home Office and Broadmoor kept *their* files, albeit with documents destroyed or missing, but as far as Scotland Yard is concerned, Kelly never existed. Why should that be?

6 From which "main" file in the series HO 45 were Kelly's supplementary registered papers separated, and where is it now?

7 Why do the Thames Valley Police have nothing on file about Kelly either? Why, despite the fact that it was in their name that the "Wanted" notice about Kelly was published, did the Wokingham Police apparently make no connection between him and the "Ripper"?

8 Why were there no replies from the Home Office when Kelly surrendered himself to the British Consuls at New Orleans and Vancouver?

9 Why, in their 1906 circular, did Scotland Yard give instructions that, should he be traced, Kelly was *not*, repeat *not*, to be arrested?

10 Why was it that the Metropolitan Police could not trace Kelly in 1906, and why were facts which would have aided his apprehension omitted from their defeatist circular?

11 Why, in view of the inquiry to them from the Home Office, was Kelly not questioned about the "Ripper" murders by Broadmoor officials when he returned to the Asylum? Or is it possible that he *was*, but that his original statement is one of the documents that has been destroyed or gone missing? Certainly the extant statement shows no evidence of his having been interrogated in detail about *anything*, and some of the phraseology seems oddly vague. Is it possible that it was virtually dictated to him, just for the record? What adds emphasis to these questions is the fact that several details not contained in the existing statement have slipped into official documents.

12 Why did Monro declare that the "Ripper" should have been caught, and why, after reading some papers which he left with his eldest son, did the latter tell his brother that their father's theory about the identity of the "Ripper" was "a very hot potato"?

A cover-up would explain:

a Why Chief Inspector Walter Dew, a Detective Constable at the time of the murders, was told, and repeated in his memoirs, that inquiries were made at asylums "all over the country, including the Criminal Lunatic Asylum at Broadmoor" but that "no useful evidence was obtained".

b Why there is no police record of *anyone* in the Convict Office, or anywhere else in Scotland Yard, or in the Wokingham Police, having made any connection between the series of murders and the escaped lunatic whom they had all been seeking only months before.

c Why the police presence in the East End was scaled down after Mary Kelly's murder.

d Why the Home Office and Scotland Yard did not want Kelly back in England.

e Why, when he *did* arrive in the country, he was able to elude capture, and instructions were given that he should not be arrested.

f Why no record remains in the Broadmoor or Home Office files of the full results of the questioning to which Kelly was subjected upon his return to the asylum, and why the Home Office should have insisted that he be kept in Broadmoor, despite the Medical Superintendent's opinion that he "would not be certifiable as insane".

g Why he was given the "chemical cosh" at Broadmoor "in order to make him an idiot".

h What "the whole matter" was that weighed on his conscience for all those years, and caused him to "burst into tears" even as late as 1927.

i Why no mention of James Kelly appeared anywhere in connection with the "Ripper" killings for over a century, until John Morrison put him forward as a suspect.

You will look in vain for Kelly's name in any of the memoirs, "discovered" documents, books or public records. They are littered with mentions of harmless Jewish lunatics, a drowned barrister, various poisoners, some society doctors, a royal duke, an assortment of Americans, a famous artist and Uncle Tom Cobley and all. Tenuous connections have been made between all of them and "Jack the Ripper", but nowhere will you find serious mention of the *only* convicted, lunatic, throat-cutting woman-killer who was known by the Home Office and Scotland Yard to have been at large during 1888.

It is now extremely doubtful whether any conclusive and incontrovertible evidence about the identity of "Jack the Ripper" will ever be discovered. Every candidate offered for consideration will therefore need to be judged upon circumstantial evidence, and I submit that, if only in that respect, James Kelly's claim to infamy exceeds by far that of any other.

Without giving any explanation, Kelly said that he had "been on the Warpath" ever since escaping from Broadmoor. I believe I know what he meant by that.

Jack the Ripper: Man or Myth

Peter Turnbull

It is the contention of this argument that the Whitechapel Murders of 1888 were not the work of one man whom today may be dubbed a "serial killer". Rather a strong case may be argued for the theory that the murders were "copycat" murders perpetrated by different men, in a highly localized area, amid a community that had worked itself up into a state of "mass hysteria".

Let us first look at the murders. Casting our net as far backwards as possible, we may take the first victim of the murderous furore to be Emma Smith. Emma was a widowed lady of 45 years who lived in a common lodging house at 18 George Street, Spitalfields. On April 1888 Emma had left the lodging house at 7.00 pm and had returned at 5.00 am the following morning suffering from serious head injuries. She reported to the deputy keeper at the lodging house, Mrs Mary Russell, that she had been robbed. She also complained of pain in her lower body and was escorted to the London Hospital. On the way to the hospital Emma was able to point the exact location of her attack, and stated that "some men" had attacked her.

At the hospital the full extent of her injuries were realized: a "blunt instrument" had been so deeply thrust into her and with such force that her peritoneum had been ruptured. She died the following day from peritonitis. Here we note that she was attacked by more than one person, that she suffered head injuries and that death was caused by a single act which was overtly sexual in nature. We also note for further reference that the coroner who held the inquest into her death was Wynne E Baxter.

The second victim was Martha Tabram, aged 39, whose body was discovered on 7 August lying on the first floor landing between 35 and 37 George Yard Buildings. She had been stabbed 39 times, the wounds being caused by two different weapons: one a dagger and the other a knife. Here we note an attack by possibly two perpetrators and of such sustained ferocity that it speaks for an emotionally charged crime, not a random attack. Martha had no known connection with the building in which she was found and it is not unsafe to believe that she was lured there, off the street, by her attacker(s), whom she knew.

The third victim and the first of the so called "canonical" victims was Polly Nichols (43) who was murdered on Friday, 31 August 1888. Her body was discovered in Buck's Row by George Cross, a carman, who went in search of a constable, and subsequently returned to the scene with PCG Mizen 56H, by which time Polly's body had been found by PC John Neil 973, who had come across her in the course of patrolling his beat. The inquest was told by the police surgeon Dr Llewellyn that Polly's throat had been cut, and that her abdomen had been slashed with deep incisions. The direction of the incision was both vertical and lateral and all wounds were caused by the same instrument. Interestingly, perhaps, is that of all the newspapers which reported the murder, only the *East London Advertiser* (which was also the only newspaper to keep its head regarding the murders) reported that Polly's body had been found at the end of a trail of blood indicating that she, despite a cut throat, had not succumbed immediately to her injuries but had dragged herself, or her lifeless body had been dragged by her murderer, to where it was found. We surmise that Polly had been attacked by a lone perpetrator.

The fourth victim was Annie Chapman, whose body was found in the backyard of 29 Hanbury Street in the early hours of 8 September. She had been strangled and then her throat cut. She had been disembowelled, a large part of her viscera removed from the scene, and a similarly large part of her intestines was left beside her head. The perpetrator appeared to have made his escape by climbing over two fences and exiting by the passageway of 25 Hanbury Street. Like Polly she had died of a cut throat, but the abdominal injuries were very, very different.

The fifth victim was Catharine Eddowes (46), whose body was found in Mitre Square on Sunday, 30 September. The inquest into her death was told that her throat had been cut which would have caused immediate death, but the incision itself was only about one inch in length. There had been abdominal mutilation and her intestines had been drawn out and placed over her left shoulder. A section of one of her kidneys had been removed and both her eyelids had been nicked with the blade of a knife. Here there is a small cut to the throat compared to the gashed throat of Polly Nichols, and no large-scale removal of the intestines, yet the small "nicks" to the eyelids suggest the perpetrator had not been disturbed and had fulfilled all the tasks he set himself.

The sixth and final victim was the young and attractive Mary Kelly who was murdered in the early hours of 9 November in her home at 26 Dorset Street. Her injuries were the most horrific: her throat was cut from ear to ear, her ears and nose had been cut off and her breasts had been cut off and placed on the table beside the bed. The stomach and abdomen had been ripped open, the face had been slashed so that she was beyond recognition, the thighs had been cut, and the kidneys and heart had been removed. Of note here is the sustained attack to the face which indicates her killer was attacking her personally. No other victim sustained such concentrated facial damage.

The argument forwarded is that despite an initial similarity between the injuries there is in fact a greater dissimilarity. Most importantly, the all important "hallmark" which enables the police to state that a series of murders are committed by a serial killer is absent from the Whitechapel Murders of 1888. The six murders were perpetrated by different perpetrators.

Before leaving the victims, I should like to address the issue of the murder of "Long Liz" Stride and do so briefly because, without minimizing the tragedy in itself, it deserves scant attention in the story of the Whitechapel Murders. It is the red herring to end all red herrings. "Long Liz" Stride was murdered on the same night as Catharine Eddowes and possibly as little as 15 minutes separates the two murders. Long Liz was found in a yard off Berner Street, just beneath the premises at the International Working Men's Club. It was thought at the time, and disappointingly, by writers who should know better, it has also been subsequently assumed, that the arrival of one Louis Diemschutz on his horse-drawn costermonger's barrow disturbed the perpetrator before he could commence inflicting abdominal injuries to Long Liz's lifeless body. An easy reading of the inquest into her death published in *The Times* and still available in every public library reveals what did happen. She had left her lover Michael Kidney a few days earlier. Just prior to her death she had been seen in the vicinity of Berner Street and accosted by two or three men who seemed to be putting some sort of emotional pressure on her, one of whom was heard to say to her, "You would say anything but your prayers." And she was heard to say "Not tonight but some other night." Michael Kidney, piqued at her refusal to return to live with him, slit her throat and fled the scene.

A few moments later a man called Gilleman, returning to the yard after walking his young lady home following an evening spent at International Working Men's Club, encountered her body and reported it to a man called Maurice Eagle. He and Maurice Eagle and some other men went to the yard, viewed the body and then left in several directions each searching for a constable. They didn't post a sentry to the body and so when, a few moments later, Louis Diemschutz arrived turned into the yard, having his pony shy to the left, then alighting to investigate and coming across the body with blood from the cut throat still in a liquid state, he understandably assumed he was the first to discover the body. He went to the Working Men's Club and reported the find to his wife and the myth of the "Double Event" was born. Long Liz was *not* a victim of the "Whitechapel Fiend", subsequently to be known as "Jack the Ripper". She would have been murdered anyway and Louis Diemschutz's arrival did not disturb anyone, or prevent anyone from doing anything. All that was to happen had happened perhaps ten minutes before he arrived. Michael Kidney sensibly allowed the assumption of the "double event" to direct suspicion from himself. He was a lucky man.

Above and beyond the lack of a distinct "hallmark" which would enable it to be stated without fear of contradiction that the Whitechapel Murders were the work of one man, the case for "Jack the Ripper" ever having existed in the form of a serial killer is further weakened when we consider the time and geographical framework of the murders. Attested serial killers have "reigns" which last for periods measured in years: Peter Sutcliffe six years, Hindley and Brady three years, Dennis Nilsen five years, the Green River killer since 1982 and still at large. Similarly their "hunting grounds" cover vast areas, such as Ted Bundy's trek from the east to the west coasts of the United States. Yet the Whitechapel Murders of 1888 were confined to an area of one square mile and the "canonical" murders all took place within a 13 week period. Jack the Ripper was not a man: he was a myth. This of course is not to deny that something dreadful happened in Whitechapel during these weeks and what probably did happen is more frightening even than a serial killer being at large.

We must now examine the conduct of Coroner Baxter, the conduct of the press, the conduct of the people and we must take our hat off to the conduct of Dr Phillips, the police surgeon, who probably saved many lives by misleading an inquest.

As already noted, Coroner Baxter had held the inquest into the death of Emma Smith, and he also conducted the inquests into the deaths of Polly Nichols, Annie Chapman and Long Liz Stride. It is during the inquest into the death of Polly Nichols that his damaging influence begins to emerge. He seemed to thrill to the pivotal role he was playing in what rapidly became a media event with the coroner's court "playing" to packed houses. In order to prolong the "entertainment" – for by his conduct no other word seems appropriate – he was prepared to overextend the duties of the office of coroner. The duty of the coroner's court, then as now, is to inquire into deaths of human beings which appear to be non-natural with the aims (a) to determine the identity of the individual, and (b) to determine the cause of death. It is not the province of the coroner's court to inquire into the history and the mode of life of the deceased, except in so far as it impinges on determining identity and cause of death, nor especially is it the duty of the coroner to hear evidence of injuries sustained *after* death. This last is clearly the province of another court, following apprehension of the perpetrator. Yet this is what Coroner Baxter did.

On 1 September for instance, the first day of Polly Nichols's inquest, her identity and cause of death had both been established. There was no reason to carry on the inquest further, yet it was continued for a further three working days after an adjournment of 14 days. The public then knew of all the details of Polly's life, from her sad decline from a respectable employment in service to life as an unfortunate who had because of alcohol abuse fetched up among the common lodging houses of East London. The inquest also heard details of her attack, conveniently summed up by the coroner: she was grabbed from behind, her throat cut so as to stifle any sound, and her abdomen then ripped open. His summing up reads as a step-by-step guide to how such a murder should be done. He even dictated the type of knife to be used: "a stout-bladed knife with a blade of 6–8 inches long". This in itself is wholly indefensible, but his conduct became alarmingly irresponsible when, using the forum of the inquest into the death of Polly Nichols, he chose to debate the similarities between her death and the other recent murders in Whitechapel, by then including the death of Annie Chapman. Not only was this quite irrelevant to the finding of the cause of death of Polly Nichols but, coming from the coroner, it authenticated the fear that gripped Whitechapel, and fascinated the Western world, that indeed a murdering fiend was prowling the streets at night. There was in fact no basis for such a supposition at all, but the press reported it, the people read it, and five days later Catharine Eddowes was found in Mitre Square, her throat cut, her intestines pulled out, the injuries being caused by a stout-bladed knife with a blade about 6–8 inches long.

Coroner Baxter, the contemporary drawings of whom show him to have been a youthful, thin-faced man, continued to indulge himself when conducting the inquest into the death of Annie Chapman. The inquest seemed to have immediately taken on a theatrical stance. Extra police had to be drafted in to control the crowd which assembled outside the Working Lads' Institute in Whitechapel Road and remained daily outside it until the completion of the inquest, and did so much, one senses, to the delight of Coroner Baxter.

At the very beginning of the inquest much was made of the fact that Annie Chapman's body had been laid in the same shell, in the same mortuary, in which the body of Polly Nichols had been laid, thus strengthening the link in people's minds between the two murders. In fact a careful analysis of the witness depositions in both inquests as reported word for word in *The Times* and other papers leads one to believe that that was all that Polly and Annie had had in common: the same shell in the same mortuary upon their respective deaths. The police surgeon, Dr Bagster Phillips, was called and allowed to give minimal evidence, addressing only the cause of death, as was appropriate. Subsequently, however, it seemed that Coroner Baxter had a change of heart, and, on the penultimate day of the inquest, Dr Phillips was recalled. After clashing violently with the coroner, Dr Phillips was then obliged to detail the post-mortem injuries, but not before the public gallery had been cleared of "all women and boys".

The Times, clearly sensitive to its female readers, allowed itself the only case of self-censorship in the entire saga of the Whitechapel Murders and reported: "The witness proceeded to give medical and surgical evidence, totally unfit for publication, of the deliberate, successful and apparently scientific manner in which the poor woman had been mutilated, and expressed his opinion that the length of the weapon was at least five to six inches, probably more, and the appearance of the cuts confirmed him to the opinion that the instrument like the one which divided the neck, had been of sharp character." It is to *The Lancet* of 29 September 1888 we must turn to discover the full extent of Annie Chapman's injuries:

> The abdomen had been entirely laid open: the intestines severed from their mesenteric attachments had been lifted out of the body, and placed by the shoulder of the corpse: whilst from the pelvis, uterus and its appendages with the upper portion at the vagina and the posterior, two thirds of the bladder had been entirely removed. No trace of these parts had been found and the incisions were clearly cut avoiding the rectum and dividing the vagina low enough to avoid injury to the cervix uteri.

Concluding his deposition, Dr Phillips becomes the unsung hero of the Whitechapel Murders because he credited the person who murdered Annie Chapman as being in possession of "great anatomical skill". He went on to say that he could not have removed Annie Chapman's uterus in less than 15 minutes, and in proper surgical conditions the operation would have taken him the best part of an hour to perform. The mystery which is solved by the report in *The Lancet* and other similar reports in the *British Medical Journal* is one which was not considered at the time, to wit, how could a man, no matter how deranged, strangle a woman, cut her throat and then calm himself sufficiently to perform a delicate operation, being the removal of the uterus, and perform the deed in what must have been the near complete darkness of a back court under a smog-laden sky at about 5 a.m. in the autumn of that year? The answer, evidently, is that he didn't. What happened is that the murderer excavated a crater in Annie Chapman's middle with a single sweep of a knife, took some of the spoil, which contained the uterus, away with him in a bag or other container, and left some of the spoil behind, close to the shoulder of the deceased. *The Lancet* credits the murderer with having "a practised hand", the *British Medical Journal* describes the murderer as being possessed of "rough anatomical knowledge".

If the murderer was acquainted with only "rough anatomical knowledge", why then did Dr Phillips credit the perpetrator with "great anatomical knowledge"? Why, instead of a rough disembowelling, did he choose to report that an operation of great delicacy had been performed?

The answer could only be that he deliberately misled the inquest for the highest and most defensible of reasons. He had just given evidence under protest and, before the term was coined, he must as a police surgeon have been familiar with the concept of what is today called "copycat" crime, which often follows as a result of wide publicity being given to an incident. He clearly feared that "copycat" killing would be consequential upon his evidence. Dr Phillips clearly attempted to stay any further killings by crediting the murderer with learned medical knowledge. In effect he was saying to the inquest, and hence the public, that in order to perpetrate a murder which might be passed off as being the work of "Jack the Ripper" then the murderer must by his mutilation of the corpse demonstrate that he is in possession of a learned anatomical knowledge – a mere cut throat and a disembowelling would not suffice.

The drawback of his ploy was that it sent the police and many many subsequent writers chasing off in the search for a deranged doctor. The great advantage of Dr Phillips's inspired initiative was that it prevented further killings. He was not able to prevent the deaths of Catharine Eddowes or possibly of Mary Kelly, but if he prevented just one slaughterman who worked in the many slaughter yards then in operation in Whitechapel and who were likely to have employed the murderers, from advancing with the requisite stout-bladed knife of the requisite length upon a woman of the "unfortunate class" and dispatching her in the manner so conveniently reported by Coroner Baxter, then Dr Phillips's deliberate misleading of the inquest was justified. In all probability Dr Phillips most probably prevented the mayhem of many other slaughtermen, each unknown to the others, advancing on many women of the "unfortunate class", each man wanting to be "Jack the Ripper" just once, making his contribution to the excitement and furore and notoriety which was briefly lifting Whitechapel out of the depression brought on by relentless poverty.

Coroner Baxter further indulged himself during the inquest into the death of Elizabeth Stride. Her identity was at first open to debate. He did not do what might be deemed to have been the sensible option of postponing the inquest to allow the police to garner irrefutable evidence as to her identity, which they could then lay before the inquest. Alternatively he could have allowed the inquest to proceed upon the issue of cause of death, thus allowing the police time to satisfy themselves as to the identity of the deceased without actually holding up the proceedings. Instead Coroner Baxter allowed witness after witness to depose until laboriously Elizabeth Stride's identity was at last determined. It was an utter waste of court time most notably with one Mary Malcolm taking up much time attempting to convince the inquest that the deceased was her sister "Long Liz" Watts, who at the time was alive and well and living in Tottenham, because of a paranormal presentiment she, Mary Malcolm, had had, and despite seeing her sister weekly was able to recognize her as the corpse only by a snake bite on her leg.

The inquest continued amid great publicity because by then the erroneous belief that a "double event" had taken place was widely held, because "Jack the Ripper" had been thus christened, and because "Long Liz" was one of "his" victims. Dr Phillips was called to give evidence and advised the inquest that the person who murdered "Long Liz" knew exactly where to cut a person's throat to cause instant death.

This evidence was probably given in the form of professional detachment, but equally it may have been seized on by Dr Phillips to promote his policy of declaring that "Jack the Ripper" must be possessed of learned medical knowledge. He was also allowed to explore the theory that Long Liz was not after all a victim of the "Whitechapel Fiend".

Coroner Baxter: Was there any other similarity between this and the Chapman case?

Dr Phillips: There is great dissimilarity. In Chapman's case the neck was severed all round down the vertebral column, the vertical bone being marked, and there had been an evident attempt to separate the bones.

Clearly there were different perpetrators and it is a wonder that the significance of this evidence was not more closely examined by the police or picked up by the press. Also, in this exchange we see an example of the many, many instances where the coroner sought to compare and contrast one murder with another, thus continuing to reinforce the notion that the murders were the work of one man. It was a highly irresponsible attitude. Inquests should not be contaminated by testimonies given in respect of other specific deaths. In this case the coroner's reference to Annie Chapman's death was idle and self-indulgent rumour-mongering.

If Coroner Baxter's conduct during the inquests was professionally irresponsible then his conduct during his summing up at the Long Liz Stride inquest verged on the criminally irresponsible and utterly inexcusable. He appears to have selected only evidence that supported what was by then the widespread notion that "Jack the Ripper" had been disturbed by the approach of Louis Diemschutz on his horse-drawn cart, and, having to flee before he could disembowel Long Liz Stride, had left the scene in search of another victim whom he found in the form of Catharine Eddowes in Mitre Square, some 15 minutes later. A wholly preposterous notion.

In his summing up he revealed an emotional immaturity by describing the difficulty of identifying the deceased as being akin to a "comedy of errors", drawing parallels with the life of "Long Liz" Watts and "Long Liz" Stride: both had the same nickname, both had been married to sailors, etc., etc., although as already stated it was a waste of court time to debate identity in the first place. The inquest should perhaps have convened only when the police had proof of Long Liz Stride's identity. The coroner then offered the assumption that she was most definitely a victim of "Jack the Ripper" by saying: "Unlike the other victims in the series of crimes in this neighbourhood, a district teeming with representatives of all nations, she was not an Englishwoman…"

It is a strange statement. One wonders about the relevancy of Elizabeth Stride's nationality (she was a Swede, née Gustafsdotter) and one further wonders if Coroner Baxter had been listening to the evidence laid before his inquest. Nowhere in the inquests was evidence offered that could link the death of Elizabeth Stride to the deaths of Polly Nichols, Annie Chapman or Catharine Eddowes. Rather, there is stronger evidence which points to the murder of Long Liz Stride as being a wholly unconnected crime. The assumption that Long Liz was a victim of "Jack the Ripper" can be traced back to Maurice Eagle who ran up Berner Street in search of a constable, and encountering PC Henry Lamb 252H called him, saying, "there has been another murder". At about this same moment Louis Diemschutz was arriving at the yard on Berner Street. One can only feel the despair of Gilleman, who first found the body, that he was not called to give evidence, or the despair of Maurice Eagle who must have realized that his testimony was ignored, because it would cause the "double event" theory to sink without trace. We can also imagine the relief at their good fortune felt by Michael Kidney and his associates, who doubtless murdered Long Liz Stride, that the acid test of logic was never applied to the "double event" theory.

Throughout the inquests he held into the deaths of Polly Nichols, Annie Chapman and Long Liz Stride the conduct of Coroner Baxter was questionable in the extreme. He appears to have unnecessarily prolonged the inquests, insisted upon evidence being given that was not the province of a coroner's court, had compared and contrasted the murders and had chosen to ignore certain facts so as to enable him to steer the inquests into the areas of most appealing sensation, fuelling local and national hysteria in the process. Fortunately, at the conclusion of the inquest into the death of Long Liz Stride his contribution to the saga of the Whitechapel Murders was complete, but the damage he had wrought was far-reaching, influencing even late twentieth-century writers, and considerable.

By contrast Coroner MacDonald completed the inquest into the death of Mary Kelly within the space of one working day. Having been satisfied of her identity, then of the cause of death, he said that that was all the evidence he proposed to take and then asked the jury if they had heard sufficient evidence. The jury deliberated openly and returned a verdict of "wilful murder against some person or persons unknown". It is tempting to speculate that perhaps the myth of a serial killer in Whitechapel in 1888 would not have arisen, nor would the "copycat" murders of Annie Chapman, Catharine Eddowes and possibly Mary Kelly have happened at all, had Polly Nichols's inquest and Long Liz Stride's inquest been conducted by Coroner MacDonald.

Before leaving the inquest of Mary Kelly it is perhaps a convenient place to expose another myth surrounding the Whitechapel Murders: the role of Inspector Abberline. He was the last person to give evidence in any court concerned with the Whitechapel Murders, and in many books and in film and television treatments of the "Jack the Ripper" myth he has been credited with being the man who led the police inquiry into the killings. In fact the only murder he investigated was that of Mary Kelly. In all other instances he seemed only to have represented the police at the inquests. Why he should have been credited so is hard to explain. Perhaps his surname has an appealing ring to it? The police officer who clearly was central to the investigation was a detective sergeant who laboured through life with the less appealing surname of "Thick".

Mary Kelly was to be the final victim of "Jack the Ripper" and with her passing something else also passed from Whitechapel. It was a phenomenon which has been recorded many times, notably in 1643 in Loudun, wherein the incumbents of the convent believed themselves and were believed to be possessed by the devil. Many people flocked to the town to witness the spectacle of young and attractive nuns, especially the beautiful Sister Agnes, "being exorcized". Closer to our own time in the town of Halifax in 1938 a series of knife attacks on women gave rise to the concept of the "Halifax Slasher". He was never caught because he never existed. The "victims" had slashed themselves, though they were not known to each other. It was the phenomenon of sexually charged mass hysteria. It is wrong to state, as it has been stated, that the Victorians didn't see the Whitechapel Murders as sex crimes. They clearly did and they clearly thrilled to them.

One aspect of the newspaper reports of the "Jack the Ripper" story may strike the reader of modern newspapers: its reporting suffered because it happened during a very quiet period of world and national news. There was little to divert attention from the events in Whitechapel during the months of September, October and November 1888. The Parnell Commission's inquiries into the activities of the Irish Land League made and still does make dull reading. *The Times* on 8 October devoted three columns on "How the British Soldier is Taught to Shoot", and on the 1st of that month had astoundedly re-reported the Krakatoa explosion of five years previously.

Another aspect of the reports is that there was no concept of "press restrictions". Everything that was said during the inquests, with the single exception of the post-mortem inquiries to Annie Chapman, was dutifully reported with all details. This would have been perhaps harmless had the newspapers still been only the "noticeboards of the rich", but just prior to the Whitechapel Murders there had come the "New Journalism" of the "penny dreadfuls", easy to read, eye-catching, and often with reporting in pictorial form. It was in these journals that, literally, fatally, the details of how "Jack the Ripper" perpetrated a murder and with what type of knife were printed. What have not, unlike the newspapers, been preserved, but which also, contributed to the hysteria were the billboard hoardings advertising the newspapers. The penny dreadfuls were published on Saturdays and the billboard hoardings advertising the forthcoming edition appeared midweek.

From the description given in *Punch* magazine, and in a letter to *The Times*, it appears that these posters were lurid, lifesize depictions of naked or near-naked women with knives sticking in their chests, and the posters were glued to every available fence and wall space. They were also brilliantly colourful – red was accentuated – and would have amounted to a constant and inescapable visual stimulus to the mass fear and mass fascination of the Whitechapel Murders. Ninety years later, by comparison, the atrocities of the Yorkshire Ripper were subject to press censorship. The police would only say that the victims had been "bludgeoned to death" and that the killer had left his distinct "hallmark". The Yorkshire Ripper murders also spanned a five-year period and competed for column inches with a massive earthquake in the then Yugoslavia and the Israeli raid on the airport at Entebbe. During those few weeks of mayhem in 1888 there was no such headline-grabbing competition and the newspapers often repeated the news of the murders in the same edition; there appeared a full and a detailed report, followed by a second equally full and detailed report, giving identical information, under the title "another account".

The influence of unbridled newspaper reporting seems to have been both considerable and sinister. The press appears to have precipitated events by prophesying them to a readership which had worked itself to an emotional state whereby it was susceptible to suggestion. The *Pall Mall Gazette*, which won praise for its crusading journalism, appeared in this instance to have been particularly irresponsible. On 7 September, for example, it published an article by one William Estall entitled "A Precedent for the Whitechapel Murder", which related the story of Andreas Bichel of Regensdorf in Bavaria who in 1806 had murdered a young woman, Barbara Reisinger. He also murdered Katherina Leidal in 1808. Both women had been lured to Bichel's remote cottage with the promise of having their fortunes told and one is further staggered by their naïvety when it was revealed that Bichel's ritual for fortune-telling involved the women allowing themselves to be tied up and blindfolded. The remains of Barbara and Katherine were eventually found beneath a pile of logs on Bichel's property. At his trial Bichel was found guilty of murder and was later beheaded. The parallel drawn by Estall was that both women had been "frightfully mutilated". The article also added that both women had been disembowelled. This is the first reference to disembowelling in the saga of the Whitechapel Murders. The day following the publication of this article Annie Chapman was murdered: she was the first of the victims to have been disembowelled.

The *Pall Mall Gazette* pursued its policy of sensationalism by reporting the death of Annie Chapman with the headline "Another murder – and more to follow". Note, there was no question mark after "follow", as if deliberately promoting a policy of causing events by predicting them. There is a feeling that the newspapermen of the New Journalism were discovering the dark side of the power of the press and were putting it to ill use. The modern equivalent of this attitude was to be found in Northern Ireland at the beginning of the "Troubles" when camera crews found that if, for example, they began filming a group of boys playing football, the boys, once they realized they were being filmed, would stop playing football and start throwing stones at the soldiers. Once this was noted the cameras remained packed away until violence started of its own accord. But the significance of this is that if people know that they are the subject of media attention then, for some reason, they will behave in the way the media expects or wants them to behave. And because of this in 1888 the New Journalism got the boost in circulation it wanted and the price was paid by Annie Chapman and Catharine Eddowes, and possibly also by Mary Kelly.

In the 1880s the penny dreadfuls and similar papers of New Journalism had a national circulation of about 1 million copies per week. If the theory that the murderous mayhem was caused in part by irresponsible reporting then we would expect that its influence was not confined to Whitechapel. In fact there appeared to have been a "murder epidemic" in the United Kingdom, wherein the murder weapon was a knife: during the weeks of the Whitechapel Murders there were 17 murders reported nationally which involved the use of a knife. In the corresponding weeks of 1887 and 1889 there was just one such murder in each year.

Jack the Ripper mania seems to have spread out from Whitechapel to engulf the British Isles. Murders which seemed clearly to be influenced by the Whitechapel Murders took place in South Wales,

Hampshire and Birmingham, but perhaps most notably in County Durham, where Jane Beetmore (28) was murdered on the night of 22–23 September 1888.

Her body was found in a field and she was noted to have sustained "horrific" injuries; her throat had been cut and her intestines were protruding. Speculation immediately spread that the "Whitechapel Fiend" had visited the North of England and officialdom also subscribed to this view because Dr Phillips and one Inspector Rootes were sent to County Durham to view the corpse. They did so and then returned to London, having rapidly concluded that the person who murdered Jane was not the same person who had murdered Polly Nicholls and Annie Chapman. They must have known that they were on a fool's errand all along. Eventually a young man, William Waddell, who was seen with Jane on the night of her murder and who subsequently had fled the district was convicted of the crime and executed at Durham Gaol one week before Christmas 1888.

Unfortunately for Waddell his hangman was William Berry. At the time the findings of the Aberdour Commission were being observed. These assumed that a blow of 1260 foot/pounds was sufficient to break the neck of the condemned, thus if this figure was divided by the weight of the condemned in pounds then it would give the length in feet of the required "drop".

The Commission also stated that when applying this formula the hangman should err on the side of generosity because if the neck failed to break the condemned would suffer a prolonged death by strangulation. Berry allowed himself a certain privilege of sentencing so that if he viewed a crime to have been especially unpleasant he would ensure that the culprit strangled. He had also made a public statement to the effect that he wished to get his hands on "Jack the Ripper". The nearest he got to "Jack the Ripper" was William Waddell, who at 22 years of age stood 5 feet 10 inches and was known to be a particularly strong man who could lift two 56-pound weights one in each hand and "knack" them together above his head with minimal effort. He was employed as a labourer and could have weighed as much as 14 stones, which by applying the findings of the Aberdour Commission would require a drop of nearly 7 feet.

Berry allowed him a drop of 5 feet, and the report of his execution was not accompanied with the usual claim that his death was "instantaneous".

Many were the people who wrote to the newspapers offering their theories about the identity of "Jack the Ripper" but one from the Reverend Barnett proposed the removal of the many slaughterhouses in Whitechapel to outlying districts of the city: "At present animals are daily slaughtered in the midst of Whitechapel, the butchers with their blood stains are a familiar sight among street passengers and sights are common which tend to brutalize ignorant natures".

Here, succinctly, is the explanation of the Whitechapel Murders. Butchers who worked in the slaughterhouses that were in operation 24 hours a day could walk about Whitechapel with blood-stained hands and clothing, go into pubs after a busy shift or as a midshift break, ride home from work on the tram, and not arouse the slightest suspicion. The nature of their trade endowed them with sufficient knowledge to inflict the injuries upon each victim. The murder quickly and ruthlessly done each man (there were probably just three or four separate murders, depending on whether Mary Kelly is seen as a victim of "Jack the Ripper" or whether she is to be seen, like Long Liz Stride, the victim of a murder which would have happened anyway) would simply walk away, the human blood merging and drying with the animal blood: another slaughterman on his way to or from his work. This was the nature and the identity of "Jack the Ripper" and we are indebted to the Reverend Barnett for his letter and the documenting of the presence of slaughtermen in large numbers, night and day, in the parish of Whitechapel.

Hysteria, like wildfire, by its nature burns out. The base behaviour of the crowd following the murder of Annie Chapman is recorded:

The scene of the fearful tragedy has been daily visited by hundreds of people who freely converse among themselves upon the absorbing topic... special writers and artists visited the spot in large numbers and many are the inquiries that have been promiscuously set on foot... by amateur detectives.

East London Advertiser

And:

> The excitement has been intense. The house and mortuary were besieged by people... people flocked in great numbers to see the blood stained spot in the yard, paying a penny each. In the Whitechapel Road "lines of terribly tragedy" were being sold and men with verses round their hats were singing them to the tune of "My Village Home". A wretched waxwork show had some horrible picture in front and people were paying their pence to see representations of the murdered woman within.
>
> *Pictorial News*

And after the "double event":

> On approaching the scene of the murders on Sunday morning it was easy to see, no nearer than a mile away that something unusual was in the air. All along the main thoroughfares a constant stream of passengers, all impelled by the same nature of horrified curiosity, was rolling towards the district... there was but one topic of conversation... the few acres of streets and houses between Mitre Square and Berner Street seemed to be the goal for which all London was making...... the two adits to Mitre Square were blocked by hundreds... and during part of the day thousands... struggling for a place where they could look at the fatal spot... the barren satisfaction of trying to peer round the fatal corner continued to be employed by the long lines of men women and children going and returning. After a glance at one place the spectators hurried away to the other... Berner Street seemed to be a sea of heads from end to end... opportunity for business was seized by costers with barrows of nuts and fruit, a shop even being opened for the purpose in Mitre Street.
>
> *Pictorial News*

It is about mid-October 1888 that by reading the newspapers and periodicals one detects the beginning of a groundswell of aversion to the hysteria of the previous weeks. There is a lessening of the incidents of apocryphal tales being reported, a lessening of drunks giving themselves up as being the Whitechapel Murderer, and a more sober-minded reporting in the press. It was a groundswell which grew to embrace the judiciary, the press and the public and was to eventually kill "Jack the Ripper".

Reading of the conduct of the people following the discovery of the body of Mary Kelly, and of the attitudes of all concerned – official, press and lay – it seems that there was a strong sense of a remarkable coming together, as if there was an intuitive but unspoken recognition of what they had conspired to create. Mass dismay and sadness greeted the news of her murder, Coroner MacDonald adopted a low-key relevance and approach and the inquest into her death was concluded in less than one working day. The press followed suit by under-reporting the inquest. Mary Kelly was a 25-year-old heavy-drinking Irish girl who had lived in Whitechapel for only a few months before she died and who, when she died, was working as a prostitute, yet several thousand people lined the route of her funeral procession and behaved as if they had been paying their respects at the funeral of an elder statesman.

And with her "Jack the Ripper" was also laid to rest.

This article is a distillation of the argument put forward in the author's book *The Killer Who Never Was*, which was published by Clark, Lawrence and is now out of print.

The Great Conspiracy

Nick Warren, FRCS

> "*Conspiracy*. A secret plan to commit a crime or do harm, often
> for political ends; a plot."
>
> *Oxford English Reference Dictionary*

Conspiracy, intrigue, machination, cover-up: choose any term you wish,
the chances are that this political expedient was perfected in Ancient
Rome. At one time every schoolboy knew that Julius Caesar was
assassinated by a number of men wielding knives on the Ides of March,
44 BC, as a result of a conspiracy led by Brutus and Cassius. The
assassins concealed the knives in their left hands, giving rise to the
uneasy meaning of "sinister". This tradition was continued through the
ensuing Byzantine Empire and the Church of Rome, culminating in
such quintessential Italianate intriguers as the Borgias and Niccolo
Macchiavelli (1469–1527). The latter was expelled from Florence by the
Medicis on suspicion of conspiracy, but he was later rehabilitated and
allowed to expand his political philosophy, which advocated the use of
unethical methods in statecraft, as exemplified by the maxim "the end
justifies the means".

Needless to say, Protestant England became highly suspicious of
such a philosophy entering the thought processes of a foreign power
(the Vatican) which could at any time attempt to subvert the country.
There had been genuine plots against the state, notably Robert
Catesby's Gunpowder Plot of November 1605, which aimed to blow up
King James I and Parliament. As a result, *praemunire*, a writ charging a
sheriff to summon any person accused of asserting or maintaining

papal jurisdiction in England, became part of statute law. There was only one prosecution for this offence, *Rex v. Crook,* in 1662, although it undoubtedly led to certain abuses of power. In 1678 a Protestant clergyman, Titus Oates, concocted a fictitious Jesuit plot to assassinate King Charles II, replacing him on the throne with the Catholic Duke of York. Thirty-five Catholics were executed as a result of this false allegation of conspiracy.

During the eighteenth century, Catholic and Protestant factions started to go underground. The Freemasons were officially founded in 1717: today they constitute 7,835 lodges. Although Freemasonary is officially open to persons of all religions, papal edict has long forbidden Catholics from joining the craft. A more overtly Protestant secret society is the Orange Order, founded in 1795 and currently comprising 1,400 lodges. Set against this trend were the Irish (Catholic) septs or clans, most notably the Clan-na-Gael or Fenian Brotherhood which was later to wage war on many fronts, including 1880s London.

In the nineteenth century this established pattern of dissent became eroded by the advent of a more secular form of conspiracy. No longer was it simply a case of Catholics versus Protestants, or "Plots" versus "Pseudo-Plots."

For the first time in history there were secular revolutionaries, infected by the prevailing mood in France: communists, nihilists and anarchists. These sentiments first took hold in Britain in the "Cato Street Conspiracy" of 1820, which was brutally suppressed by the authorities. Civil unrest in London was still an issue in 1887 when Sir Charles Warren, Commissioner of the Metropolitan Police, ordered police and troops to disperse a riot in November, after the unemployed had congregated in London's Trafalgar Square. In this disturbance, the original "Bloody Sunday" of 13 November 1887, nearly 100,000 unemployed converged on the Square, to be confronted by 4,000 police and 600 soldiers. One person was killed and over 150 injured. Various of his senior officers however, may have disagreed with his emphasis, feeling that the threat still came from the "Enemy Without," rather than the "Enemy Within."

Chief among these senior officers were two men seconded to the Metropolitan Police at Scotland Yard with no police experience whatsoever. They were, in short, a couple of Establishment grandees sent to clear muddied waters when the Jack the Ripper killings became a press sensation. The first of these was Sir Robert Anderson (1841–1918), born in Dublin and educated at Trinity College. He was given work reviewing Fenian activities around 1863, thanks to his elder brother Samuel, Solicitor-General in the Viceregal administration. In 1867 he came to London as deputy head of the anti-Fenian intelligence branch. In his memoirs, he remained firmly convinced that Jack the Ripper was a Jew. The second was Sir Melville Leslie Macnaghten (1853–1921). He became known to his later colleague, James Monro, then Inspector-General of Bengal Police, in 1881, when he was attacked by Indian land rioters. He was descended from one of the original Prentice Boys of Derry[1] (and so an Orangeman). Educated at Eton, he later came to believe that the Ripper murders were the result of a Catholic plot.

The idea of a Catholic plot has resurfaced in modern times. In 1975 a book, *The Ripper File* by Elwyn Jones and John Lloyd, based on an earlier BBC TV series, highlighted the theory that Prince Albert Victor ("Prince Eddy"), heir presumptive to the throne in 1888, had contracted an unofficial marriage with a certain Elizabeth Crook of 6 Cleveland Street, London W1, so marrying a Catholic. This theory was later expanded in two further books by Stephen Knight and Melvyn Fairclough, but the reality is that the whole scenario, as a cause for scandal, is absurd. (Annie) Elizabeth Crook (1862–1920) was not a Roman Catholic. In any event, her alleged secret marriage would automatically have been set aside under the Royal Marriages Act (1772) as it was contracted without the Sovereign's permission.

Today, we can view the "conspiracy" theory of the Ripper crimes under the following headings:

1 That the police knew the identity of the murderer, but suppressed it.

2 That the crimes were carried out by a secret society that transcended, in some way, the powers of the police.

1 Martin Fido, *The Crimes, Detection and Death of Jack the Ripper* (1987), p. 148. In 1613 Derry was granted to the City of London for colonization and became known as Londonderry. The Prentices came from a background of ancient crafts, crafts which some would adjoin to Freemasonry.

3 That there was some secret link between the crimes and the true identity of the final victim, Mary Jane Kelly, whose identity, always mysterious, was finally physically obliterated.

The first two possibilities were raised at the time the murders took place. There has been considerable expansion over ensuing years, mainly on these two parts, but also latterly on the third.

Regarding the theory of the suppressed identity of the murderer, this question has been channelled in four directions in the past: the murderer could have been a doctor, a policeman, a prominent politician, or a member of the Royal Family. The first theory, as a medical practitioner myself, I find entirely risible, but not for reasons as one might suppose. The idea was initially developed in *The Mystery of Jack the Ripper* (1929) by Leonard Matters, who adduced the theory that the murderer was a "Dr Stanley", a prominent London surgeon whose only son had died from syphilis acquired from the final victim, Mary Jane Kelly. Matters made two serious mistakes. Most importantly, syphilis takes 20 or 30 years to kill someone.

Shortly afterwards, the idea of a doctor was taken up by the maverick medium Robert James Lees (1849–1931) who just before his death claimed in the *Daily Express* to have solved the crime and received a royal pension for his pains. The clairvoyant said that on the occasion of one of the murders he had followed the Ripper from a London omnibus to the expensive mansion of a great West End physician, whom he subsequently denounced to the police. Even the late Stephen Knight, whose 1976 book *Jack the Ripper: The Final Solution* makes much of the Lees story, admitted the following: "The chief objection to the Lees story is that several commentators have claimed it did not appear in print until 1931 ... a letter received at Scotland Yard on 25 July 1889 (however) says, 'Dear Boss, You have not caught me yet you see, with all your cunning, with all your Lees, with all your blue-bottles. Jack the Ripper.'" It is an unfortunate fact that the current whereabouts of this key document are quite unknown.

Over the years various other candidates apart from the pseudonymous "Dr Stanley" have been put forward for a medical Ripper. So far as is known, only one, Dr Thomas Barnardo, who took in the East End waifs and strays and who was a familiar sight on streets in the neighbourhood at night, was questioned by the police at the time. This was almost certainly a routine enquiry, since East End doctors were under suspicion. (Indeed, Scotland Yard appears to have been so preoccupied with the idea at one time that they mistook a major suspect, M.J. Druitt, for a doctor when he was in reality a barrister.) Names put up by recent writers have included Dr William Withey Gull and Sir Frederick Treves. Gull was Physician-in-Ordinary to Queen Victoria. He suffered a stroke in 1887, one year before the murders began. Nevertheless, Gull was first implicated by Stephen Knight in his 1976 book, although some claim that he was anonymously alluded to in an article in *The Criminologist*, written by Dr Thomas Stowell in 1970. Either way, the evidence against him appears minuscule. Sir Frederick Treves appears only ever to have been implicated because of his association with the Elephant Man. In other words, both had connections with the East End of the 1880s, and with the London Hospital in Whitechapel in particular. This line of argument leads us inevitably to the case of Dr Robert Donston Stephenson, another medical man who had connections with the London Hospital and whose candidacy as Jack the Ripper has been promulgated through three books by the author Melvin Harris. Certainly to date, he has not proved his case.

What is most risible about this conspiracy theory is that the Victorian police would not have hesitated in arresting a doctor on a charge of capital murder. They had arrested several before, and almost all had been hanged. Famous cases include several poisoners. Dr Edward Pritchard, who poisoned two relatives with antimony, was publicly hanged in Glasgow on 28 July 1865 before a crowd of 100,000. Dr William Palmer, a Bart's graduate, became the "Rugeley Poisoner", murdering up to 14 people with antimony in order to finance his losses on the turf at Shrewsbury races. He was hanged outside Stafford Goal on 14 June 1856, in front of a large crowd shouting "Poisoner!" Dr George Lamson murdered his crippled brother-in-law with aconitine (wolfs bane) in December 1881 and was hanged privately at Wandsworth Prison on 28 April 1882. Dr Thomas Neill Cream, the "Lambeth Poisoner", was a Canadian medical graduate when he indulged in the crimes of arson and murder, poisoning a number of London prostitutes with strychnine before his execution on 15 November 1892. This trend for medical poisoning has persisted into the twentieth century. The last infamous practitioner, however, Dr Hawley Harvey Crippen, who poisoned his wife with the unusual alkaloidal drug hyoscine in 1910, was, technically speaking, an American dentist. He was also executed on the gallows, almost 25 years after the Ripper murders.

It has to be said that the legal profession has always been notably adverse to executing their own kind. Welsh solicitor Harold Greenwood was duly acquitted in 1919 on a charge of poisoning his wife with arsenic. Unfortunately for himself, another Welsh lawyer, Herbert Rowse Armstrong, was convicted of the copycat arsenic murder of his own wife and hanged in 1922, the only solicitor to suffer this fate in the history of capital punishment in the UK. Needless to say, even today, the lawyers are trying to rehabilitate his memory. (See for example, *Dead not Buried* by fellow solicitor Martin Beales, 1995.)

The theory that Jack the Ripper was a policeman is really not that old, or that original. During 1888 a number of police officers were denounced to their superiors at Scotland Yard as the murderer, for very obvious reasons. The Yard file containing these names has now been lost, but I doubt that its contents were ever very significant. Certainly they were never taken seriously by the investigating officers at the time. Only one senior police officer has been denounced in recent times, Sir Robert Anderson, who was Assistant Commissioner at Scotland Yard during the latter part of the enquiries, was named as part of a Ripper conspiracy in Stephen Knight's 1976 book, without a scintilla of evidence being adduced in support of such an allegation.

In short, the policeman-as-murderer theory, however ingenious, is unlikely to be proved in this case. Police officers *have* murdered people, but they are considerably less likely to be serial killers than some of the doctors mentioned above. In any event, Stephen Knight's idea was far from original. Another London serial murderer of prostitutes, known as "Jack the Stripper" (1963–64), was rumoured to be a senior CID officer who lived with his mother in West London. These rumours went on to implicate the late Detective Chief Superintendent Arthur "Tommy"

Butler, who retired from the Metropolitan Police CID, in 1968; he later wrote a series of articles in the *Sun* newspaper in 1972, claiming that the original Jack the Ripper had been a deranged midwife-abortionist with an accomplice somewhat improbably named "Fingers Freddy". Needless to say, there is not the slightest evidence that Arthur Butler was the uncaught 1960s "Jack the Stripper," but the implication is that he clearly had enemies at Scotland Yard. Even today, most Jack the Ripper "policeman" theories emanate from that source. Yet the theory lacks vigour. Policemen, like doctors, have occasionally been convicted of murder without evidence of public horror or hint of scandal. The simple truth is that Scotland Yard by the 1880s was already notorious for serious CID corruption cases, such as the Great Turf Frauds of 1876.

So we are obliged to fall back upon what can only be termed the "blindingly obvious" scenario. If it was not the identity of a prominent doctor or policeman that had to be covered up, it could only be that of a member of the establishment, a senior politician or a member of the Royal Family. Surely, the argument runs, only such figures could wield the necessary clout to pervert the course of justice.

For a long time rumours have circulated that a member of the Royal Family was implicated in the murders. The origin of this quirky idea appears to have been Queen Victoria's idiosyncratic personal interest in the investigation of the crimes, which appears in turn to have culminated in the presence of royal courtiers at the scene of Eddowes's murder in Mitre Square, as recounted by correspondents of the popular press. Such regal interest culminated in the suggestion that Queen Victoria's grandson Prince Albert Victor ("Eddy"), heir presumptive to the British throne, who died from influenza in 1892, was himself Jack the Ripper. The theory was first mooted in print by the Frenchman Phillippe Jullien in his 1962 study of King Edward VII which also implicated the Duke of Bedford as an accomplice. It was taken up in 1970 by Dr Thomas Stowell, who communicated it over lunch at his club to the crime writer Colin Wilson, who continued to reiterate its essence in his 1987 book. Nevertheless, the "Prince Jack" hypothesis reached its apotheosis in a 1978 book by an American Frank Speiring, whose "evidence" proved to be entirely evanescent. Unfortunately for Jullien, Stowell, Wilson and Speiring, Prince Albert Victor had watertight alibis for *all* the Ripper crimes. According to court circulars and other state papers, he was engaged on various official duties at the relevant times, well away from London.

To date, only two senior politicians have been placed in the frame. The first of these is the Right Honourable William Ewart Gladstone (1809–98), a member of the Privy Council and in 1888 Leader of Her Majesty's Opposition. Gladstone was four times a British Liberal Prime Minister (1868–74, 1880–85, 1886, and 1892–4). Interestingly, he campaigned in favour of Home Rule for Ireland and oversaw the passing of the Irish Land Acts. No doubt, many in London saw these actions as blatantly pro-Catholic. It should be remembered that one of the key issues placed before Parliament in 1888–9 was Parnellism and the question of Irish Home Rule. The only "evidence" against Gladstone is that, ever since his undergraduate days, he had vowed to clear the streets of the evil of prostitution. He carried out his plan in a very naïve way, inviting streetwalkers home for tea and conversation. The accusation smacks more of political propaganda than anything else.

The other senior politician implicated is Lord Randolph Henry Spencer Churchill (1849–94), a Conservative statesman who was the son of the 6th Duke of Marlborough and the father of Sir Winston Churchill. The candidacy of Lord Randolph Churchill as a potential Jack the Ripper was aired in newspaper articles prior to its appearance in book form in Melvyn Fairclough's *The Ripper and the Royals* (1991). Once again, the evidence against Lord Randolph consists of nothing more than innuendo. He died from general paralysis of the insane, an advanced form of syphilis. Today he is best remembered for various street names in his former Paddington constituency, notably Randolph Avenue.

It is instructive to analyze the precise political arithmetic which allowed Gladstone to return to power. In June 1885 the Liberals under Gladstone were defeated in the Commons because the Irish members voted with the Opposition. Charles Stewart Parnell, leader of the Irish Nationalists, in spite of having only 85 members, held the balance of power between the Liberals and the Conservatives. After Gladstone's defeat, Lord Salisbury formed a minority Conservative government, but six months later Gladstone was back with a majority over the

Conservatives of 86. By this time the "Grand Old Man" had undergone a conversion to the cause of Irish Home Rule. The election of 1886 was fought purely on the Irish issue. Salisbury's Conservatives returned 316 seats and remained in power throughout the key years until 1892. Their supporters over Home Rule, the Unionists, gained 78. Overall, the Liberals won only 191 seats and the Parnellites 85.

By way of appeasement, perhaps, Lord Salisbury was determined to retain his only Catholic cabinet minister. Henry Matthews, the first Roman Catholic minister of cabinet rank since the reign of Elizabeth I, held the post of Home Secretary throughout the administration, as the direct boss of the Metropolitan Police. He was elevated to the peerage as Viscount Llandaff in 1895. Once again the Catholic issue was smouldering in England, reincarnated after nearly 300 years. It is little wonder that James Monro, Commissioner of the Metropolitan Police from 1888–90, succeeding Sir Charles Warren who had been eased out of office by Henry Matthews, regarded the whole affair of the Whitechapel Murders of 1888 as a "very (political) hot potato," even after his own resignation from the same office under Matthews.

In any event, a political smear in 1888 against Gladstone would have been a smear against the Irish Nationalists. In the same way, a contemporary smear against Churchill would have told against the Loyalists (Orange) Lodges and so, in turn, the Freemasons.

Various secret societies under suspicion can be classified into two groups: the Irish Catholics and their Protestant adversaries. The political situation in London during 1888 was both unusual and highly charged. In addition to Home Secretary Henry Matthews being the first Roman Catholic minister to hold Cabinet rank for three hundred years there were interesting appointments to the police force itself, possibly to redress the balance, or possibly for more sinister reasons. Either way, it is quite certain that two senior officers with views inimical to the Irish cause were appointed at key times in the development of the Ripper enquiry.

The first was Sir Robert Anderson, the Home Office Fenian expert, duly appointed Assistant Commissioner of the Metropolitan Police CID, and nominally in charge of the Ripper investigation from 6 October 1888. The second was Orangeman Sir Melville Macnaghten, who took over responsibility for the unsolved enquiry upon his appointment as Assistant Chief Constable, CID in 1889.

Apart from a single clue these political tensions of the 1880s lay dormant until the Irish Catholics re-emerged with a vengeance in London, with IRA bomb outrages in the capital during the 1970s. In these same years, curiously enough, Scotland Yard decided to "leak" some information. Gordon Honeycombe, chronicler of Scotland Yard's Black Museum, has summarized the situation as follows: "The IRA is a segment of the oldest terrorist organization in the world. Nationalists opposed to English rule in Ireland began a long war of underground resistance when the English invaded Ireland in 1169... In the 1850s that resistance found expression in the Fenian Society, an Irish-American movement."

Needless to say, such Irish-Americans were embittered emigrants from the Great Potato Famine. The IRA bombing campaign on "mainland" Britain commenced after another "Bloody Sunday", this time in Londonderry in January 1972. The first bomb, in Aldershot, killed seven people, including five women and a priest, in February of that year. In March 1973 one person was killed and 244 injured by car bombs in the Old Bailey and Whitehall, old Fenian targets. In November 1974 a bomb explosion killed two near Woolwich barracks. The death toll was much higher outside London.

At some time during January 1973 certain BBC researchers had lunch with a senior Scotland Yard man who, while unnamable, was regarded as "an impeccable source". He had come to renew the old *spiel*. He asked if the researchers had any contact with a man called Sickert "who has some connection with the artist" and knew of a marriage between the Duke of Clarence, son of Edward VII, and a Catholic. Nothing much came of this briefing, at least at first. The BBC researchers obtained a statement from Joseph "Hoboe" Sickert in July 1973 regarding the Ripper's final victim, Irish Catholic Mary Jane Kelly, and a Catholic wedding plot. Tellingly, and uniquely at that time, Joseph Sickert went on to say: "You have to remember it was a time when the possibility of revolution was thought to be a very real one – and the problems and violence surrounding Ireland were at their height." And so the Fenians were firmly in the frame. But what of their rivals? At the end of their quest the BBC researchers laid the blame on quite a different secret society. It would appear that their Yard briefing had gone seriously awry. The fruits of their research pointed to the Freemasons as conspirators in the Ripper murders. An anonymous source advised them that an allusion to the cutting of the throat, the penalty for revealing Masonic secrets, constituted "the Sign of the Eternal Apprentice". The Goulston Street graffito then became a Mason's message and, worse yet, the Commissioner of Police for the Metropolis, Sir Charles Warren, was revealed as a Freemason himself. He joined the Order in Gibraltar in 1859, entered the Grand Arch in 1861 and was made a Knight Templar in 1863. Since 1886 he had been heavily involved in founding the first Quattor Coronati Lodge of Masonic Research.

The essence of the case against the Freemasons, albeit weak, has long been misunderstood. It is nothing more than a simple case of counter-propaganda. The Freemasons are cognate with the Lodges of the Orange Order, and it remains inconceivable that a controversial series of murders in London would have benefited Orange interests. William of Orange defeated the Catholic James II at the Battle of the Boyne in 1690. The Orange Order, founded in 1795, organized as Freemasons' Lodges, spread beyond Ireland to Britain and many parts of the former British Empire. Clearly, it had reached Gibraltar by 1859.

The solitary clue alluded to above consists of an opinion attributed to Sir Melville Macnaghten (1853–1921), who became Assistant Chief Constable of Scotland Yard's CID in 1889, the year after the Ripper murders, but this opinion is problematic because it is at variance with Macnaghten's only surviving notes on the case, written in 1894. It is contained in a book called *The Rise of Scotland Yard: A History of the Metropolitan Police* by Douglas P. Browne (1956). Mr Browne died some years ago; he based the book on notes made from Scotland Yard papers by his friend Ralph Straus, who had himself died after completing only 11 of the book's eventual 27 chapters. To quote Browne directly: "A third head of the CID, Sir Melville Macnaghten, appears to identify the Ripper with the leader of a plot to assassinate Mr Balfour at the Irish Office."

What is vitally important about this enigmatic observation is the fact that Ralph Straus undoubtedly *did* see confidential Scotland Yard papers on the Ripper many years before they were opened to other researchers. On the previous page, for example, Browne states: "The assumed medical knowledge of the murderer then turned the thoughts of the police to medical students and doctors, and in a letter to the Home Office in November Sir Charles Warren refers to inquiries being made about a demented student living in St John's Wood." Indeed he did, the student in question being John William Smith Sanders (1862–1901) of Abercorn Place, St John's Wood. Today the relevant papers are in the public domain, lodged at the Public Record Office in Kew under classifications MEPO 3/140 and HO/144.

As an aside, but one of considerable interest, the same page of Browne's book contains a footnote to the effect that a friend of the writer owned one of two surgical knives "said to have been left by the Ripper beside his victims". This is undoubtedly a reference to Dorothy Stroud, who knew Mr Browne. The current author would only amend the above statement to read "said to have been left by the Ripper beside his *final victim* [my italics]."

So as not to be accused of chasing phantoms, it is necessary to re-emphasize the political situation in London in 1888. Macnaghten, albeit a dyed-in-the-wool Orangeman with ancient allegiances, is unlikely to have held such a controversial opinion either lightly or flippantly. Barely 100 years previously London was brought to its knees by anti-Catholic riots. The "Gordon Riots" erupted between 2 and 9 June 1780 and left approximately 300 people dead. Their immediate cause was a petition presented in Parliament by Lord George Gordon against the relaxation on the holding of landed property by Roman Catholics. Cavalry troops were called in to quell the riots. Sir Charles Warren's "Bloody Sunday" of 1887 was a pale imitation of these earlier events. Sir Melville Macnaghten, a senior Yard official charged with the maintenance of public safety and order in the Metropolis, is hardly likely to have wished to rekindle the smouldering Catholic issue without good reason.

From which source did Macnaghten acquire his knowledge of the Balfour plot? Almost certainly the answer is James Monro, the man who befriended him as Inspector-General of the Bengal Police and who later recommended him for high office at Scotland Yard. Monro (1838–1920) ran the Secret Department (Section D) at Scotland Yard between 1887 and 1890. Section D (officially the Home Office Crime Department, Special Branch) was the forerunner of the Yard's existing Special Branch, which deals with certain acts of terrorism and counter-intelligence. Historical documents show that Monro was at one time preoccupied with an assassination attempt on Mr Balfour.

Why was A.J.Balfour so detested? The answer seems to be a simple case of mistaken identity. He is supposed to be the originator of the Irish "shoot-to-kill" policy, in fact inaugurated by a telegram sent by the Divisional Magistrate for Cork district in 1888, reading as follows: "Deal very summarily with any organized resistance to lawful authority. If necessary do not hesitate to shoot (signed) PLUNKETT."

James Monro was responsible for a most important Home Office memorandum, issued at the time of the murders. On 22 September 1888 the following memo was written by the Home Secretary, Henry Matthews, to his Private Secretary, Evelyn Ruggles-Brise: "Stimulate the police about the Whitechapel Murders. Monro might be willing to give a hint to the CID people if necessary." What did Monro know that he could only hint at to the regular detective force? Perhaps it was all a matter of Irish terrorism.

Detective Chief Inspector John George Littlechild, once a subordinate of Monro, revealed in a 1913 letter that he believed the Ripper to be a Dr Francis Tumblety (1883–1903), an American-Irish physician. The expert researchers Stewart Evans and Paul Gainey have established that Tumblety had weak associations with the Fenian movement, but rather stronger ones with the London homosexual scene, jumping police bail around the time that the Ripper crimes ceased.

It is an unpleasant fact that terrorism often goes hand-in-hand with the sexual humiliation of its victims, or traitors. Western hostages held in Beirut were allegedly subjected to buggery, as was T E Lawrence (of Arabia) when captured by Ottoman Irregular Forces. This trend remains active today in the Irish terrorist movement. One infamous case featured in a report in *The Times* of 17 March 1998, regarding the murder of David Keys in Ulster's Maze prison, apparently by members of the

Loyalist Volunteer Force, giving the following details: "A security official said last night, 'even by the standards of these people it was an appalling killing, they are psychopaths.' Another security official said Keys had also been anally assaulted."

Ever since 1888 rumours have persisted that the Ripper's final victim, Mary Jane Kelly, had been sodomized (or "anally abused"). Some authors have chosen to refute these rumours, certainly unaware of the state of forensic pathology, or indeed the state of Kelly's corpse, at the relevant time. Extant medical reports have nothing to say about the examination (if any) of her anal canal, but there is good evidence that original pages from these reports are now missing.

Sir Charles Warren, Commissioner of Police for the Metropolis at the time of the murders, like Macnaghten, had interesting views on the case. He considered "this series of murders as unique in the history of our country" (thereby, albeit inadvertently, creating the concept of a serial murderer). According to official papers seen by Michell Raper while researching a radio play *"Who Killed Jack the Ripper?"* (commissioned in 1971 and broadcast on 1 June 1972), Sir Charles believed that the notorious Goulston Street graffito was written by an Irishman.

The background to this statement is given in a letter alluded to as follows (broadcast transcript page 35): "Some months ago, a personal acquaintance researching into old documents for a history of Scotland Yard, came upon a letter written by Warren to a Home Office colleague. It was in a file marked private and as the file was of miscellaneous material, not directly concerned with the Whitechapel Murders, it is possible that this is the first time the letter has been made public." The letter goes on to suggest that illegal measures, such as "searching houses without a warrant etc." could be employed in the hunt for the murderer. What remains abundantly clear is that both Ralph Straus and Michell Raper's acquaintance had access to official Ripper papers, which have since disappeared, long before these papers were opened to the general public.

We should perhaps consider the conspiracy theory as it was presented in the contemporary press of 1888. Needless to say, it reflected the ancient debate between Catholic and Protestant interests:

A Unionist Theory

We are on the track of the murderer at last! ... It has been reserved for a lowly Scotch "Meenister" to evolve the truly new and the newly true theory from his inspired cranium. THE EMISSARIES OF THE IRISH-AMERICAN SECRET SOCIETIES says this ingenious scribe, were thwarted in all their efforts to terrorise London with dynamite, & May it not be possible that one of their most dare-devil agents has taken this plan to annoy and engross the Metropolis? ... Here is some ground for Warren's successor to work on, and if he wants the name of the author of the theory the editor of the (of course) Unionist *Scotsman* will no doubt give it to him." *Star*, 19 November 1888.

In fairness to Macnaghten, it should be pointed out that he is by no means the only source for the Balfour assassination plot. Douglas Browne, in his 1950s book, states that in June 1889 Monro sent to the Home Secretary what he described as a direct incitement to the murder of Mr Arthur Balfour. In his recently recovered personal memoirs, Monro elaborates on the circumstances as follows: "The Fenians... resolved to inaugurate a system of assassination of eminent persons, Mr Balfour especially, to be carried out by Irishmen, not Irish Americans. The agent chosen for this rascality was J S Walsh, a resident of Brooklyn, and a well-known ruffian who had been concerned in the Phoenix Park Murder." This key link between Phoenix Park in Dublin and the Whitechapel murders of 1888 will be fully explored at the end of this essay.

There remains one final component to this unresolved conspiracy theory. Uniquely, among her fellow victims, final victim Mary Jane Kelly presented serious problems in identification. For this reason, if not for some other, her death occasioned the first crime scene photographs in the Metropolis. In recent years, some authors have come to question the fact that the final victim really was Kelly at all, suggesting that someone else was murdered in her stead, then subjected to severe mutilation. Only the fact that the body was found in Kelly's room at Miller's Court, they argue, points to its being hers. The only reason ever stated for Kelly being singled out as a victim, later to be

saved from her fate or not, was that she was a police informer (this is
the version given by Joseph Sickert to author Melvyn Fairclough). The
whole argument becomes even more complex when you consider that
"Kelly" may have been a false name in the first place!

The corpse was identified by Kelly's erstwhile boyfriend Joseph
Barnett, described as an Irish cockney. His identification was made by
(the colour of) the hair and eyes, or the eyes and (unusual shape of) the
ears; accounts vary. There are two unusual aspects to this. Firstly, the
body was still clothed in a chemise, which Barnett was not apparently
asked to identify as the property of the deceased. Secondly, Kelly is said
to have had highly unusual frontal dentition, and dental peculiarities
had been used to establish identity for centuries.

Barnett gave details of Kelly's relations to the police and at the
subsequent inquest. Over the years researchers have failed to confirm
any of these details for someone called Mary Jane Kelly, born in 1863 or
1864 – or, indeed, in other years – in Limerick. Her parents, many
siblings, her own date of birth and details of her marriage to a
Welshman named Davies have all proved strangely elusive. The best
"match" to date is the birth of a Mary Kelly at Castletown,[2] County
Limerick in 1864 to a John Kelly and Ann McCarthy. This has been
linked to newspaper reports that Mary Jane Kelly habitually used the
surname McCarthy (see for example *The History of the Whitechapel
Murders* by Richard K Fox, New York, 1888, which is essentially a
compilation of such reports). It has even been suggested that Kelly's
landlord, John McCarthy, could have been a cousin or uncle, explaining
the reason she was allowed to run up large arrears of rent.

Which leads us directly to the unique mystery surrounding Kelly's
death: the fact that not a single member of her family came forward
after her death or to attend her funeral, in spite of documented efforts
by the Royal Irish Constabulary to trace any family in Ireland, and
attempts by Post Office officials to trace the source of letters written to
her from there. It seems highly unlikely that the supposed stigma of
prostitution, family illiteracy(?) or even the confusion over surnames
could have resulted in not a single relative being traced. Perhaps the
explanation was more sinister; her relatives may have feared some form
of reprisal in her native land for guilt by association. Certainly Kelly

2 Possibly Castletownbeare, Co Limerick

told Barnett that she feared for her own safety, apparently believing that she knew who Jack the Ripper was.

So now we come to what crime novelists like to call the denouement. Although tentative, it does explain a number of enigmatic facts and *could* be correct, given the paucity of real clues which remain in this case. It does explain why the Ripper murders generated such enormous Home Office interest and paperwork, while a parallel series of unsolved prostitute murders – the "Thames Torso" crimes of 1887–9, in which dismembered bodies were dumped in or near the River Thames and its associated waterways – generated no great interest at all. The essential connection is a notorious double murder which took place six years previously, in Dublin.

These crimes are known in history as the Phoenix Park Murders. On the evening of 6 May 1882, Lord Frederick Cavendish, Balfour's Liberal predecessor as Irish Secretary, and a senior Irish civil servant, were assassinated as they walked across the park to the Viceregal Lodge at 7.00 pm. They were attacked by a gang of 11 "Invincibles" (a splinter group of the Fenians, themselves formed in New York in 1857) which consisted of seven accomplices and four assailants. The assailants were named Brady, Kelly, Delaney and Caffey. Of these only two, Tim Kelly and Joseph Brady, inflicted mortal wounds. Thomas Burke, the civil servant, apparently the main target of the assassins, had his throat cut (the precise modus operandi of Jack the Ripper); Cavendish, who came to his rescue was stabbed repeatedly.

What is most unusual about these murders is the choice of weapon used. Twelve "long surgical knives" had originally been purchased by a man posing as "Dr Hamilton Williams" (undoubtedly a pseudonym), a colonial surgeon of Demerara, British Guyana. These knives were subsequently smuggled across the Irish Sea by female couriers using rope scabbards, disguising their bulk under their clothing as false pregnancies.

The Phoenix Park murders smack of ritual – a latter-day assassination of Julius Caesar, or a forerunner of the Night of the Long Knives. A reward of £10,000 for information was put up, enabling Superintendent Mallon of the Dublin Metropolitan Police to apprehend the guilty. In spite of an exhaustive search, which included the use of electromagnets to drag the River Liffey in Dublin, only three of the 12 knives were ever recovered by the police. What became of the rest? The answer, it seems, is that they later turned up in the Ripper enquiry. Modern research has shown that the knives in question "had twelve-inch blades" and were purchased at "Weiss's, the instrument-makers of Bond Street (London)" (Tom Corfe, *The Phoenix Park Murders*, Hodder and Stoughton, 1968). These details allow us to identify the knives, supplied by John Weiss and Son of 287 Oxford Street (adjacent to Bond Street), as top of the range. They were undoubtedly No 20 in the contemporary catalogue, double-edged amputating knives designed by the Napoleonic surgeon Lisfranc, having 12-inch blades, and priced at 12 shillings and sixpence each. The odds against such idiosyncratic weapons turning up again in a major murder enquiry are highly remote, yet they did so.

In the early 1970s Ripper author Don Rumbelow was presented with "Jack the Ripper's knife" by Dorothy Stroud, the inspectress of the Sir John Soane museum. She had been given it by Major Hugh Pollard in 1937, a time when interest in the Ripper case was all but dormant. Its exact provenance remains uncertain: Pollard was at various times an associate of Robert Churchill, the Scotland Yard ballistics expert, and Intelligence Officer to the Chief of Police in Dublin during the "Troubles". Originally the knife was one of a pair, contained in a box lined with heavily bloodstained blue silk. Rumbelow's knife has a truncated blade measuring 8 inches and a black handle bearing the manufacturer's name John Weiss.

Dorothy Stroud died in January 1998. I had been able to interview her some years previously. She was characteristically lucid and coherent, recalling the knife well, and recalling with ease the details of its history. During the Second World War, with steel in short supply, it had doubled as a meat carver and a garden tool. Employed in the latter function, digging up a privet hedge, the long blade had snapped. She took the knife to a cutler off Sloane Square who bevelled off the broken blade and put in a thumb grip and guard near the handle. He thought it was a veterinarian's knife (in this he was wrong as John Weiss never made veterinary instruments, but this is a possible origin for the belief that the Ripper was a veterinary student).

Some years ago I pointed out that one injury on a Ripper victim, depicted on the second photograph of the corpse of Mary Jane Kelly, clearly showed an injury which had been inflicted by an axe or hatchet, rather than a knife: the splitting of the thigh bone. Correspondents kindly pointed me towards the following confirmation of this observation, as published in *The Globe* of 16 February 1891, describing a visit to the Convict's Office/Department at Scotland Yard, where the reporter saw: "A hatchet by the door, used by the Whitechapel murderer to hack and disfigure the first [sic] poor girl who fell a victim to his fiendish fury in Dorset Street." Reference to Dorset Street establishes this crime as the murder of Mary Jane Kelly. The hatchet was presumably among the items found in Kelly's room.

"The Convict Office/Department at Scotland Yard" appears to be an early description of the Black Museum, which was housed at the relevant time in a small back room on the second floor of the Convict Supervision Department in Great Scotland Yard. My argument is simple: if a hatchet ever disappeared from the Museum, so too could have two knives. Supposing that all three weapons were found at Miller's Court, this would make sense. This was the tightest spot the Ripper ever had to escape from, so it makes logical sense that he abandoned the tools of his trade at the scene.

The Phoenix Park knives might have meant little to the regular CID officers, but to others they would have sent out shockwaves. An amnesty was put up, and a reward offered, for any accomplices not actually instrumental to murder. Behind the scenes, I am sure, the following political deal was duly brokered.

The Ripper knives firmly connected the Irish Nationalist cause with a series of murders which would not just have brought down their own political aims, but also the entire Liberal opposition. Therefore the Conservative government of the day negotiated the following settlement. Details of the murder investigation would be suppressed in return for calling off the dynamite attacks on London and the attempts on the lives of Balfour and Queen Victoria. And so the murders of five London prostitutes would be subsumed to the interests of the political status quo. Police enquiries (in a half-hearted way) persisted into 1889, just to make sure that the uneasy truce was being maintained.

No wonder James Monro referred to the entire affair as a "political hot potato".

Jack the Ripper, a Novelist's Speculation

Derek Raymond

Long before 1888 – the year of the initial murders attributed to Jack the Ripper – Frederick, Duke of Cambridge, son of Queen Victoria and fourth in line to the crown, made a new friend; Walter Sickert, a Danish portrait painter whose work had so impressed His Majesty that he was taken under the wing of the Royal Family and became a familiar face at Court.

Frederick and Sickert were both of a similar age and quickly became friends. One might have thought that the painter would prove envious of the Duke's power, social status and his wonderfully elevated life at Buckingham Palace. Far from it, it was Frederick who came to be envious of Walter Sickert.

The painter was a character whose notoriety was growing fast amongst London society; he was being commissioned from all parts to deliver portraits; he had installed himself in a magnificent studio and, more importantly, he benefited from absolute liberty of movement, and like any commoner could choose to go where and when he wanted at all times. He took advantage of this liberty, like all artists and bohemians do, to make acquaintance with people from all layers of society: rich people, the middle-classes...and the creatures from the lower depths.

Which was exactly what Frederick would have liked to have been able to do. The Duke was, from all appearance, an intelligent young man who felt constrained by his position. Above all, he also liked to go out to clubs, drinking, to be in the company of pretty women (even if they were from a different social class from his own) and walk the streets in all freedom at any given time of the day, or night. However, the Duke could not escape an unadjustable problem: he was too famous to go unnoticed on such escapades. On the rare occasions when he had been adventurous, his actions had provoked complaints which, even though of a discrete nature, had alarmed the Palace. As a result, he was almost condemned to seldom set foot outside of Court.

This was in the mid-1880s, a time when the Palace worried all too easily. Seldom, since the previous century, had the working classes of British society felt so troubled. This unrest had first manifested itself with a series of demands, calling for some basic form of social justice. These demands, inspired by a new and terrifying phenomenon, then known as "socialism", a brand new word in the vocabulary, were in part responsible for a bloody riot, known as the "Gordon riots", after their principal instigator; a protest march which quickly degenerated into a mob so severe that troops had to be called upon and the police armed. A dozen people died on this occasion.

What alarmed the Crown most was the fact that, during the riot, repeated calls were heard time and again demanding that the Palace should be laid siege to, and the monarchy overthrown. As a result, after calm was achieved again, the Royal Family were keen to avoid any bad gossip to be spread (however anecdotal) that might in one way or another concern a member of England's throne and likely to tear open the smokescreen behind which the Palace was taking shelter.

This was the situation in the summer of 1888, the year when Frederick, half crazed with boredom in his enforced retreat, proposed a secret expedition to his painter friend for the first time; a proposal Sickert did not turn down.

Sickert in fact led a double life. Although he earned a living painting classical portraits of members of the irreproachable bourgeoisie and aristocracy, he was naturally driven to paint canvases, for which he was becoming famous, depicting the faces of East End prostitutes. Under cover of darkness, many of these damaged beauties would travel to the West End to sell their wares; Sickert, however, preferred finding his models on their home patch, in the ill-famed districts of Whitechapel, Wapping and Mile End, and enjoyed spending his days and nights in down market pubs full of often dozing and vindictive drunks of all sexes, including children. He drank with them, under the poor light of gas lamps, amongst the constant hiss of their white light reflected by dull mirrors.

Which is why, more and more often, as night fell, a closed carriage with darkened windows would wait close by Buckingham Gate, a decent distance from the Palace, awaiting two furtive gentlemen. Once they had settled in the carriage, the horses would turn eastwards and make their way towards the City.

In the police archives of those days, or at any rate those that can be looked up today, there are no elements undeniably proving that Maria was a whore. It could well be that, although she was friendly with so many prostitutes, Maria wasn't actually one herself. Her only sin was likely to have been born into a very poor East End family, and to have worked as a saleswoman in a tobacconist on Cleveland Street, one of the West End's least alluring areas, in the labyrinth of streets between Middlesex Hospital and Euston Road. Neither do we know for sure whether Frederick and Sickert ever met her in the tobacco shop, or, more likely, if they made her encounter in the East End where she still lived.

What is certain, on the other hand, is that Maria and Frederick fell madly in love with each other at first sight, which Sickert of course was witness too, and the latter had to swear to the Duke he would keep the matter secret – a secret he kept until his own death in 1939. But he did leave a single clue; the portrait of a rather pretty if tired woman. Young, modestly attired but not without charm, she stands in a dark room full of shadows, in front of a mirror set above a marble chimney. She is half looking into the mirror and also peering sideways at a tall empty chair behind her. Her eyes are infinitely sad, almost lost, so that I feel, having compared this image to the only photograph in existence of Maria, that it is in fact her portrait and that the empty chair, which you might expect to be occupied by a man, symbolizes Frederick's absence.

In spite of Sickert's reservations – he implored the Duke to terminate the relationship before matters went too far – the mutual passion of the two lovers was too strong for this to happen and, well before Maria became pregnant, the couple were already envisaging marriage.

No secret; no escape. Even though her Royal suitor had ordered her to keep silent, it's likely that Maria, like any woman (or man) in love, was unable not to reveal the incredible news to four of her closest friends, to share her joy with them. And then of course, despite Maria swearing her friends to absolute secrecy, at least one of them could not resist the temptation to divulge it. It was established later that each of Jack the Ripper's victims knew Maria well. What is known is that right from the outset of Maria's pregnancy, rumours began to circulate. These rumours were, of course, quickly picked up by the press, insofar as any negative news concerning the Royal Family was assiduously sought after. It goes without saying that the Queen, once all the gossip was spread across the newspapers, summoned her son to establish whether there was any truth in the terrible gossip.

Frederick categorically denied it all, but the flow of rumours continued unabated. Which is when the murders began.

The killings were repugnant, terrifying, brutal and more savage than any previously known acts of violence in London or the East End.

They were also puzzling murders insofar as all four had certain characteristics in common. First of all was the way the bodies had been eviscerated, which would have required a certain mastery of surgical techniques. It was very unlikely that a mere madman from the lower depths – at first the accepted idea of Jack the Ripper – could have had the wherewithal to have committed such a complex operation, and even more unlikely that he would have known how to cut out the kidneys and livers with such precision (and, furthermore, with the poise certainly required, as if the killer had been able to operate with all the time in the world). Which is why one of the initial suspects, a particularly unstable Polish Jew immigrant, was soon released. Although he had confessed to the four murders, claiming as his motivation his wish to avenge himself of the racial abuse he had been a victim of – all the prostitutes in the area refused to go with him – it was soon established that he had no surgical experience whatsoever. When shown one, he could not even recognize a scalpel. Similarly, a second suspect, a medical student, was released as he could not explain in any way how none of the victims had actually been killed where they had been found, and the police could not establish how, with no one else's help, he could have moved the bodies from one place to another. As the suspect pointed out to the police, had he had to act alone, there was no way he could have dragged each body down streets and alleys, even had he a reason to do so. Another somewhat irritating fact for the police was that the murders were still being committed as the suspect in question was under lock and key.

But there was yet another troublesome detail; there was almost no blood under the bodies, where they were being discovered, whereas a normal human body holds at least half a dozen litres of blood.

Nonetheless, the image of a demented madman brandishing a butcher's knife and literally stronger than ten men combined and fuelled by alcohol and delirium quickly took hold of the imagination the London sketch writers and helped sell hundreds of thousand of newspapers. These "special editions" devoted to the Ripper sold out in minutes. There was no other subject of conversation, and frightened folk took refuge in their homes behind locked doors and windows.

The third bizarre element in the case were the scribblings left behind by the killer. In doorways or even across the doors themselves, messages were found, written in chalk and sometimes in pencil, an often clumsy and uncultured proletarian form of writing, signed Jack the Ripper. But despite the constant presence of police officers at the scenes of the crimes, these graffiti disappeared within two or three days, if not within hours; not before, however, some had been photographed by enterprising journalists with then cumbersome photographic equipment.

These messages across walls were not the only forms of communication of the murderer, as "Jack the Ripper" soon made a habit of writing both to the newspapers and to the police at Scotland Yard. Sometimes, he would just send a parcel – a chunk of liver or kidney, cooked but undeniably of human origin, or again a piece of ear, a finger, accompanied by brazen confessions in the style of "I've eaten some of Eddows' liver today with bacon. It was verry god. Signed, Jack the Ripper."

It was then that a young and dynamic inspector from the criminal investigation forces (still a nascent section of the police in those days) made an interesting discovery concerning the messages and informed his superiors. The samples he had examined, he explained, were in fact the first ever examples he had witnessed of an uncultured person's ability to trace, on repeated occasions, the Greek letter "*e*", or epsilon. In his opinion, there was no way this could not be the handwriting of a manual worker, but more likely that of a cultured person trying to pass himself off as a partial illiterate.

This remarkable discovery, which has never been disproved, alarmed the young policeman's superiors so much that he was severely reprimanded, and asked to keep quiet or else seek new employment.

The fourth amazing fact about the Ripper case, was the particular position in which all the bodies of the victims were found. Far from being abandoned in an ugly heap in the way they would have had they fallen to the ground after being assaulted, they had all been carefully lowered to the ground and been eviscerated. In all cases, an ear or a finger were missing, as well as the kidney or liver, and the corpse's right hand was invariably placed over its left shoulder, and the face of the body was turned towards the right.

But no one attached much significance to this fact, with the exception of one journalist who pointed out the ritual aspect of this position, as determined by the rules, for murders committed by freemasons. In those days, the freemasons were still something of an ultra-reactionary secret organization, with powerful international links, a powerful group of people including bankers, judges, ministers and even royalty.

The article however went quite unnoticed, and no one, including the police, would take any note of it. On the Scotland Yard front, everyone was in agreement as to the facts; apart from the arrests of the two suspects mentioned earlier who had since been released, the investigation was visibly going nowhere, which didn't help defuse the general air of panic and quiet anguish that dominated London and had folk shying from all dark alleys and areas barely illuminated by dimmed gaslights.

A final point of interest, and even more so with the advantage of hindsight, is the fact that all the murders were committed over a brief period of time, and that the crime spree ended as suddenly as it had begun, with no credible suspect ever having been arrested who could be proven to be the culprit. All the slanderous gossip about the Palace ceased at the same time, as abruptly, and no one expressed any astonishment at this, at any rate publicly.

As for the Palace, apart from some messages of condolence for the families of the victims, it had nothing to say on the subject, and the government even less so. The discreet, unflappable veil of British silence floated across the corridors of power, in total contrast to the reaction to successive murders on the street.

Sir William Gull, the queen's surgeon, had been given a title upon his appointment to the post, as per tradition. Because of his function, he was often in attendance at Court. He was a freemason, had a busy practice but was also the owner and director of an insane asylum situated 80 kilometres from London, where he took a lively interest in the study of madness. At the time, this area of medicine was no more than a hobby for any doctor; it was not in the public eye and just about anyone could pretend to be an "alienist", a speciality which reaped neither official nor financial rewards. What few people realized of Sir William, even amongst his closest friends and private acquaintances (a very limited circle, as he was not a particularly communicative person) was that his interest in mental disturbances had already pushed him well beyond his studies of the subject, almost to the point of madness himself. One of the few people to actually be aware of how disturbed he had become was evidently Lady Gull, who shortly after the Ripper murders took an extraordinary decision – an act both scandalous and unprecedented for a woman of the Victorian age. She discreetly but clearly left him. A scandal was averted as neither party began actual divorce proceedings.

At Scotland Yard, the Metropolitan Police Commissioner was a freemason; he was often seen at Court, as one of his responsibilities was to look after the Palace's security. From the outset of the affair, he proclaimed – an unprecedented decision for someone of his rank – that he would personally take charge of the Ripper investigation, arguing that his interest in the case would assist the public's confidence. As a result, it is likely following his instructions that the pregnant woman, Maria, was placed under discreet surveillance by the police, on the basis that all known friends of the victims had to be protected. It is also interesting to note (although it could also prove to be sheer coincidence, and no one made a note of it at the time) that the hospital where Maria gave birth was precisely the university hospital where Sir William Gull mostly operated as a surgeon.

The fascinating and ambiguous character who served as a driver for Sir William Gull's carriage was something of a colossus, and knew both horses and London's streets inside out. He had been a servant of the surgeon's for many years. However, shortly after the Ripper killings ceased, and public curiosity had faded along with the press's interest in the subject, he suddenly came into a substantial inheritance and left the country, possibly for Australia.

Maria gave birth to a girl and informed the hospital authorities that she wished to make a statement about the identity of the child's father. Before she could meet up with the relevant authority however, she was declared not to be in full control of her mental powers. As the child could not be separated from its mother, they were both transported to an insane asylum where they both died shortly after in solitary confinement.

By a strange coincidence, the owner and director of the asylum in question was Sir William Gull who shortly after became insane himself.

Frederick, Duke of Cambridge, committed suicide.

"Jack the Ripper" has never existed; which is why he was never caught. "Jack the Ripper" was a conspiracy including at least four men, three of whom were freemasons. Gull's servant drove a closed carriage whose windows remained closed. Inside the carriage sat Gull and probably Sickert, who was there to specifically identify the victims. When there was a knock on the roof of the carriage, the coachman would stop the carriage, jump to the ground and once the men seated inside had confirmed it was the right person, would quickly seize the victim and throw her inside in the vehicle. It was here that the woman's throat was cut and that she was eviscerated and mutilated. Once Gull had finished with her, the body would be left on another street, a few minutes away. This is why no one could ever explain how the bodies had been transported between locations.

Then the carriage returned (where to? maybe the Palace?), with its macabre load, where it was meticulously cleaned up.

The official enquiries never succeeded, because the Police Commissioner saw to it that they did not make progress, reprimanding his own staff on occasion, rubbing out traces and concealing evidence where necessary.

This is all just a hypothesis, but one thing is certain. There is a trait which both the freemasons and the Crown share, particularly in difficult times; a dislike of riots and popular uprisings clamouring for social justice.

The preceding explanations are just that; a hypothesis. And everything that has happened since keeps it that way. Because if there was a single culprit at the origin of the whole conspiracy behind the serial murders it could well have been the Queen of England herself. And we all know that murderous monarchs have survived through history by carefully protecting their own interests.

Carl Feigenbaum – aka Jack the Ripper

Trevor Marriott

Jack the Ripper; man or myth, fact or fiction? Whoever he was, up until now his identity remained a mystery. The horrendous murders attributed to the unknown killer spread terror among the residents of London' s East End. The name Jack the Ripper was known and feared the world over.

More than a century has passed since the Ripper's crimes were committed, yet the search for his identity has been ongoing. In fact the mystery had deepened so much that the truth about the murders is thoroughly obscured. Innumerable press stories, books, plays, films and even musicals have dramatized and distorted the facts, with the unfortunate result that the public have now accepted the fiction more readily than the reality.

As a modern day British Murder Squad Detective I had been interested in the case for many years but due to a heavy workload, I never had the time to study the case in great detail. However in 2002 with more time at my disposal I decided to re-investigate the murders. I felt that all the experience, knowledge and insight into the criminal mind I had gained over the years by interviewing and talking to murderers, rapists and robbers would be invaluable in my attempt to view the murders not only through the eyes of an experienced investigator but through the eyes of the killer. So I set out to conduct a twenty-first century investigation into this series of nineteenth century murders.

I looked closely at the murders themselves, the victims, and the suspects at the time, and both the evidence originally available and the new evidence and new suspects that have emerged in the intervening years. I analyzed and assessed the new evidence recently put forward, which I hoped would either prove or disprove some of the accepted theories about the murders, which have also been with us for many years. In doing so I hoped I might find something new that would unlock the mystery and lead me to the identity of Jack the Ripper

It has been widely accepted that Jack the Ripper killed only five women all of whom were prostitutes. However, my investigation revealed that eight women were in fact murdered. All were killed in similar circumstances and all the murders occurred in or near Whitechapel, East London, between August 1888 and February 1891, and all were prostitutes. All had their throats cut, and some suffered mutilations and in the case of two of the victims it was suggested that the killer also removed vital organs taking them away with him from the crime scenes.

The East End of London was a very cosmopolitan area, as it still is today. It was also a particularly violent area, with brutal crime a common occurrence, and knives were widely carried for use in criminal acts as well as for self-protection. Over the years it has been suggested that the cutting of the victims' throats was unique to these crimes and therefore linked them as having been committed by the same person. However, it was a fact that the accepted method of killing a person was to cut their throat in this violent society. So, while the Whitechapel victims were all killed in this manner, it was not unique to these murders. This means of killing was far more common than it is today, when very few murders that are committed with a knife are the result of the victim's throat being cut.

So, has everyone been wrong all these years? Were the police of the day blinkered in the way they investigated the murders? Did the Ripper kill the canonical five women? Or was it more? Or was he responsible for fewer murders than have been attributed to him? Could another person or persons have murdered some of the victims? All are interesting questions that I hoped to be able to answer as a result of my investigation.

So who were these poor unfortunate souls who fell victim to Jack the Ripper? The first murder I uncovered was that of Martha Tabram. A plump, middle-aged prostitute, she was stabbed to death in George Yard on 7 August 1888.

On the previous evening Tabram was seen with another prostitute in various pubs in Whitechapel. At around 11.45 pm she was seen going into George Yard with a soldier, presumably to have sex. There were no more sightings of her before her body was found at 4.45am on the stairs in George Yard Buildings. Her lower garments were in a state of disarray, suggesting intercourse had taken place. She had been stabbed repeatedly with 39 wounds to her chest and one different size stab wound to her abdomen, suggesting that perhaps her killer was armed with two knives. The police failed to identify her killer or trace any witnesses to the crime.

The second murder occurred on Friday 31 August. The victim was Mary Ann Nichols, known as Polly, aged 43. She was found murdered in a narrow, cobbled street called Buck's Row. Nichols was last seen alive around 2.30 am and was found in the street at 3.45 am. Witnesses who found her suggest she may have been clinging to life. If that was so, the killer was very lucky not to have been seen either committing the murder or making good his escape. Nichols had been stabbed several times in the stomach and abdomen and her throat had been cut to the point that she was almost decapitated. Bruising found around the neck and throat suggests she may have possibly been strangled before having her throat cut. It was suggested that she was murdered with a long bladed knife.

There were no witnesses and no descriptions of anyone seen with Nichols before her death or at the spot where she was murdered. Her killer vanished unseen into the darkness and the mist.

The next victim was Annie Chapman aged 47, she was found dead in the back yard at 29 Hanbury Street on 8 September 1888. Her throat, like Mary Ann Nichols's, was dissevered deeply. She had been disembowelled and her uterus was found to be missing at the time of the post-mortem. Her intestines had been placed over her right shoulder and other parts of her stomach were on her left side.

She was last seen alive at around 5.30 am, talking to a man near to where her body was found. This man was described as shabbily dressed, over 40 years of age, with a dark complexion, possibly of foreign appearance. He was wearing a brown deerstalker hat and what is believed to have been a dark overcoat.

The main issue with this murder was the removal of the organs, which for many years experts have suggested was done by the killer at the scene. The doctor who went to the murder scene made a cursory examination and did not record any organs having been removed at that time. However he found the uterus had been removed when conducting the post-mortem some seven hours later and stated that the person who removed the organ must have had some anatomical knowledge and stated that it would have taken a skilled medical man like himself 15 minutes to carry out such a removal.

We now have a killer who takes a female into a back yard of a house in the early hours, while it is still dark. He kills her and supposedly disembowels her. Hospital surgeons normally require a great deal of light to locate the organs and either operate on or remove them. But in this murder the killer is supposed to have removed a specific organ (the uterus) and cut it out with medical precision in almost total darkness. I cannot disagree with the doctor's finding that the uterus was removed with precision. So could the killer have been a highly trained medical man? If he was, why savage and mutilate the body? The police enquiry into this murder also proved negative.

Elizabeth Stride a 45-year-old prostitute was the next victim and was the first of the so-called "double event". Her body was found in Dutfield's Yard, off Berner Street, at about 1.00 am on the night of 30 September 1888 by a salesman returning with his pony and cart. She died from a single cut to her throat, believed to have been made by a small knife. There were no other wounds found on her body. Speculation at the time suggested that the killer was disturbed.

The crucial question in the Stride murder is; was she a victim of the Ripper or simply an unconnected victim? It would have been foolhardy to dismiss any possibility lightly. After carefully assessing all the facts surrounding her murder. My conclusion was that Stride's murder was not connected to any previous or later murders and she was not a Ripper victim. In fact the police doctor at the time also came to the same conclusion. The murder location was different from the rest. The time of the murder was signifcantly earlier; the knife used was also different.

As with the previous murders the killer disappeared into the night. No one was ever arrested in connection with her murder.

The second victim of the bloody night of 30 September, was Catharine Eddowes, known as Kate, a prostitute aged 46. At 1.45 am she was found brutally murdered in a darkest corner of Mitre Square. Eddowes's head, like that of Polly Nichols, had been almost severed. Her body was gashed open from breastbone to stomach and her intestines had been cut out and placed over her right shoulder. The post-mortem, which did not take place until twelve hours later, showed that her kidney and uterus had been removed, again with medical precision. Her face had been brutally mutilated, and there was no doubt she had been the victim of the most frenzied attack to date.

Eddowes's murder is almost identical to those of Annie Chapman and Polly Nichols, the only significant difference being that those two victims were killed much later at night. The alleged removal of Eddowes's organs and the placing of her intestines on her shoulder mirrors the murder of Chapman.

The murder of Eddowes is a case that raises more questions than answers. The first is in relation to the removal of the organs and I suggest that there must be grave doubt as to how exactly the organs were removed from these victims, when they were removed, and by whom?

In those days the medical sciences were less advanced than they are now and many areas were being investigated. This research would have called for the use of organs and body parts, which were very difficult to acquire by conventional means. I suggest that Annie Chapman's and Catharine Eddowes's organs were expertly removed, not at the crime scenes by the murderer, but after the bodies had been taken to the mortuary and before the post-mortems were carried out.

Body parts were a valuable commodity and it would have been easy for a mortuary keeper, in particular, to provide these or allow them to be removed by a third party. He may well have had sufficient medical skill himself to remove organs from bodies in his care, although it is more likely that he allowed a medical researcher or a doctor to do so. In either case he would, no doubt, have received a substantial reward. The removal of organs would have been even easier in cases where the body had already been opened up, as with Chapman and Eddowes. The findings of the post-mortem would, quite naturally, have left everyone thinking that the killer had removed the organs at the murder scene.

You may be asking why, if Chapman's and Eddowes's organs were removed, as I suggest, why weren't any removed from the other victims? The answer is simple; these were the only two victims who were savagely mutilated to the extent that their abdomens were ripped open and their intestines removed. The other victims were not mutilated to this degree, so it would have been impossible to remove the organs for fear of their absence being noted at the post-mortem.

Adding more weight to this the coroner in the Chapman inquest mentioned that an American had recently been trying to purchase organs and had been prepared to pay a high price. Even more reason for a mortuary keeper, or another to be a party to the theft of Chapman's and, later, Eddowes' s organs. The police failed to trace any witnesses to this crime.

Eddowes's murder differs in a further respect from the previous murders described above. After her body was discovered, some two hours later there came to the notice of the police two different pieces of what have been regarded as "evidence" which at the time were suggested as being material to the murder and have generally been accepted up until the present day.

Both pieces of evidence were found in a stairwell leading to dwellings in Goulston Street, a 20-minute walk from the Eddowes crime scene. Having examined all of this evidence carefully, I now suggest that perhaps the police and other experts have been wrong all this time about this evidence.

The first item of "evidence" was a wet piece of apron spotted with blood. This was later examined closely and found also to have on it a smearing of faecal matter. The piece of apron was later identified as coming from the apron of Catharine Eddowes, and was described as having been cleanly cut. The second item was chalk writing found scrawled on a wall at the spot where the piece of apron was found. At the time the police believed that the killer might have written this. This read "The Juwes are the men that will not be blamed for nothing". Did the writing have any connection with the Eddowes murder, any of the previous murders or any of the later murders? The answer is definitely no. This is the only writing ever found which has been suggested as being connected to any of the murders. However, it was not found at the scene of Eddowes's murder and the content does not refer to either this murder or any other murders before or after. I am sure that a search of the area would have revealed countless other scrawlings on walls and in alleys, some of which would have had meaning for the writer alone, as this example may have done. But the idea that a killer making his escape would stop to write a message on a wall is unbelievable.

Moving on to the piece of apron, later identified as having come from Eddowes's apron, several questions arise. When was it removed? By whom? For what reason? And how long had it been at the location where it was found? At the time the police put forward several theories. One suggestion was that the killer had cut the piece from the apron to wipe away the blood from his hands and/or the knife, and that he may have even used it to carry her organs away. The police also believed the apron piece showed the direction in which the killer had escaped, regardless of whether he had deliberately left it or dropped it accidentally.

I disagree with all these suggestions and have my own theory based on my research. First, let us assume that the killer did not reside in Whitechapel. He kills Eddowes at a location on the edge of Whitechapel and then flees into the misty, murky, dimly lit streets of the City. If the police theory, which has been widely accepted, is correct, he then makes his way back almost into the centre of Whitechapel, where he either deposits or loses the piece of apron. Even if I am wrong and he did live in the heart of the area and decided to go to ground there, he was taking a huge risk in making his way back home knowing that there would be a large police presence in response to Eddowes's murder and Stride's a short time earlier. We are asked to believe he would have risked being stopped, searched and possibly apprehended.

I must also ask why the killer would have cut off a piece of the apron. Perhaps it was for the reasons the police suggested at the time. But there is no evidence of a similar act in any of the other murders. If it was to clean his knife with, he could have done that at the scene with one swift wipe across her clothing. If it was to clean his hands with, he could have done that at the scene without cutting off and taking away a piece of apron. Even if he did cut it off, surely he would have discarded it long before reaching Goulston Street. He would not have wanted to be seen walking down the road wiping his bloodstained hands. Besides, the killer may have worn gloves and not needed to clean his hands.

If we accept that the piece of apron was correctly identified, as coming from Eddowes's apron but the killer did not cut it off, what other explanation could there be? I will put forward one, which, many experts have foolishly chosen to disregard. However, as there is very little direct evidence it is unwise to dismiss anything which may add additional weight to existing evidence and, likewise, new theories which could suggest that earlier theories have been wrong all these years.

First, the apron piece. This was made of cotton and was wet when found; it was spotted with blood and was smeared with faecal matter. It was found screwed up and lying in the stairwell of the tenement building. This area of Whitechapel was no doubt used as a short cut from one part to another and could have been used by Eddowes at some time that day or after her release from police custody shortly before her death.

The answer I believe revolves around matters of personal feminine hygiene, which would account for the blood and faecal matter on the apron piece. In Victorian times women of the lower class, when menstruating, did not use sanitary towels, as we know them today. If they bothered to use anything at all, it was a cotton rag. In addition the use of public toilets was unheard of among this class owing to the fact that a penny was required (hence the saying "to spend a penny") and most could not afford this. When outdoors, they would relieve themselves wherever they could: waste ground; alleyways and stairwells, for example. How do we know that the piece of apron was not cut by Eddowes herself from her apron for this purpose and then discarded when totally soiled or when she used the stairwell in Goulston Street as a toilet while passing through at some time before her murder? After all, there was a six-hour gap *from* when she left home until her arrest *for* being drunk at approximately 8.30 pm, and almost an hour after her release from police custody before her murder. She was in the area earlier that day, before being arrested for being drunk. The apron piece was in the stairwell, so if it had been raining it would not have become wet with the rain. Maybe the wetness was caused by Eddowes's urine. The blood spotting is also consistent with the menstruation cycle.

Going back to the removal of the organs of Eddowes. As she was found murdered in the darkest area of Mitre Square, I would suggest that it would have been almost impossible *for* anyone to have removed these organs with any medical precision in total darkness. The same would also apply to the removal of Chapman's organs. So this in itself must cause grave doubt about the accepted theory that the killer removed these organs. The police were unable to trace any witnesses to this crime.

The next victim in chronological order was Mary Kelly. Unlike the other prostitutes, who were killed on the streets where they worked, Kelly had her own private room. She met her death on 8 November 1888, at 13 Miller's Court, off Dorset Street, where she was disembowelled, disfigured and dismembered in a fury of madness. The post-mortem found no defensive wounds, nor any signs of a struggle. She may even have been killed as she slept or rendered unconscious first. Some of her vital organs had been removed from the body and found in various parts of her room, but none were taken away and there was no suggestion that they had been removed with any medical precision. I think this fact alone adds more weight to my earlier suggestion that the organs removed from Chapman and Eddowes were not removed by their killer.

The nearest the police came to obtaining any form of description of Jack the Ripper was obtained after Kelly's murder when a man named George Hutchinson came forward several days after the murder and told the police he had seen Kelly with a man near to her house and gave them a 'detailed' description. His statement is interesting. Hutchinson seems to have been the last person to see Kelly alive. The description he gave of the man he saw with Kelly was "too accurate" to be plausible. He described the man as having a dark complexion and a heavy, dark moustache, turned up at the corners, dark eyes and bushy eyebrows. He was "Jewish looking". He wore a soft felt hat pulled down over his eyes, a long, dark coat trimmed with astrakhan and a white collar with a black necktie fixed with a horseshoe pin. He wore dark spats over light, button-over boots. On his waistcoat there was a massive gold chain with a large seal with a red stone hanging from it.

The problem with Hutchinson's account is that at that time and in that location it would have been very dark. He stated that he was standing under a street light, but we do not know how far away he was from the man. To have taken note of so much detail, he would have had to have been very close to him. Hutchinson described seeing a red stone hanging from a large gold chain. All dark colours look the same in half-light, so how could he have been certain it was red? He described the man as wearing a horseshoe pin, but this too would not have been easy to notice unless he was very close to him. Hutchinson said the man's eyes were dark and his eyebrows bushy. As the man and Kelly passed him the man lowered his head, he said, yet he was still able to describe the colour of his eyes and the form of his eyebrows. It would have been difficult to be sure of either in those conditions.

After Hutchinson was interviewed the police were happy to accept his account as correct. Or were they? This was the most savage murder to date and the police had nothing to work on except his statement. Public outrage was growing at the unsolved crimes, but the police would have been able to save face to some extent by saying the description given by Hutchinson was the nearest they had come so far to identifying Jack the Ripper, although I suspect that they thought he could in fact be the Ripper. If the police had dismissed his statement and the press had found out, there would have been more adverse criticism of their work on the case. For this reason, I suspect, they chose outwardly to accept Hutchinson's description but continued to investigate him discreetly.

Some researchers even suggest that Hutchinson was the Ripper. But, if Hutchinson was the Ripper, why did he come forward with a statement? He had not been seen by anyone else at the murder location, so it would have been sensible for him to keep quiet. Was he really there at that time? Or was he just an attention-seeker who made up this story in an attempt to obtain money from the press? By the time he came forward, he would have known that the police had no other witnesses and so his credibility would not be questioned. I do not believe him to have been Jack the Ripper nor did the police at the time.

Mary Jane Kelly is said to have been the last of the Ripper's victims. But as stated earlier my investigation uncovered several other murders of prostitutes in the Whitechapel area that are worthy of consideration in deciding whether the Ripper continued killing after Kelly.

Forty-year-old Alice McKenzie died in Castle Alley on 17 July 1889 of wounds to the left side of her neck. Her abdomen showed signs of superficial mutilations. Her clothes were up around her chin. She was last seen alive at 11.40pm and her body was found at 12.50 am in the same alley that a police officer later stated he patrolled some 20 minutes before this time and saw nothing suspicious. Two doctors agreed that a "sharp-pointed weapon" was used to inflict the wounds, but also that it could have been smaller than the one used in the previous killings. However neither the doctors nor the police could agree on whether McKenzie was a Ripper victim. Police failed to trace any witnesses to this murder.

My ability to state conclusively that this murder was connected to the previous killings is not helped by the failure of the two doctors and the police to agree. However, in the light of my theory as to how and when the organs were removed from the earlier victims, I believe Alice McKenzie was indeed a Ripper victim.

Twenty-three-year-old Frances Coles was the last possible UK Ripper victim and perhaps the prettiest of them all. She was murdered in the early hours of 13 February 1891 under a railway arch in Royal Mint Street. Her throat was slashed only moments before a policeman arrived on the scene. There were no abdominal mutilations. She had injuries to the back of her head consistent with being thrown to the pavement and her throat had been cut while she was lying on the pavement. The policeman who discovered the body heard footsteps walking away, but police rules required that he stay with the body, as she appeared to be still alive. Had he followed the footsteps, he may have caught the murderer.

Coles was last seen alive at 1.45 am and found dying at 2.15 am. At 1.45am she had bumped into fellow prostitute Ellen Gallagher in

Commercial Street, passing "a violent man in a cheese cutter hat". Apparently Gallagher remembered the man as a former client who had given her a black eye and warned Coles not to entertain him, but Coles ignored her friend's advice and solicited the man. She and the stranger headed toward the direction of the Minories. This was the last time she was seen alive. It appears that no enquiries were carried out by the police to trace or identify the man.

Was Frances Coles a Ripper victim? Her throat was cut, but unlike in the other Whitechapel slayings, a blunt knife was used. There seems to have been no evidence of strangulation. There was no mutilation of the abdomen and the clothes were not disarranged. The murder site, as in the case of Elizabeth Stride, was south of Whitechapel Road.

Could the Ripper have ceased his onslaught for eight months and then resumed his slayings with Frances Coles? Or was she just another victim of the violent world of Whitechapel of the time? My initial impression is that her murder is perhaps not connected to any of the others, but during the latter part of my investigation I uncovered other evidence which suggested she and all the other victims I have mentioned with the exception of Liz Stride were killed by Jack the Ripper.

Before considering any likely suspects I had to see if there was any direct evidence I could use after analyzing the murders that would help me to identify the killer. There was none. All I had to go on were vague descriptions of men seen with some of the victims before their deaths and the MOs – the *modus operandi*, or method of killing – used in each murder. As I looked at each suspect my aim was to see if any of them matched any of these descriptions, but, even if they did, I knew that this fact would be no more than weak circumstantial evidence. In reality those assortment of descriptions obtained by the police who saw the victims with or talking to male persons prior to their deaths was of no help.

I then looked at the evidence, which had been put forward against the main suspects, only one of which was ever arrested for the murders, and several of these have only been put forward in recent years. These suspects were Montagu Druitt, who at the time of the Whitechapel murders was a barrister and a teacher, Aaron Kosminski, a local barber.

George Chapman also a barber, John Pizer a leather worker and Michael Ostrogg a petty criminal.

Prince Albert Victor, Duke of Clarence, and the grandson of Queen Victoria. Walter Sickert famous English painter recently put forward by writer Patricia Cornwell, and Francis Tumblety an American "quack" doctor living in London at the time of the murder of Mary Kelly and arrested for gross indecency with a male person around the time of Kelly's murder. Joseph Barnett the estranged boyfriend of Mary Kelly, Sir William Gull physician to Queen Victoria, and James Maybrick cotton merchant from Liverpool who became a suspect when a diary emerged in the mid-1990s which was purportedly written by Maybrick in which he confessed to being Jack the Ripper. However this diary has now been proved to be a forgery.

After lengthy enquiries I could find no tangible evidence other than weak hearsay evidence to suggest any of these suspects could have been Jack the Ripper.

So having eliminated the prime suspects I asked myself many times who the killer was. Was he a tinker, tailor, soldier, sailor, rich man, poor man, beggar man or thief? It is probably true to say that, over the years, representatives of all of these walks of life and many occupations besides have been suspected, with a list of over 140 likely suspects. I've always believed that, should the truth ever come out, the killer would be revealed as someone who did not fall under suspicion at the time and has not been mentioned by any researcher to date. After investigating these "prime" suspects and satisfying myself that none of them was Jack the Ripper, this conviction was even stronger.

For a long time I personally suspected that Jack the Ripper may have been a merchant seaman. I could find nothing to suggest that the police had pursued this specific line of enquiry at the time. This was strange and suggested to me that they were perhaps very blinkered in their approach to solving the murders. They should have seen, after the double murders on 30 September, that a pattern was beginning to form. In short, since St Katharine's dock and the London Dock were so close to the murder locations, they should have looked at the possibility that the killer was a merchant seaman. Ships use docks, prostitutes are attracted to docks, merchant seaman seek out the prostitutes when their boats dock. Between 30 September and 7 November 1888 police had ample opportunity to explore this line of enquiry, and had they done so, after Mary Kelly's murder they would have been in a position to take positive action (with regard to this particular line of enquiry) and see a pattern to the murders.

In view of my suspicions I decided to broaden my lines of enquiry to try to ascertain if there were any other Ripper-like murders in other parts of the world. I came across unconfirmed newspaper reports of a string of murders of prostitutes in Managua, the capital of Nicaragua. These murders supposedly took place within a ten-day period in January 1889. All the victims were killed and mutilated in similar fashion to the Whitechapel victims. All of the crimes were undetected.

In addition, I discovered the murder of a woman, which occurred in October 1889 in the German seaport town of Flensburg. Again the victim was killed and mutilated in Ripper like fashion with no one being apprehended. The merchant seaman theory was now becoming a reality with the dates of the murders all fitting into a pattern suggesting the same killer could have been responsible for all the murders, and that killer was a merchant seaman.

I then re-focused on the Whitechapel killings. My first line of enquiry was to try to establish the details of any boats docked in London Docks and St Katharine's Dock on the dates of the murders, to see if any of them were berthed on all the murder dates between August and November 1888. After combing through the records I discovered that a German merchant vessel registered in Bremen named *The Reiher* was berthed in St Katharine's dock on all the murder dates save for 30 September.

The reason it was not in London on that date was the fact that it had been taken out of service for a time following a collision in the River Thames previously. However another vessel from the same line was here on that date. Furthermore *The Reiher* was also here on the date of the Alice McKenzie murder on 17 July 1889. The records also show that two merchant vessels from the same line were also here on the date of Frances Coles's murder, 13 February 1891. So now the investigation was moving towards the killer being a German merchant seaman but, could I identify him?

I managed to trace crew lists for *The Reiher* but found them incomplete. Unlike crew lists for British vessels, which showed a crewman's name, age, place of birth and previous boat, the lists from Bremen showed only the name, previous boat and occupation on the present boat. These crew lists showed that the majority of the crew on these vessels were German and that the majority were present when the vessels were in London on all the murder dates. However, the lists did not give the ages or other personal details of the crew. It was also common practice for seaman not to give their correct details when signing up.

I then uncovered similar Ripper-like murders in the US and Germany, all occurring after the cessation of the Whitechapel murders. These took place between 1891 and 1894. All have a very similar MO and fit into a significant time pattern, and all remain undetected save for one, which would become very significant and subsequently lead me to the identification of Jack the Ripper.

11 April 1890, Hurley, Wisconsin USA – Laura Whittlesay
28 April 1890, Benthen Germany – un-named female (prostitute?)
24 April 1891, Jersey City, USA – Carrie Brown (prostitute)
25 October 1891, Berlin, Germany – prostitute named Nietzsche
31 January 1892, New Jersey USA – Elizabeth Senior
3 April 1892, Berlin Germany – un-named prostitute
31 August 1894, New York – Juliana Hoffman

The last murder was the most interesting and occurred on 31 August 1894 while the location was close to the scene of the Carrie Brown and Elizabeth Senior murders. The most significant point in relation to this crime was that the perpetrator was apprehended moments after committing the murder while attempting to flee the scene of the crime. He was found with traces of blood on his hands. The murder weapon was a long knife with a six-inch highly sharpened blade that was found nearby. When examined by a doctor, it had traces of what was believed to have been the blood of the victim. When a later search of the suspect's room was conducted police found a cloth bag, which they suggested was where the knife had been kept. Also found in the room was a whetstone for sharpening the knife. The suspect had been residing with the victim and her son for only a few days as a lodger. Further enquiries showed that he had been travelling around the New York area as well as other parts of the US.

The man arrested was later convicted and sentenced to death for this murder. After losing his appeal he was finally executed in the electric chair in Sing Sing Prison on 27 April 1896. The killer's name was Carl Feigenbaum. He was known to have used several aliases around the country, of which Anton Zahn was one that he is positively known to have used. It has been suggested that this may have been his real name. Other aliases he was known to have used are Carl Zahn, and Carl or Anton Strohband.

From all the facts I had gathered through my long protracted enquiry into the Whitechapel murders my suspicions led me to suspect that this man could in fact be the elusive Jack the Ripper.

I ascertained that Feigenbaum was born in Germany around 1840 and had also worked as a fireman on German merchant ships owned by the same merchant fleet that operated vessels between Bremen and London at the time of the Whitechapel murders. Furthermore records show that he was still working as a fireman on ships sailing between the US and Germany when the murders in Germany and the US occurred. Following his arrest in 1894 there were no more Ripper-like murders.

I realized that despite gathering all this circumstantial evidence I was a long way from being able to positively say that Feigenbaum was Jack the Ripper. But then what I now believe to be the final pieces of the jigsaw came together in the form of an unsolicited statement from his attorney William Sandford Lawton following the execution of Feigenbaum. Lawton when speaking to the press, stated that he himself believed that Feigenbaum was Jack the Ripper, and broke his code of confidentiality to say that during the time he had been representing him Feigenbaum had confessed to having a hatred of women and a desire to kill and mutilate them. This prompted Lawton to research the Whitechapel murders and the other, previously mentioned, US murders. The outcome being, that Lawton from his own enquiries ascertained that Feigenbaum had been in London between the dates of some or all of the murders, and when confronted with this Feigenbaum made no denials to these facts. Feigenbaum was also asked if he had killed the Whitechapel women to which he gave a non-committal answer.

This statement made by Lawton was crucial to my investigation. When Lawton made his statement he invited the police to investigate Feigenbaum and his movements in relation to the Whitechapel murders. Neither the New York Police nor the Metropolitan Police in London appeared to have pursued this line of enquiry, and I have to ask why not? Surely, if they had spoken to Lawton he could have given them details of the enquiries he conducted, and this is where Lawton's credibility as a witness is confirmed. Lawton would not have made that statement if the facts contained in it were false or untrue. He would have known that facts mentioned by him would likely be closely scrutinized and tested. So yet another reason to accept his statement as being correct. The other issue is, that if Lawton was fabricating his statement, as I am sure some will suggest he was, then why did he not simply come out and say that Feigenbaum had actually confessed to being Jack the Ripper. After all who could rebut this, certainly not Feigenbaum.

The sad fact surrounding Feigenbaum is that very little is known about him or his movements in his early years. By the time he was finally arrested he was 48. In a way, Feigenbaum was unique in that his killing spree was not restricted to one country. Thus making him the world's first transcontinental serial killer. Nowadays most serial killers tend to kill their victims within specific localized areas.

At 11.00 am on 27 April 1896, the final chapter on Jack the Ripper was about to be written. Feigenbaum was transferred from the condemned cell on death row in Sing Sing Prison to the execution chamber. Warden Sage, two keepers, and Father Creeden of Sing Sing prison, attended him. During his death march he repeated the prayers of the Roman Catholic Church and kissed the crucifix, which he carried before him.

Feigenbaum was composed and took his seat in the electric chair without any urging. As the straps were being buckled, he took Warden's Sage's hand, kissed it warmly and, with a smile, wished the warden and the priest goodbye. He then took off his spectacles and handed them to Father Bruder, with the request that they be buried with his body.

The death mask was then adjusted and at 11.16 am an electric current of 1.820 volts with amperage of 7.5 was turned on and continued for 20 seconds when it was reduced to 300 volts. This level was kept for 40 seconds and then turned off. After a few seconds a second shock of 1,820 volts was given, when it was turned off doctors pronounced Feigenbaum dead.

Feigenbaum's body was then removed to the operating room where an autopsy took place. It showed that death must have been instantaneous which is more than can be said for many of his victims. He made his will that same morning supposedly leaving money in a German bank in New York to his sister reserving $90 to pay his funeral expenses.

The warden and the clergyman said that he even protested his innocence of the crime for which he was convicted right up to the moment that he went to the electric chair.

Following his execution prison records show that his body was taken to a Roman Catholic cemetery in Poughkeepsie, New York where he was buried. This was probably St Peter's Roman Catholic Church Cemetery; it was the only Roman Catholic church cemetery in that area at the time. Burial records from this cemetery were apparently destroyed in a fire in the 1900s, so the actual whereabouts of his grave are unknown.

The full details of my investigation can be found in *Jack the Ripper – The 21st Century Investigation* published by Blake Publications (ISBN 9781844543700 in paperback form).

A Lifetime in Ripperology

Colin Wilson

I suppose I must qualify as one of the first Ripperologists, since I became interested in the murders when I was seven or eight, in 1938 or 1939. My father, who worked in the boot and shoe trade in Leicester, brought home from work a book he had borrowed called *The Fifty Most Amazing Crimes of the Last Hundred Years*, published by Odhams Press in 1936. Each article has a sketch of the murderer beside its title; but the article on Jack the Ripper – by F. A. Beaumont – had only a huge black question mark. The piece was called "The Fiend of East London", and it made my hair stand on end. But then, children rather enjoy gruesome tales.

I asked my maternal grandfather about the murders. He could remember them clearly, having been born about 1880, eight years earlier, and he recalled being warned to be indoors by six o'clock in case Jack the Ripper got him. My grandfather took the weekly magazine *Titbits*, and it was in one of these that I saw an article that I later recalled as being written by General Booth of the Salvation Army. In my recollection, Booth had stated his belief that Jack the Ripper was his secretary, a man who had "dreams of blood", and who one day told Booth that "Carroty Nell will be the next to go".

I was mistaken. More than 40 years later, the Scotland Yard librarian, David Streatfield, tracked down the article, and included it in his Ripper Bibliography (for which he adopted the pen name Alexander Kelly.) It was actually by Salvation Army Commissioner David C Lamb, and appeared on 23 September 1939. Kelly thought the Ripper was a signwriter he had employed, who had visions of blood (not dreams), and who made the prophecy about Carroty Nell around February 1891. Carroty Nell's real name was Frances Coles, and she was found with her throat cut on 14 February 1891. Most Ripperologists are in agreement that she was almost certainly not a victim of Jack the Ripper, whose activities were confined to the year 1888, but Commissioner Lamb thought she was, and believed that the signwriter was Jack the Ripper – an unlikely theory, since he would hardly announce the murder in advance.

In "The Fiend of East London", Beaumont suggests that Jack the Ripper was a doctor who was obsessed with tracking down the woman who had given his son syphilis – Mary Kelly, the final victim. He had killed the other women in the course of his search to prevent them revealing to Mary Kelly that he had been asking questions about her, and he removed the inner organs "to add to his collection of specimens, one of the finest in the world."

This theory had first been suggested by a Member of Parliament named Leonard Matters, *The Mystery of Jack the Ripper*, published in 1929, the first book on the murders (and the only one when I first read about them). Matters claimed that he had come across the theory in a newspaper in Buenos Aires, which contained an account of the death-bed confession of a doctor, formerly a London surgeon, who had died recently: according to this doctor, Jack the Ripper had been his former teacher, a certain Dr Stanley. Matters claimed that he had searched the records of the Medical Council of Great Britain for anyone who sounded like Stanley, but had failed to find him.

The truth is that Matters almost certainly made up the whole story. To begin with, Mary Kelly was not suffering from syphilis, as the post-mortem showed. And Matters phrases his story so vaguely – even implying that Stanley was not his suspect's real name – that he makes an impression of shiftiness.

In 1939, the second book on the murders appeared: *Jack the Ripper: A New Theory*, by one William Stewart, who described himself on the title page as "Artist". At the age of eight, I was not aware of it, and in any case, I doubt if my local junior library would have stocked it. But I read it 12 years later, in 1951, when I moved to London. I had married shortly before my 20th birthday, and one of the first things I did in London was visit Whitechapel and look at the murder sites. The stable door in Buck's Row (now Durward Street), where the body of Mary Ann Nichols, the first victim, had been found, was still there; so was the back yard at 29 Hanbury Street, where the Ripper murdered Annie Chapman, his second victim. Berner Street and Mitre Square, the two locations of the "double event" of 29 October, still looked much as they had in 1888. Only Miller's Court, where Mary Kelly had been butchered, had long since vanished.

I also succeeded in getting a reader's ticket for the Reading Room of the British Museum, and there studied the original reports of the murders in *The Times* for 1888. And I took the opportunity to read William Stewart's "new theory", which suggested that Jack the Ripper was a woman, a sadistic midwife. Stewart's evidence was that the postmortem had disclosed that Mary Kelly had been pregnant; he thought that she had called in the midwife to procure an abortion. The midwife had killed and dismembered Mary Kelly, then burned her own bloodstained clothes in the grate, and left the house wearing Mary Kelly's spare clothes. I was unconvinced. To me, the murders seem so obviously motivated by some sexual obsession that I found it impossible to believe that the killer was a woman. Besides – as some Ripperologist has pointed out – Mary Kelly had no spare clothes, and if she had, they would probably have been in the pawn shop.

And why was I spending my Saturday afternoons in Whitechapel and the British Museum? Not out of morbid curiosity, but because I was writing my first novel – *Ritual in the Dark* – which was based on the Ripper murders. My killer was a sadistic homosexual who hated women, particularly prostitutes; I learned something of the psychology of the criminal sadist from Professor Karl Berg's book *The Sadist*, which I also discovered in the catalogue of the British Museum. It was a study of the Düsseldorf murderer Peter Kürten, who caused a panic in the late 1920s. During his "reign of terror", he used various weapons – including a hammer, knife and scissors – to attack women and children (and even a man). Kürten was obsessed by strangulation and by the sight of blood and, when he was beheaded in 1931, he said that his dearest wish was to hear the sound of his own blood running into the basket.

As I read Berg's book, I felt I was getting closer to the psychology of Jack the Ripper. He was not a "religious maniac" – as a doctor called Forbes Winslow had suggested in 1910 – but a man who almost certainly experienced a sexual orgasm as he killed.

These insights went into *Ritual in the Dark*, which I wrote assiduously in the Reading Room during the early 1950s. The year 1954 found me sleeping on Hampstead Heath in a sleeping bag to save rent, and spending my days in the British Museum, where the novelist Angus Wilson – who was the superintendent of the Reading Room – saw me scribbling away assiduously, and asked me what I was writing. When I told him it was a novel, he offered to read it, and, if he liked it, to show it to his own publisher.

That Christmas, 1954, Angus took away the unfinished typescript of *Ritual* to read over the holiday; on Christmas Day I, having nothing better to do, decided to begin a study of romantic misfits. By the time Angus returned, with a cautiously favourable opinion of *Ritual*, I had already started to write *The Outsider*. By good luck it was accepted by the first publisher to whom I submitted half the typescript. It came out in May 1956, and immediately became a bestseller, both in England and America; by the end of the year it was being translated into 16 languages.

Overnight "fame" was a vertiginous experience, and as interviewers enquired about my next book, I found myself wondering whether I was ever going to finish *Ritual*; after many struggles, I scrapped the earlier versions of the novel, and began rewriting from the beginning. I finished the book in late 1959, having been working at it, on and off, for about ten years. And it was soon after that there finally appeared the third full-length book about Jack the Ripper, Donald McCormick's *The Identity of Jack the Ripper*.

McCormick tells the story of the murders, from Martha Turner to Carroty Nell, then reviews the theories – Dr Stanley, "Jill the Ripper" and the East End barber-surgeon George Chapman, hanged in 1903 for poisoning three of his wives. (Inspector Abberline, the head of the team that hunted Jack the Ripper, was convinced that Chapman was the Whitechapel Murderer, apparently unaware that poisoners do not usually kill with knives, or vice versa.) But the theory McCormick favoured is one put forward by the writer William Le Queux, who, in *Things I Know* (1923) claims to have seen a manuscript on great Russian criminals, written by the famous (or infamous) Rasputin. Le Queux said it was written in French, and that it was found in the cellar of Rasputin's house in St Petersburg. And according to Rasputin, said Le Queux, Jack the Ripper was a criminal lunatic called Alexander Pedachenko, who was sent to London – which had become a refuge for Russian anarchists – by the Tsarist secret police to embarrass Scotland Yard.

This story struck me as absurd, and when I met Rasputin's daughter Maria in Los Angeles a year or so later, she pointed out to me that her father did not speak French (let alone write it), that his house had no basement, and finally, that he was not in the least interested in criminals.

But McCormick claimed he had another source for the Pedachenko story, a manuscript called *Chronicles of Crime*, by Dr Thomas Dutton, which asserted that Pedachenko was the double of the barber-surgeon George Chapman, and that Pedachenko worked in Walworth, south London, for a barber named Delhaye. Unfortunately, few other people have seen Dutton's manuscript, and no one else has had any success tracing Pedachenko. On the whole, it seems likely that he never existed outside Le Queux's imagination.

Still, Ripperology was looking up. In 1959, my friend Dan Farson devoted one of his television programmes in the series *Guide to the British* to Jack the Ripper, and I took part in it. Dan had done an interesting piece of detective work. In *Mysteries of Police and Crime* (1898), Major Arthur Griffiths had mentioned that there were at the time three leading suspects, one of whom was a doctor who had been found drowned. Griffiths had obtained his information from Sir Melville Macnaghten, who succeeded Sir Charles Warren in 1889 as Commissioner of CID. Dan tracked down notes on the Ripper made by Macnaghten, which were in the hands of his daughter, Lady Aberconway. And Macnaghten names the drowned doctor as Montague John Druitt. For some reason, Lady Aberconway asked Dan not to disclose Druitt's full name, and Dan referred to him only by his initials on the programme.

Ritual in the Dark appeared in 1960, received some good reviews, and sold well. I also wrote a series of five articles on the Ripper in the London *Evening Standard* from 8–12 August 1960 and went around the sites with a press photographer. The barber – a Mr Brill – who ran the shop at 29 Hanbury Street, where Annie Chapman was murdered, allowed us to go into the back yard where her body was discovered. There was a lavatory in the yard, and Mrs Brill told me how, one day, a visiting friend had asked to use the toilet, and had been sitting there placidly, chatting to Mrs Brill (who stood outside), when Mrs Brill pointed to a spot a few feet away, and remarked that Jack the Ripper's second victim had been found right there. The lady gave a shriek, leaped to her feet, and ran indoors without pausing to pull up her knickers. It was an amusing example of how much fear the name of the Ripper could still inspire more than 60 years after the murders.

Druitt was the first name to emerge as a really credible suspect in the Ripper murders, yet for some odd reason, Dan Farson failed to follow up his discovery. He told me later that all his notes had been stolen from his office, but I suspect that this was not the only reason that he failed to follow it up. Dan, who died in January 1998, was a heavy drinker, and in the 1960s he compounded his problem by buying a pub in East London, all of which left him little time for serious research.

The person who actually did the research on Druitt was an American called Tom Cullen, who finally revealed Druitt's name in *Autumn of Terror* in 1965. But Cullen's researches also revealed why Druitt was an unlikely suspect. According to Macnaghten, Druitt was a doctor, who lived at home with his family. In fact Druitt was actually a barrister (and a very unsuccessful one) who lived in chambers in Lincoln's Inn. Obviously, Macnaghten knew virtually nothing about him. He also claims that Druitt's mind snapped after his "awful glut" in Miller's Court, and that he committed suicide the day after. In fact, Druitt committed suicide on 3 December 1888, five weeks after Mary Kelly's murder. And we also know that he killed himself because he believed he was going insane, like his mother.

Since the theory that Druitt was Jack the Ripper rests solely on Macnaghten's words, and since it is obvious that Macnaghten was basing his opinion on some garbled piece of information heard from colleagues, there seems to be little doubt that there was never any real basis for the Druitt theory. When I pointed this out to Dan (whose book *Jack the Ripper* had finally appeared in 1972), during a visit to Cornwall, he said dryly: "You can go off some people".

My series in the *Evening Standard* led me to another suspect. Among the letters I received was one from a doctor who signed himself Thomas E. A. Stowell, who said that I very obviously knew the identity of Jack the Ripper. I wrote back to say that unfortunately, that was not the case, at which Dr Stowell invited me to lunch at the Athenaeum Club. He proved to be a charming old gentleman, probably in his 70s, and as we had a sherry in the lounge, he told me why he thought I knew the Ripper's identity – I had described him as a well-dressed young man. I explained that I was merely quoting the witnesses. PC Smith had described the man he saw speaking to Elizabeth Stride as wearing a deerstalker hat, about 28 years of age, and of respectable appearance. Matthew Parker had described the same man with a deerstalker ...

At the lunch table, Dr Stowell told me the name of the man he believed to be Jack the Ripper: the Duke of Clarence. I have to confess I was less than amazed – as he obviously expected me to be – for I did not have the slightest idea who the Duke of Clarence was. I had a vague idea that he was a historical character who drowned in a butt of Malmsey. But he was, it seemed, the grandson of Queen Victoria, son of the man who became Edward VII, and the heir to the throne of England. In one of the best-known photographs, he is wearing a deerstalker hat.

Stowell explained to me that, in the 1930s, he had been approached by Caroline Acland, the daughter of Queen Victoria's physician Sir William Gull. She had found among her father's papers some documents about the Duke of Clarence, which asserted that he did *not* die in the 'flu epidemic of 1892, as the history books assert, but in a mental home near Sandringham, suffering from a softening of the brain due to syphilis. There were also ambiguous remarks about Jack the Ripper, which made it sound as if the Duke of Clarence – known to everyone as Eddie – knew his identity.

Now there was a well-known story about a famous medium called R. J. Lees, who had seen Jack the Ripper in a dream, and had one day recognized him sitting opposite him on a bus. He followed the man to a house in Park Lane, and was told that it was the house of a well-known doctor. The story – which I heard from my wife, who knew Lees's daughter – went on to claim that the police had been so impressed by Lees's story that they had kept watch on the house, and arrested the doctor late one night as he set out from home carrying a large knife concealed in a black bag. The doctor, according to this tale, was incarcerated in a mental home at Ascot.

Caroline Acland had told Stowell that a detective had called at her father's house in Park Lane, and asked him some impertinent questions which infuriated her, all of which made it sound as if the police thought Sir William Gull was Jack the Ripper. But that was unlikely – Gull had had a stroke in 1887, the year before the murders, and died of a second stroke three years later. No, the mysterious references to the Duke of Clarence convinced Stowell that *he* was Jack the Ripper, and that Gull knew all about it.

The following day, I rang Stowell to ask if he would mind if I published the story; he said he would prefer me not to, because it might "upset Her Majesty". So accordingly I kept silent, although in retrospect I believe that Stowell actually *wanted* me break my word and publish the story, so that he would have the satisfaction of seeing it made public property while being able to blame me for a breach of confidence.

In December 1970, Stowell told the story in *The Criminologist*, edited by my friend Nigel Morland. He did not actually name the Duke of Clarence, but referred to him as "S", and remarked that he was "the highest in the land". It did not take the newspapers long to learn the identity of the suspect – to begin with, I had told a few close friends, like the journalist Kenneth Allsop – and the resulting publicity proved far more than Stowell had anticipated. The strain proved too much and he died a few weeks later.

A journalist on *The Times* proved that the Duke of Clarence could not have been Jack the Ripper by simply checking the court circular, and learning that Eddie was in Balmoral, in Scotland, on the day after one of the murders. He *could* have made the long journey in a day, but it seems unlikely.

In 1971, about a year after Stowell's death, my old friend Michael Harrison re-examined the Stowell theory, and came to the interesting conclusion that Stowell had got hold of the wrong end of the stick.

Michael told me in a phone conversation in 1971: "I have a letter from Jack the Ripper on my desk in front of me now." Michael had noted that Stowell's description of "S" in his article did not fit Clarence – for example, he says that "S" resigned his commission at the age of 24, but Clarence never resigned his commission. And why did Stowell choose to refer to his suspect as "S"? Was it because Gull's original papers called him "S"?

In other words, was there some close friend or associate of Clarence whom Stowell's description *did* fit? In fact, there was: Clarence's close friend – and Cambridge tutor – James Kenneth Stephen, the son of Sir Leslie Stephen, and cousin of Virginia Woolf. J. K. Stephen died insane, after receiving a head injury when he was thrown from his horse. Michael speculated that Stephen and Clarence had had a homosexual affair at Cambridge, but that Eddie avoided his former tutor after leaving Cambridge – to Stephen's distress. Michael also pointed out that Stephen had published some poems that revealed a strange hatred of women, particularly "common" women, and went on to suggest that Stephen became pathologically jealous of Eddie's romantic attachments to women, including Princess Alix of Hesse, who preferred to marry Tsar Nicholas II of Russia. All this led to the mental breakdown that led him to find a way of expressing his hatred of common women ...

I find it impossible to believe that either Eddie or J. K. Stephen could have been Jack the Ripper. Both were foppish young men about town, and it seems to me unlikely that either could have become sadistic serial killers. In fact, virtually all serial killers so far have been working class, from the French "Ripper" Joseph Vacher in the 1890s to Fred West and Andrei Chikatilo. I am not sure why this should be so, except that the kind of violence associated with serial killers seems to be incubated by the frustrations of a working-class childhood. I would say that it is certainly true that serial murder springs from deep-seated anger, and that it is rare for middle-class (or upper-class) young men to reach the degree of frustration that leads to sex murder.

Michael Harrison's biography of Clarence appeared in 1972. And by now, as the Ripper's centenary drew near, new theories about his identity began to appear at a rate of at least one a year. In 1973, I received a letter from a BBC producer called Paul Bonner, who wanted me to act as consultant to a series of programmes on Jack the Ripper. Donald Rumbelow, the policeman to whose *Complete Jack the Ripper* (1975) I would write an introduction, was a fellow consultant.

The Ripper theory Bonner outlined to me was certainly the strangest I had heard so far. It appeared that an artist named Joseph Sickert, son of the Victorian painter Walter Sickert, had made an extraordinary claim: that the Duke of Clarence had had an affair with an artist's model named Annie Crook – introduced to her by Walter Sickert, a well-known rake – and had married her secretly. The Queen learned of the marriage, and was outraged. Annie was a Catholic, who, in 1885, had given birth to Eddie's child, a daughter named Alice.

The Prime Minister, Lord Salisbury, decided on drastic action. Annie was kidnapped from her home in Cleveland Street, and interned in a mental home. But there was another menace. Alice Crook's nurse was a pretty Irishwoman named Mary Kelly who had drifted downhill and become a prostitute in Whitechapel. Mary and her friends knew about the secret marriage; it was essential to silence them. The man chosen to do this was Sir William Gull, who was driven to the East End of London in a magnificent royal coach by a coachman named Netley. He would entice his victim into the coach, and there disembowel her. Netley later died as a result of a fall from his driving seat. The child, Alice, later became the mistress of Walter Sickert, and bore him a child – Joseph Sickert.

I met Bonner in a pub opposite Scotland Yard, where I happened to be lecturing that evening, and it was there that he told me this preposterous story. I said it sounded like nonsense. But, said Bonner, they had discovered that Annie Crook *did* live in a basement in Cleveland Street (the rent book said "Cook", obviously a misprint, he thought), just as Joseph Sickert had claimed. Moreover, Netley *did* exist, and had indeed died of a fall from his coach.

I said that I still thought the story was nonsense. The idea of Sir William Gull dragging prostitutes into a coach was laughable. Predictably, my scepticism lost me the consultancy job.

Nevertheless, the theory appeared in a six-part television series in 1973, with the crimes discussed at length by the fictional policemen Barlow and Watt (of *Z Cars*). Later, it was turned into a paperback called

The Ripper File (1975) by Elwyn Jones and John Lloyd. It remains one of the best factual books on the case, and certainly one that deserves to be reprinted.

A young journalist named Stephen Knight found it all so interesting that he tracked down Joseph Sickert and decided to write his story. The result was one of the most successful books on the Ripper so far, *Jack the Ripper: The Final Solution* (1976), which made some excellent and convincing points, for example, that Walter Sickert had shown himself to be obsessed by the Ripper murders. A friend of Sickert, Marjorie Lilly, told Knight: "After the stroke, Sickert would have 'Ripper periods' in which he would dress up like the murderer and walk about like that for weeks on end." Many of Sickert's pictures contain gruesome-looking heads of women, one looking as if the flesh has been stripped off her skull. Another strange painting shows a young woman in a large drawing room, standing underneath a bust. It is called *Amphytrion, or X's Affiliation Order*. An affiliation order fixes the paternity of an illegitimate child. And Amphytrion tells how Jupiter disguised himself as a mortal to seduce an ordinary woman, who becomes pregnant by him. If the young woman in the painting is supposed to be the one who was seduced by Jupiter, then presumably the bust above her is her seducer. This certainly sounds very like evidence for the story of Eddie's seduction of Sickert's model Annie Crook.

But the rest of Stephen Knight's book is so absurd that it is impossible to take seriously, particularly his view that Sir William Gull mutilated the prostitutes in some Masonic ritual (Gull was a Freemason). In fact, Knight's theory will not stand scrutiny. And shortly before its publication in paperback (1977), Joseph Sickert admitted to a *Sunday Times* journalist that his Ripper story was an invention (a statement he confirmed to me when I met him in 1995). It *was* true, he claimed, that his mother was Alice Crook, the illegitmate daughter of the Duke of Clarence, and that therefore he was a member of the Royal Family (he told me he often went to tea with the Queen). But all the stuff about Gull and Jack the Ripper was nonsense.

In the early 1980s, Simon Wood, the editor of a magazine called *The Bloodhound*, decided to track down information on Annie Elizabeth Crook, who, according to Knight, had been the victim of a brain operation by Gull (to remove her memory), after which she was incarcerated in a lunatic asylum for the rest of her life. But Wood's investigation revealed that Annie Crook had been alive and at liberty – even if destitute – from the late 1880s until her death in 1920; she had been admitted briefly to the Endell Street Workhouse in 1889, together with her daughter Alice, and got fourteen days in prison in 1894 for some undisclosed offence. In 1903, admitted to the St Pancras Workhouse, her occupation was given as a "casual hand" at Crosse and Blackwell's factory. She died in a lunacy ward of the Fulham Road Workhouse in 1920, and the report of her death lists her religion as Church of England – not Catholic, as Knight declared. Wood states that he showed Knight his evidence, but Knight was "smilingly unrepentant", i.e. preferred to ignore it.

I came to know Stephen Knight fairly well, and he and his wife stayed with us twice in Cornwall. On the strength of his Ripper book, he had decided to retire from journalism and make a living as an author. I always found him immensely likeable, and find it hard to blame him for refusing to let a few facts spoil a good theory, which no Ripperologist took seriously anyway. (Incidentally, I invented the word Ripperologist in a review in *Books and Bookmen* – possibly the one in 1976 in which I damned Stephen's book.) Knight repeated the whole preposterous theory in his bestselling book on the Freemasons, *The Brotherhood*, in 1984. Regrettably, he had by that time learned he was suffering from a brain tumour (oddly enough, as a result of volunteering for a brain scan for a BBC programme), and he died in 1985. No doubt someone will one day write a book proving he was murdered by the Freemasons.

And from then on, as the Ripper centenary approached, new theories came in a flood. I myself was one of the few Ripperologists who had no new suspect to suggest. I and my old friend Robin Odell collaborated on a book called *Jack the Ripper: Summing Up and Verdict* (1987), in which Robin advanced his own theory – dating from a few years earlier (*Jack the Ripper: Fact and Fiction*, 1965) that the Ripper was a shochet, or Jewish slaughterman. I myself was inclined to feel that a more likely suspect was an unknown man who had written to Dan Farson in 1959, and signed his letter "G.W.B.". "Georgie" told how he had lived in Whitechapel at the time of the murders, and how his father had been a drunkard, who had beat his wife and children until Georgie grew old enough to threaten to thrash him. After that, they ceased to be on speaking terms. In 1902 Georgie emigrated to Australia, and it was on the evening before he left that his father confessed to him that he was Jack the Ripper. He drank heavily and, when drunk, experienced sadistic feelings towards women. (Many serial killers have been stimulated to kill when drunk – presumably the alcohol releases some repressed sadism.)

Georgie's father said that he would confess before he died, and therefore advised Georgie to change his name; but the promised confession never came.

To me it all sounded credible. Why should "G.W.B." write a long letter to Dan Farson if it was all invention? On the other hand, it seems highly probable that Georgie's father "confessed" to Georgie in a paradoxical attempt to gain his sympathy – he claimed that he had become a drunkard because he had wanted a daughter, and his first child, a girl, was mentally retarded, while his later children were all boys.

In 1987, new theories now came tumbling head over heels. In *The Crimes, Detection and Death of Jack the Ripper*, my friend Martin Fido, an actor turned writer, came down in favour of another suspect mentioned in Macnaghten's papers, "Kosminski, a Polish Jew" who went insane from indulgence in "solitary vices". (When I was a child, masturbation was supposed to make you blind.) One Aaron Kozminski was committed to the Colney Hatch asylum in 1891, and became an incurable imbecile. Another Polish Jew called David Cohen was arrested in 1888, rambling incoherently in Yiddish, the only language he spoke. He died in 1889 in Colney Hatch of "exhaustion of mania". But there is nothing to suggest that either Kozminski or Cohen might have been Jack the Ripper. Besides, it seems unlikely that the Ripper's victims would have gone with a man who rambled incoherently in Yiddish.

Keith Skinner and Martin Howells, two writers I came to know well, produced an impressive piece of research in *The Ripper Legacy* (1987). They tried to track down a relative of Druitt (mentioned by Dan

Farson), Lionel Druitt, in Australia, but it turned out – at the end of a long trail – that the man was a wife killer called Frederick Bailey Deeming, hanged in Melbourne in 1892 for murdering (among others) his wife and children. Skinner and Howells go on to suggest that Macnaghten's Druitt *was* after all the Ripper, and that he was murdered by former Cambridge friends – members of a society called the Apostles – to avert disgrace, his death being made to look like suicide in the Thames. A few years later, both admitted to me that their theory had been a little far-fetched, but at least their book shows a commendable new trend in Ripperology – immensely detailed and patient research.

In *Sickert and the Ripper Crimes* (1990), Jean Overton Fuller even suggests that Walter Sickert himself was the Ripper, a theory I am inclined to discount on the grounds that *no* artist in history has ever committed a premeditated murder, perhaps because artistic expression drains away the potential for homicidal violence.

The "magician" Aleister Crowley was told by a lesbian named Vittoria Cremers that Jack the Ripper was a doctor and journalist named Roslyn D'Onston Stephenson, who committed the murders as part of a magical ritual, and that the sites of the murders, when joined together on a map, formed a Calvary cross (which, of course, is untrue). This theory was resurrected by Richard Whittington-Egan in *A Casebook on Jack the Ripper* (1976) and subsequently developed by Melvin Harris in *Jack the Ripper: The Bloody Truth*, and its two sequels. Unfortunately, in spite of some excellent research, Harris is unable to prove any connection between D'Onston and the Ripper, although he certainly deserves a high mark for persistence.

Over the years, I have become a kind of clearing house for theories on Jack the Ripper. Pat Pitman, my co-author on *An Encyclopedia of Murder* (1961) believed – on no discernable grounds – that he was the novelist George Gissing.

A later correspondent, a Norwich accountant named Steward Hicks, had looked through the records of the Lunacy Commissioners in London, and came upon a patient in the Coton Hill Asylum in Staffordshire named John Hewitt, who was also a doctor. He recollected how Sir Osbert Sitwell had told a story of a Camden Town landlady whose lodger, a young vet, was named John Hewitt; he had been obsessed with the murders, and had died a few months later of consumption.

If Dr Hewitt had been admitted to the asylum after November 1888, then he was certainly a possible candidate for the Ripper. Mr Hicks was unable to obtain the information from the asylum, because only relatives were allowed access to the records, but in 1986 I tried ringing the head of the Staffordshire Health Authority, David Elliott, who was able to tell me that Hewitt had been admitted before November 1888, but since he had been a voluntary patient, he had been able to absent himself at will.

So *if* the records – which were due for release in 1988 – showed that Hewitt had absented himself on the dates of the Ripper murders, there would be virtually no doubt that Steward Hicks had finally identified Jack the Ripper. Sadly, the papers finally showed that Hewitt was safely behind bars when the murders were committed.

Oddly enough, Mr Hicks refused to accept this. I had, of course, promised him silence about his theory, but when the asylum papers proved that Hewitt could not be the Ripper, I felt free to tell the story in *The Mammoth Book of True Crime 2*. To my astonishment, I received an angry phone call from Mr Hicks, reproaching me for breaking my word. I pointed out that his theory had been disproved when the papers were placed in the Public Record Office, and was staggered when he refused to admit that. And I realized, with a certain rueful perplexity, that Mr Hicks was so obsessed with his theory that he simply refused to admit that it could be untrue.

I still feel I did him a favour. He would never have published his theory – he has since died – and I was able to afford him at least a kind of minimum of recognition; his name can also be found in that Bible of modern Ripperologists, *The Jack the Ripper A–Z* by Paul Begg, Martin Fido and Keith Skinner.

Over the years, my list of new – and unlikely – suspects continued to swell. One Scottish correspondent, Tommy Toughill, thought that the Ripper was Oscar Wilde's friend, the artist Frank Miles. Another correspondent had written a book to prove that the Ripper was a Japanese named Takahashi, who had travelled around the world committing atrocities, and who had later been responsible for the appalling Evengelista murders in Detroit in 1929, when a family of six was decapitated. (To spread the Ripper's murderous career over 40-odd years, my correspondent had to posit that he had been a precocious teenager in 1888.) And an American child-therapist named Richard Wallace, was convinced that Jack the Ripper was the writer Lewis Carroll, author of the Alice books. Wallace's researches into Carroll, which had led to an earlier book, *The Agony of Lewis Carroll*, had convinced him that Carroll was a tormented man who suffered from deep sexual frustration. The sheer research involved in *Jack the Ripper: "Light-Hearted Friend"* so delighted me that I agreed to write an introduction to the book, which was privately printed in America in 1996. It is a fascinating piece of work, but it ended by convincing me that a sufficiently skilful researcher could assemble evidence to prove that Queen Victoria or Mark Twain was Jack the Ripper. Richard Wallace certainly deserves to be remembered as the man who has produced the (so far) most wildly improbable theory of the Ripper's identity.

Another American, Bruce Paley, who contacted me in the late 1970s, was convinced that Jack the Ripper was the man with whom Mary Kelly had been living, Joseph Barnett. Bruce came to believe that Barnett, a nervous man who stammered, was so deeply opposed to Mary's life of prostitution that he began killing the friends he felt were trying to lure her back into it, and ended by killing Mary herself. The book in which he presents this theory, *Jack the Ripper: The Simple Truth* (1995) is a brilliant piece of research into the London of the 1880s, by far the most evocative book on the period. The main objection to Barnett is that he was an intelligent man, more sensitive and literate than the average East End labourer, and that he had no record of violence. Jack the Ripper was obviously a man of extremely high dominance; when interrupted after killing Elizabeth Stride, he went off to Mitre Square and found himself another victim, Catharine Eddowes. Somehow, I cannot see Joseph Barnett as Jack the Ripper, and I explained why in the introduction I wrote for Bruce's book.

The theories have continued to proliferate. The latest at the time of writing (February 1998) is *The Jack the Ripper Whitechapel Murders*, by Kevin O'Donnell, based on the researches of a couple named Andy and

Sue Parlour. They lived in a village called Thorpe-le-Soken, where Queen Victoria's physician Sir William Gull lies buried. According to local legend, Gull's grave contained a coffin filled with stones. Gull, the Parlours believe, did not die in 1890; he went insane out of remorse at his involvement in the Ripper murders, and was confined in a mental home; it was only after his death seven years later that his grave was opened by night and his corpse laid to rest.

And what was Gull's involvement in the murders? It seems that Queen Victoria's son Bertie (later Edward VII) had an affair with a young Irish Catholic prostitute, Mary Kelly, and became the father of her child. When the Prime Minister, Lord Salisbury, found out, he called a meeting of various distinguished men, including Gull, Lord Randolph Churchill, and Sir Charles Warren (the Commissioner of Police), and they decided to silence Mary Kelly and her friends. The two men chosen to carry out the slaughter were Montague John Druitt and J K Stephen. Gull was placed in charge of the whole operation, but both killers found their grisly work so horrifying that they had nervous breakdowns; Druitt committed suicide and Stephen died insane. The Parlours even suggest that if the murder sites are joined up on a map, they form an arrow which points straight at the Houses of Parliament, although they ignore one of the sites that fails to fit their pattern.

And whom do I personally believe was Jack the Ripper?

It was not until 1992 that I finally came upon a theory that struck me as the most convincing so far. I will not say that I am as totally convinced as its leading exponent, Paul Feldman, but the more I have looked into it, the more I have come to feel that this is almost certainly the only plausible answer.

I met Paul Feldman in London as a result of a phone call that he made to my home in Cornwall, telling me that he was confident that he had at last solved the problem of the Ripper's identity. And a few weeks later, he disclosed to me – under a promise of secrecy – that a diary signed "Jack the Ripper" had been discovered, and that the evidence revealed clearly that its author was James Maybrick, the Liverpool cotton broker who had died of arsenic poisoning in 1889, the year after the murders; it would be published the following year.

The diary had apparently found its way into the hands of an out-of-work scrap dealer named Mike Barrett, who lived in Liverpool; Barrett claimed he had been given the manuscript notebook by a friend named Tony Devereux, who had since died. Barrett had read the scrawled notebook with increasing fascination. Its author seemed to live in a house named Battlecrease. And when Barrett read a book on poisons, and learned that James Maybrick and his wife Florence had lived in Battlecrease House, he understood the astonishing implication: that "Jack the Ripper" had been a victim of poison, apparently administered by his wife, who was sentenced to death, although this was later commuted to life imprisonment.

The diary soon found a publisher, Robert Smith of Smith Gryphon, and an author, Shirley Harrison, was commissioned to write a book in which a facsimile would be reproduced.

At this stage, Paul – who had bought the film rights from the publisher – did not believe Mike Barrett's tale about Tony Devereux, and when he heard that Barrett's estranged wife Anne had worked in the office formerly occupied by James Maybrick, he was inclined to believe that Anne Barrett had found it there in some hiding place, or perhaps just a dusty old cupboard. This alternated with the suspicion that the diary had been found by workmen carrying out electrical installations at Battlecrease House, perhaps under the floorboards, and that a workman had handed it to Tony Devereux, who happened to drink in the same pub.

Robert Smith was naturally anxious to keep the diary a secret until its publication. Unfortunately, Barrett himself spoiled this by talking about the book to a local journalist he met on a train. In due course he complicated the issue still further by "confessing" that he had forged the diary – then withdrawing his confession a day later, insisting that he had made it to spite his estranged wife Anne. Yet in spite of a *Sunday Times* "exposé", declaring the diary a forgery, Shirley Harrison's book *The Diary of Jack the Ripper* soon became a bestseller after its publication in October 1993.

The notion that James Maybrick was the Ripper struck me as highly plausible. A self-made man, he had fallen in love with the 18-year-old Florence on a ship crossing the Atlantic to Liverpool in 1881; Maybrick was then 41. But when Florence found out that he not only had a mistress and illegitimate children, but that he was continuing to see her, she denied Maybrick her bed, and began engaging in a series of flirtations, one of which, with a man called Alfred Brierly, resulted in three nights spent together in a London hotel. Maybrick was insanely jealous, and believed that Brierly was not the only man to whom his wife had surrendered herself. He was quite probably correct.

Now it so happened that Maybrick was a drug addict, and – oddly enough – the drug to which he was addicted was arsenic. It is, in fact, a powerful stimulant, and doctors in the nineteenth century often prescribed weak doses, – not only of arsenic, but also of strychnine, and other drugs which, in larger quantities, can be deadly. Maybrick was addicted to most of them, and his local chemist in Liverpool even made him up his own special mixture. Sooner or later, Maybrick would have died of arsenic poisoning anyway; he had for years been taking doses that were large enough to kill any normal man.

Maybrick and Florence had quarrelled violently about Brierly after returning from the Grand National on 29 March 1889, and Maybrick had given her a black eye. A month later, Maybrick became ill with diarrhoea and vomiting, and he died on 11 May. The housekeeper, who disliked Florence and suspected her of poisoning her husband, had wired his elder brother Michael to hasten back even before Maybrick died. A servant had seen Florence soaking arsenic flypapers in water in her bedroom. Florence would insist that she was simply using it for a beauty preparation and, in fact, the recipe was found later, but not soon enough to prevent her being charged with her husband's murder and found guilty.

The diary seems to be written by a man who is on the verge of nervous collapse, and a handwriting expert has pronounced that it is written by a man who is mentally unstable and capable of violence. Yet there is one problem: the handwriting is totally unlike that of Maybrick's will, which is the typical neat copperplate of the day. This was the main thing that bothered me when Paul Feldman showed me a photocopy of the diary. On the other hand it is full of fragments of information that suggested its genuineness. For example, the writer knew that the police had found two brass rings and two farthings by Annie Chapman's body. Many Ripper "experts" have denied the existence of the farthings and even the rings, but Feldman found a report in the *Daily Telegraph* which verified their existence.

I must mention another piece of evidence from the *Daily Telegraph* which is certainly not conclusive, but is undoubtedly bizarre. On 6 October 1888, the *Telegraph* published an artist's sketch, based upon the description of a witness, of a man seen talking to Elizabeth Stride in Berner Street. It shows a man with a moustache, wearing a bowler hat; the mouth and chin are distinctly weak. Paul Feldman would eventually print this in his book *Jack the Ripper: The Final Chapter*, together with a photograph taken of James Maybrick in the year before the murders. The resemblance is so close that it looks as if the drawing must be taken from the photograph. Yet clearly, this resemblance proves nothing, since the artist himself had not seen the suspect in Berner Street. I still find myself unable to look at the two pictures without a prickling of the scalp.

Among the most vociferous critics of the diary was Melvin Harris, who was totally convinced that it *had* to be a modern forgery. An American handwriting specialist, Kenneth Rendell, further confused the issue by declaring that the diary *was* a forgery, but that it dated to around 1921, give or take a dozen years. That was absurd, since the diary was clearly either a modern forgery, or it was genuine; why should anyone have taken the trouble to forge it in 1921, then hidden it away for 60 years? An ink expert, Alec Voller, declared unhesitatingly that the "bronzing" of the ink proves that it is at least 90 years old.

By now another piece of evidence had turned up which certainly seemed to support the hoax theory. Just before publication of the diary, a man called Albert Johnson, from Liverpool, announced that he had bought a watch with scratches inside the back of the case; under a microscope, these scratches were revealed as the writing: "J Maybrick", and the words "I am Jack". There were also initials of Mary Ann Nichols, Annie Chapman, Elizabeth Stride, Catharine Eddowes and Mary Kelly. Surely this had to be a fake? Apparently not. Metallurgist Dr Stephen Turgoose examined the scratches under a microscope, and in two of the scratches found brass particles from the tool with which they were made; the surface of these particles showed corrosion due to ageing, which meant they had to be at least several decades old.

At a party given in the "Jack the Ripper" pub in Commercial Street, Whitechapel, for the launching of Paul Feldman's video about the diary, I met Albert Johnson and examined the watch. It was obvious that he was transparently honest, and had no motive for perpetrating a hoax. He had bought the watch from a jeweller's shop in Wallasey for £225, and had the receipt to prove it.

So the watch alone would seem to prove the diary's authenticity. James Maybrick certainly wanted to pose as the Ripper, whether he was or not.

There was much argument about the ink of the diary, and Melvin Harris had his own analysis performed, which seemed to support his objection that it contained a modern chemical called chloracetamide. Melvin rang me several times to try to convince me that the diary *had* to be a fake, perpetrated by Mike Barrett. He also talked to my wife Joy, who was at the time reading Alexander MacDougall's *Treatise on the Maybrick Case* (borrowed from the London Library) and the *Notable British Trials* volume. Joy was more than half convinced by many of Melvin's objections, as I was myself. The only thing that bothered me was that Melvin had obviously invested as much emotional energy into proving the diary a fake as Paul Feldman had invested in proving it genuine. But then, Paul had invested a great deal of money too. As to myself, I didn't really give a damn; if it was proved a fake, I would shrug and forget it.

Meanwhile, Paul had made an interesting breakthrough. Anne Barrett, Mike Barrett's wife, suddenly telephoned him to ask him to stop harassing members of her family in his search for the diary's provenance. If he would agree, she would tell him the simple truth. Paul promptly agreed, whereupon Anne told him that *she* was the original owner of the diary. It had been passed on to her by her father, Billy Graham, who had received it from *his* father.

Anne explained that Mike's fecklessness and alcoholism had resulted in estrangement. But she knew Mike wanted to be a writer. He had published a few interviews in local newspapers. She thought that perhaps the diary would give him a subject to which he could devote his total attention. She knew nothing about Jack the Ripper. In fact, she thought that he was mythical, like Spring Heel Jack. Since she and Mike were on such bad terms, and he already felt guilty because she was going out to work to support him, she decided not to give it to him directly, but via his friend Tony Devereux, who was instructed to say nothing about its source. Devereux agreed, and handed over the brown paper-wrapped notebook with the words: "Do something with it." In fact, Mike suspected that Anne was behind it, but said nothing.

Paul finally persuaded her to allow him to interview her father, Billy Graham. She was reluctant, because Billy was dying of cancer. But she agreed. The result was the most astonishing surprise so far.

Paul suspected that Billy Graham was a descendant of one of James Maybrick's many illegitimate children. Yet he also knew that Florence Maybrick had chosen to call herself Graham when she came out of prison. And during the interview with Billy Graham, Billy dropped the incredible statement that his father, William, was Florence's illegitimate child. (Anne was as flabbergasted by this revelation as Paul was.)

It was amazing. Florence was only 18 when she married James, and they had two children. Yet apparently Florence had borne an illegitimate child when she was 16. The father had been a Liverpool ship-owner named Henry Flinn; Paul went to see his grave. His research (which he details in his book *Jack the Ripper: The Final Chapter*, 1997) left him in no doubt that Flinn (who was then 20) impregnated the 15-year-old Florence, who was at that time on a visit to Liverpool with her mother. The child was called William, and was "farmed out" with a family called Graham. Billy Graham was his son. William Graham knew that his mother was the notorious Florence Maybrick. (In his book, Paul includes photographs of Florence Maybrick at 77, William Graham, and William's daughter Mary; the resemblance is remarkable.) Feldman believes that the diary was passed on to William Graham by Florence's solicitors in 1941, after Florence's death. Billy Graham said he first saw it in 1943. In due course, he gave it to Anne, who was not particularly grateful about it. She felt there was something vaguely "nasty" about the book, and kept it behind a dresser in her bedroom.

At that stage Paul wanted me to write the book about his investigations, and I had agreed. We intended to go 50/50 on the royalties. (Later, in fact, I urged Paul to write it himself, since he knew the case more intimately than anyone.) Yet I still had my doubts. In

September 1995, Paul asked me to spend a few days in London, looking
over his vast file of Maybrick Ripper material. He also wanted me to go
to Liverpool to meet Anne Barrett.

I decided to take Joy with me. To begin with, she now knew as much
about the case as I did. Second, she was more sceptical than I was. On
the way to London, she asked me: "What if you finally decide you're
not convinced by Paul's material?" I had already brooded on that
eventuality. I said: "In that case, I'll have to take a deep breath and tell
him I can't write the book."

Within an hour of arriving at Paul's flat in St John's Wood, my
doubts were already evaporating. Shirley Harrison rang while I was
there to tell him that she had learned that chloracetamide, far from
being a "modern" chemical, has been in use since at least 1857. It was
used in the treatment of paper. The analysis paid for by Melvin Harris
had revealed only one-billionth part of chloracetamide, while diomine
ink (which Mike Barrett originally claimed he had used for forging the
diary) has 0.26 per cent chloracetamide – 260 million times more. It
sounds as if the billionth part might easily have come from the paper.

But by that time, I had totally dismissed Melvin's conviction that
Mike Barrett had forged the diary, so this hardly mattered. What *did*
worry me was whether Anne Barrett, and her now deceased father,
were telling the truth when they claimed that the diary had been in the
family for decades.

The following day, that doubt was also laid to rest. Paul drove us to
Liverpool, and we met Anne and her teenage daughter Caroline. There
could not be the remotest possible doubt that Anne was totally honest.
Everything she said was too spontaneous to be invention. It was
obvious, to begin with, that she had no ulterior motive in claiming to be
the original owner of the diary. She had not made a penny from it. (The
royalties had been split between Shirley Harrison and Mike.) She was
so obviously honest that I later begged Melvin Harris to meet her,
certain that five minutes with her would leave him in no doubt that she
was telling the truth.

But Melvin explained that to meet her would be a violation of the
"investigator's protocol", which demanded rigid detachment. He failed
to explain how assessing an important witness might somehow damage

his detachment, since by the same principle, no witness would ever get examined...

We also went to meet Albert Johnson again, and again I felt that this man was telling the whole truth about the watch. Paul had decided that Albert was actually a descendant of James Maybrick, and that that is why he had invented the story of buying the watch at a jeweller's (in a desire not to be known as a descendant of Jack the Ripper). Albert denied this, and I believed him.

So when I returned to Cornwall from London, my doubts had vanished. It was impossible to doubt that both Anne Barrett and Albert Johnson were telling the truth. And, like myself, Joy was totally convinced. In which case, Maybrick had to be the author of the diary and the owner of the watch.

That, of course, did not make him Jack the Ripper. But it certainly meant that, for whatever reason, he wanted to believe he was. Perhaps, like Walter Sickert, he enjoyed playing morbid games.

I wrote Melvin a long letter about my Liverpool visit and about my conclusions. He did not reply, and has not been in touch with me since. But he has decided that Mike Barrett was not the forger after all; he has continued to write to Paul Feldman, now insisting that the diary was forged by a committee.

But what about the handwriting? Certainly, the scrawl of the diary bears no obvious resemblance to Maybrick's signature on the will. But when Joy and I attended a Jack the Ripper conference, organized by Stewart Evans in Ipswich in 1996, Paul was there with his latest discoveries – a number of other samples of Maybrick's handwriting, which he had tracked down in America and London. The first thing he showed me electrified me; it was a sample of Maybrick's handwriting from 1881, and Paul had placed it beside the famous "Dear Boss" letter, Jack the Ripper's first known piece of correspondence, sent to the Central News Agency and the letter that had first introduced the *nom de guerre* Jack the Ripper. As far as I could see, the handwriting was identical. Maybrick's signature also bore a strong resemblance to a further Jack the Ripper signature on another letter from the Metropolitan Police files. (All three are reproduced in Paul's book.) Paul had also unearthed some of Maybrick's handwriting from a Bible he presented to an early mistress, Sarah Robertson, in the days when Maybrick, as a young man, worked in Whitechapel. The various samples of Maybrick's handwriting display so many differences, as well as similarities, that the handwriting of the diary no longer seems so uncharacteristic. And the handwriting of a man suffering from paranoia and destroying his nervous system with arsenic and strychnine is likely to show a steady deterioration.

When *Jack the Ripper: The Final Chapter* finally appeared in 1997, I reviewed it for the *Literary Review*, and was startled to see how forcefully and concisely Paul has presented his case. Since that trip to Liverpool, I had forgotten just how powerful this is.

On the face of it, it sounds, I agree, unlikely that Jack the Ripper kept a diary and scratched his victim's initials in the back of a watch. Yet the more I look at the evidence, the more irrefutable it seems. I have little doubt that Jack the Ripper and James Maybrick were the same person.

Patricia Cornwell Names The Ripper

Barry Forshaw

Unless a dusty doctor's bag is found with bloodstained scalpels and a signed confession, or a long-suppressed Scotland Yard document is released in which royalty is implicated in the grisly work of history's most famous serial killer, we'll never really know the facts about Jack the Ripper. And, even then, Jack's identity will still be essentially unknown. Which, of course, is precisely why we are so fascinated – even in the twenty-first century – with Saucy Jack. Had he been caught, he'd be like so many everyday murderers, all of his nigh-mythical status drained away. We've had a slew of films based on the subject and bookshelves are groaning under the weight of speculative books. What are the known facts, keeping eccentric speculation at bay? There are the lesser-known suspects (the ones who are hardly household names – Druitt, Ostrog and Tumblety). There there's the more glamorous Dr Gull, Chief Surgeon to Queen Victoria (who works well in movies, where a vast Masonic conspiracy can be invoked). And the mysterious Kosminski – for some – a key suspect. And we know the photographs, such as the famous one of prostitute Mary Kelly, the only one of Jack's victims murdered indoors, giving him time to indulge his ghastly hobby to the full. But, yoking all the facts together, can a convincing solution be formulated? Many have tried – but one woman has achieved poll position – as much because of her notable celebrity as her theories. Patricia Cornwell is – by a comfortable margin – one of the world's best-selling crime writers. She is also the woman who claims to know – with some degree of certainty – a secret that has eluded writers and policemen over the centuries; the identity of Jack the Ripper. And, a campaign to prove the truth of her deduction has cost her a great deal of money, while giving her a best-selling book, *Jack the Ripper: Case Closed*. And, as a corollary, Cornwell has suffered a great deal of hostility (not least from those who admire her number one suspect – a celebrity of the Victorian era).

Cornwell's books featuring forensic pathologist Dr Kay Scarpetta are one of the great success stories of modern crime fiction. Although the veteran crime writer Ed McBain was somewhat irritated by the fact that his innovation (foregrounding forensic science in crime novels) was parleyed into greater success by Cornwell, there is no denying that she developed the concept with great skill and rigour. The army of imitators she has inspired invariably have cover blurbs on their books which boast "as good as Patricia Cornwell", and rarely is the boast justified. She won acclaim for her very first novel, *Post Mortem*, in 1990, and the momentum with which this book launched her on her career (not to mention the various prizes it bagged) guaranteed Cornwell one of the most imposing bank balances in the US (financial resources that proved useful later in her quest for the identity of Jack the Ripper).

American-born Cornwell (she was born in 1956) is, like many other US crime writers, a great anglophile, and when she received the Crime Writers' Association Dagger for her work, she pointed out what an honour it was to receive it in the country of one of her great idols, Agatha Christie. Cornwell has long noted an interest in the most famous serial killer in history, and to some degree this ties into her anglophilia. But, the fact that she decided to name the Ripper as the great English Impressionist painter, Walter Sickert, (though it was not, in fact, a new theory), brought much ridicule and opprobrium down on her head. These facts, together with the psychological portrait of the painter's psyche (as Cornwell saw it) in his paintings – along with his proximity to the Whitechapel locations of Jack the Ripper's murderous sorties – pointed Cornwell in the direction of this irresistible conclusion. As has often been noted, Cornwell is not the only writer to think along these lines, and in *Sickert and the Ripper Crimes* (published in 1990) Jean Overton Fuller reached a similar conclusion.

Cornwell is notoriously prickly, but she was particularly irked that the greatest hostility to the theories she proposed in *Jack the Ripper: Case*

Closed came from the country she so admired; the UK. Shaking her head in exasperation when this fact was put to her, she exclaimed, "Why do the British in particular treat this idea with such suspicion? I didn't get this reception for the book in the United States!" (Perhaps English journalists were too polite to point out that Saucy Jack – despite being a monster – was still an *English* monster, and perhaps there was some resentment at the fact that a Yank had appeared, claiming she'd solved a case that had baffled hundreds since the Victorian era.

But why did Cornwell elect to name the much-respected Walter Sickert as a bloody, knife-wielding maniac? Sickert was a key painter in the field of nineteenth-century British art, utilizing elements of the Impressionism made famous by French masters Claude Renoir and Edgar Degas, but forging a very individual path within the constraints of the technique – notably in terms of the subject matter (and it's here that Cornwell found the clues that set her off on what some would say was a wild goose chase). Sickert's most celebrated paintings are, of course, those known as the Camden Town series, which portray an unsentimental, bleak vision of British life with an honesty not usually to be found in the arts of the time. These great painting now hang in many of the most important art galleries of the world, and ensure that Sickert's reputation (as a painter, at least) is totally secure. The novelist and essayist Virginia Woolf was one of many writers inspired by the dark world conveyed by his paintings, and regarded his psychological perception as akin to that beginning to appear in the novel (notably in terms of the disturbing dramas played out before, during and after the scenes that Sickert chooses to show us in his work).

German-born Sickert came from Danish stock, and his hardworking father was an inspiration. Sickert's was a family of achievers; his mother may perhaps be best remembered for simply becoming extremely wealthy after a legacy, but Sickert, his father and sister (the latter an early feminist) all made their mark. When the family moved to London in 1868, Sickert's first experiences of violence and drunkenness at the school he attended were strongly reminiscent of the accounts given by Charles Dickens. He subsequently became a pupil at University College School and King's College, developing the artistic skills that had long been apparent but also wasting his time in an abortive career as an actor. A significant moment was his decision to become an assistant to the painter James McNeill Whistler, followed by a period in France working with the great Impressionist Edgar Degas (Sickert's impeccable draughtsmanship owes something to the example of his French teacher in art – Degas was the greatest draughtsman of the Impressionist school). A period in Italy followed, and Sickert's early attraction to criminality (at least as perceived by the Victorians) was, ironically, piqued by a meeting with the disgraced playwright Oscar Wilde after his imprisonment for homosexual offences. At the same time, Sickert met Aubrey Beardsley, another artist attracted to darker notions of eroticism.

Sickert's great work was notably at odds with that of many of his contemporaries. Instead of society beauties, he preferred to paint women from the underclass (often prostitutes) in squalid surroundings – and the considerable individuality of his vision was underpinned by the levels of psychological penetration; it is impossible to look at these Sickert paintings of desperate, unhappy men and women of the streets without being affected by the disturbing undercurrents discernible in the subjects. He was an admirer of the French writer, Balzac, another artist perfectly prepared to confront the non-respectable side of life (and, like Sickert, another artist who suffered from the prudery of those moral guardians who felt that the arts should not reflect these avenues of life). Sickert's home life was giving him no pleasure – his marriage to the daughter of a Liberal politician in 1885 was unhappy (Ellen, his wife, was considerably older than him). Sickert had affairs with his models (and may even have fathered illegitimate children); he lived in the same fear as Dickens – that his double life would be exposed and the full weight of Victorian piety would come down on his head (though the latter had more to lose, not being given to directly confronting conventional Victorian morality except in terms of exposing its hypocrisy concerning the poor and the exploited).

In 1888, in the East End of London, five prostitutes were brutally killed – not far from the area where Sickert had his studio. And, it was while reading about this that Patricia Cornwell's interest in Sickert became acute. Cornwell was particularly struck by the sequence of 1909 paintings called "The Camden Town Murders", clearly inspired by the

Jack the Ripper killings that had so horrified the country. The fact that a painting by Sickert was described as Jack the Ripper's bedroom was groundbreaking for a whole variety of reasons. Certainly, while Sickert's master Degas had specialized in painting subjects very much from everyday life (women yawning, or stretching and clutching their back after ironing, or attempting to wash themselves in an ungainly fashion in tin baths), Sickert was virtually unique in the grimness of his subject matter. The fine arts had long traded in the gruesome and the grisly (notably in many blood-soaked renditions of Judith hacking off the head of Holofernes, while Goya's unsparing depictions of the horrors of war, featured grotesque mutilation and horror), but Sickert's uncompromising vision located such grimness directly in the world of his contemporary viewers, and touched public consciousness in a way that few painters had before. In his defence, Sickert cited the great American writer Edgar Allan Poe who had similarly transmitted elements of the macabre into artistic conceptions, but the painter's utilization of such terms as "truth" and "beauty" did not persuade his straight-laced Victorian audience, who looked at these pictures of the less salubrious side of life with dismay.

Patricia Cornwell had noted that, like his contemporary James McNeill Whistler, Sickert was not content to simply create his visions from the imagination in his studio, but was something of a nighthawk, prowling the dangerous streets unknown to those around him. But what was he really making such expeditions for? To gather material for his work? Or, had there been a far more disturbing agenda? By now, Sickert was the leading light of the Camden Town Group, which was a collection of artists (including Wyndham Lewis and Pissaro) who regarded themselves as iconoclasts, less interested in flattering the egos of patrician patrons than in rendering uncompromising truths in pigment on canvas.

None of the artists in the Camden Town Group were concerned with representations of the beauty of landscape; the truth (as they perceived it) of human existence was their pre-occupation. In the teaching field, many of Sickert's pupils remarked on the fact that he was a charismatic individual, with a winning sardonic quality and attractive appearance – all of which gleaned him a devoted following amongst his female students. He led a peripatetic existence, moving from Dieppe to Margate to Bath, and enjoying success for his commercial endeavours while having the requisite number of signs of academic recognition laid at his feet. He married numerous times, and died in 1942.

Patricia Cornwell had developed a fascination for the artist, and was clearly struck by another writer's analysis of Sickert's work. Virginia Woolf (who knew the artist) pointed out that many of his paintings had clear narrative elements, notably a canvas he painted in 1913, "Ennui". This celebrated vision of the dark, ambiguous relationship between a man and woman suggests (like much of the artist's work) elements of the psychosexual. And, as in many of the artist's canvases, there is a strong suggestion of off-kilter eroticism – unlike such Impressionist painters as Renoir, Sickert was not interested in celebrating the joys of sexuality or the carnality of the female body – his concerns were clearly elsewhere, and it was this that attracted Cornwell's attention. The American writer noted that Sickert (who held his teacher and contemporary Whistler in the greatest esteem) was deeply affected by the latter's marriage and honeymoon with his new love. Cornwell noticed that this experience had something of a traumatic effect on Sickert, perhaps destabilizing the relationship that he imagined he held with his colleague. But (as in her highly accomplished crime thrillers), Cornwell was fully aware that a variety of circumstances were necessary to prove her thesis – that Sickert was the Ripper – and she was well aware that her ideas would be considered outrageous by many. She adduced another fact to add more detail to her *Portrait of a Killer*. Sickert had been, she pointed out, born with a deformity of the penis – a condition that resulted in several extremely painful childhood operations. It is this disfigurement that struck a particular chord. Cornwell noted a letter of the day in which it was theorized that the killer had been badly disfigured, and this Cornwell construed as the seat of Sickert's mental disorder – a man whose genital mutilation meant that he had to squat like a woman in order to urinate would be predisposed to the most horrific psychological traumas. She further speculated that the painter was probably not able to obtain an erection.

Even Cornwell's most passionate opponents could not accuse her of a lack of thoroughness. One source of her conclusions were the famous letters sent by Jack to the police, crowing his delight at their inability to catch him. Cornwell commissioned a team of forensic scientists to examine the DNA to be found on the Ripper letters, which were compared with similar missives from the painter – there was, Cornwell and her team concluded, a match. Watermarks were also adduced as further corroboration. The fact that the Ripper letters were full of misspellings and the crass misuse of language – hardly the characteristics of a member of The Royal Academy – were easily explained; Sickert had adopted these tactics as a diversionary measure. The fact that the provenance of the letters is still open to dispute is (needless to say) something of a problem for the conclusions in *Portrait of a Killer*. A more serious objection was, of course, the DNA evidence – Cornwell's opponents pointed out that the letters were over a hundred years old and had been handled by so many individuals that the DNA Cornwell *et al* utilized for their argument could not be identified with any certitude. As for the evidence of the watermarks, the most common objection raised to this theory was simply the massive availability of such materials of this kind to the Victorians. And, the other argument to which Cornwell gives some weight – the use of the word "Nemo" in the Ripper letters is also contentious. "Nemo" may have been a stage name utilized by Sickert when he trod the boards, but the name also conveyed "no-one" to the Victorians and it would not be impossible that the Ripper (whether or not he was the illiterate that the letters appear to convey) would have used the name as shorthand for no-one, i.e. the unknown.

However, the aspect of Cornwell's arguments to which many took exception (including fellow crime writer Caleb Carr) was the clues to be found in the paintings themselves. Cornwell tells her readers that many of the paintings contained visual indexes and clues relating to the Ripper, including a knowledge of the locales of the murders, rendered in a detail which proves that Walter Sickert himself had been present to record his locations with such accuracy. Another point; one of the best-known photographs of one of the Ripper's victims is that of Catharine Eddowes, but this is in fact a mortuary shot, and not photographed at the actual location in which the luckless prostitute was killed. It has also been observed that a Victorian audience quickly became familiar with the relevant images, as the news media of the day did not observe the censoring mechanisms so firmly in place today. As to such factors as where Sickert was when the murders took place, Cornwell points out that his exact location was not proven. It goes without saying that a writer as intelligent as Patricia Cornwell would not be rash in her conclusions and would certainly marshal the evidence she had access to when giving what she saw as the most persuasive pointer to the truth of her thesis. However, (as she quickly found), a virtual army of nay-sayers came together to repudiate her findings. Particular outrage was expressed by lovers of British art, when it appeared that Cornwell had appeared to purchase paintings by Sickert and then destroyed them in her quest for evidence – but, as Cornwell pointed out, this was not in fact the case, although the canvases were scientifically analyzed. Cynics quickly pointed out that these real-life endeavours certainly echoed the fictitious activities of Cornwell's alter ego, Dr Kay Scarpetta – and that the corollary activities of Scarpetta's creator probably helped the sales of her crime fiction (this, however, is one of the counter-arguments that hardly bears water – when she wrote *Portrait of a Killer*, Cornwell was (and is)riding high at the top of the book sales charts, and hardly needed to massage her sales with what she must have known many would describe as a jaw-dropping series of constructions based on a handful of facts).

Of course, what has given the Cornwell/Sickert drama such a long and healthy life is the perception that the author herself became somewhat obsessive about the subject. Rather than simply meeting all objections that were levelled at her conclusions – or even adopting a "take them or leave them" approach (a course of action that several pundits observed would have been by far the most sensible approach), Cornwell bristled and fumed at every objection to her theories, and pointed out that such factors as the amount of money she had spent coming to her conclusions pointed to the persuasiveness of her theory. Cornwell made a TV documentary version of her book, immediately compromised by maladroit dramatizations of the killings, and "the lady doth protest too much" scenario seemed even more unmistakable in this simplified visual form. Even the fact that Cornwell took the issue seriously enough to put her own reputation for veracity on the line was not calculated to win over the doubters, as the sense of desperation (already evident in the book) was here much more palpable. Regarding the TV programme, it also seemed ill-advised to present to viewers the team of specialists that Cornwell had assembled, who hardly presented a convincing appearance in the cold light of day at an airport parking lot. Finally, Cornwell and her director employed the age-old trick of using a freeze frame when looking at a film of Sickert as an old man, the sinister-looking freeze frame suggesting a malignancy in his manner. At this point, many who were predisposed to give Cornwell the benefit of the doubt might have felt suspicious simply because someone can look malignant when viewed in a certain light – which hardly proves that they are the most famous serial killer in history.

Most notoriously, Cornwell paid for a four-page advertisement in the *Independent* newspaper based in London, offering a very defensive plea that her work should be accorded the seriousness and respect that she felt it deserved. She has frequently reminded us that she has spent $2 million of her money to prove her case. Cornwell reminded readers that the Ripper's victims deserve justice even at this distant point in history, but many felt that this was rather akin to apologies by modern-day politicians for the slave trade – the distance in time is simply too great to make such concepts more than nebulous notions. And, some were worried by the fact that Cornwell – once applauded for writing crime fiction as unambiguously grisly as any male writers – could make such feminist-sounding pleas for justice for downtrodden women of a distant era.

Of course, Cornwell is too good a writer (in a whole variety of senses) to write something that is sheer meretricious, however much the reader may choose to disagree with the conclusions. But – *Jack the Ripper: Case Closed*? No, it isn't – and it is a case that will, of course, never be closed.

Further Evidence

Further Reading

Other Suspects

Robert D'Onston Stephenson
(changed his name to Roslyn D'Onston) (1841–?)

Our source for this story is Baroness Vittoria Cremers (died 1937), widow of Baron Louis Cremers, who recounted her memoirs to journalist Bernard O'Donnell between 1930 and 1934. Cremers was a friend of fellow theosophist, novelist Mabel Collins, who became Stephenson's lover. Cremers herself became Stephenson's business partner in the Pompadour Cosmetics Company in Baker Street, London in the 1890s.

At the time of their meeting in 1890, Stephenson is described as tall, fair and moustachioed. His hair was thinning at the sides, his teeth discoloured. He was of unassuming appearance, his eyes were "dead" and he was, says Cremers, the most "soundless" man that she had ever known. He almost never ate, in consequence, he maintained, of a "Chinese slug" – a bullet, we assume, rather than an invertebrate – in his gut.

Stephenson was a magician, and avowed a fear of "some horrible Presence" against which he protected himself by tracing an upturned triangle on the door of any room he entered. Plainly widely travelled, he told Cremers tales of having killed the seducer of his favourite cousin, dipping the girl's handkerchief in the man's blood. He claimed to have been party to the murder of a Chinaman during the Californian goldrush and to have performed appendectomies without benefit of anaesthetic while a doctor with Garibaldi's army.

Stephenson recounted that he had once also held a commission in the British Army. On a visit to London, he had fallen in love with a prostitute named Ada and she with him. He determined to marry her, but his outraged family cut off his allowance. Stephenson therefore gambled and lost heavily. In desperation, he asked his father for help which was given only on condition that he gave up Ada and married an heiress. Ada, so the story went, flung herself from Westminster Bridge. Stephenson maintained that candles made from human fat were essential in the practice of black magic, together with "a preparation made from a certain portion of the body of a harlot".

In time, Mabel Collins and Cremers became convinced that Stephenson was Jack the Ripper. Collins left him, and Cremers, rummaging among his things, found a few ready-made black ties, stained with what may have been blood. Soon afterward, Stephenson informed Cremers that he had known the Ripper. He was a surgeon (Morgan Davies), he said, who had cut the women's throats from behind them. He had carried the uteri home with him "in the space between his shirt and his tie".

So much for Stephenson's own version of his life. He was, in fact, born in 1841, the son of a Hull mill-owner. From an early age he had practised mesmerism and been fascinated with black magic and the occult. He had studied chemistry under Dr James Allen in Munich, and been initiated into black magic lore by Sir Edward Bulwer Lytton before volunteering for Garibaldi's Foreign Legion. He returned to Hull where he took up a post with HM Customs, but was dismissed. It seems that there may have been some truth in the tale of his love affair with a prostitute named Ada. In 1876, he married one Anne Deary, formerly his mother's servant. She was still alive in 1886, but then appears to have disappeared completely. Stephenson is then found living in Brighton, but, on 26 July 1888, now calling himself "single", he booked into the London Hospital in Whitechapel, complaining of neurasthaenia. He remained there until 7 December. He was thus two minutes' brisk walk from the site of Nicholls's death, within easy walking distance of Chapman's, Stride's and, for a fit man, Eddowes's.

On 16 October, he wrote a perceptive letter to the City of London Police:

The London Hospital

Sir,

Having read Sir Charles Warren's Circular in yesterday's papers that "It is not known That There is any dialect or language in which The word Jews is spelt JUWES."

I beg to inform you That The word written by the murderer does exist in a European language, Though it was not JUWES.

Try it in script – Thus,

The Juwes. etc.

Now place a dot over The Third upstroke (which dot was naturally overlooked by lantern light) and we get, plainly, The Juives which, I need not tell you, is the French word for Jews.

The murderer unconsciously reverted, for a moment, To his native language.

Pardon my presuming to suggest That There are Three parts indubitably shown (2 another probably) by the inscription.

1 The man was a Frenchman.

2 He had resided a long time in England To write so correctly; Frenchmen being, notoriously, The Worst linguists in the World.

3 He has frequented The East End for years, to have acquired, as in The sentences written, a purely East End idiom.

4 It is *probable* (not certain) That he is a notorious Jew-hater: Though he *may* only have written it To Throw a false scent.

May I request an acknowledgment That This letter has safely reached you, & That it be preserved until I am well enough to do myself The honour to call upon you personally.

I am Sir,

Yr Obedt Servant

Roslyn D'O Stephenson

PS. I can tell you, from a French book, a use made of the organ in question – "d'une femme prostituee", which has not yet been suggested, if you think it worth while. R D'O S.

The capitalization of the letter "T" and, on one occasion, "W" as initial letters in this document is nowhere explained, nor its explanation essayed, but the same idiosyncrasy can be noted in the "Juwes" graffito. This raises three possibilities: 1. Stephenson was the murderer; 2. Stephenson was not the murderer, but wrote the graffito; 3. Stephenson wanted the police to believe that he was the murderer; 4. Stephenson recognized this trait in the graffito as symbolically representative of some cult in his ken.

Stephenson subsequently wrote an article which appeared in the *Pall Mall Gazette* of 1 December 1888, once more outlining the "Juives" theory (but, deliberately or otherwise, wrongly stating that the message was written above Eddowes's corpse) and offering a necromantic explanation of the murders. He supplies a shopping list for the black magician: "strips of the skin of a suicide, nails from a murderer's gallows, candles made from human fat, the head of a black cat which has been fed forty days on human flesh, the horns of a goat which has been made the instrument of an infamous capital crime, and a preparation made from a certain portion of the body of a harlot." Enumerating six, not five murders, he also hypothesizes that the sites of the murders form the pattern of a sacrilegious cross.

Stephenson, an habitual drinker and drug-taker, now courted the favour of George Marsh, an impressionable fantasist with dreams of becoming an amateur detective. Stephenson informed Marsh that he knew the Ripper, and even named him as Dr Davies. He said (again wrongly) that the Ripper had buggered his victims and slashed their throats from behind. He demonstrated this procedure so convincingly that Marsh believed that he was watching the real murderer. Marsh duly made a statement to Inspector J Rootes on Christmas Eve 1888, naming Stephenson as the Ripper. Two days later, Stephenson too wrote to Scotland Yard, fingering Dr Davies. Stephenson was taken in for questioning on two occasions, but it appears that his cultured manner and eagerness to assist the police with arcane knowledge evoked their admiration rather than their suspicion. The *Sunday Times* of 30 December 1888, however, indicates that someone matching the description of Stephenson was under police observation.

In the summer of 1889, Stephenson met Mabel Collins and seems to have lost interest in the black arts, and his publication of *The Patristic*

Gospels in 1904 is taken by some to prove that he underwent conversion, thus explaining the cessation of his crimes. Shortly after the book's publication, Stephenson, by now a sick man, completely vanished. No death certificate for him has been discovered.

The strongest argument for Stephenson's candidacy is his advocate – Melvin Harris, a responsible and sceptical Ripperologist – in his well-researched *The True Face of Jack the Ripper* (1994). Certainly Stephenson's stay at the London Hospital provides him with a perfect bolthole and a perfect excuse for being at the hub of the area where the murders took place. He appears to have known the East End intimately and to have had a cultured, inoffensive, if impassive manner, which would have won the trust of his victims. He had been (by his own account) in love with a prostitute and had contracted venereal disease from others of her kind. It may be that he murdered his wife, and he claimed to have killed others and to have kept black ties stained with his victims' blood. He claimed too to have candles made from human fat and to know arcane purposes to which uteri could be put.

The principal problem with Stephenson as a suspect is that we are heavily reliant on his own testimony, both as to the depths of his heartlessness and iniquity and as to his activities. Cremers, our principal witness, was closely linked to Aleister Crowley, and Stephenson's air of mystery and his somewhat theatrical, throwaway boasts of wickedness anticipate Crowley's own romancing. The candles and the ties may well have been theatrical props designed specifically to have the effect which they had – to frighten two impressionable women. The story of the ties needs some explaining. Exactly how is a human uterus secreted "in the space between" a man's shirt and his tie, and exactly what is this space?

Harris believes that Stephenson was deliberately trying to obfuscate when he made out that there had been six murders (including that of Martha Tabram and that of a woman whose torso was found "in the new police-buildings", but excluding that of Kelly) and that the "Juwes" legend was found above the body of Catharine Eddowes. He bases this assumption, however, upon the reminiscences of Cremers as reported by a professional journalist, both of whom would have known that the five "canonical" murders had been established beyond doubt, and would hardly have reiterated Stephenson's error. Physically, Stephenson does not match the descriptions of Schwarz, Hutchinson or Long. He was too fair and, at 5 feet 10 inches, too tall, and, at 47, too old.

Stephenson remains a strong suspect in that he was on the spot, he was interested in the black arts, and he at least believed himself to be seriously wicked and heartless. The sudden cessation of the crimes, however, supposedly due to conversion, remains a problem, not least because Stephenson for years after the murders continued to lecture on the occult and to enjoy tormenting the likes of Cremers and Collins with hints which do not speak of remorse or of the sort of mental anguish which must have afflicted any such convert.

Alonzo Maduro/Alios Szemeredy

We have not seen elsewhere the linking of these alleged suspects, yet the resemblances between their legends and between their names satisfy us that they are one and the same. Maduro is said to have been a Buenos Aires businessman. Griffith S. Salway had met him through his own work in a City brokerage firm. On the night of Emma Elizabeth Smith's murder (see *Other Victims?*), Salway met Maduro in Whitechapel. Maduro later stated that all prostitutes should be killed. Later still, Salway claimed to have found surgical knives among Maduro's effects. Salway told this tale to his wife shortly before his death in 1952.

Alios Szemeredy described himself at one time as an American surgeon, at another as a sausage-maker. He too hailed from Buenos Aires (though is thought to have been of Austro-Hungarian origin), where he was incarcerated in a lunatic asylum after being accused of robbery and murder. In August, 1889, he was in Vienna, claiming that he was bound for America. He was next spotted in Vienna again in 1892, where he was arrested for murder and robbery. He committed suicide while on remand. Viennese rumour cast him as the Ripper.

Maduro's candidacy is imponderable. His statement that all prostitutes should be killed is not in itself significant. We have heard apparently sane people delivering themselves of similar opinions with regard to homosexuals and rapists in our own time. All that we know, then, is that a violent Argentinian lunatic may have been on the loose in London in or around the period of the Whitechapel murders.

"Fogelma"

Apparently a Norwegian seaman. Another mysterious lunatic. His identification, quoted by Melvin Harris, occurs in the *Empire News* of 23 October 1923, where a student of criminology writes:

Every head of police knows that Jack the Ripper died in Morris Plains Lunatic Asylum in 1902.

He was sent there from Jersey City in 1899, and was, for a time, employed in the infirmary of the institution. He was not a "permanent"; he had fits of insanity, and I, who knew him as a patient, gave information to the Mulberry Street authorities concerning the patient's identity.

He was not "wanted" in the United States, so the Detective Department of New York took no steps in the matter. A letter giving the facts in the case was sent to Scotland Yard, and, as nothing further was heard of the matter, it was allowed to lapse.

The man was not a Russian. He was a native of Norway and had no knowledge of surgery. He was just a simple sailor suffering from an incurable and terrible disease.

During the three months before his death, two women called to see him. One was known to the patient as Olga Storsjan, and the other – who said she was his sister – gave her name as Helen Fogelma.

As Fogelma the patient was entered in our books. He was subject to fits of terrible depression, and before his death became a fearful coward.

He had all the weird superstition of his race, and on one occasion I heard him scream out in the night, calling upon God to have mercy on his soul.

But during the intervals when his brain worked, he muttered of scenes and incidents that connected him clearly with the atrocious crimes of 1888.

His sister, to whom I mentioned these muttered facts, became fearful for his life, but when I assured her that, being now certified a lunatic, he was immune from the death penalty, she told me that he had done some terrible things in London.

She showed me cutting [*sic*] from the Press of New York and from the London papers. These she had found in the trunk of her brother, who after he landed in New York lived with her at 324 East 39th Street.

Many of the passages were underscored, and marginal notes, in sarcastic vein, gave an insight into the working of the madman's brain.

His sister told me that in his native town of Arendal he was known as a good-living youngster. His passion was for the sea, and he came to London with no idea of staying there.

Then for a year or so, she lost sight of her brother, and heard no more of him until in 1898 he came to her and the other girl, both of whom had come to New York to seek a living.

When he appeared in their flat at the above address, the girls did not know him. He was worn to a skeleton, and in rags. They kept him for some months, and all the time he had to spare he would read over again the cuttings relating to the Ripper crimes.

Olga Storsjan was the old-time sweetheart of this awful wreck of a man, and soon after his coming to their flat she decided to leave it. She went to Jersey City, but the man followed her, and it was upon her information to the police that he was arrested and committed to the asylum.

Before he died this man sent for the Rev J Miosen, the pastor of a Nestorian church in New York. To him the dying man told enough to connect him with the crimes committed in London.

Three letters found in his tin trunk were copied, and one of these is in answer to a letter to one Carol Mackonwitch. In it he makes mention of a great necessity to leave England, and the money appears to have been supplied by the man Carol.

This candidate is imponderable. This is one of the more frustrating of the many documents identifying "Rippers" worldwide. There is a deal of circumstantial detail in the account – the names of the patient, the pastor, the sister, the sweetheart, the benefactor, even the New York address – but the author omits any physical description of Fogelma and omits to identify himself. The most frustrating thing is that such details as we have about Fogelma correspond to the type to which we would expect the murderer to match. A tormented imbecile with a progressive disease occasioning occasional fits of insanity. His obsession with reading and rereading accounts of the murders is entirely characteristic.

Since too, it is plain that the Whitechapel Murderer either died, was incarcerated or sailed to another port, and since none of our Colney Hatch inmates or suicides has proved an entirely satisfactory candidate, the notion of a seaman is particularly persuasive, explaining as it does the sudden beginning and ending of the series of murders. The sightings of the suspect in a sailor's cap is suggestive, as is the oilskin parcel spied by Hutchinson, credibly posited by Mark Daniel to be a knife-wallet. When we consider, too, that a series of similar murders was committed in Jamaica, starting in December, 1888, and that more drunken prostitutes were similarly murdered and disembowelled in Managua, Nicaragua, in the following year, it may be that a study of *The Times* shipping columns, and its equivalent in Kingston, might prove more rewarding than trawling through London prisons, workhouses and asylums.

Michael Ostrog (born 1833?)

This is one of the suspects mentioned in the Macnaghten Memorandum, in which Sir Melville Leslie Macnaghten rejected the identification of Thomas Haynes Cutbush (*qqv*) as the murderer and suggested, as alternatives, Druitt, Kosminski (*qqv*) and Ostrog.

Ostrog was a Russian or Pole and a lifelong rogue, charlatan and thief. He described himself as a former surgeon in the Russian Navy or Imperial Guard, and, from his first recorded conviction for pilfering in the colleges and swindling hoteliers in Oxford in 1863, for which he was sentenced to ten months' imprisonment, he toured the country under countless aliases. The following year, as a rogue and vagabond, he received three months for swindling the good burghers of Bishops

Stortford and Cambridge. In July, 1864, as Count Sobieski (now a royal Pole), he was at it again in Tunbridge Wells, Kent. December of the same year found him in Exeter, where he was sentenced to eight months for fraud and felony committed at Tormoham, Devon. In January, 1866, he was in Gloucester, where he was acquitted of obtaining food, lodgings and money to the value of £7 14/-. Back in Kent, this time in Maidstone, he stole a gold watch and other chattels, and in Chatham, again he stole from a man whom he had befriended. He was arrested (this time as Bertrand Ashley, alias Ashley Nobokoff, 22), and sentenced to seven years penal servitude.

In 1873, after stealing silver from Woolwich Barracks, befriending Eton assistant master Oscar Browning (later to be sacked for taking "too personal an interest in the boys") and thus gaining access to the school, from which he stole silver and a coat and books from Browning's library, Ostrog announced that he was returning to Russia, but he was arrested in Burton on Trent.

Here he demonstrated that, far from being a mere harmless but habitual sneak-thief, he was a desperate man capable of violence. The arresting officer, Superintendent Oswell, only escaped with his life by using main force to turn Ostrog's revolver back on him. On this occasion, at Bucks Quarter Sessions, Ostrog was sentenced to ten years' imprisonment. On 28 August 1883, however, he was discharged on licence. Soon afterwards, the *Police Gazette* listed him as wanted for failing to report.

He escaped further arrest until July 1887, when he returned to Woolwich Barracks and stole a tankard. On this occasion, he discovered that he had chosen the wrong targets. The massed cadets gave chase across Woolwich Common, and Ostrog, this time calling himself Dr Bonge, was taken into custody. By now his stability was decidedly questionable. He swallowed, or made out that he had swallowed, nux vomica on his way to the police station, and attempted to throw himself under a train as he was taken on remand to Holloway. How far this instability was genuine is questionable. He behaved very oddly in court, maintaining that he had felt impelled to run on Woolwich Common and thought that he was running a race when the cadets gave chase, that all his brothers had committed suicide and that his wife had been unfaithful. At one point, he picked up his coat and announced to the court that he was off to France, if they didn't mind. They did, and he was restrained. At the Old Bailey, Ostrog pleaded insanity but was disbelieved and sentenced to six months hard labour. He persisted in his sham, if sham it was, and was soon transferred to the Surrey Pauper Lunatic Asylum suffering from "mania". He was discharged on 10 March 1888.

In October, 1888, Ostrog was again a wanted man for failing to report to the police while on licence. Startlingly, for an habitual thief and recidivist, we hear nothing more of him, though Macnaghten (an honest, but not altogether reliable witness) appears to know more than the records show:

> Michael Ostrog, a mad Russian doctor and a convict and unquestionably a homicidal maniac. This man was said to have been habitually cruel to women, and for a long time was known to have carried about with him surgical knives and other instruments; his antecedents (previous convictions) were of the very worst and his whereabouts at the time of the Whitechapel murders could never be satisfactorily accounted for. He is still alive.

This last statement – "he is still alive" – written in 1894, coupled with Macnaghten's statement that Ostrog was a serious suspect for the Ripper's crimes, presumably implies that Macnaghten had kept tabs on Ostrog, although, so far as we can tell – and somewhat improbably – Ostrog had not reoffended. Was he perhaps, as his behaviour leads us to believe, slowly going mad and, after the Ripper murders, confined under one of his many pseudonyms? And, if so, why does Macnaghten not tell us of his whereabouts?

Ostrog remains a perfectly possible candidate, impossible to verify or discount until we know something of his career during and after the Ripper murders. He was too tall (5 feet 11 inches) and too old for those who believe that the Ripper was spotted at the scenes of the murders, but it is plain that he was a violent, vain, vengeful man on the brink of insanity. The fact that his "previous convictions" give no indication of the sort of inclinations manifested by the Ripper is discouraging, though to some extent that discouragement is vitiated by Macnaghten's (unsupported) assertion that he was "said to have been habitually cruel to women" and (again unsupported) "unquestionably a homicidal maniac".

The fact that Ostrog apparently retired from his criminal career after the Ripper murders is at once improbable if he was the Ripper and astonishing if he was not, unless, as has been conjectured of other suspects, the flaying of Mary Jane Kelly finally tipped him into insanity. Otherwise, under some pseudonym or another, we can expect to find Ostrog cropping up in some Court, somewhere in the world, between 1888 and 1894.

Nicolai Wassili (1842–?)

The existence of this suspect must be proved before his criminality can be mooted. His myth is almost certainly linked to that of Pedachenko (*qv*), and has been concocted layer by layer, the initial whisper compounded and elaborated by other superstitions, legends and suppositions. Wassili is one of many suspects in the class of the "Very Odd Foreigner", which must have consoled the bemused Briton. Born in the Ukraine and educated at the University of Odessa, Wassili is said to have joined the self-castrating sect of the Shorns, who despised all sexual congress and impulse.

Driven from his homeland by the Orthodox Church's proscription of the Shorn cult, Wassili moved to Paris, where he made it his sinister business to persuade perfectly healthy and jolly French tarts to adopt his sombre principles. A young woman named Madeleine (it could, I suppose, have been Marguerite or, a few years later, Mimi, just as well), fell in love with Wassili and he with her, but, on discovering his firm principles (and, it is to be supposed, his want of firmness elsewhere), quite reasonably rejected him.

Wassili was demented by grief at her fickleness, and took to saving prostitutes wholesale by killing them. He had saved five such by stabbing them in the back before he was caught and sent to an asylum. He was released on 1 January (when else?) 1888, and is said to have arrived in London just in time to learn his way around before resuming his campaign, this time with additional elaborations.

There is no proof of Wassili's existence, crimes or committal. In common with most VOF (Very Odd Foreigner) theories, it seems to spring from the oddness and foreignness (the very fact that a cult such as the Shorns existed), rather than from any link between the crimes and the candidate.

Dr Alexander Pedachenko (1857?–1908?)

This is another VOF candidate (*see* Wassili), this time with medical expertize and espionage chucked in for good measure. This story posits an obstetrician from Tver who also happened to be an agent of the Secret Police or Ochrana. He worked for a while in Glasgow, then moved with his sister to Walworth. He performed the Ripper murders in order to discredit the Metropolitan Police, whom the Tsarist Ochrana thought to be far too nice to dissidents, socialists and anarchists. Once Sir Charles Warren resigned, Pedachenko was smuggled back to Russia, but unfortunately had got into the habit of murdering women, as one does ("If once a man indulges himself in murder," wrote De Quincey, "very soon he comes to think little of robbing; and from robbing he comes next to drinking and sabbath-breaking, and from that to incivility and procrastination") and had to be sent to an asylum.

Unfortunately, the alleged sources for this story are all deeply suspect. Its original source is said by William Le Queux in *Things I Know* (1923) to be none other than Grigor Efimovich Rasputin, whose documents, so Le Queux claimed, were entrusted to him by Kerensky's Duma. Rasputin is an unreliable source, not least because he had a vivid imagination and had innumerable axes to grind. Furthermore, we have no evidence that Rasputin ever had knowledge of the Ochrana, nor that he ever wrote such a document, nor that he spoke French, in which it was written, nor that it was sent to Le Queux. A poor start.

Then we come to Donald McCormick, who, though a journalist of probity, did not abide by the conventions current in the discipline of history. As the authors of *The Jack the Ripper A–Z* have it, "The conventions of his generation led McCormick to invent dialogue and eschew sources for many of his interesting discoveries and revelations, which means that some data traced back to him ... rest on his unverifiable assertions." McCormick has proved consistently reluctant to supply other researchers with documentary verification of his assertions in his book, *The Identity of Jack the Ripper (1954)*, from which we draw a further elaboration of the Pedachenko theory. McCormick couples the Pedachenko identification with that of Severin Klosowski (*qv*) who was, of course, George Chapman (*qv*). According to McCormick, Klosowski/Chapman was, apparently, Pedachenko's double. Pedachenko, he says, was a barber-surgeon employed by one William Delhaye, and worked part-time at St Saviour's Infirmary, at which Tabram, Nichols, Chapman and Kelly were all patients. McCormick goes further. Pedachenko, he says, citing a Russian publication which has yet to be traced, was the alias of Vassily Konavolov – surely none other than Nikolai Wassili (*qv*) – who killed a woman in Paris.

So the slender threads unravel into a floss, dense, impenetrable but, in the end, nigh weightless. We must be careful, however, not to dismiss every strand simply because it has been woven into something intrinsically worthless. The fact that folklore, street lore and populist journalism picked up on these stories and elaborated them beyond credibility does *not* mean that they had, originally, no germ of truth. On the contrary, we are persuaded that several, if not many, of the inhabitants of the East End at the time probably had a fairly shrewd idea as to the Ripper's identity, and that legend, if carefully plucked free of its more outlandish and garish ornamentations, can supply us with important information. Prejudice and archetypes, however, cannot.

George Chapman (1865–1903)
see Severin Klosowski

Frederick Bailey Deeming (1853–92)

Plumber and mass murderer Deeming killed his wife and four children in Rainhill, Liverpool, in 1891, then escaped to Melbourne where, the following year, he murdered his second wife. He buried his victims under hearthstones. It seems likely that he killed others, and rumours abounded, both in Australia and in Britain, at the time of his conviction. Deeming was said to have confessed to "the last two" Whitechapel Murders while awaiting execution. His solicitor, however, denied that he had done so.

Frederick West among others has demonstrated that the domestic murderer can extend his indoor games to more random outdoor contact sport, though, in West's case at least, it appears that he killed his first wife and children because they threatened the continuation of his depredations. Deeming plainly was a homicidal maniac, but his connection with the Whitechapel Murders is founded only upon rumour springing from horror at his crimes. Overall, he is one of the least likely suspects in the canon.

Dr Thomas Neill Cream (1850–92)

A suspect only in the mythology, Cream poisoned four Lambeth prostitutes in 1891, was arrested, convicted and hanged.

There is no support for this candidate. Different method, different place, different time, different man. Cream was in prison in Illinois for the murder of one Stott at the time of the Whitechapel Murders.

Severin Klosowski (1865–1903), aka George Chapman

This multiple murderer was a persistent suspect since 1903, when Inspector Frederick George Abberline identified him to the *Pall Mall Gazette* as the Whitechapel Murderer. Abberline is alleged to have said to Detective Inspector George Godley, when he arrested Klosowski, "I see you've got George Chapman at last."

Born in Nagornak, Poland, Klosowski was apprenticed in 1880 to Moshko Rappaport, a senior surgeon. In 1885, having completed his apprenticeship, he attended a practical surgery course at Praga Hospital, Warsaw. He left for England at some point in 1887, and took up a post as assistant hairdresser in Abraham Radin's barber shop at 70 West India Dock Road. By early 1889, he is listed as running his own business at 126 Cable Street, St George's-in-the-East. In October 1889,

Chapman married a woman named Lucy Baderski. By 1890, he was working as an assistant at a barber's in the basement of the White Hart pub at 89 Whitechapel High Street, calling himself (according to Wolff Levisohn, a witness at Klosowski's trial) Ludwig Zagowski. September saw Klosowski running the premises and living there with Lucy and their newborn son.

The baby died on 3 March 1891, and Chapman and his wife soon afterwards boarded a steamer (name unknown) for New York. In Jersey City, Klosowski once more set himself up in business, but it seems that he was flirting with other women. There was a row. Klosowski attacked his wife with a knife. Lucy, once more pregnant, fled back to London in February 1892. She lodged with her sister at 26 Scarborough Street, Whitechapel, and bore her daughter there on 15 May, just before Klosowski returned and re-entered their lives.

In 1893, Klosowski took up with a woman called, coincidentally, Annie Chapman, and Lucy Klosowski is heard of no more until questioned by George Godley's men in 1902. Late in the following year, however, Klosowski introduced another woman into his menage, and Annie, pregnant by him, stormed out. Klosowski henceforth retained her surname. In 1895, Klosowski resolved that getting married was altogether too much trouble. Encountering a married woman named Mary Spink, living apart from her husband in Forest Road, Leytonstone, he announced to their landlord, John Ward, on 27 October, that they had married according to the rites of his – that is, the Jewish – people. This was untrue, nor was Chapman/Klosowski of the Jewish faith. Mary Spink gave her new "husband" a £500 legacy that she had received. He used the money to take out a lease on a barber's shop in Hastings.

Although the "Chapmans" presented a happy and unified face to the world, and their business thrived accordingly, Chapman was said by subsequent witnesses to have beaten Mary, and to have played fast and loose with the women of the town, particularly a domestic servant named Alice Penfold. Chapman had by now decided that breaking up with wives was now as redundant as marrying them. On 3 April 1897, he bought an ounce of tartar emetic, a soluble powder containing antimony, from pharmacist William Davidson on Hastings High Street.

Returning to London, Chapman became landlord of the Prince of Wales, a pub in Bartholomew Square, off the City Road. Mary by now was slowly and agonizingly dying, wasting away as she purged and vomited up every food and liquid that she ingested. Chapman prepared the drugs prescribed by her doctor. He was heartless towards his wife as she died, and opened the pub, as ever, on the day of her death, Christmas Day 1897.

Antimony is colourless, odourless and tasteless. Having administered it once with total success (the doctor attributed Mary's death to pthisis), Chapman hunted no further through the pharmacopoeia. Essentially conservative, he also fastened upon a way of recruiting concubines and, incidentally, victims. He advertised for barmaids. Bessie Taylor was the first. Again they went through a fake marriage. Again Chapman abused her at their new pub, the Monument in Union Street, Southwark. She died of "intestinal obstruction, vomiting and exhaustion" on 13 February 1901. Next, in August of the same year, 18-year-old Maud Marsh entered his employment at the Crown, 213 Borough High Street. This was Chapman's last pub and last victim. Chapman fixed upon a new barmaid, Florence Rayner, as his next fancy; Maud died on 22 October 1902. The doctor, who had attended Bessie Taylor, declined to sign a death certificate. Prompted by Dr Francis Grapel, Maud's family doctor from Croydon, Dr Stoker had Maud's stomach and its contents sent to the Clinical Research Association. Maud's internal organs contained massive quantities of antimony. On 25 October, Inspector George Godley, who had worked on the Whitechapel Murders, arrested George Chapman at the Crown.

In November and December, Bessie Taylor and Mary Spink were exhumed. Mary Spink's body was unchanged, Bessie's mould-covered but intact. Antimony preserves bodies. Chapman was hanged at Wandsworth on 7 April 1903.

Chapman had never been a suspect for the Whitechapel Murders until Abberline (for all his brilliance as a detective and his knowledge of the East End, by now a fallible witness) became convinced, on reading details of his trial, that Chapman was his man.

The most notable objection to the identification of Klosowski/Chapman with the Whitechapel murders is the modus operandi. In general, this objection is found to be a valid one. The knife-wielding disemboweller does not become the cautious poisoner. More particularly, however, the Ripper's victims were of a kind: inebriate drabs, whom he clearly despised. Chapman's victims were respectable, attractive women, and his heterosexual competence and ability both to charm and to inspire affection and loyalty are beyond doubt. He never killed until he had tired of his victim and found a replacement. He was callous and cruel, but he was rational. The Ripper's crimes, on the other hand, were humane but irrational. At 36, Klosowski could run a business and inspire the love of 18-year-old Maud Marsh. Why then, at 23, did he feel the need to skulk in the shadows and, at enormous risk, slash up old bruisers like Annie Chapman *without sexual congress*?

Above all, how did the Ripper suppress the urges which caused the Whitechapel Murders over nine years of hard work and philandering following the death and orgiastic mutilation of Mary Jane Kelly, only to make his first, initially tentative attempts at poisoning? Is it possible for a man who has stripped a woman to the skeleton to philander at all?

These objections are not unanswerable with hypothesis, but they remain stumbling blocks. Against them must be set Klosowski's dandyism and physical description, which make him (nigh) indistinguishable from the man seen by Hutchinson with Kelly. That man, it will be recalled, was "Jewish-looking", wearing a long dark coat with astrakhan collar and cuffs, a dark jacket and trousers, a black tie with a horseshoe pin, a thick gold chain and spats. He had a pale complexion and a slight moustache, curled up at the ends. The description matches Klosowski in every regard save one: his age. Twenty-three and 35 might be confused in half-light, but Hutchinson heard the man's voice, and that (particularly at that lowered pitch expressive habitual in sexual arousal) should have given the game away.

Add to this the dubious theatricality of Hutchinson's description (elsewhere referred to), absent in his initial description, and the hour at which he saw the man with Kelly, and this link is at best circumstantial. This is not to rule out Klosowski/Chapman, but, until we have further evidence (which, though undisclosed, may, of course, have existed) to support Abberline's contention, he must be regarded as a rank outsider.

Dr Stanley (dates unknown)

This candidate presents another garbled mish-mash of familiar material. Here is a brilliant doctor again, and here, somewhat surprisingly, a recurrence of Buenos Aires in the mythology. Stanley, posited by Leonard Matters, is a cancer specialist at "X" Hospital, much favoured by the fashionable. Alas, his beloved son "Herbert" or "Bertie", whose achievements were to have been the crowning glory of our doctor's career, enjoyed a brief liaison with Mary Jane Kelly after celebrating the Boat Race too well in 1886 and contracted an extraordinarily virulent form of syphilis that promptly killed him. Stanley, therefore, for all the knowledge of disease and clinical detachment acquired over years, swore vengeance upon the whore who had clapped his son, and, for good measure, all her friends. He then travelled widely and ended his life in Buenos Aires.

Where do we start? Stanley is stated by Matters to be a pseudonym, so we have no way of disproving the hypothesis, but the world-record-breaking spirochetes, which do not seem to have affected Kelly, give cause for suspicion, as does the notion of a doctor avenging a disease upon one affected by it, as does the even more outlandish idea that he would first kill and mutilate, at great personal risk, four other women who may or may not have known her. This story appears, in one form or another, to have been current in the folklore of the time, hence the recurrence of so many familiar features.

The father of "GWB"

An interesting candidate, regarded favourably by novelist and criminologist Colin Wilson for the perfectly acceptable reason that the story "rings true". An Australian correspondent, signing himself "GWB", wrote to the late Dan Farson, claiming that, when he was a boy playing in the London streets at night, his mother would call to him, "Come in, Georgie, or Jack the Ripper will get you." One night in 1889, GWB's father, hearing this, patted the boy's head and told him, "Don't worry, Georgie. You would be the last person Jack the Ripper would touch."

This man, a brutal, wife-beating drunkard, had been born in 1850 and had married in 1876. He had pined for a daughter, but his only girl-child was born an imbecile. He therefore took to drink and, when all his subsequent children proved to be boys, he grew violent and at last demented.

GWB stated that, after a showdown in which he threatened his father with a thrashing, the two men never spoke to one another again until the son declared his intention to emigrate to Australia and was urged by his mother to make his peace with the older man. At this valedictory meeting, the father told his son that he had committed the Whitechapel Murders in, it appears, a sort of drunken fugue. He stated that he had worn two pairs of trousers on his nocturnal forays, and, after the murders, would remove the outer pair and dispose of them in the manure which it was his business to deliver. He advised his son to change his name when he settled in Australia because, so he said, he intended to make a full confession before he died. The son did change his name, but no such confession was ever made.

Colin Wilson is right. In certain regards, this story does have the ring of truth. The domestic detail – the jokey warning from the mother, the occasional benevolence of the drunken father, the showdown between father and son, the story of the imbecile daughter, the final remorseful confession – is persuasive. Either "GWB" missed a vocation as a novelist or he was telling the truth. Unfortunately, that does not mean that his father was. A drunken fantasist subject to blackouts may well have convinced himself that, during his debauches, he had indeed killed, or he may simply have derived malicious pleasure in persuading his son of his accursed ancestry (and of his father's place in history). Of course, his story may have been true, and certainly the want of a rational motive makes this a more plausible case than most.

The only question marks arise in the father's account. Just how many pairs of trousers could such a man afford? All in all, however, a credible theory involving a common man, a drunk (see Schwartz's evidence) and a bully in the grip of dementia rather than a prince, a surgeon or a master criminal. Unfortunately, the tale cannot be substantiated and the sources – one anonymous, the other an habitual drunk – are far from reliable.

Dr Francis J Tumblety (1833–1903)

A new candidate was identified by the Littlechild letter (see Key Texts), written in 1913 by Chief Inspector John Littlechild, head of Special Branch at the time of the murders. This letter was uncovered by Stewart Evans in 1993, and formed the starting-point for the book *The Lodger* by Evans and Paul Gainey.

Of Irish ancestry, Tumblety was born in Canada. Although he appears to have been uneducated, he became a rich and successful homoeopath and mixer of patent nostrums. He was despised by many for his self-aggrandizing tall stories and his fraudulence, but his foppishness and grandiloquence persuaded many others. He was known to have a deep-seated hatred of women, and especially prostitutes (it is believed that he was tricked into marriage by a prostitute), and kept a "museum" of anatomical parts, including many uteri. In 1865, in a case of mistaken identity, he was arrested as a suspect following the assassination of President Abraham Lincoln, but released. This incident damaged his reputation in America, and he became a frequent visitor to London.

In 1888, he took lodgings in Batty Street, where, it is plain, he was watched by police. He was arrested on 7 November for "unnatural offences" – usually a reference to homosexuality – and released on bail on 16 November. As Littlechild writes, Tumblety jumped bail and escaped to Boulogne with the police at his heels. From Boulogne, Tumblety managed to obtain a passage to New York, where police staked out his lodgings, but Tumblety escaped them and was not, to our knowledge, further pursued. He died after a long and painful illness in St Louis.

Loud-mouthed, eccentric, controversial: Tumblety does not fit in with our perception of an unobtrusive character who would arouse no suspicion in his victims or notice from witnesses, yet the case made by Evans and Gainey is a powerful one. Tumblety was a rogue. He does appear to have disliked women. He was in the East End at the time of the Whitechapel Murders, and the police did take a considerable interest in him.

It is plain that, whatever Tumblety's supposed crime for which he was arrested (and the Act under which he was charged proscribes procuring young girls as well as homosexual acts), this was a holding charge merely. A simple case of cottaging would hardly have initiated an international pursuit involving the police forces of three different countries. The police plainly suspected Tumblety of being the Whitechapel Murderer.

There is just one problem, which must have occurred to them too. If Tumblety was the Whitechapel Murderer, who did him an enormous favour by copying and exceeding his previous crimes by flaying Mary Jane Kelly to the bone *while Tumblety was still in police custody*? Because if Tumblety is our man, we must fly in the face of all opinion, at the time and since, and declare that Kelly was not a Ripper victim. For all that, an intriguing suspect and a nasty bit of work. More research will be needed, however, to establish claims about Tumblety.

Montague John Druitt (1857–1888)

Named in the Macnaghten Memoranda (*qv*), to which Major Arthur Griffiths had access, this suspect was also known of by journalist George Sims. After 1898, both men suggested, without naming him, that Druitt had been the Whitechapel killer. His true identity and history, however, were not known until Daniel Farson rediscovered the original memoranda.

Druitt was a gentleman, educated at Winchester and Oxford and called to the bar, who was found drowned in the Thames on 31 December 1888. His pockets were weighted with stones. A verdict of suicide was returned by the Coroner's inquest of 2 January 1889.

Druitt had been teaching at a school until late in November, when he was dismissed for "a serious offence". The train ticket found in his pocket suggests that he may have made his last journey on, or soon after, 1 December. The tormented man is supposed to have left a message addressed to his brother declaring that, "since Friday" (possibly 30 November, which appears to have been the date of his dismissal), he had felt that he was going to be like his mother, who had been sent to a Clapham asylum in July 1888, and that he deemed it best that he should die.

It has been conjectured that Druitt lost his job because of homosexuality. There is no evidence for this, but certainly many of Druitt's background would have considered homosexual feelings to be indicative of insanity. Druitt had had a hard time. His mother's committal and his own dismissal must have preyed on the mind of one who was plainly of melancholic and anxious temperament. His maternal grandmother had been a suicide, and his older sister was also to kill herself. He had ample cause, given the standards of his era and his time, to feel suicidal, without adding the Ripper's chronicle of savagery to the horrors already burdening him. The suicide letter, rendered in a gloss in the *Acton, Chiswick and Turnham Green Gazette* on 5 January – "Since Friday I felt I was going to be like mother" – simply does not make sense if this man, about to die, had been slaughtering women wholesale over the past four months. We know of no evidence connecting Druitt to the murders with the exception of the memoranda and, just possibly, White's report (*qv*). This may, of course, be explained by the statement in Macnaghten's memoirs. "Certain facts, pointing to this conclusion (the murderer's suicide after Kelly's murder) were not in possession of the police till some years after I became a detective officer (1890)". These facts, he implies, for reasons of decency or discretion, have been withheld. George Sims records in 1902 that the police were searching for a man who must surely be Druitt "alive when they found him dead", and, in 1903, Sims again tells us that he was suspected "by the chiefs of Scotland yard, and by his own friends." He plainly was suspected by the Yard, but the basis for such suspicion is unknown. See *The Jack the Ripper Whitechapel Murders*, and their contribution to this book, by Sue and Andy Parlour for one hypothesis regarding Druitt's involvement.

(Aaron?) Kosminski

"Kosminski" is one of the prime suspects mentioned in the Macnaghten Memoranda (*qv*), and is also named by Swanson (*qv*) and apparently described by Anderson (*qv*). It is generally believed that their references are to Aaron Kosminski, a Polish Jew, who was admitted to Mile End Old Town Workhouse Infirmary for three days in 1890, having been attested insane for two years. His brother took him into his care on his release, but was plainly unequal to the task, for Aaron Kosminski was committed to Colney Hatch Lunatic Asylum on 7 February 1891, with no known history of violence. The lay witness committing him declared that he ate bread out of the gutter (as did many, were they lucky enough to find it) and refused food at the hands of others. The lay witness, however, Jacob Cohen, was a fellow Jew with an interest in preserving his tribe's reputation, and his assertion that Kosminski was a harmless imbecile may be untrustworthy. Kosminski died in 1919. Macnaghten, Swanson and Anderson do not precisely agree about the history of their suspect.

James Maybrick

Well, why not? A drug-taking cotton merchant in Liverpool, already well known to criminologists of the period, is considerably likelier a candidate than, say, the Pope or Queen Victoria. Maybrick died in dubious circumstances in May, 1889 – a good time for the Ripper to die. His wife, Florence, was convicted of poisoning him with arsenic. The trial was a notable travesty. Florence was released in 1904 and died in 1941.

The story of Maybrick's diary is found in Shirley Harrison's contribution to this book. Colin Wilson and Melvyn Fairclough will also be found supporting his claims. We find much suspicion about the "diary" upon which his association with the Whitechapel Murderer is based, but accept that, inured to Ripperologists' fantasies, we are now sceptical to the point of cynicism. We eagerly await definitive proof of the diary's bona fides.

Other Victims?

At the time of Polly Nichols's murder, it was already assumed that a serial killer was on the loose in the East End and that this was only the latest of three killings. Only subsequently, when the Whitechapel Murderer's signature, as it were, became familiar, did it become clear to most, but not all people that the earlier crimes had been committed by other hands.

Emma Elizabeth Smith

She was 45 at the time of her death, which like Martha Tabram's occurred on a Bank Holiday. Emma Smith was a widow and occasional prostitute. She too was a drunk. She left her common lodging house at 7.00 am on 2 April (Easter Monday) 1888, and returned between 2.00 am and 3.00 am, her face bruised and livid, one ear nearly torn off, and suffering from acute pains in her groin. The deputy keeper, Mary Russell, immediately took her to the London Hospital. It emerged that Smith had been raped, assaulted and robbed by (or by components of) a gang of three. One was only about nineteen years old. A blunt instrument had been forced into her vagina and had ruptured the perineum. On the morning of 4 April she died of peritonitis.

Emma Smith occupied a common lodging house at 18 George Street, Martha Tabram (*qv*), who was killed in August 1888, lived at another at No 19. Tabram frequently used the name, "Emma". In the case of a solitary psychopath, we look to modus operandi. In the case of gang killings, however, no such particularity prevails. Contemporary rumour put both killings down to the Old Nichol gang of the Jago, presumably because the victims had not paid protection fees or because they had invaded Old Nichol pitches. On the other hand, there may have been a new breed of Mohocks on the rampage. Either way, both killings were achieved on Bank Holidays, when the maximum number of people would have been milling in the streets (look at the "bumper crop" of witnesses for the "double event", when it was pouring with rain), both appear to have been deliberately unpleasant, *pour encourager les autres*, and the victims are remarkably similar. If the "Ripper" had had the sexual confidence to rape Smith, then to replicate the offence with a broomstick or whatever, he had had no need so tentatively, then so adventurously, to probe the interior of the dark, mysterious continent of femininity.

Martha Tabram

Pulchritude was, it appears, of no interest to the Whitechapel Murderer. Mary Jane Kelly was pretty, Stride lively and once, at least, attractive. Otherwise, his victims were gin-soaked drabs. Even Annie Chapman, however, might have conceded last place in a beauty contest to Martha Tabram. Tabram had been married, but her passion for drink had caused her to be rejected by her husband, warehouseman Henry Samuel Tabram, and by her long time lover, William Turner. On 6 August 1888, Martha was several times spotted with soldiers. Mary Ann Connolly, also known as "Pearly Poll", related that she and Tabram had picked up two guardsmen, a private and a corporal, who had treated them to drinks at various pubs. At last, the two couples separated in order that each should have intercourse in adjacent yards, Martha accompanying the private into George Yard (now Gunthorpe Street).

At 3.30 am, Alfred George Crow climbed the stairs of George Yard Buildings and saw what he thought to be a sleeping tramp on the first floor landing. At 4.45 am, another tenant of the tenement, John Saunders Reeves, found Tabram's body there. She had been stabbed 39 times, all over her torso. The stab wounds appear to have been made with a penknife save one, at the breastbone, made with "some long, strong instrument", which could have been a bayonet. For all that the liver, heart and spleen were punctured, the cause of death was deemed to be loss of blood. The astonishing feature of so savage and painful a murder is that tenants living mere yards away heard nothing. Newspapers allege that Tabram might have been at least partially strangled, but we have no evidence to that effect. Suspicion at once fixed upon the soldiery – first the Scots, then the Coldstream Guards – but Pearly Poll, having volunteered information to the police in the first flush of indignation at her friend's killing, now proved a recalcitrant and unreliable witness. The murderer was never identified.

The reasons for rejecting Tabram as a Whitechapel Murderer victim are manifold and manifest. The Whitechapel Murderer was cool and avoided pain, Tabram's killer(s) was frenzied and sadistic. The Whitechapel Murderer slashed with the cutting edge of a ground blade; Tabram's killer stabbed. The Whitechapel Murderer concentrated his attentions upon the groin; Tabram's killer was far less discriminating. Tabram's murderer demonstrates none of the obsessive interest and curiosity displayed by the Whitechapel Murderer. His aim, was only to cause pain and death. The Whitechapel Murderer had more devious and intricate furrows to plough.

Alice McKenzie

If there is one "non-canonical" victim who just might be a victim of the Whitechapel Murderer, it is Alice McKenzie. A lodging-house dweller, occasional drunkard and tart, she was murdered on the night of 16–17 July 1889. There is nothing exceptional about her final movements. She was drunk, and was last seen in Brick Lane at around 11.40 pm. She was walking fast, and would not pause for conversation with friends. At 12.50 am on 17 July, in Castle Alley, which had been patrolled by two separate policemen in the previous 35 minutes, the latter at about 12.25 am, McKenzie was found dead. Her throat had been cut and her abdomen mutilated. The killer cut through the carotid artery from left to right, as did the Whitechapel Murderer. These cuts, however, were no more than 4 inches long whereas our man had slashed from ear to ear. McKenzie, like the "canonical" victims, had been lying on the ground when killed. Dr Bond, however, who also performed the autopsy on Mary Jane Kelly, declared that McKenzie's killer had stabbed her throat, then dragged the knife through the flesh. The abdominal injuries, too, indicate a copycat killing by one returning to the tentativeness of Nichol's killer (or one who had read only the more decorous reports in the press), rather than the deep, bold opening of the cavity performed by the Whitechapel Murderer. For all that, the murderer's technique in laying down the victim and executing her were startlingly similar to those used by the Whitechapel Murderer, and Alice Mckenzie had the tell-tale bruises high on her chest. To accept McKenzie as a Ripper murder, therefore, it is necessary to picture the killer now debilitated by age or disease. A copycat is far more likely.

Weather Report

Prevailing Weather conditions on the nights of the Whitechapel Murders:

30–31 August 1888, Mary Ann Nichols
Partly cloudy but dry and becoming fine during the night. Second day of the moon's last quarter.

7–8 September, 1888. Annie Chapman, aka Siffey
Partly cloudy but dry, and becoming fine during the night. Second day of the new moon.

29–30 September, 1888. Elizabeth Stride, aka Kidney ("Long Liz") and Catharine Eddowes, aka Kelly (also used the names Mary Jane and Mary Ann)
Cloudy with rain, clearing after midnight. A chilly night with minimum temperature 43°F (6°C). Second day of the last quarter.

8–9 November, 1888. Mary Jane Kelly, née Davies
Overcast with rain all night. Cold, with minimum temperature 38°F (3°C). Fourth day of the new moon.

Geographical Note

For the benefit of those who would follow in the Ripper's footsteps, Buck's Row is now Durward Street, while Berner Street has been renamed Henriques Street.

Bibliography

The early literature concerning the Whitechapel murderer is not noted for factual accuracy. The two most famous contributions to the corpus are Marie Belloc Lowndes's hugely successful novel, *The Lodger* (1911) and Leonard Matters's *The Mystery of Jack the Ripper* (1929), a story apparently founded upon hearsay evidence.

In modern times, dating from Daniel Farson's rediscovery of the Macnaghten Memoranda (*qv*) in 1959, five works demand special attention – Tom Cullen's *Autumn of Terror*, Donald Rumbelow's *The Complete Jack the Ripper*, Paul Begg's *Jack the Ripper: The Uncensored Facts*, *The Jack the Ripper A–Z*, by Paul Begg, Martin Fido and Keith Skinner, and, last and best, the magisterial *The Complete History of Jack the Ripper* by Philip Sugden. (Special mention should also be made of Alexander Kelly's admirable bibliography, and Donald McCormick's entertaining but dubious theories dependent upon highly elusive sources.)

These, then, are the ground-breaking works which, stage by stage, have transformed Jack the Ripper from bogeyman of legend to a genuine murderer susceptible to serious investigation and speculation. It is doubtful, however, if any of these has had so much impact on the popular imagination as the late Stephen Knight's *Jack the Ripper: The Final Solution*. This astonishing book, positing the thesis that the murders were committed in a carriage by a remarkable trio – the royal physician, Sir William Withey Gull, the artist, Walter Sickert and an obscure coachman "John Netley", attracted extraordinary attention, not least because it was theorized that Queen Victoria's son and heir, Prince Albert Victor, Duke of Clarence (1864–92) had secretly married the previously unknown Annie Crook. While this thesis is with good reason generally discredited (but see Melvyn Fairclough's and the Parlours' contributions in *Current Views*), it is impossible to exaggerate the attention (some of it, admittedly, undesirable) which it attracted to the mystery of the Whitechapel murders.

The serious interest has not waned, but the public furore died down again until the emergence of James Maybrick's alleged diary, a document which has aroused fierce controversy and is discussed at length by several of our contributors. This is not the place to detail the arguments, but Colin Wilson at least has given the document his imprimatur, and we must await further developments.

It is always dangerous to assert that any one book is "definitive", but certainly, until further discoveries be made, any history of the murders was superfluous since the publication of Philip Sugden's remarkable book. As to the identity of the murderer, however, as the debate in *Current Views* makes clear, the jury is still out. Further information will, we are confident, be forthcoming, and further theorists will detect method amid the mayhem. Ripper Bibliographers will not be out of work for many years to come.

Books about the Jack the Ripper Case

All are published in the UK unless otherwise noted.

1888 G Purkess, *The Whitechapel Murders, or the Mysteries of the East End*
1888 Anonymous, *Jack the Ripper at Work Again: Another Terrible Murder and Mutilation in Whitechapel*
1888 Richard Kyle Fox, *The History of the Whitechapel Murders: A Full and Authentic Narrative of the Above Murder With Sketches* (USA)
1888 Samuel Hudson, *Leather Apron, or the Horrors of Whitechapel* (USA)
1889 W J Hayne, *Jack the Ripper, or the Crimes of London*
1889 Anonymous, *The Latest Atrocities of Jack the Ripper* (Germany)
1889 Anonymous, *Jack lo Squartatore* (Italy)
1908 Carl Mussmann, *Hvemm var Jack the Ripper?* (Denmark)
1924 Tom Robinson, *The Whitechapel Horrors, Being an Authentic Account of the Jack the Ripper Murders*
1929 Leonard W Matters, *The Mystery of Jack the Ripper*

1933 Jean Dorsenne, *Jack L'Eventreur: Scènes Vécues* (France)

1935 Edwin Thomas Woodhall, *Jack the Ripper, or When London Walked in Terror*

1939 William Stewart, *Jack the Ripper: A New Theory*

1953 Allan Barnard, *The Harlot Killer: Jack the Ripper in Fact and Fiction* (USA)

1959 Donald McCormick, *The Identity of Jack the Ripper*

1965 Tom Cullen, *Autumn of Terror: Jack the Ripper – His Crimes and Times*

1965 Robin Odell, *Jack the Ripper in Fact and Fiction*

1972 Alexander Kelly, *Jack the Ripper: A Bibliography and Review of the Literature*

1972 Daniel Farson, *Jack the Ripper*

1972 Michael Harrison, *Clarence: the Life of HRH the Duke of Clarence and Avondale 1864–1892*

1975 Michell Raper, *Who Was Jack the Ripper?*

1975 Elwyn Jones and John Lloyd, *The Ripper File*

1975 Donald Rumbelow, *The Complete Jack the Ripper*

1976 Stephen Knight, *Jack the Ripper: The Final Solution*

1976 Richard Whittington-Evans, *A Casebook on Jack the Ripper*

1978 Frank Spiering, *Prince Jack: The True Story of Jack the Ripper* (USA)

1979 Arthur Douglas, *Will the Real Jack the Ripper?*

1983 John Morrison, *Jimmy Kelly's Year of the Ripper Murders 1888*

1987 Martin Fido, *The Crimes, Detection and Death of Jack the Ripper*

1987 Roland Marx, *Jack L'Eventreur et les Fantasmes Victoriens* (Belgium)

1987 Melvin Harris, *Jack the Ripper: The Bloody Truth*

1987 Martin Howells and Keith Skinner, *The Ripper Legacy*

1987 Terence Sharkey, *Jack the Ripper: One Hundred Years of Investigation*

1987 Peter Underwood, *Jack the Ripper: One Hundred Years of Mystery*

1987 Colin Wilson and Robin Odell, *Jack the Ripper: summing up and Verdict*

1988 Anonymous, *Aleister Crowley and Jack the Ripper*

1988 Paul Begg, *Jack the Ripper: The Uncensored Facts*

1988 Winston Forbes-Jones, *Who Was Jack the Ripper?*

1989 Melvin Harris, *The Ripper File*

1990 Jean Overton Fuller, *Sickert and the Ripper Crimes*

1990 Katie Colby-Newton, *Jack the Ripper: Opposing Viewpoints* (USA)

1991 Paul Harrison, *Jack the Ripper: The Mystery Solved*

1991 Melvyn Fairclough, *The Ripper and the Royals*

1991 Paul Begg, Martin Fido and Keith Skinner, *The Jack the Ripper A–Z*

1991 Stephane Bourgoin, *Jack L'Eventreur* (France)

1992 David Abrahamsen, *Murder and Madness: The Secret Life of Jack the Ripper* (USA)

1993 Shirley Harrison, *The Diary of Jack the Ripper*

1993 A P Wolf, *Jack the Myth*

1993 Frater Achad Osher, *Did Aleister Crowley Know the Identity of Jack the Ripper?* (USA)

1993 John Wilding, *Jack the Ripper Revealed*

1994 Theo Aronson, *Prince Eddy and the Homosexual Underworld*

1994 Patricia Cory, *An Eye to the Future*

1994 John de Locksley, *Jack the Ripper Unveiled*

1994 Philip Sugden, *The Complete History of Jack the Ripper*

1994 Camille Wolf, ed., *Who Was Jack the Ripper?*

1994 Melvin Harrls, *The True Face of Jack the Ripper?*

1994 John de Locksley, *The Enigma of Jack the Ripper*

1995 Stewart Evans and Paul Gainey, *The Lodger: The Arrest and Escape of Jack the Ripper*

1995 Bruce Paley, *Jack the Ripper: The Simple Truth*

1995 William Beadle, *Jack the Ripper: Anatomy of a Myth*

1996 Peter Fisher, *An Illustrated Guide to Jack the Ripper*

1996 John de Locksley, *A Ramble With Jack the Ripper*

1996 Scott Palmer, *Jack the Ripper: A Reference Guide* (USA)

1996 Ross Strachan, *Jack the Ripper: A Collectors Guide*

1996 Richard Wallace, *Jack the Ripper: Lighthearted Friend* (USA)

1996 Peter Turnbull, *The Killer Who Never Was*

1996 A J Richards, ed, *Ripper Roundup*

1997 Robert Desnos, *Jack L'Eventreur* (France)

1997 Paul Feldman, *Jack the Ripper: The Final Chapter*

1997 James Tully, *The Secret of Prisoner 1167: Was This Man Jack The Ripper?*

1997 Andy and Sue Parlour, *The Jack the Ripper Whitechapel Murders*

1997 M J Trow, *The Many Faces of Jack the Ripper*

1998 Bob Hinton, *From Hell …The Jack the Ripper Mystery*

1998 Stephane Bourgoin, *Le Livre Rouge de Jack L'Eventreur* (France)

1998 John F Plimmer, *In the Footsteps of the Whitechapel Murders*

1998 Stewart P Evans & Paul Gainey, *Jack The Ripper: First American Serial Killer* (USA)

1999 Anne E Graham and Carol Emmas, *The Last Victim*

1999 Stephen Wright, *Jack The Ripper: An American View* (USA)

1999 Robert Graysmith, *The Bell Tower* (USA)

1999 Maxim Jakubowski & Nathan Braund, *The Mammoth Book Of Jack The Ripper*, 1st Edition

1999 Gary Coville & Patrick Lucanio, *Jack The Ripper: His Life And Crimes In Popular Entertainment* (USA)

2000 John Douglas & Mark Olshaker, *The Cases That Haunt Us* (USA)

2000 R Michael Gordon, *Alias Jack The Ripper: Beyond The Usual Whitechapel Suspects* (USA)

2001 John J Eddleston, *Jack The Ripper: An Encyclopedia* (USA)

2001 Mark Whitehead & Miriam Rivett, *Jack The Ripper*

2001 Karen Trenouth, *Epiphany Of The Whitechapel Murders* (USA)

2001 R Michael Gordon, *The Thames Torso Murders Of Victorian London* (USA)

2001 Stewart Evans & Keith Skinner, *Jack The Ripper: Letters From Hell*

2002 L Perry Curtis, *Jack The Ripper And The London Press* (USA)

2002 Peter Hodgson, *Jack The Ripper: Through The Mists Of Time*

2002 Alexander Chisholm et al, *News From Whitechapel: Jack The Ripper In The Daily Telegraph*

2002 Stewart P Evans & Keith Skinner, *Jack The Ripper And The Whitechapel Murders*

2002 Denis Meikle, *Jack The Ripper, The Murders And The Movies*

2002 Patricia Cornwell, *Portrait Of A Killer: Jack The Ripper Case Closed* (USA)

2003 Ivor J Edwards, *Jack The Ripper: Black Magic Rituals*

2003 David Spears, *Jack The Ripper: Crime Scene Investigation* (USA)

2003 R Michael Gordon, *The American Murders Of Jack The Ripper* (USA)

2003 Seth Linder, Keith Skinner & Caroline Morris, *Ripper Diary: The Inside Story*

2004 Shirley Harrison, *Jack The Ripper: The American Connection*

2004 Natalie M Rosinsky, *Jack The Ripper*

2004 Paul Begg, *Jack The Ripper: The Definitive History*

2004 Dan Norder et al, *Ripper Notes: America Looks At Jack The Ripper* (USA)

2004 Dan Norder et al, *Ripper Notes: Murder By Numbers* (USA)

2004 Stan Russo, *The Jack The Ripper Suspects* (USA)

2004 Paul Begg et al, *Ripper Notes: Madmen, Myths & Magic* (USA)

2005 Wolf Vanderlinden et al, *Ripper Notes: How The Newspapers Covered The Jack The Ripper Murders* (USA)

2005 Christopher Scott, *Will The Real Mary Kelly?*

2005 Matthew Sturgis, *Walter Sickert: A Life*

2005 Calum Reuben Knight, *Jack The Ripper, End Of A Legend*

2005 Wolf Vanderlinden, Dan Norder & Stewart P Evans, *Ripper Notes: Suspects And Witnesses* (USA)

2005 Trevor Marriott, *Jack The Ripper: The 21st Century Investigation*

2005 Wolf Vanderlinden, Dan Norder & Rob Clack, *Ripper Notes: Death In London's East End* (USA)

2005 Tony Williams, *Uncle Jack*

2005 Deborah McDonald, *The Prince, His Tutor & The Ripper* (USA)

2005 Robert J McLaughlin, *First Jack The Ripper Victim Photographs*

2005 Susan McNicoll, *Jack The Ripper: Murder, Mystery & Intrigue In London's East End*

2006 D J Leighton, *Ripper Suspect: The Secret Lives Of Montague Druitt*

2006 John Wilding, *Jack The Ripper: Revealed And Revisited*

2006 Bryan Lightbody, *Whitechapel* (USA)

2006 Euan Macpherson, *The Trial Of Jack The Ripper: The Case Of William Bury*

2006 Wolf Vanderlinden, Dan Norder & Tom Wescott, *Ripper Notes: The Hunt For Jack The Ripper* (USA)

2006 Vanessa A Hayes, *Revelations Of The True Ripper*

2006 Wolf Vanderlinden et al, *Ripper Notes: Written In Blood* (USA)

2006 Robin Odell, *Jack The Ripper: A Study Of The World's First Serial Killer And A Literary Phenomenon* (USA)

2006 John Barber, *The Camden Town Murder*

2007 Stephen P Ryder, *Public Reactions To Jack The Ripper* (USA)

2007 Paul Begg, *Ripperology: The Best Of Ripperologist Magazine* (USA)

2007 Wolf Vanderlinden, Tom Wescott & Dan Norder, *Ripper Notes: Jack The Slasher* (USA)

2007 Val Horsier, *Jack The Ripper: Crime Archive*

2007 Alexandra Warwick & Martin Willis, eds, *Jack The Ripper: Media, Culture, History*

2007 Karen Trenouth, *Jack The Ripper: The Satanic Team* (USA)

2007 Charles Van Onselen, *The Fox And The Flies*

2007 Richard Jones & Sean East, *Uncovering Jack The Ripper's London*

2007 Stewart P Evans & Donald Rumbelow, *Jack The Ripper: Scotland Yard Investigates*

2007 Neal Shelden, *The Victims Of Jack The Ripper*

2007 Paul Roland, *The Crimes Of Jack The Ripper* (USA)

2008 R Michael Gordon, *Poison Murders Of Jack The Ripper: His Final Crimes, Trial And Execution* (USA)

Filmography

Farmer Spudd and his Missus Take a Trip to Town (England, 1915),
dir: J V L Leigh.

Das Wachsfigurenkabinett (The Waxwork Cabinet) (Germany, 1924),
dir: Paul Leni, with William Dieterle, Emil Jannings, Conrad Veidt.

The Lodger (England, 1926),
dir: Alfred Hitchcock, with Ivor Novello.

Die Buchse der Pandora (Pandora's Box, or Lulu) (Germany, 1928),
dir: G W Pabst, with Louise Brooks.

Die Dreigroschenoper (The Threepenny Opera) (Germany, 1930),
dir: G W Pabst.

The Lodger (England, 1932),
dir: Maurice Elvey, wth Ivor Novello.

The Lodger (USA, 1944),
dir: John Brahm, with George Sanders, Merle Oberon, Cedric
Hardwicke.

Room To Let (England, 1950),
dir: Godfrey Grayson, with Valentine Dyall.

El Hombre Sin Rostro (The Man With No Face) (Mexico, 1950),
dir: Juan Bustillo Oro, with Arturo de Cordova.

Here Come the Girls (USA, 1953),
dir: Claude Binyon, with Bob Hope, Arlene Dahl.

Man in the Attic (USA, 1954),
dir: Hugo Fregonese, with Jack Palance.

Jack the Ripper (England, 1958),
dir: Robert S Baker, Monty Berman, with Eddie Byrne, John le Mesurier.

Lulu (Austria, 1962),
dir: Rolf Thiele, with Nadja Tiller, Mario Adorf.

Die Dreigroschenoper (The Threepenny Opera) (Germany/France, 1963),
dir: Wolfgang Staudte, with Sammy Davis Jr, Curt Jurgens, Gert Frobe,
Lino Ventura.

Das Ungeheuer von London City (The London Killer) (Germany, 1964),
dir: Edwin Zbonek, with Marianne Koch.

A Study in Terror (England, 1965),
dir: James Hill, with John Neville, Robert Morley, Anthony Quayle.

Night after Night (aka *He Kills Night After Night* and *Night Slasher*)
(England, 1969),
dir: Lewis J Force (Lindsay Shonteff), with Justine Lord, Jack May.

Dr Jekyll and Sister Hyde (England, 1971),
dir: Roy Ward Baker, with Ralph Bates, Martine Beswick.

Hands of the Ripper (England, 1971),
dir: Peter Sasdy, with Eric Porter, Angharad Rees.

Jack el Destripador de Londres (Jack the London Ripper) (Spain, 1971),
dir: Jose-Luis Madrid, with Paul Naschy.

The Ruling Class (England, 1972),
dir: Peter Medak, with Peter O'Toole, Alastair Sim, Arthur Lowe.

Terror in the Wax Museum (USA, 1973),
dir: George Fenady, with Ray Milland, Elsa Lanchester, Broderick Crawford, John Carradine.

A Knife For the Ladies (aka *Jack the Ripper Goes West*) (USA, 1973),
dir Larry G. Spangler, with Jack Elam.

The Groove Room (aka *Champagne Gallop*, *A Man with a Maid* and *Tickled Pink*) (Sweden/England, 1973),
dir: Vernon Becker, with Diana Dors.

From Beyond the Grave (England, 1973),
dir: Kevin Connor, with Peter Cushing, David Warner.

Le Nosferat (The Nosferat) (Belgium, 1974),
dir: Maurice Rabinowicz.

Black The Ripper (USA, 1975),
dir: Frank R. Saletri, with Hugh Van Patten.

Jack the Ripper (Germany/Switzerland, 1976),
dir: Jesus Franco, with Klaus Kinski, Josephine Chaplin.

Lulu (USA, 1978), dir: Ronald Chase, with Elisa Leonelli.

Time After Time (USA, 1979),
dir: Nicholas Meyer, with Malcolm McDowell, David Warner, Mary Steenburgen.

Murder by Decree (England/Canada, 1979),
dir: Bob Clark, with Christopher Plummer, James Mason, David Hemmings, Donald Sutherland, Genevieve Bujold, John Gielgud.

Lulu (France/Germany/Italy, 1980),
dir: Walerian Borowczyk, with Ann Bennent, Udo Kier.

Bridge Across Time (aka *Arizona Ripper and Terror on London Bridge*) (USA, 1985),
dir: E W Swackhamer, with David Hasselhoff, Adrienne Barbeau, Clu Gulager.

Amazon Women on the Moon (USA, 1985),
dir: John Landis, Joe Dante and others, with Michelle Pfeiffer, Henry Silva, Carrie Fisher.

The Ripper (USA, 1986),
dir: Christopher Lewis, with Tom Savini.

Jack's Back (USA, 1988),
dir: Rowdy Herrington, with James Spader, Cynthia Gibb.

Jack the Ripper (England, 1988),
dir: David Wickes, with Michael Caine, Armand Assante, Jane Seymour, Ray McAnally.

Edge of Sanity (England, 1989),
dir: Gerard Kikoine, with Anthony Perkins, Glynis Barber.

From Hell (USA, 2001),
dir: Hughes Brothers, with Johnny Depp, Heather Graham, Ian Holm.

Television

Jack the Ripper has also appeared in episodes of the following television series:

The New Adventures of Sherlock Holmes (USA, 1955)
The Big Story (USA, 1956)
Alfred Hitchcock Presents (1957)
The Veil (USA, 1958)
Cimarron City (USA, 1958)
Thriller (USA, 1961)
The Twilight Zone (USA, 1963)
Star Trek (USA, 1967)
The Green Hornet (USA, 1967)
The Avengers (England, 1969)
The Sixth Sense (USA, 1972)
Kolchak: The Night Stalker (USA, 1974)
Till Death Us Do Part (England, 1975)
The Two Ronnies (England, 1976)
Fantasy Island (USA, 1980)

Index